MW01105477

Blood Money

Blood Money

A History of the First
Teen Slasher Film Cycle

Richard Nowell

continuum

2011

The Continuum International Publishing Group
80 Maiden Lane, New York, NY 10038
The Tower Building, 11 York Road, London SE1 7NX

www.continuumbooks.com

Copyright © 2011 by Richard Nowell

All rights reserved. No part of this book may be reproduced, stored in a retrieval
system, or transmitted, in any form or by any means, electronic, mechanical,
photocopying, recording, or otherwise, without the written permission of the
publishers.

Library of Congress Cataloging-in-Publication Data
Nowell, Richard.
Blood money : a history of the first teen slasher film cycle / Richard Nowell.
p. cm.
Includes bibliographical references and index.
ISBN-13: 978-1-4411-1705-2 (hardcover : alk. paper)
ISBN-10: 1-4411-1705-9 (hardcover : alk. paper)
ISBN-13: 978-1-4411-2496-8 (pbk. : alk. paper)
ISBN-10: 1-4411-2496-9 (pbk. : alk. paper) 1. Slasher films—United States—History
and criticism. 2. Slasher films—Canada—History and criticism. I. Title.

PN1995.9.S554N69 2010
791.43'6164—dc22   2010019839

ISBN: HB: 978-1-4411-1705-2 (hardcover)
PB: 978-1-4411-2496-8 (paperback)

Typeset by Pindar NZ, Auckland, New Zealand
Printed and bound in the United States of America

Contents

Acknowledgements

First of all, thanks to everyone at Continuum for making this project possible, especially to David Barker who was as helpful, patient, and upbeat an editor as any writer could hope to have. I would like to express my gratitude to Peter Krämer for the guidance and encouragement he has shown me over the years in which this project has taken shape. I am also incredibly grateful to Dr. Rayna Denison, Prof. Diane Negra, Prof. Yvonne Tasker, and Prof. Mark Jancovich for their helpful advice, as well as to Prof. Steve Neale for his gracious, kind, and much appreciated words of support. To the postgraduate community at the University of East Anglia's School of Film and Television Studies, my thanks too, particularly to Oliver Gruner for his insight and patience. And, very special thanks to Jindřiška Bláhová who offered invaluable comments and pointers, posed tough but necessary questions, and who, it would be fair to say, went through more than most teen slasher film heroines as *Blood Money* was taking shape. The advice of the aforementioned was taken seriously and on board, and any errors or over-sights are my own. Finally, to my parents, Clive and Pamela Nowell, I thank you from the bottom of my heart.

Richard Nowell is a film scholar who has lectured at leading universities in the UK and Germany. His work can also be seen in *Cinema Journal*, the *Journal of Film and Video*, and *Post Script*.

List of Illustrations

Figures

Tables

Introduction

Co-ed Frenzy

As students party in their college dorms, a mysterious figure heads toward a bathroom where a female student is showering. The prowler is revealed to be a hunched, middle-aged man, with an unhinged and lustful gleam in his eye. He approaches his oblivious, naked, vulnerable prey, rips aside the shower curtain, and raises an enormous blood-soaked blade. The young woman turns, her eyes widen, her lips part, and she screams.

Shot on grainy film stock and mostly through subjective (or POV) shots, this sequence opens *Blow Out* (1981), a big-budget conspiracy thriller about a soundman (John Travolta) who inadvertently records a political assassination while working on an assignment. The victim's scream pierces the air: not a spine-chilling wail but a feeble squeal. It sparks laughter. 'What cat did you strangle to get that?', snaps a producer to his sound engineer as they screen footage of their latest picture. A starlet's vocal inadequacies provide an unwelcome disruption during post-production of the cut-price shocker 'Co-ed Frenzy', the making of which seems to be governed by considerations of blood, money, and precious little else (see Figure 0.1).

FIGURE 0.1   'Independent filmmaking practices' in *Blow Out*.

Blow Out perpetuates a prevalent misconception about the conduct and the output of the North American independent sector at the dawn of the 1980s.[1] The film depicts a central protagonist that works for a shady producer of low-budget horror, a man operating at the outer margins of the American film industry, both economically and creatively. Sitting in a dirty screening room, their professional existence is portrayed as being far removed from the glamour of Hollywood — the product, conduct, and power of which *Blow Out*'s financier-distributor Filmways had made its mission to emulate. Similarly, the cheap, sleazy, sexist little movie to which the filmmakers in *Blow Out* anchor their dreams of making a quick buck seems a world away from the artistic pretensions of Brian De Palma; the writer-director of *Blow Out*; the new 'master of suspense'; the heir-apparent to Alfred Hitchcock.

With the opening frames of *Blow Out*, Filmways, a small company that recently had merged with B-movie studio American International Pictures (Anon., 1978f, pp. 3, 63), and Brian De Palma, a man who was subject to sustained accusations of misogynistic filmmaking (Kapsis, 1992, pp. 201–210), made a bid for respectability by drawing a firm line between themselves as 'big-time producer-distributor' and 'serious artist' respectively, and the amateurish hacks that supposedly churned out sexist schlock from the shadows of the American independent sector. In short, precisely the kind of filmmakers to which De Palma was referring when he made the following disparaging remarks. 'A horror film is usually born when a group of young filmmakers is sitting around and asking "How can we become commercial directors?"', began De Palma, '[o]ne person will invariably say, "Hey, let's get some friends together and make a movie about a maniac who goes berserk and cuts every-body up with a knife"' (quoted in Morrisroe, 1980, p. 101).

For the 'Co-ed Frenzy' sequence to function effectively it needed to showcase a high-profile trend that was associated specifically with independent filmmaking. The same effect would not have been achieved had De Palma aped a sci-fi epic or a romantic comedy. The 'Co-ed Frenzy' sequence thus suggested that the films comprising the trend had achieved enough visibility to be discernible to *Blow Out*'s target audience; Filmways had tailored its marketing campaign to attract the American youths that had largely ignored De Palma's previous film, a thriller about a cross-dressing misogynist knife-killer entitled *Dressed to Kill* (1980), in favor of attending cut-price independently produced films about shadowy maniacs preying upon their on-screen surrogates — *Silent Scream* (1979), *Friday the 13th*, and *Prom Night* (both 1980) (Frederick, 1980, p. 14; Anon., 1980k, p. 6; Harmetz, 1980d, p. C15). The object of De Palma's scorn was not lost on Gary Arnold of the *Washington Post* who described 'Co-ed Frenzy' as '[a] "Friday the 13th" clone astutely parodied' (1981c, p. D1). Yet, with its emphasis on misogynistic content and amateurish filmmaking practice, 'Co-ed Frenzy' was more a calculated misrepresentation of independent production and output than a parody.

De Palma was capitalizing on a sea-change in the popular reception of films like *Friday the 13th* to take a swipe at his competitors and distinguish himself from the independent sector, of which he had been, and, strictly speaking, continued to be, a part. On the back of controversy over De Palma's film *Dressed to Kill*, a small but vocal band of journalists, led by Gene Siskel and Roger Ebert of Chicago's *Tribune* and *Sun-Times* newspapers, had begun in late 1980 to claim that *Friday the 13th* and its youth-market contemporaries were polluting America's shopping mall multiplexes with the most sadistic showcases of femicide ever committed to celluloid — all to end the social and professional gains advanced by second-wave feminists. Here was the moment at which the dominant perception of tales of blade-wielding killers stalking young people started to shift from light-hearted entertainment to dangerous social menace, thus laying a firm foundation for popular and scholastic treatments of the earliest examples of the film-type that came to be known as the teen slasher film.

In her influential 1987 article, 'Her Body, Himself', Carol J. Clover opened by summarizing the type of film that was being misrepresented in *Blow Out*'s 'Co-ed Frenzy' sequence. 'Down in the cinematic underbush', she began, 'lies — horror of horrors — the slasher' (1987, p. 187).[2] Suggesting that the film-type was '[d]renched in taboo and encroaching vigorously on the pornographic' (ibid.), Clover, like De Palma, portrayed films such as *Halloween* (1978) and *Hell Night* (1981) as having surfaced from a disreputable underbelly of the American film industry. Clover was using the teen slasher film to advance a revolutionary cross-gender identification model, whereby actual male viewers of films like *Halloween* identified with heroic females or 'Final Girls'. Her work was received as a significant contribution to film studies, ensuring that most scholars cited Clover as the leading authority on teen slashers despite the fact that Robin Wood (1983) and Vera Dika (1987) had published more meticulous and, I feel, more measured, overviews of early teen slasher content. Clover's remarks exerted a lasting influence on scholarly and popular perceptions of the teen slasher. Her suggestion that early examples of the film-type were fashioned as vehicles of horrifying male-on-female violence to be consumed exclusively by the young male patrons of 'drive-ins

and exploitation houses' echoed and reinforced the nascent strand of
1980s popular discourse touched upon above, informed early-nineties
social science (Cowan and O'Brien, 1990; Molitor and Sapolsky, 1993),
shaped fan-oriented publications (Whitehead, 2000; Rockoff, 2002;
Armstrong 2003; Harper 2004), and has been recycled in interpretive
text-based scholarship on the film-type (Lewis, 1992, pp. 66–68; Creed,
1993; Pinedo, 1997; Nolan and Ryan, 2000; Reiser, 2001; Gill, 2002;
Shary, 2002a, pp. 147–168; Koven, 2006, pp. 159–171; Koven, 2008,
pp. 113–134).[3]

Claims about the motives and logic that underwrote early teen slasher
film production and content have been made despite the absence of a
rigorous examination of the North American film industry's stakes in
early teen slasher film production and distribution. The sizable volume
of industrial film history examining independently produced and/or distributed horror and youth-oriented product of earlier historical periods,
which includes Kevin Heffernan's study of the horror film business from
1953 to 1968 (2004), Eric Schaefer's work on classical-era 'exploitation'
films (1994, 1999, 2004, 2007), and Thomas Doherty's exploration of
1950s teen films (2002), is not matched by work focusing on the late
1970s and early 1980s, even though the period witnessed a production
boom in these types of film.[4] *Blood Money* begins to fill that void by providing the first industry-focused history of the first teen slasher film cycle,
one which sheds new light on the decision-making processes that shaped
teen slasher film production and distribution, and which challenges
standard thinking on the film-type.

Thus, where scholars have, to date, commonly applied psychoanalytic
models to representations of gender in early teen slasher films in order
to claim that they were formulaic, excessively violent exploitation films
that were fashioned to satisfy the misogynist fantasies of male visitors
to grind-houses and fleapits, by examining the commercial logic, strategies, and objectives of the American and Canadian independents that
produced the films and the companies that distributed them in the US,
this book demonstrates that filmmakers and marketers actually went to
extraordinary lengths to make early teen slashers attractive to female
youth, to minimize displays of violence, gore, and suffering, and to
invite comparisons to a wide range of post-classical Hollywood's biggest
hits, including *Love Story* (1970), *Saturday Night Fever* (1977), *Grease*, and
Animal House (both 1978).

Despite being one of the most high-profile shifts in film production
of the last half-century, the teen slasher film boom of the late 1970s and
early 1980s has yet to be explained by historians. From January 1980 to

April 1982, the American film market hosted fifteen teen slashers. Ten of the films opened between May 1980 and August 1981, a remarkable ratio of a new teen slasher every six weeks.[5] Yet, as David A. Cook recognized, speculative references to the influence of earlier films like *Peeping Tom*, *Psycho* (both 1960) and *The Texas Chainsaw Massacre* (1974) (Clover, 1987, p. 192; Kapsis, 1992, p. 159; Prince, 2000, pp. 224–225, 351–352), do not account for the industrial conditions that led to this explosion of activity. 'For whatever reason', conceded Cook, 'there was a significant boom' (2000, p. 237). This book reveals the conditions under which the teen slasher film emerged and became a key component of the North American film industry's repertoire of youth-market product.

The surge in teen slasher film production was highlighted by Steve Neale as a textbook example of a film cycle, which he defined as 'a group of films made within a specific and limited time-span, and founded, for the most part, on the characteristics of individual commercial successes' (2000, p. 1). By emphasizing similarities between early teen slashers, scholars have approached the films that belonged to that cycle somewhat a-historically, thus minimizing the influence of historically specific industrial developments on production, content, marketing, and distribution. However, to gain greater insight into the decision-making processes that shaped industry conduct vis-à-vis early teen slashers, it is necessary, as Gregory A. Waller pointed out, to focus on discontinuities and to examine the ways in which early teen slashers intersected with and were impacted by contemporaneous trends in film production and promotion (1987, pp. 8–12).

Blood Money therefore proposes a groundbreaking model of film cycle development, which promises to be transferable to other types of film, other historical periods, and the films of other nations. By treating cycles as a series of chronologically distinct phases of activity so as to illuminate the ways in which industrial developments, market shifts, and changing commercial imperatives underwrite production and distribution of a film-type as well as the content of individual films and their marketing campaigns, this book hopes to make important contributions to genre studies. *Blood Money* uses this methodological tool to explain how the advent of the teen slasher in 1974, its gradual rise to prominence by 1980, and its swift, albeit temporary, demise in 1981, was bound up with perceptions of the commercial viability of other film-types, from prestige horror and glossy thrillers to youth-oriented fare like gross-out or 'animal' comedies and female-centered coming-of-age dramas. In doing so, *Blood Money* shows that conceptions of gendered consumption, the transnational approach of Canadian filmmakers and financiers, the enterprise of the American independent sector, and changes in Hollywood business practices contributed to the first teen slasher film cycle.

By applying the cycle development model to a film-type that was produced independently but often distributed by major studios, *Blood Money* also offers timely new insight into the under-examined interaction of American and Canadian independents and 'New' Hollywood. Scholarship on these branches of the North American film industry has tended to contrast major studio releases to films produced or distributed 'independently' in North America. The due attention that has been paid to blockbuster filmmaking at this time (Schatz, 1993; Hall, 1998; Krämer, 2005),[6] as well as to maverick, visionary, 'independent spirited' employees of the majors such as Hal Ashby and Robert Altman (Kolker, 1980; Gilby, 2003), to small producer-distributors including New World Pictures and Dimension Pictures that unlike the majors did not belong to the Motion Picture Association of America (MPAA) (Hillier and Lipstadt, 1981, 1986; Hillier, 1992; Lowry, 2005), and to creatively oriented Canadian filmmakers (Leach, 1986, 2006), has left a significant gap in the history of the North American film industry. These tendencies have obscured the fact that a different breed of independent filmmaker existed, one that targeted MPAA-members (Hollywood) by offering them for distribution completed films which had been tailored to meet their needs. Thus, although it has been shown that the majors were, by the late 1970s, releasing film-types and mobilizing content and themes that had been hitherto associated with independent studios like New World (Schatz, 1983, 1993; Hall, 1998), and that those companies increased their production budgets and gentrified their films so as to compete head-to-head with the majors (Hillier, 1992; Tzioumakis, 2006, pp. 204–205), the responses of that other breed of independent filmmaker have drawn scant scholarly attention. By showing that the exchange of content between the majors and independents was a complex two-way process, *Blood Money* demonstrates that the conduct of the majors and North American independent filmmakers was more heavily intertwined in the late 1970s and early 1980s than has commonly been thought, and that, rather than always existing in opposition to one another, the MPAA-members and some independent filmmakers, like those behind the teen slashers, forged a mutually beneficial existence.

Blood Money also provides a new perspective on the role gender played in early teen slashers by revealing the remarkable lengths to which filmmakers and distributors went to make the films attractive to teenage girls and young women. To date, scholars have applied interpretive textual analysis to sequences of threat and bloodshed to conclude that first cycle teen slashers were misogynistic films that offered little to female audiences.[7] Such claims have been incredibly enduring, restated, as they are, in even the most recently published work (Koven, 2006, 162–168; Connelly, 2007). For example, Valerie Wee's (2005, 2006) suggestion that the *Scream* films (1996, 1997, and 2000) were radically innovative teen slashers because they were female youth-orientated, hinges on the supposedly male-youth-orientation of earlier entries. '[T]he [*Scream*] trilogy', argues Wee, 'made the genre relevant to the adolescent female moviegoer — a segment of the audience that had been largely dismissed by previous practitioners of the genre' (2005, p. 57). While rightly emphasizing the extent to which the perceived interests of young females were considered in the assembly and market-ing of late-nineties teen slashers, such work has further obscured the important role that conceptions of female youth played in early teen slasher film production and promotion. Films like *Halloween* and *Prom Night* are thus positioned as an anomaly among horror films, for, as sev-eral scholars have shown, the American film industry has endeavored tirelessly to sell scary movies to female theatergoers. Cynthia Erb has detailed how studio management, creative personnel, and exhibitors attempted to secure a female audience for *King Kong* (1933) (1998, pp. 41, 61–62). Both Rhona Berenstein (1996, pp. 70–87) and Tim Snelson (2009) have demonstrated that, during the classical era, studios commonly angled horror to women. Similarly, Thomas Austin (2002) has documented the recent implementation of this strategy in the produc-tion and promotion of *Dracula* (1992). By examining the often fleeting moments of 'stalk and slash' action alongside non-violent content, which dominated teen slasher screen-time and featured heavily in promotion, and which reveals much about how industry-insiders perceived and cultivated the films' target audience, *Blood Money* shows that the com-mercial investment in making teen slashers that would be appealing to young females was part of much broader industrial developments and shifts.

With little archival documentation available, the job of the film histo-rian, focusing on the conduct of the American film industry toward the end of the twentieth century, is always done with one hand tied behind his or her back. And this study is no different. It therefore draws on those resources available, particularly the American trade and US and Canadian popular press and, toward the end of the period covered, the only major horror fan publication, *Fangoria*. These sources pro-vide a wealth of information which was readily available to industry professionals involved in teen slasher filmmaking and marketing and was therefore likely to have impacted (or covered events that had impacted) their conduct. Particularly relevant are records of films' commercial performances and statements by filmmakers, distributors and, occasionally, audience-members. To measure industry-insiders' perceptions of the commercial potential of particular film-types and elements of film content, I refer to *Variety*'s annual box-office charts.[8] I also draw on the comments of industry-watchers, who provide the only accessible information about the way teen slashers, and other films, were received contemporaneously, so as to demonstrate that my observations about film content are not the product of diachronic reading positions. On occasion my analysis is supported with post-facto testimony from filmmakers and distributors concerning their logic, strategies, and ambitions.

The first chapter presents three frameworks that structure subsequent chapters. It begins by outlining the textual model that characterized the teen slasher films of 1974–1981: a story-structure which enabled filmmakers to incite not only horror, but thrills, intrigue, and amusement. From there, the principles that governed early teen slasher film production are set out as I argue that the overarching goal of securing a major studio distribution deal led independent filmmakers to craft teen slashers that would be marketable to female as well as male youth, that avoided the X-rating, and which evoked a range of contemporaneous hits. The chapter concludes by presenting the model of film cycle development that is to be applied across the remainder of the book, outlining the distinct forms of commercial logic and objectives that govern each of the four chronically distinct modes of production that comprise film cycles, what I call: Pioneer Productions, Speculator Productions, Prospector Cash-ins, and Carpetbagger Cash-ins.

The second chapter offers a radically different account of the teen slasher film's emergence than those proposed to date. Focusing on the period 1974–1978, it questions standard narratives that detail how radical breaks from filmmaking convention in *Psycho* and *The Texas Chainsaw Massacre* ushered in the teen slasher on the back of artistic vision, arguing instead that the teen slasher's advent was the product of astute commercially driven activity among ambitious filmmakers working on both sides of the North American border and their shrewd re-combination of film content that boasted a track-record of box-office success. The chapter begins by explaining how the teen slasher's distinct story-structure emerged by way of a case-study of the first teen slasher, the Pioneer Production *Black Christmas*, a female-centered politically engaged whodunit that began life as the first calculated blockbuster to receive production subsidies from the Canadian government, became a film that a major American studio expected to be one of the highest earning youth-centered films in US history, and turned out to be a box-office disaster. The chapter then examines the first film that suggested an audience existed for tales of youth being menaced by psycho-killers, the Speculator Production *Halloween*. While this female-centered small-town-set horror film is commonly held up as the only creatively innovative teen slasher, the chapter shows that *Halloween* was in fact crafted to capitalize on developments in blockbuster filmmaking and tap into the growing confidence that Hollywood placed in light-hearted 'female friendly' teen films like *Carrie* (1976).

Chapters three and four focus on the development of the teen slasher by examining *Halloween*'s impact on the two national film industries that contributed to the cycle.

Concentrating on the American film industry, chapter three begins by revealing that in 1979 American filmmakers were reluctant to model films on *Halloween* because they placed greater confidence in other horror and youth-oriented film-types. Against this backdrop, it is suggested, that the conduct of the producers of the only American-made teen slasher Prospector Cash-in, *Friday the 13th*, must be re-evaluated. Rather than being dismissed as a cynical act of exploitation, the production of this relatively gory animal comedy-infused murder-mystery is better understood as having been a perilous undertaking that required a series of strategies to offset risk, including the mobilization of 'painless' set-piece killings from *The Omen* films (1976, 1978) and extracting material from light-hearted comedy hits. The chapter concludes by revealing that industry and audience responses to *Friday the 13th* indicated that teen slasher films offered independent filmmakers a low-risk opportunity to realize their commercial objectives.

The Canadian film industry's proactive response to *Halloween* is taken up in the fourth chapter. While the teen slasher is usually seen as an exclusively American phenomenon, the chapter reveals the influence of non-American production on the film-type and its first cycle, particularly in terms of making the films highly marketable to female youth. The chapter begins by charting the transnational industrial conditions that shaped Canadian-based filmmakers' willingness to attempt to capitalize on *Halloween* at a point in time at which most of their American counterparts were reluctant to do so, arguing that the production of two female youth-oriented Prospector Cash-ins was the culmination point of a long-standing state-inspired initiative to foster a sustainable Canadian film industry by enabling producers to break into the American market.

Thereafter, my attention shifts to the most influential of the films, *Prom Night*, showing that its creators made female youth the film's prime target audience. The chapter concludes by arguing that *Prom Night*'s release indicated that angling teen slashers to female youth not only offered filmmakers a competitive edge in the battle for distribution deals, but offered distributors a way of generating profit in a crowded marketplace.

The fifth and final chapter focuses on a period of boom and bust in teen slasher film production, a remarkable twelve months from late 1980 to late 1981 during which the teen slasher film underwent a spectacular transformation from being arguably the most commercially attractive film-type of its time to being considered wholly unviable, both commercially and politically. The chapter opens by outlining the conditions that generated over-production of teen slasher Carpetbagger Cash-ins like the Canadian films *My Bloody Valentine* and *Happy Birthday to Me* and the American contributions *Friday the 13th Part II* and *Hell Night* (all 1981). From there it is shown that the teen slasher filmmakers' already slim chances of attracting a major distributor lengthened further due to a lack of product differentiation among their films, as the achievements of previous teen slashers, in combination with other youth-market developments, resulted in a tidal wave of female-centered animal comedy-infused murder-mysteries and signaled that the US market soon would be saturated with similar films. The chapter concludes by looking at the economic, institutional, and socio-political developments that brought about a dramatic drop in teen slasher film production, arguing that high-profile media controversy, market-saturation, and derivative marketing campaigns ensured that teen slasher film production and distribution ceased to be viewed as financially viable — albeit temporarily.

Three decades after *Blow Out* hit theaters and the first cycle of the teen slasher film ended, the 'Co-ed Frenzy' sequence recalls a much larger group of films than its makers could have envisaged. Yet, before De Palma's thriller had been completed, the American trade and popular press were characteristically prophesying the end of the film-type derided in its prologue (Harmetz, 1980d, p. C15; Knoedelseder, 1980a, p. N3). With both *Variety* and the *Los Angeles Times* predicting that the lengthening odds in 'the killer-with-a-knife sweepstakes' would trigger a shift to the production of teen slasher parodies, films in the vein of *Halloween*, *Prom Night*, and *Friday the 13th* were already being seen as a fleeting craze (Pollock, 1981b, p. H1; Carl., 1980, p. 20). However, two of those films spawned franchises that have spanned five decades, and all three of them, like many of their contemporaries, have been re-made or 're-envisaged' for twenty-first-century audiences. Between the releases of *Halloween* (1978) and *Halloween* (2007), *Prom Night* (1980) and *Prom Night* (2008), and *Friday the 13th* (1980) and *Friday the 13th* (2009), new teen slasher films have opened in the US almost every year, amounting to almost 200 films in total. An additional three teen slasher film cycles have unfolded, first from 1984 to 1989, then from 1996 to 2000, with the most recent beginning in 2005 and continuing unabated. In that time, shrewdly marketed teen slasher franchises propelled two small independent companies to mini-major status and made them attractive take-over targets for multinational media conglomerates (Wyatt, 1998). Indeed, the killers of New Line's *A Nightmare on Elm Street* (1984–2003) films and Miramax's *Scream* trilogy stepped out of the shadows to become iconic images of threat on a scale that had not been seen since Universal's classic monsters of the 1930s. The teen slasher film, contrary to the gloomy expectations of industry-watchers in fall 1980, has become one of the North American film industry's most prominent weapons in its ongoing battle to serve the prime movie-watching audience, yet it remains one of its most misunderstood products.

Chapter 1

'There's more than one way
to lose your heart'

The teen slasher film-type, production strategies, and film cycle

A teenage girl showers, unaware of the masked intruder creeping down her hallway. The prowler slips into the bathroom and rips aside the shower curtain. The youth turns, screaming as the madman projects his blade towards her midriff. She grabs her assailant's wrist and struggles valiantly, but the weapon inches mercilessly towards her flesh. Inevitably, the maniac's weapon reaches the girl's skin. But the blade bends pathetically on impact — it is rubber. Confused, but unhurt, the plucky teenager unmasks her attacker to reveal a grinning boy. 'Joey!' she yells. Her kid brother laughs and flees (see Figure 1.1).

So begins *The Funhouse* (1981), not a teen slasher, but leading horror director Tobe Hooper's playful tribute to fifty years of American horror. Made for Universal Pictures in late 1980, when teen slasher film production and distribution had been gaining momentum, *The Funhouse* misleads audiences into anticipating a film modeled on the most high-profile teen slasher of the time, *Halloween* (1978). 'The parody of *Halloween*', remarked Bruce F. Kawin, 'is entirely explicit' (1987, p. 105).

The opening of *The Funhouse* captured the essence of the teen slasher's distinct content, the commercial logic that underwrote its production in the mid-to-late 1970s and early 1980s, and its status as a nascent film-type. Encapsulated in the scene is the combination of everyday locations, fun-seeking young people, and shadowy knife-killers that set teen slashers apart from other films. Similarly, by inviting parallels to a hit like *Halloween*, promising but not delivering brutal violence, and showcasing light-hearted material oriented to youths of both sexes, the prologue to *The Funhouse* reflected the strategies implemented by teen slasher producers to make their product economically viable. Finally,

FIGURE 1.1   Evoking the teen slasher film in *The Funhouse*.

by inviting, but refusing to allow, audiences to anticipate a film like *Halloween*, Hooper and his collaborators position *The Funhouse* in relation not only to *Halloween* but to similar films that were hitting American theaters at the time, and, in doing so, evoke the on-going process that was making teen slashers part of American film culture. The opening scene of *The Funhouse* gestured in light-hearted fashion to the American film industry's understanding of teen slasher film production, which is the focus of this chapter.

This chapter provides three conceptual frameworks that structure the industrial analysis presented across subsequent chapters, outlining the textual model employed by teen slasher filmmakers, identifying the strategies they implemented to help to realize their commercial objectives, and proposing a model of film cycle development which illuminates the ways in which filmmakers conduct was impacted by developments specific to the point in time at which they contributed a film to the cycle. By abandoning the assumption that early teen slashers were made solely to horrify male drive-in patrons, irrespective of when they were produced, this chapter permits the book to approach the films as multifaceted products that were fashioned to permit astute businesspeople to realize relatively lofty ambitions. In doing so, it suggests that, only by treating film-types as complex networks of elements designed to provoke diverse types of audience engagement and to fulfill different commercial objectives, can the conditions underwriting production and the mobilization of content be identified.

'An easy-to-follow blueprint': the Teen Slasher Film-Type

At its core, film genre is a system of communication comprising two components, the label and the corpus. A name is assigned to a number of films because they are considered to share similarities that distinguish them from other films, thus bringing order to relative chaos. However, as Steve Neale (1993), James Naremore (1998), and Rick Altman (1999) have shown, that order is somewhat illusionary because the relationships between the label and the corpus rarely are stable. The application of the label and the choices of films are impacted by countless factors including 'personal taste', knowledge of, and investment in, the films, as well as by geographic and temporal conditions. For example, Mark Jancovich (2000) revealed that horror fans possess distinct conceptions of the texts that constitute the horror film, while Neale (1993) demonstrates that melodrama originally referred to male-oriented action films, not emotionally wrought female-audience films. The contestation and flux characterizing genre has led some scholars to adopt one of two approaches. Approaching genre as a primarily discursive activity, scholars including Naremore (1998) and Jancovich (2000) have examined the roles played by genre in film reception such as journalism and fan commentary. The second approach, advocated by Neale (1990), and employed by, among others, Thomas Doherty (2002), Tico Romao (2003), and Kevin Heffernan (2004), maintains that, through rigorous empirical research, film historians can reveal the temporal specificity of film categories so as to gain insight into production, promotion, distribution, and exhibition practices.

Yannis Tzioumakis' work on 'American independent cinema' (2006) has shown that the two approaches are not always incompatible. For Tzioumakis, 'independence', in the American context, is both a discursive activity that distinguishes films from an imagined 'mainstream', and an institutional category denoting films that are not handled by major studios (ibid., pp. 1–14). Tzioumakis shows that a strong correlation exists between discursively and institutionally 'independent' American films. While there may be some debate as to whether

'American independent cinema' constitutes a genre, it certainly provides a way of categorizing and distinguishing films in much the same way as universally accepted genres like the Western or the horror film. Much like 'American independent cinema', the films of the mid-to-late 1970s and early 1980s that came to be known as teen slasher films offer a prime example of discursive activity and industrial conduct exhibiting a high degree of regularity — albeit for a brief time.

Even though, as we shall see below, no stable labeling system had become established by 1980 and 1981 to describe what I and many other scholars now call teen slasher films, it is clear that, at this point in time, individuals speaking from all levels of North American film culture, from producers, distributors, and exhibitors to industry analysts, reviewers, casual moviegoers, and fans, recognized the existence of a new type of film that was distinguished from other films by virtue of the story it told — the story of a blade-wielding killer preying on a group of young people. In this respect, the teen slasher fulfilled three of the four criteria laid out by Altman (1999) as constituting what he calls a genre or what I call a film-type. Its distinct story exemplifies what Altman termed the 'structure' i.e. shared content (ibid., pp. 14–15). That story provided a 'blueprint', the general model used by filmmakers to fashion new examples of the film-type (ibid.). And, the fact that audiences recognized the film-type's distinct story demonstrates that existing between teen slasher film producers and consumers was what Altman described as the 'contract' (ibid.), a state reached when viewers hold firm expectations of the 'structure' that will be delivered by films made to the 'blueprint'. Missing is what Altman dubbed the 'label', a name that conveys relatively unambiguously the alignment of 'structure', 'blueprint,' and 'contract' in such a way as to demonstrate that speaker/writer and listener/reader recognize that a film features a 'structure' because it has been fashioned to a 'blueprint' thus establishing a 'contract'. Instead, numerous etiquettes circulated contemporaneous to the early teen slasher films. Many were hyphenated labels comprised of different combinations of terms that communicated the film-type's distinct story, others, as is elucidated in the next section, were descriptive phrases that emphasized the links between examples of the film-type. The fact that none of these etiquettes have been widely adopted and that those etiquettes which did gain currency at a later date — teenie kill-pics (Wood 1983, 1987), stalker films (Dika, 1990; Rubin 1999), slasher movies (Clover 1992), and teen slasher films (Wee, 2005, 2006) — were not used when the films were produced and first released, indicates that a more reliable gauge of whether or not several films are perceived to represent a coherent group (or genre or film-type) is provided by efforts to communicate that sense of belonging rather than by the existence of a single label.

Because of ambiguities concerning the manner in which films about young people being menaced by blade-wielding killers subsequently have been labeled by scholars, concerning the films to which scholars have applied the label 'slasher', and concerning the complex interplay between the two phenomena, it is essential to provide a definition of the films to which this study applies the term 'teen slasher film'. Although many scholars recognize that the term 'slasher' is commonly applied to films about young people being menaced by blade-wielding killers and that films featuring this content commonly are labeled 'slasher films', 'slasher' has also been used as a synonym for so-called splatter films (filmic showcases for gore), in reference to films which feature blade-wielding killers irrespective of their targets' ages, and to youth-centered horror films irrespective of the monster presented therein, while films about blade-wielding killers preying on young people have, as noted above, been given numerous labels in academic writing. More so than any other factor, however, confusion has been caused by the fact that many of the writers that outlined as their locus of interest tales of blade-wielding killers preying on young people and that presented detailed descriptions of the films' distinguishing content, actually jettisoned their definitions when illustrating their arguments. This tendency, and its consequences, are nowhere clearer than in the case of the much-cited article, and later book chapter, 'Her Body, Himself', in which Carol J. Clover forwarded the concept of cross-gender identification, not with reference to the youth-centered 'slasher films' she described across the majority of the piece, but mainly with adult-centered thrillers like *Psycho* (1960), *Eyes of Laura Mars* (1978), and *Dressed to Kill* (1980) (1992, pp. 46–50). Such slippages, whether calculated or otherwise, are not without their implications. Clover's assimilation of the two distinct film-types that Robin Wood (1983), four years earlier, had called the 'teenie kill-pic' and the 'violence against women film', so as to form a critical category that, I maintain, did not exist on celluloid in the years before her piece was published, influenced scholarly and popular perceptions of the teen slasher profoundly. Appearing in what was widely received as groundbreaking film scholarship, Clover's definition provided an imme-diate reference point for academic and popular writers (Whitehead, 2000, pp. 7–16; Rockoff, 2002, pp. 5–22; Armstrong, 2003, pp. 1–19; Harper, 2004, pp. 31–61), who, by restating its key tenets, proliferated, gave credence to, and reinforced misconceptions of teen slasher content, particularly the erroneous, but remarkably enduring, claim that the films showcased psychosexually disturbed male sadists torturing and murdering scores of beautiful, independent young women (see for example Prince, 2000, pp. 298–306, 351–353; Wee, 2005; 2006).

Amidst such confusion and misunderstandings, I aim to represent the textual model that distinguished, and was recognized contemporaneously as distinguishing, from other films, the content of the teen slashers of 1974–1981: a story-structure that could be articulated differently and combined with content drawn from a variety of sources and which enabled filmmakers not only to provoke audience horror, but also to incite intrigue, thrills, and amusement. While expressed in terms used by structuralist scholars, I am not suggesting that the story-structure imposed a mode of engagement on individual viewers, as structuralists have done. Rather, the story-structure is designed to distinguish what I call teen slasher films from other tangentially similar films in such a way as to reflect, in as organized and articulate a way as possible, the manner in which the films were perceived upon their original releases, based on the recorded testimony of industry-insiders, industry-watchers, and audiences.[1]

By late 1980, the film-type that came to be known as the teen slasher film was recognized widely across the North American film industry, in the trade and popular press, and by theatergoers soon thereafter, as industry-professionals, industry-watchers, and young people spoke openly and articulately about the content that distinguished it as a new type of film. Producers and distributors, even those who had never even made a teen slasher, spotlighted its distinct features. 'It's all a game', explained horror filmmaker Christopher Pearce, 'a group of coeds are endangered. Who is it? What is it?' (quoted in C. Williams, 1980, p. E1). A similar point was made by a top US distribution executive. 'If you get the audience to identify with young teens in trouble and you do a knife movie', suggested Avco Embassy's Don Borchers, 'it's always going to work' (quoted in Knoedelseder, 1980a, p. N3).

Films about young people being menaced by shadowy maniacs, far from having been 'never even written up' by American journalists, as Morris Dickstein suggested (1984, p. 74), had in fact initiated a light-hearted competition to coin an appropriately descriptive and catchy generic label among writers at the most widely read newspapers in North America. Alongside terms like 'horror', 'thriller', and 'mystery', which Jancovich (2009) shows have often been used interchangeably by reviewers to describe films now commonly thought of as 'horror movies', countless sobriquets spotlighted the combination of young people and blade-wielding killers that industry personnel noted as distinguishing the film-type.[2] Ed Blank wrote in the *Pittsburgh Press* of 'slash-your-local teenager features' (1981, p. 6), the *Los Angeles Times'* Linda Gross discussed the 'young-folk-getting-killed-genre' (1981b, p. H7), and, at the *New York Times*, Aljean Harmetz examined the 'homicidal-maniac-pursues-attractive-teen-agers' sweepstakes (1980d, p. C13). But *Washington Post* employees were the most gleeful participants, with Tom Shales commenting on 'endangered teen-ager movies' (1981, p. C2), Joseph McLellan speaking of 'the 'kill-the-teenagers' cycle' (quoted in Arnold et al., 1980, p. F1), and Judith Martin taking aim at 'the teen-age Blood Film' (1981, p W19). Not to be outdone by these epithets, Gene Siskel of the *Chicago Tribune* described *Happy Birthday to Me* (1981) as a 'typical "teen-age girl takes violent revenge on kids who have been mean to her" flick' (1981b, p. B10). By November 1981, a *Variety* reviewer seemingly felt that it was high time to discontinue this labeling one-upmanship. A plot synopsis that highlighted 'the mysterious murderer' and 'grad[uate students]', s/he concluded, communicated sufficiently that *The Prowler* (1981) belonged to 'the seemingly endless procession of chillers' that comprised 'the now familiar subgenre' (Klad., 1981, p. 22).

Interviews conducted in summer 1981 and published in the *Los Angeles Times* demonstrate that that 'now familiar subgenre' had also been recognized by America's theatergoing youths, adding weight to Jay Scott's observation in Toronto's *Globe and Mail* the previous fall that '[t]he premise — a crazed killer abused years before returns to wreak vengeance on the young — is so familiar that the audience can predict (. . .) every shock' (1980b). Whereas a group of teenagers that attended urban high schools in the Venice area expressed their views on '*Happy Birthday to Me, Prom Night, Friday the 13th* and stuff like that' (quoted in Caulfield and Garner, 1981, p. L22), graduates from an elite academy in the wealthy suburb of Irving discussed movies in which a 'killer goes crazy and kills 15 people', and having viewed '*Happy Birthday to Me* (. . .) and films like that' (quoted in Garner, 1981, p. L29).

Recognition of the teen slasher across North American film culture was often accompanied by cogent descriptions of the narrative model that distinguished the new film-type. 'It's a new type of horror film', wrote Canadian journalist Richard Labonté in respect to what he dubbed a 'litany of recent films, each with essentially the same plot' (1980b, p. 202). Later Labonté was even more specific: 'It's a genre which, like any other trend, is rooted in a formula and has a portable plot, in this case, the common denominator was the knife (hatchet, cleaver, pointed stick)-wielding psychopath stalking darkened suburban streets in search of teenage prey' (1980c, p. 27). Labonté's colleague at the *Ottawa Citizen*, Hugh Westrop, was equally direct, announcing in his review of *Terror*

Train (1980) that the 'plot device of a psychopathic killer stalking the nubile young is back, this time involving a crowd of college kids partying on a train' (1980, p. 203). South of the border, *Los Angeles Times* film industry analyst William K. Knoedelseder Jr. considered the impact of that 'plot device' on filmmakers. 'The formula provides an easy-to-follow blueprint, he outlined, '[g]iven some teens in trouble, all you need is someone or something to stalk them [and] a weapon for doing them away' (1980a, p. N3). Yet, perhaps the most detailed and precise summary of the new film-type's content came in April 1981, when the first teen slasher cycle had yet to enter its most intensive phase of releases, from Tom Sowa of the *Spokesman-Review.*

> In films like (. . .) "My Bloody Valentine," "Prom Night," "Silent Scream", "Friday the 13th," and "Terror Train,", the basic pattern always holds. Young, sometimes innocent teens get together to party or just share a little free spirit. Along comes the bogey man, and in his/her hands there's a knife, ax or other means of mutilation. (. . .) By film's end the bad guy always gets his, but by that time the survivors are outnumbered by the hacked-up, impaled, garrotted, mutilated, decapitated and dismembered victims (Sowa, 1981, p. D14).

Based on the films' contemporaneous reception and extensive research conducted across American distributors' entire output up to the year 2003, it is possible to outline a filmmaking model that has been remarkably resilient to change since it emerged in 1974.[3]

The teen slasher story-structure depicts a shadowy blade-wielding killer responding to an event by stalking and murdering the members of a youth group before the threat s/he poses is neutralized (see Figure 1.2). This sequence of events comprises three parts: the setup, featuring story-point one (trigger) and story-point two (threat); the disruption, featuring story-point three (leisure), story-point four (stalking), and story-point five (murders); and the resolution, featuring story-point six (confrontation) and story-point seven (neutralization). The setup, explains why the killer is targeting the youth group. The disruption oscillates between the youth group members' recreational interaction, and the killer stalking and murdering them. During the resolution, the killer is confronted by the surviving character(s) and the threat that s/he poses is extinguished.

Bound to the teen slasher story-structure are three iconographic elements: a distinct setting, a shadowy killer, and a group of youths. Action is confined largely to a single non-urban location which, as a result of being labyrinthine, remote, and sparsely populated, transforms the

Part One: Setup

1. Trigger: Events propel a human (the killer) upon a homicidal trajectory.
2. Threat: The killer targets a group of hedonistic youths for killing.

Part Two: Disruption

3. Leisure: Youths interact recreationally in an insular quotidian location.
4. Stalking: A shadowy killer tracks youths in that location.
5. Murders: The shadowy killer kills some of the youths.

Part Three: Resolution

6. Confrontation: The remaining character(s) challenges the killer.
7. Neutralization: The immediate threat posed by the killer is eliminated.

FIGURE 1.2   The teen slasher film story-structure

everyday sites of the American middle-class into ideal arenas for activities that otherwise would be restricted, enabling youths to pursue and realize their hedonistic urges and, as Martin Rubin notes, permitting a lone blade-wielding stalker to pose a grave and unnoticed threat to a collective of physically fit young people (1999, p. 162). The teen slasher killer is a shadowy prowler, who monitors young targets before, as Timothy Shary recognizes, dispatching 'instant death, although little suffering' (2002a, pp. 60–61), through close-proximity assaults like stabbings and strangulations or attacks from distance with longbows, spear-guns, and other weapons. Whereas stalking undermines potential sympathy for the killer by demonstrating that his/her actions are premeditated, depicting a killer as 'depersonalized, devoid of psychological detail, and faceless' (Rubin, 1999, p. 163), enabled filmmakers to sidestep suggestions that s/he acts sadistically by mobilizing a human monster that, while uncompromising and merciless, behaved like a focused and efficient assassin. Youth group members undertake activities that require them to engage with each other recreationally, from mildly transgressive deeds like casual sex and recreational drug taking, to innocuous free-time activities, including sports, games, and general horseplay (Dika 1990, p. 56). The inclusion of sketched character-types in the group minimizes characterization to prevent audiences from becoming saddened or shocked by their deaths.

Whereas teen slashers tend to be discussed by academics and popular writers as horror films, the film-type's distinct story-structure enabled filmmakers to provoke intrigue, thrills, horror, and amusement. Industry-watchers were acutely aware of these qualities at the time the first teen slasher film cycle unfolded. For example, in a review published in the *Los Angeles Times* in October 1980, Kevin Thomas described *Terror Train* as 'a real jolter of a horror film' and 'a pure thriller', noted its 'atmosphere of mystery', and recognized the filmmakers' attempts to 'lighten it with a saving of dark humor' before concluding that *Terror Train* was 'scary fun' (1980b, p. H19). By drawing on cognitive models developed by Noël Carroll (1990, 1996, 1999) and David Bordwell (1985) light can be shed on the ways the makers of teen slashers like *Terror Train*, which Richard Labonté called 'a skilled mimic of its type' (1980b, p. 202), employed the film-type's story-structure to engage an imagined audience. In doing so, subsequent chapters are provided a framework in which to show that teen slasher film production and content was impacted not only by other horror films, but by films that were widely thought to have been made to provoke one or more of the other responses.

The teen slasher story-structure enabled filmmakers to provoke intrigue in one of two ways, what Rubin called 'the whodunit format' and 'the cipher format' (1999, pp. 163–164). In the whodunit format, elements of story-point one (trigger) are withheld until near the end of the plot (the arrangement of story-points in the film), encouraging viewers to ask: 'who is the killer?' and, when relevant, 'why is s/he killing?' In the cipher format, explains Rubin, 'the question becomes not so much whodunit but whatdunit', as story-point seven (neutralization) is used to provoke intrigue (ibid., p. 164). With the swift revelation of the killer's identity, the audience is invited to wonder 'how can the killer be stopped?'. Bordwell's cognitive model indicates that both formats provoke intrigue because they withhold from viewers information that is required to comprehend causal links between plot-points, the absence of which prevents them from reconstructing completely the plot into the chronologically-organized cause-and-effect sequence of actions that comprise its story (1985, pp. 50–57).

Two points of the teen slasher story-structure, story-point four (stalking) and story-point six (confrontation), enabled filmmakers to excite audience thrills. Carroll proposes that thrills are generated when viewers are presented a situation with two outcomes, one of which is undesirable but probable and one that is desired but unlikely (1996, pp. 100–101). During the period in which both outcomes remain possible, audiences, in theory at least, experience the suspenseful sensation of wanting deeply that which appears improbable. In both sequences of stalking and the confrontation between the killer and the surviving character(s), viewers are presented scenarios in which the killer's targets, for which they are invited to root, are placed in mortal jeopardy, unaware of the danger or ill-equipped to defend themselves. The outcomes of these story-points, especially story-point four (stalking), enabled filmmakers to provoke the response that is most associated with teen slashers.

Story-point five of the teen slasher story-structure (murders) enabled filmmakers to attempt to horrify audiences. For Carroll, horror generated by fictions is an emotional response resulting from exposure to an incongruous threat — a dangerous entity which disturbs natural order — that generates the visible or audible signifiers of horror from characters it menaces (ibid., pp. 27–35, 43–49). Thus in story-point five, viewers are confronted by the fear and loathing of the killer's targets as they acknowledge they will fall victim to a maniac, who, as an emotionless stalker-killer, is stripped of the clearest markers of humanity, seeming thus, as several scholars recognized, at once inhuman and superhuman (Clover, 1992, p. 30; Maltby, 2003, p. 356).

Sequences of young people enjoying themselves that comprise story-point four (leisure) lent themselves ideally to the invitation of amusement, which in turn enabled filmmakers to craft teen slashers that were likely to produce what Isobel Christina Pinedo has called 'recreational terror', 'a bounded experience that will not generate so much distress that the seasoned horror audience will walk out' (1997, p. 40). Amusement is generated, argue incongruity theorists such as Carroll and Paul Lewis, when viewers, shaped by clusters of moral, cultural, aesthetic, philosophical, cognitive, and scientific knowledge, resolve what they perceive initially to be an unthreatening but baffling combination of ideas. 'The resolution of some perceived incongruity occurs in the appreciation of most humor', writes Lewis, 'it is the joyful click of something making sense that had been briefly puzzling that sparks a humor response' (P. Lewis, 1989, p. 11). Whether as a result of pranks or verbal jokes, sequences of young people interacting recreationally offered filmmakers a 'tone-lightening' mechanism which served, much like the amusing moments that Geoff King suggests are utilized strategically in violent action films, as 'a source of comic relief from the otherwise serious implications of the material presented' (2002, p. 172). Thus, amidst the assumed intrigue, thrills, and horror of viewing a mysterious prowler trailing and executing young people, scenes of fun and high-jinx were used to permit viewers to enter what Kawin described as, 'the funhouse of the genre' (1987, p. 105).

In sum, the tales of shadowy maniacs preying upon young adults that came to be known as teen slasher films were widely recognized contemporaneously as having been made to a narrative model that set them apart from other films. Building from the teen slasher's contemporaneous reception it has been possible to identify a unique three-part seven-point story-structure that distinguished the films and which enabled their makers to attempt to intrigue, thrill, and amuse audiences, as well as to horrify them. The teen slasher story-structure provided a filmmaking model with which to fashion the plots and content of their films. 'These films are easy to make', a studio executive had remarked to the *Chicago Tribune*, 'their storytelling pattern is obvious' (quoted in Siskel, 1980d, p. D6). The simplicity of the story ensured that it was recognized quickly by industry-insiders and industry-watchers. It soon became apparent that sagas of young people being menaced by a shadowy killer constituted a new film-type, which, as Neale argued (2000, pp. 231–233), offer industry-professionals a way of rationalizing and reducing financial risk. The commercial objectives of the filmmakers that employed the teen slasher story-structure from 1974 to 1981 are taken up in the next section, in which it is shown that, contrary to standard thinking, the so-called merchants of menace behind the films had far loftier ambitions than to see their efforts 'rubbing shoulders with sex pictures', as Dickstein (1984, p. 74) and others (Clover, 1992, p. 21) have suggested.

Merchants of Menace:
the Goals and Strategies of Teen Slasher Film Production

Unlike industries based on the Fordian model of producing multiple exact copies of a commodity, films need to be different, meaning that film-types like the teen slasher 'provide a cost-effective equivalent to lines and ranges' (Neale, 2000, p. 231), which, as Neale points out, enable a film industry 'to regulate demand and the nature of its product in such a way as to minimise the risks inherent in difference and to maximise the possibility of profit on its overall investment' (ibid., p. 232). As Neale has shown, the production of films to a type is characterized as much by difference between the films as their similarities, and teen slashers were no different, a notion flaunted in the tagline that promoted *My Bloody Valentine* (1981): 'There's more than one way to lose your heart'.

The teen slasher story-structure was, and is, flexible enough to be articulated in countless ways, in terms of the order of its story-points, the frequency with which they are mobilized, and the duration they are afforded in the plot, and could also be supplemented with additional material. The many possible permutations of expressing on-screen the story-structure increased further when it was invested with strategies that filmmakers employ to enhance their films' box-office prospects. For, as Altman (1999) has shown, filmmakers seek to maximize their chances of transforming their investments into financially successful products by combining elements of previous hits and economically viable film-types into new films. Rather than seeking solely to mobilize the characteristics of a single recognizable film-type, Altman suggests that 'popular film producers have always understood the value of merging the qualities of multiple successful films' (ibid., p. 132). One could reduce this industry logic to killing two birds, or even a whole flock, with one stone. Altman identifies two motives that drive this sort of 'calculated hybridity', the first of which is to widen attendance. 'The goal', he proposes, 'is of course to attract those who recognize and appreciate the signs of a particular genre, while avoiding repulsion of those who dislike the genre' (ibid., p. 128). The second motive concerns the ability of distributors to secure the patronage of multiple target-audience segments. 'The desire to aim publicity at a wide range of narrowly defined audiences', writes Altman, 'in turn puts pressure on producers to conceive films as a mix of as many genres as called for by targeted audiences' (ibid., p. 129). Altman therefore is arguing that filmmakers combine elements of hit films to provide distributors with an array of commercially viable material for a film's marketing campaign. This strategy affords marketers consider-able flexibility, enabling them to spotlight marginal textual elements and/or play down prominent material if market-conditions indicate that it will attract theatergoers. It also permits distributors, as Altman, Barbara Klinger (1989, pp. 3–19), and Lisa Kernan (2004) have demonstrated, to frame a film as one which offers a multitude of attractions. This way ticket sales can be maximized by appealing to a range of audience segments and taste-formations. The implementation of these strategies can be seen in Cynthia Erb's production history of *King Kong* (1933), in which she details that efforts to attract a cross-section of the American public led to the film being made and marketed so as to display 'a discernible pastichelike quality, rooted in an assembly of a number of formulas and popular conventions that circulated in the 1920s and early 1930s' (1998, p. 32).

The simultaneous production of different films, the makers of which have drawn content from earlier hits and contemporaneously-made film-types, leads, as Tino Balio (1993), Steve Neale (2000), and Peter Stanfield (2001) have demonstrated, to significant intersections of film content between film-types. For example, Balio shows that during the

1930s numerous elements of film content intersected among the major studios' six 'broad production trends': prestige pictures, musicals, the women's film, comedy, social problem films, and horror films (Balio, 1993, p. 179). So, whereas the Great Depression, dramatized in many social problem films, also provided a backdrop for comedies like *Modern Times* (1936), the European elites that were the principal protagonists of prestige pictures appeared as ghoulish aristocrats in horror films like *Dracula* (1931) (ibid., p. 192). It becomes swiftly apparent that filmmakers of the period located the characteristics of one 'trend' into films produced as part of another 'trend'. The phenomenon of 'intra-cyclic development' is particularly pronounced in cases where distinct films share a target audience and when they are made to similar models. As detailed below, teen slasher film production and content was bound up with developments in youth-oriented and horror filmmaking and with thrillers and murder-mysteries, including glossy whodunits, demonic child films, female-centered coming-of-age dramas, and roller-disco movies.

Employing a textual model and combining elements from hit films are not mutually exclusive modes of film production. Whereas the model is fixed, the landscape of financially successful films is subject to shifts and changes, being reshaped constantly by new hits and misses. Balio, for instance, shows that the central protagonists of the biopic cycle of the 1930s prestige picture started the decade as Europeans but by decade's end were mainly American heroes (1993, p. 192). With the range of commercially viable films and film-types from which to draw content changing rapidly, films produced to a particular model will also exhibit substantial differences from one another across brief periods of time, as a film-type that prompts widespread confidence can be soon viewed with deep suspicion a few months later if commercial promise is not fulfilled and potential sleeper hits and calculated blockbusters turn out to be costly flops. The constantly evolving background of hits coupled with the existence and employment of a filmmaking model enables the films made to a textual model to be positioned simultaneously in several content-focused generic categories (not to mention those defined by industrial or institutional factors, such as independent film or blockbuster hit), and ensures that, across time, a broad range of textual difference is exhibited among films that have been produced to a particular model. Thus, most films are at once 'genre films' and hybrid products, constructed, to some extent, from existing textual material. If genre, whether in reference to film or other cultural products, appeared to bring some semblance of order to, what seemed at first sight, to be a chaotic mass of output, the notion of generic hybridity, that most, if not all, films are complex matrices of content intersecting with, and locatable in, numerous other generic categories in almost never-ending series of Venn diagrammatical circles, seemed to re-impose much of that initial chaos, albeit in a reassuring cloak of scholastic progress. Yet, logic underpins the industrial application of generic hybridity.

Filmmakers do not combine, in wholly random fashion, elements of hit films, whether it is in conjunction with the employment of an established textual model or not. Indeed, when Altman quotes a scene from *The Player* (1992), in which film producers brainstorm unlikely projects such as '*Ghost* (1990) meets *The Manchurian Candidate* (1962)' (1999, pp. 130–131), the informed viewer/reader is invited to balk or laugh at the incongruous synthesis of seemingly incompatible films. The key to gaining insight into the commercial logic underwriting the industrial employment of hybridity at the level of film production, and, for that matter, film promotion, lies in the identification of the imperatives and objectives that govern production of the film-type generally during a particular period and those that govern the production of individual examples of the film-type at specific points in time. By recognizing the manner in which a film is designed to return a profit, and from whom those monies are expected to be generated, light is shed on the decision-making processes that lead content to be mobilized and the sources from which that content has been drawn. It would, for example, make little sense commercially for a producer-distributor attempting to turn a profit by securing the attendance of young urban black males to draw content from films which have proven, or are perceived, to appeal exclusively to elderly white female suburbanites. At the risk of mischaracterizing their audiences, a project along the lines of '*Shirley Valentine* (1989) meets *Menace II Society* (1992)' would seem an incredibly risky venture. However, as Suzanne Mary Donahue, whose groundbreaking work on American film distribution in the 1970s and 1980s is referenced throughout this chapter, pointed out, film producers do not always make their money directly from audiences, rather, some filmmakers aim to sell their films to distributors or exhibitors (1987, p. 263).

Perceptions of the requirements of the target market, whether it is audiences or middlemen like distributors, exert a profound influence on film content and the films and film-types from which content is drawn. It is crucial to establish the kind of company that producers target, because, as producers are well aware, the conduct and requirements of individual distributors and exhibitors often vary, governed, as they are, by different imperatives, some corporate, others relating to agreements they may make with powerful organizations like the Motion Picture Association of America (MPAA). Moreover, producers that aim to sell films to other companies will be aware of the ways in which executives at those companies perceive the audiences for whom they wish to cater. Producing films with a view to enabling second parties to target an audience necessitates that filmmakers draw conclusions about what executives believe will appeal to their target audiences, and thus provide content that is likely to generate executives' confidence based on its assumed capacity to attract their target audience. Thus, for example, it would seem like economic suicide for a production company to lace a film with hardcore pornography if it hoped to sell it to an American television network. It would appear equally inadvisable to offer a children's station like Nickelodeon a film that had been modeled on gory horror films such as *Saw* (2004) and *Hostel* (2005). It is therefore crucial to recognize three ways in which producers envisage product entering into circulation. First, it is important to recognize the producer's target market. So, when approaching an independent production called *Friday the 13th*, one must ask: to which companies did the film's producer-director Sean S. Cunningham hope to sell the film? Once the producer's target market has been established, it is important to consider what the producer perceives the requirements of his/her target market to be. So, if Cunningham was looking to sell his film to Disney, he would have to take into account the fact that Disney specialized in family films and would not handle an R-rated horror film, and thus tailor his film's content accordingly. Then, having established the producer's buyer of choice and what s/he sees as the requirements of the preferred buyer, it is important to consider the ways in which the producer thinks the buyer perceives its target market — the source of the buyer's revenue — usually audiences. Thus, if Cunningham was to conclude that Disney, based on its recent output, preferred to target families with animated features about animals embarking on adventures in exotic lands, it would be in his interest to abandon a live-action tale of a psycho-killer menacing young adults in favor of say a cartoon about a nomadic gerbil searching the Sahara for hidden treasure. Such an approach illuminates the logic that drives filmmakers to mobilize film content which in turn enables the multiple borrowings that permit films, even those fashioned to a textual model, to be hybrid product connected to numerous film-types and individual films.

To enable later chapters to explain the logic behind the production of individual teen slasher films and to identify the films and film-types from which their makers drew content, this section outlines the commercial objectives of teen slasher film production and the principal strategies that teen slasher film producers employed to realize their objectives.

In stark contrast to the bumbling amateurs portrayed in the 'Co-ed Frenzy' sequence from *Blow Out* (1981), a synopsis of which opened this book, early teen slasher producers were resourceful, professional, and opportunistic entrepreneurs who labored tirelessly to make a living at the periphery of the American film industry in the hope of carving out long-term careers. Having invested large sums of money, usually obtained from private financiers, teen slasher filmmakers sought to generate profits for themselves and for their backers so as to generate income and increase their chances of securing future employment. As Christopher Pearce, the horror producer behind *Schizoid*, *New Year's Evil* (both 1980), and *X-ray* (1982), explained of teen slashers, 'these pictures aren't too different from those that have gone before, and what makes them work is more craft than art' (quoted in C. Williams, 1980, p. E1). Such sentiments were echoed by individuals involved in teen slasher production. 'It's all very nice to talk about "art of cinema"', explained *Friday the 13th*'s producer-director Sean S. Cunningham, 'but in this business you need a hit to survive' (quoted in Morrisroe, 1980, p. 101). Cunningham's filmmaking partner, and the writer of *Friday the 13th*, Victor Miller, explained what was on the line. 'I am happy to be a working writer. There are quite a few of us whose names are hugely unknown', he wrote, 'we feed our families by our efforts (. . .) we love our families and we pray for a hit' (1980a, p. K1). Miller's peer William Gray, who, while scraping by as a freelance journalist, had scripted a teen slasher film, was equally pointed about his perceptions of his profession. 'I'm not an artist (. . .) I'm the kind of guy who writes what people suggest (. . .) I'm a hired writer', explained Gray, '[w]hat's done it for me is *Prom Night*, a good commercial movie' (quoted in Anon., 1980l, p. 102).

The teen slasher films made from 1974 to 1981 (and beyond) by Gray, Miller, Cunningham, and their contemporaries were not crafted for audiences per se, but for distribution companies. The teen slashers were independent productions, in the sense that they belonged to what film industry analyst A. D. Murphy described in 1976 as the 'outside world' of North American moviemaking, in which pictures were made despite having 'no ready entree into major distribution companies [and] no bank loan guaranteed by a major studio' (1976b, pp. 1, 37). As *Variety* reported, production of this sort was perilous, with almost 50 per cent of films remaining unreleased and therefore in the red from 1970 to 1980 (Anon., 1980o, p. 10). To turn a profit on the $0.3m–$3m they invested in production, the entrepreneurs behind early teen slashers needed a company to buy the domestic (US and Canadian) theatrical distribution rights to their completed films in an arrangement known as a 'negative pickup' deal. Films were acquired in this way by most distributors, from fly-by-night outfits, small but established independent companies like Dimension Pictures, and top independent distributors such as New World Pictures, to the super heavy-weights of the American film industry, the MPAA-members (Hillier, 1992, pp. 38–73; Lowry, 2005, pp. 41–53; Wyatt, 2005, pp. 229–245).

Teen slasher filmmakers' reliance on reaching the American theatrical market was a consequence of the contexts in which their films were produced and their films' status as youth-oriented horror films. For one, it was felt that independently produced horror and youth-oriented films could not depend upon overseas distribution because American-made action films were thought to be significantly more profitable abroad (Donahue, 1987, p. 272). Moreover, home video had yet to open up an alternative route for independent filmmakers to turn a profit (Wasko, 1995), and films that had not been distributed by MPAA-members were rarely broadcast on network television (Donahue, 1987, p. 228), with even leading independent producer-distributor New World estimating that 97–98 per cent of its pictures never reached the small screen (cited in ibid.). If a film failed to secure domestic theatrical distribution, its chances of turning a profit for its makers were slim.

While it is often claimed that teen slashers were crafted as exploitation product destined for rundown exploitation houses, teen slasher filmmakers did not target the independent distributors that supplied these sites. Most exploitation distributers operated on shoe-string budgets, releasing one or two films annually, conditions which, as Donahue pointed out, commonly prevented them from releasing a film even if they felt it was a surefire hit (ibid., p. 219). Other independent outfits, she explains, specialized in one film-type, which made them unwilling to handle product about which they knew little (ibid., p. 280). These companies also struggled to make money from films they handled because they struggled to secure bookings from exhibitors who were wary of films that had not secured an established distributor (ibid., p. 286). Even larger independent distributors like Dimension Pictures and American Cinema Releasing were unappealing to teen slasher filmmakers because they purchased films on terms that were unfavorable to producers. Operating under tight financial restraints, these companies were unable to pay upfront the $1–4m that teen slasher filmmakers needed to turn a profit (Schreger, 1977, p. 28; Anon., 1980d, pp. 1, 606). Rather, they only could afford to pay filmmakers once a pickup had generated ticket sales. Under this arrangement, filmmakers lost money if the film flopped.

The conditions of independent distribution also meant producers faced long odds and longer waits to receive their share of the box-office dollar. Independently distributed films were routinely deprived of premium play-dates because many exhibitors, with a limited number of screens on their premises, tended to prioritize the MPAA-members' films because the MPAA-members supplied greater quantities of films and, crucially, almost all of the big hits (Donahue, 1987, p. 113). Even if independent distributors secured a reasonable number of play-dates, budgetary restrictions prevented them from giving their films the best chance of attracting large audiences. These small companies could not afford to open a film widely in multiple domestic territories or employ a sophisticated promotion campaign fashioned by a top Madison Avenue marketing firm, and they could not afford to implement the kind of cross-media blitz-marketing that announced the film's imminent arrival or presence in theaters to as wide as possible an audience (ibid., p. 280).

Standard conduct among exhibitors also ensured that, even if an independently distributed film did attract crowds of moviegoers, it needed to sell significantly more tickets than an MPAA-member's film to return the same amount of money to the distributor. It was common knowledge that exhibitors offered independent distributors significantly less favourable terms than they did MPAA-members. Whereas companies like Paramount could use their ability to guarantee delivery of large numbers of films, including certain hits, and could threaten to withhold top films as leverage in the negotiation of favourable distributor-exhibitor contracts, independents could not (ibid., p. 214). Exhibitors therefore increased house nut costs (the monies removed from gross ticket sales to cover a theater's operating costs) (ibid., p. 135), and imposed on independents take-it-or-leave-it offers that saw them, the exhibitors, retain the lion's share of remaining revenue (ibid., p. 114). These factors meant that independent distributors had to wait longer than MPAA-members to accumulate the monies that enabled them to break even on their investments, a situation which was exacerbated by the fact that, in this time, bank loans they used to run their businesses would accumulate interest, thus delaying even further the moment at which the producers of the pickup would see their payments.

Even if an independently distributed film became against-the-odds a hit, there was no guarantee that producers would make a dime. In the time it took to receive payments, producers' profit margins could be

erased by crippling interest incurred on the bank loans that they had
taken to fund the production in the first place (Anon., 1980d, p. 606).
Independent distributors were also notoriously unstable businesses that
often folded as a result of a single box-office failure (Anon., 1979d, pp. 5,
40). In such cases, the producers of other films that the company was
distributing also bore the brunt and tended to be left empty-handed.
Moreover, many small distributors were thought to be controlled by
organized crime syndicates that routinely withheld filmmakers' payments (Gage, 1975, p. 1). For example, it was widely reported that the
producers of *The Texas Chainsaw Massacre* (1974), rumored to have performed fairly well in the mid 1970s, had to pursue their cut of the film's
profits through the courts after their mob-run distributor, Bryanston
Distributing, filed suddenly for bankruptcy (Farley, 1977, p. O1). With
most independent outfits seen to be heavily disadvantaged when marketing and releasing films thought of as financially unstable, and sometimes
run by unscrupulous sharks, teen slasher producers courted the only
distributors that could pay upfront for films, thus ensuring that profits
were made swiftly.

From 1974 to 1981, the independent filmmakers that made teen
slasher films, like most of their peers, targeted the wealthy, stable,
and well-regulated members of the MPAA: the majors Columbia,
MGM/UA, Paramount, Twentieth Century Fox, Universal, and Warner
Bros., and (after 1979) the mini-major Avco Embassy. *Friday the 13th*'s
producer-director, Sean S. Cunningham, has since made it clear that he
appreciated that, other than the MPAA-members, commercially viable
distribution options were limited for filmmakers like himself. '[A]t the
time', explained Cunningham, 'the whole idea of a second feature, that
plays drive-ins and exploitation houses, almost didn't exist anymore as a
viable alternative to conventional distribution' (quoted in Bracke, 2005,
p. 27). It was, however, incredibly difficult to secure a pickup deal from
a company like Universal. Hundreds of films without distribution were
being made each year but MPAA-members purchased only a fraction of
that number because they felt they exerted greater control over their
product by financing production themselves (Anon., 1980d, p. 10).
Supply had outstripped demand, it was a buyer's market, and MPAA-
members could choose which films they purchased. Competition was so
fierce that *Variety* recognized that one teen slasher producer had realized 'the ambitions of most independent filmmakers' when he secured
a pickup deal from Paramount Pictures (Anon., 1980i, p. 25).

MPAA-members, as Jon Lewis pointed out, picked up films which
enabled them to capitalize on commercially successful trends more

quickly and less expensively than if they made similar films themselves (2002, p. 224). Distributors of this caliber were not thinking in general terms. They were interested in specific content, which, based on recent box-office success, seemed capable of generating sufficient ticket sales to enable them to make a profit. In fall 1980, for example, MPAA-member executives including Fox's vice president of advertising Robert Cort, and Don Borchers, a man who the *New York Times* described as 'project coordinator for creative affairs and resident production expert on horror at Avco Embassy Pictures' (Harmetz, 1980d, p. C15), distinguished between the commercial potential of two kinds of monster. Whereas body-snatchers were seen as box-office poison, both men felt that maniacs still exhibited some financial potential (Robert Cort and Don Borchers cited in ibid.). With Hollywood distribution executives, and not theatergoers, determining whether teen slasher film production was a profit-making venture, the films' makers needed to show gatekeepers like Cort and Borchers that their films offered an MPAA-member a reasonable chance of turning a profit. The drive to secure a distribution deal from an MPAA-member gave rise to three principles which governed teen slasher film content: to evoke a combination of hits, to demonstrate marketability to female as well as male youth, and to avoid the X-rating.

Teen slasher filmmakers sought to demonstrate to distributors that their films could be marketed to a large and reliable audience. Industry-insiders and industry-watchers all considered the prime audience for teen slashers to be youth; a demographic that was commonly defined as 12–29-year-olds of both sexes, with a core of 15–25-year-olds (Murphy, 1975a, pp. 3, 74; Murphy, 1975b, pp. 3, 34). 'Kids with loose change are what summer movies are all about, of course, and Frank Mancuso, the marketing whiz behind "Friday the 13th," aimed his $4.5 million promotional budget squarely at the 17- to 24- year-old set' wrote David Ansen and Martin Kasindorf in *Newsweek*, before adding: 'It may be a movie only teen-agers can enjoy and be scared by; for better or worse, they seem to love it' (1980, p. 74). Elsewhere, Jim Moorhead of the *St. Petersburg Independent* remarked that *Silent Scream* was 'aimed primarily at young audiences' (1980b, p. 3B), at Toronto's *Globe and Mail* Jay Scott discussed *Halloween*'s 'high school audience' (1979a) and Rick Groen (1981) commented on the 'predominantly school-age viewers' and the 'nubile teenies in the audience' of *Friday the 13th Part II* (1981), and, in the *Hollywood Reporter*, Vernon Scott maintained that *Hell Night* and other teen slashers appealed to 'teens between roller-skating and college-going age' (1981). The producers and distributors of the teen slashers also spoke of their films' target audience. Whereas Peter Simpson, who bankrolled *Prom Night*, described the film as his 'teenybopper horror picture' (quoted in Anon., 1980r, p. 36), Martin Antonowsky, president of marketing and research at Columbia Pictures discussed the need to promote *Happy Birthday to Me* to its target audience. 'In this case, its teen-agers', declared Antonowsky, 'that's the market for this picture' (quoted in Boyles, 1981, p. H1). There were compelling reasons to consider youth the prime audience for films about young people being menaced by maniacs.

When the early teen slashers were made, young people had been seen as the principal audience for youth-centered and horror films for a quarter of a century, and had been recognized for over a decade as America's prime movie-going demographic. As Thomas Doherty (2002) and Kevin Heffernan (2004) have shown, the American film industry had considered youth to be the principal market for horror and youth-centered films since the 1950s. Indeed, in the late 1970s and early 1980s, it made particular sense for independent filmmakers to offer MPAA-members films that were marketable to young people and for MPAA-members to target those films to young people. At this time, youth was the American film industry's prime audience. In 1979, MPAA market research concluded that 12–20 year-olds accounted for 49 per cent of US theatrical admissions (Anon., 1979o, p. 120). Top industry-insiders also spoke of their conviction that the youth-market determined the commercial achievements of horror. 'Young people are the principal audience for scary films, and they are the major market for movies', explained Robert Rehme, president of Avco Embassy, 'It has always been that way. When I was a kid, I loved the "Dracula" and "Frankenstein" pictures' (quoted in B. Thomas, 1980). The most highly prized segment of the American theatergoing public, as Thomas Schatz (1993, pp. 189–191) pointed out, was unsurprisingly the one which had dominated attendance since the late 1960s: educated middle-class 15–24-year-old males. The prevalence of this view among industry-insiders is said to have given rise to the widespread implementation of the 'Peter Pan Syndrome', a filmmaking doctrine developed by American International Pictures (AIP) in the 1950s that suggested that appealing to 19-year-old males would also secure the attendance of their younger siblings and their female peers (Doherty, 2002, p. 128). In line with this thinking, it would seem safe to assume that teen slasher films were fashioned exclusively or primarily to be marketable to teenage boys and young men, particularly given that it was thought at the time that they were the principal consumers of horror films; 'The audience for horror films', proclaimed *Variety* in August 1980, 'is predominantly male and aged 15–25 years' (Watkins, 1980, p.33).

However, as Rick Altman has argued (1999, p. 129), a central tenet of commercial filmmaking has been the desire to widen attendance beyond the core audience segment. Accordingly, teen slasher filmmakers aimed consistently to make films that also were marketable to female youth.

The makers of teen slashers fashioned films that could be sold to female as well as male youth because they promised to enable MPAA-members to capture the largest possible share of the youth-market so as to offset the cost of purchasing teen slashers, promoting the films, and delivering them to theaters. To produce teen slashers that were marketable to only one sex threatened to reduce by almost half their audience and, by extension, ticket sales. But by making teen slashers marketable to female and male youth, independent filmmakers could offer MPAA-members inexpensive films which they could target to half of the theatergoing population of the US. Thus a teen slasher that could be angled to young people of both sexes offered producers and distributors a better chance of turning a profit. It was also astute to pre-sent distributors films that also would appeal to young females because attendance had, in recent years, been fairly evenly split between the sexes, and because, even though it was thought that, for couples aged twenty-four and under, men decided which movies to attend, some film-makers, including the writer-producers of the 1979 teen slasher *Silent Scream*, Jim and Ken Wheat, felt that young women, like their elder peers, selected films they and their partners viewed together. Indeed, the duo revealed that they had written a strong female lead solely to encourage young women to select the film for themselves and their partners, stating: 'women like to see strong women characters' and 'women decide who goes to the movie more than men' (Jim Wheat and Kim Wheat inter-viewed in 'Three all-new featurettes', 2009). The Wheat brothers were in esteemed company in their assessment of the power of the female horror audience. The view was also held by one of the most powerful figures in American independent production. 'You can never go wrong with a movie' explained Jere Henshaw production vice president at AIP, 'that makes a girl move closer to her date' (quoted in B. Thomas, 1980).

The near-absence of gender-specific referents, relating either to males or females, in the comments made by industry-insiders and industry-watchers about teen slasher audiences cited above testifies to the widely held belief in the 1970s and early 1980s that the American youth-market was composed of young people of both sexes and that, irrespective of whether it was a teen romance like *The Blue Lagoon* (see Harmetz, 1980e, p. C5) or a raunchy comedy about high school boys pursuing casual sex like *Porky's* (1981) (see Byron, 1982, p. 50), youth-oriented films were to be made for, marketed to, and consumed both by teenage boys and young men and by teenage girls and young women. Nevertheless, connections between teen slashers and young female audiences surfaced from time to time. For example, writing of a romantic subplot involving two college students that featured in *Silent Scream,* Jim Moorhead of the *St. Petersburg Independent* remarked, '[i]t's a foregone conclusion that they'll make love eventually, which is a turn-on for the boys and girls who are watching' (1980b, p. 3B). In addition, Tom Sowa noted in the *Spokesman-Review* that a leading exhibitor had told him that his twelve year-old daughter viewed teen slashers regularly (Steve Friedstorm cited in Sowa, 1981, p. D14.). And, as chapter five shows, by 1980, a studio report had concluded that teen slasher films were attracting disproportionately large numbers of teenage girls. By virtue of making films that could be targeted both to female and male youth, teen slasher filmmakers, like most other makers of youth-oriented product, saw themselves, and were seen by industry-watchers, as being in the 'date-movie' business. This is not to say, as the term 'date-movie' suggests, that these companies were making films that were expected only to be viewed by courting-couples. Rather, it means, as Geoff King indicates (2002, p. 73), that they were making youth-centered films that could be angled to young people of both sexes, irrespective of whether they attended alone, as dating heterosexual couples, in single-sex pairs or groups, or as mixed-sex groups. To show that their films could be sold to male and female youth, the makers of the teen slashers aimed to provide MPAA-members with content that could be transferred to marketing materials so as to clearly mark the films for young people as product that had been designed specifically for their consumption.

On-screen depictions of the target audience were perhaps the most valuable hooks. Industry-insiders and industry-watchers believed emphasizing the presence of young people in horror films like teen slashers would be commercially viable, not only because horror film attendance was dominated by youths, but because the American film industry has commonly assumed that spotlighting a demographic in a film and its marketing campaign communicates that the film is intended for that demographic, without necessarily alienating others. The *Hollywood Reporter*'s Vernon Scott noted '[t]hose unfortunate victims, as a rule, are themselves played by teen actors, all the better to provide age-group identification for young viewers' (1981), while Patrick Goldstein of the *Los Angeles Times* observed that '[t]he majority of the current victims are school kids — by clever coincidence the same age as most horror moviegoers' (1981, p. L7). The same logic is apparent in statements made by producer-distributor Irwin Yablans, the so-called 'Merchant of Menace', about his 1981 teen slasher *Hell Night*. 'It's about college kids, again, young people in jeopardy', he told the *Hollywood Reporter*, '[i]t's young people who go to the movies and they love to fantasize themselves in the same circumstances' (quoted in V. Scott, 1981). *Terror Train*'s writer-producer Daniel Grodnik did not use cod psychology to illuminate his thinking. 'It involved young people', he explained, 'because that's the market' (Daniel Grodnik quoted in Knoedelseder Jr., 1980a, p. N3). Robert E. Kapsis' production history of the 1981 teen-centered horror film *Fear No Evil* shows that MPAA-members shared this view (1992, pp. 163–164). Kapsis was told by Robert LaLoggia, the film's writer-director, that Avco Embassy would probably have withdrawn its offer to distribute the film had he not emphasized the depiction of young people, content that initially had been a minor element (cited in ibid.). Predictably, the promotion of *Fear No Evil* emphasized teenagers. 'Alexandria High . . . Class of '81 . . .' began the film's tagline.

In addition to reflecting on-screen the films' target audience, teen slasher filmmakers looked to increase their chances of realizing their commercial objectives by acquiring a detailed and up-to-date under-standing of industry developments. As, Mark Tenser, president of Crown International Pictures, put it, 'an independent in today's marketplace has to be on top of the trends' (quoted in Donahue, 1987, p. 229). By monitoring box-office statistics, scrutinizing distribution rosters, and reading the trade press, individuals like Gary Sales, a producer of the 1981 teen slasher *Madman*, aimed to identify which film-types and what film content to replicate so as to appeal to MPAA-members. Explaining that he and his collaborators 'realized that you need a project for which there is a ready-made market', Sales revealed to *Variety* that they made *Madman* because Paramount recently had enjoyed some commercial success with an independently produced teen slasher (cited in Anon., 1982b, p. 20). These strategies, while not guaranteeing success, enabled filmmakers to draw informed conclusions about content that improved their chances of securing MPAA-member distribution. If possessing a comprehensive and up-to-the-minute understanding of the American film market provided the bedrock of research and development in the independent sector, combining material from several hit films provided the cornerstone of production.

To ensure that the youth-centered and youth-oriented content high-lighted by MPAA-members in their marketing campaigns not only demonstrated to young people that the teen slashers had been made for their consumption but that large numbers of young people actu-ally attended screenings, teen slasher filmmakers drew content from films and film-types which were assumed recently to have secured a sizable young audience — blockbuster hits and youth-oriented hits. As is elucidated in subsequent chapters, the hits from which teen slasher filmmakers drew content were varied, and while including some horror blockbusters, tended not to be horror films. Initially, it may seem puzzling that the makers of low-budget horror films incorporated elements drawn from non-horror blockbuster hits and moderate hits, however, as Peter Krämer has pointed out (2005, p. 11), the influence of the industry's biggest earners can be expected to be considerable. In much the same way as Krämer shows how the imitation of blockbuster hit content was seen to increase the box-office prospects of the majors' next wave of calculated blockbusters, such strategies were of equal importance to filmmakers endeavoring to provide the same companies with their next sleeper hits. In addition, by evoking big hits, which displayed, at the very least, high production values, teen slasher filmmakers could mask the shoestring budgets on which they were operating and obscure the fact that the films emerged from the same sector of the industry that churned out micro-budget, often brutal exploitation films, so as to offer MPAA-distributors product that was not entirely different from their existing output and which, as a consequence, would not look wholly out of place on their distribution rosters. Thus, when it came to making a youth-centered horror movie like a teen slasher film, mobilizing content from a smash hit youth romance like *Love Story* (1970), a mega-earning disco gang movie like *Saturday Night Fever* (1977), or a chart-topping example of the tales of youthful high-jinks that William Paul labels 'animal comedy' (1994, pp. 85–112) like *Animal House* (1978), was, in effect, no different from aping elements of horror hits like *The Exorcist* (1973), *Jaws* (1975), and *The Omen* (1976); they were all, at specific points in time, commercially viable properties which had appealed to the assumed audience of teen slasher films. By enabling prospective distributors to draw parallels between teen slashers and these major attractions, teen slasher filmmakers looked to provide themselves with an edge in a fiercely competitive market place in which MPAA-member pickup deals were highly prized and in limited supply. Although independent production companies discussed openly the fact that they tailored film content in the 1970s for marketing purposes (Donahue, 1987, p. 89), filmmakers tend to be guarded about borrowing content from other films. And the makers of early teen slashers were no exception. Their conduct was, however, pinpointed by journalists, who, as subsequent chapters show, spotlighted similarities between individual teen slashers and hit films routinely. As their observations indicate, teen slasher filmmakers plundered contemporaneous hits extensively.

The extraordinary lengths to which teen slasher filmmakers went to provide MPAA-member distributors with product to serve their prime audience, amounted to nothing if the films were awarded the institutional category that MPAA-members were loathed to see stamped on their films — the dreaded X. Claims that the teen slashers were made to push the envelope of filmic violence, particularly misogynistic violence, overlook the fact that this type of conduct would have jeopardized the filmmakers' chances of realizing their commercial objectives by alienating completely the very companies upon which they relied to generate a swift profit on the hundreds of thousands or even millions of dollars they had invested in production. Because the producers of teen slashers aimed to secure MPAA-member distribution deals, they were required to craft films that would receive the R-rating from the MPAA's film certification office, the Classification and Ratings Administration (CARA). While the MPAA-members occasionally had released X-rated films in the early 1970s, they had all but abandoned the practice by the time the teen slashers were being made. 'An X-rating is so tainted', explained Bob Clark, the producer-director of *Black Christmas* (1974), 'it kills your film — no major distributor will touch it' (quoted in Heller Anderson, 1982, p. 19). Even if an MPAA-member distribution contract was not forthcoming, it was in teen slasher filmmakers' interests to avoid the X-rating.

The commercial prospects of X-rated films were poor because of restrictions placed on their promotion, exhibition, and consumption. Due to the rating's association with hardcore pornography, TV networks were barred from advertising X-rated releases (Donahue, 1987, p. 43), many newspapers refused to publicize them, and the vast majority of US theaters would not book them (Lewis, 2004, pp. 164–171). Most importantly, an X, unlike the R-rating, prohibited the attendance of under-17s. When rated R, a film could be viewed by any spectator, including minors who were accompanied by guardians of 17 years and over. Moreover, because the R-rating was used voluntarily by the American film industry, exhibitors could not be enforced by law to follow to the letter its stipulations (Donahue, 1987, p. 42). It was widely known, although usually denied officially, that unaccompanied minors were admitted to R-rated films or would otherwise find an older-looking teenager to pass off as their guardian, points which were hammered home shortly after the teen slasher cycle ended when the American popular press drew attention to the lax policing of the R-rating by published thought-provoking images of gangs of pubescent girls queuing for the aforementioned teen sex comedy *Porky's* (Heller Anderson, 1982, p. 19). The under-17s were seen to be a crucial market to the distributors of teen slasher films. Comprising roughly a quarter of all admissions and half of the youth-market, 12–17-year-olds had the power to make or break a teen slasher film for a distributor. 'The young crowd is the prime audience', declared Irwin Yablans, the man behind *Halloween* and *Hell Night,* 'the greatest response [to teen slasher films] seems to come from the 11–12 age group' (quoted in B. Thomas, 1980). Indeed, as the *New York Times* reported in 1980, unpublished studio reports had indicated that as much as 45 per cent of tickets for teen slashers had been sold to spectators aged between 12 and 17 years, significantly higher numbers than those generated for contemporaneous adult-centered horror films like *Dressed to Kill* (1980) (Harmetz, 1980d, p. C15). With the X alienating preferred distributors and excluding a significant portion of the teen slasher's target audience, the receipt of an R-rating was nothing short of essential.

The conditions which reduced drastically the commercial potential of X-rated films gave rise to a mode of filmmaking that Kevin S. Sandler (2002, pp. 203–208) called 'Incontestable R', whereby filmmakers, like those behind the teen slashers, tailored content to satisfy the (shifting) boundary that separated the R and X ratings. To help filmmakers avoid an X-rating, the MPAA even published a code of self-regulation, a revised edition of which was issued in 1977 (reprinted in Lewis, 2002, pp. 307–314). Of most interest to teen slasher filmmakers were those points related to the depiction of violence. 'Restraint shall be exercised in the taking of a life', stated the document, 'detailed and protracted acts of brutality, cruelty, physical violence, torture and abuse shall not be presented' (reprinted in ibid. p. 310). With the cost of certification as high as $8000 and with CARA having overturned only twelve of the roughly 3500 certificates it had issued (Donahue, 1987, p. 40), there were strong incentives for filmmakers to follow the MPAA's guidelines carefully, and to make certain that content was controlled in such a way as never to approach the threshold of the X-rating — editing footage for resubmission was a costly exercise that, based on historical precedent, seemed futile. As subsequent chapters show, most teen slasher filmmakers went to great lengths to limit on-screen aggression, suffering, and bloodshed, and to ensure that most violent acts were committed by men against men.

In sum, the independent filmmakers behind the teen slasher films of 1974 to 1981 (and beyond) were sophisticated businesspeople who possessed a detailed and up-to-date understanding of the shifting industrial landscape in which they operated. They realized that their best chance of making a profit was to sell their films to the only companies that could afford to pay upfront in one lump sum an amount of money larger than the films' production budgets — the member studios of the MPAA. To increase their chances of realizing this highly-prized objective, teen slasher filmmakers endeavored to offer MPAA-members product which could be released in any theater, which could be advertised openly, which promised to be marketable to a reliable theatergoing demographic, and which shared features with films that boasted a proven track-record of securing the attendance of that demographic. Accordingly, teen slashers were crafted to be R-rated date-movies that could be target marketed to male and female youth based on the presence of content shared with a range of youth-market hits and blockbuster hits. The combined results of applying this production model to the textual model outlined above, across the seven year period from 1974 to 1981, was the first cycle of a new film-type. The next section focuses on the structure of that cycle, breaking it into a series of chronologically distinct phases of production operations so as to illuminate how the commercial objectives of teen slasher film producers, as well as the content of their films, was impacted by the points in time at which they contributed films to the cycle.

From Pioneers and Speculators to Prospectors and Carpetbaggers: A Model of Film Cycle Development

Scholars are in general agreement that a considerable portion of film output is released in cycles. That is to say, relatively large quantities of similar films are made and released over a limited period of time before production declines markedly or ceases altogether, sometimes temporarily, other times permanently. The concept of the film cycle thus places a film industry's conduct in terms of production and distribution at the heart of genre scholarship. However, despite calls from Alan Williams (1984) and Steve Neale (1990), film cycle scholarship has often played down the commercial imperatives and objectives, and the industrial conditions that shape film production and distribution decisions and that underwrite decisions of whether or not to mobilize certain film content, be it individual textual elements or textual models — conduct that ultimately determines whether or not a film cycle develops.

The reluctance to position industrial and institutional forces at the centre of studies of film cycles has given rise to two tendencies. On the one hand, scholars have concentrated on tracing the evolution of content and/or themes across a historically specific group of films. Thus, where Thomas Schatz (1983) once theorized that a genre evolves through phases of increasing self-consciousness that lead to parody, Koven (2006) has shown that shifts in the content of Italian popular cinema evolved across the 1970s and 1980s, leading to, among others, supernatural films, murder-mysteries, and police procedurals. Other scholars have attempted to explain film cycles as by-products of broad social or cultural currents. Effectively sidestepping the industrial decision-making processes that govern the production, content, and distribution of individual films (the cumulative effect of which is the development of the film cycle itself), these scholars link the proliferation across films of shared content and themes to developments taking place outside of, or independent to, the mechanisms of film production. For instance, Vera Dika (1990) links the 'stalker cycle', a selection of higher-profile teen slasher films released between late 1978 and mid 1981, to the American public's apparent dissatisfaction with the foreign and domestic policies of President Jimmy Carter's administration. I will be offering a different account below. In such cases, social forces are presented as triggers for the intensive mass-scale production of films made to a certain type, rather than as catalysts which may, or, clearly have, informed the mobilization of some elements of film content.

In the four decades that have passed since Lawrence Alloway (1971) introduced the notion of film cycles to film studies, no attempt has been made to explain the different forms of commercial logic that underpin the production of a particular film-type at different points across a cycle. This section seeks to fill that void by presenting what, to my knowledge, is the first attempt to provide a model of film cycle development from an industrial perspective, one which explains the manner in which film cycles unfold rather than shifts in film content, and one that provides a lexicon with which to describe the chronologically distinct phases of film production operations that comprise a film cycle. By enabling film cycles to be approached as a series of chronologically distinct phases of film production and distribution operations that are each characterized by specific sets of commercial imperatives and micro-industrial contexts, both of which directly influence production and distribution decisions, the model promises to assist in the identification of the precise points in time at which a film-type is produced and in what numbers in order to make it easier to draw conclusions about the specific sets of conditions which impacted production levels, including dips and surges in production as well as the temporary or permanent suspension of production. While developed retrospectively based primarily on research conducted on patterns of teen slasher film production in North America from the

1970s to the early 2000s, with particular emphasis placed on the period 1974–1984, the model of film cycle development has thus far demonstrated remarkable levels of applicability to other film-types made in the period. Therefore, in the course of this book, the model will be applied, along with its associated terminology, to other film-types being made for the American market around the time of the first teen slasher film cycle.

Because film-types offer film industries one of the most significant ways in which to rationalize conduct and manage the risks of operating in a capital intensive and highly unpredictable business environment (Neale, 2000), they provide an ideal starting point at which to gain insight into the logic and decision-making processes that shape output. It is therefore my hope that the model of film cycle development offers scholars a useful tool with which to account for patterns in film production and distribution. And, although the conclusion of this book will speak to the model's potential transferability to contexts beyond the American theatrical film industry of the late 1970s and early 1980s, its use-value hinges on it being applied to different types of film, different historical periods such as the classical era and the present day, to the filmic output of other nations, to other sectors of film production and distribution including art film, avant-garde, and hardcore, as well as industries specializing in non-theatrical markets like home video/DVD, television, and the internet. It is therefore my hope that the model may become part of an ongoing scholarly process, one which could reinvigorate the study of 'genre' by encouraging scholars to rethink the links between film industries' conduct and their products.

The term 'film cycle' has, for two main reasons, impeded scholars' abilities to develop a deeper understanding of the stratification of film production patterns, and thus, more importantly, to comprehend the conditions that inform the continuation, discontinuation or suspension of a film-type or, for that matter, the escalation, reduction, or stagnation in the quantities of that film-type being made. First, the term 'film cycle', implying an organic process of birth, life, and death, suggests misleadingly that the widespread production and distribution of a film-type is bracketed by periods of complete inactivity. However, the conduct of large numbers of industry-professionals working at any given time ensures that production of a film-type tends not to begin and then, after a brief intense period of production, end, either permanently or for a lengthy period of time, but instead tends to continue to some degree after such bursts of activity, at what could be called 'base level production'. Base level production refers to a low level of production that is specific to the film-type in question and which will invariably be affected by production costs, meaning that capital intensive projects like biblical epics or disaster films are likely to have a considerably lower base level production than comparatively inexpensive ventures such as gang movies or teen slasher films. Base level production is a result of a film-type essentially being 'out there' once it has become established as part of an industry's range of products. There is nothing to stop film-makers from producing an example of the film-type, which they often do. Thus, whether it is because of a failure to recognize that a film-type is no longer commercially viable, as happened with demonic child films in the late 1970s, or because it has been concluded that relative inactivity has opened up a potentially profitable niche, the 1996 teen slasher film *Scream* being a case in point, most film-types are usually being made. The film cycle is thus ideally perceived as a specific spike-pattern in production levels during which a film-type is made in larger quantities than at its base level. Second, the term film cycle, not unlike the term genre, has been applied to several distinct patters of film output. Of specific relevance here is Neale's (1990) observation of the differences between industrial categories of film genre (product-types defined contemporaneously by industry-professionals like the 1970s car-crash films examined by Tico Romao (2003)) and critical categories of film genre (groupings such as film noir that have been designated post facto by writers to form the basis of critical projects). For some writers film cycle has become a byword for film genre, thus becoming a catch-all label in much the same way as Neale pointed out vis-à-vis 'genre'. An example here would be what Jacinda Read (2000) calls the 'rape-revenge cycle' which, by encompassing such diverse product as the 1977 exploitation film *I Spit on your Grave* and the 1992 calculated blockbuster *Batman Returns*, falls firmly into Neale's critical category. Beyond Neale's categories, the term film cycle has been used in reference to different patterns of industry conduct: to an element of content shared by a small number of disparate films (Heffernan, 2002); to low levels of production that are restricted to a brief period of time (Grant, 1996; Dika 1990); to the protracted proliferation of a film-type across stretches of time as long as a decade or more (Doherty, 1988). Given that these distinct patterns of film production and distribution result from different sets of industrial conditions, it is advantageous to distinguish conceptually and lexically between these patterns and think in terms of 'fads', 'clusters', 'staples', and, 'cycles'.

A 'fad' is an individual textual element or theme mobilized across film-types with some regularity during a particular period. It may therefore be, but is not limited to, a character-type like the wise-cracking male protagonists that Yvonne Tasker (1993) shows were common to 1980s action films, but which also appeared in countless contemporaneous comedies, and even distinguished the killer of the later *A Nightmare on Elm Street* films (1987–1991), or it may be the young heroines of rape-revenge films (Read, 2000), some teen slashers (Clover, 1992), and 'violence-against-women' thrillers (Wood, 1987) of the late 1970s and early 1980s. A fad may also be a setting such as a summer camp or a high school, which, as James Hay and Stephen Bailey (1998, pp. 218–235) indicated, and as later chapters show, were used in various youth-oriented film-types of the early 1980s, from female-centered coming-of-age dramas to teen slashers. Or it may be set-piece spectacle such as sequences of disco-dancing, which, in addition to appearing in 1979's roller-disco movies, featured in the aforementioned youth-oriented film-types, most notably in the teen slasher *Prom Night*. A fad may also be a theme that rises to prominence across a series of contemporaneous but otherwise different films, such as liberation through recreation, which, as shown in later chapters, was a common strand running through examples of the youth-oriented film-types cited above. In contrast to the fad, a staple is no flash-in-the-pan craze among filmmakers working with different film-types.

By staple, I mean a film-type that is produced with a high degree of consistency and in regular numbers across a long period. For example, as Balio (1998) points out, American-based companies, particularly Disney/Pixar and Dreamworks Animation, followed *Toy Story* becoming the highest grossing film of 1995, by releasing, every year since 1998 (the earliest point at which similar films could be completed) digitally animated adventure films including *A Bug's Life* (1998), *Shrek* (2001), *Madagascar* (2005), and *Up* (2009). Had these big-budget calculated blockbusters been expensive flops, it is inconceivable that they would have continued to be made. However, because they were, and remain, highly profitable ventures that usually finish in the annual top ten theatrical earners, production is unlikely to stop soon. Twelve uninterrupted years (and counting) is, in my opinion, too long to consider these CGI adventures a film cycle. Rather, they have become a long-standing fixture of Hollywood's repertoire of 'family-friendly' films (Krämer, 2002). If fads and staples exist at the outer extremes of the spectrum, the 'cluster' and the 'cycle' occupy the middle-ground, distinguished as patterns of output by the number of chronologically distinct phases, during which production of a film-type rises above base level production.

As elucidated below, I consider a film cycle to be comprised of either three or four stages. Each stage consists of a chronologically distinct phase of production operations during which films are produced to a specific filmmaking model — what Altman (1999) called the 'blueprint'

— such as the teen slasher story-structure. Although it may be preceded by a film that fails commercially but is considered to exhibit some economic potential (stage one), the process of cycle development begins when a film that differs from contemporaneous hits is adjudged to have performed well commercially (stage one or two). Thereafter, follow two chronologically distinct phases of film production operations. During the first of these phases (stage two or three), at least one additional hit is generated, usually from a fairly small quantity of similar films. During the second of these phases (stage three or four), more textually similar films are made, usually in greater quantities than the first phase. Thereafter, production drops to base level. The process can, and often is, repeated if a new hit interrupts a commercially unsuccessful period of base level production. With production of the film-type contained within distinct periods of time, subsequent phases begin once the films made during the previous phase have begun to be released and producers are able to respond by producing new examples of the film-type.[4]

While a cycle is a surge in production/distribution of a film-type followed by a period of sustained production/distribution and a decline in production/distribution, a cluster is characterized by the absence of sustained production. The cluster, ostensibly an undeveloped cycle, is the product of confidence in a film-type rising quickly and evaporating suddenly after the first phase of post-hit production. As later chapters show, gang movies, the large-scale production of which was restricted to 1978, and roller-disco movies produced only in 1979, are quintessential film clusters.

A cycle does not unfold without what I call a Trailblazer Hit, the film that is seen to have been commercially successful and which content-wise is seen to differ significantly from contemporaneous hits. This development occurs in one of three ways. In terms of new film-types, a single film provides both a new textual model and demonstrates its economic viability, or two films produced at different times serve these functions separately. For cycles of an established film-type, which includes the second, third (and so on) cycle of a film-type, a single film establishes anew the commercial potential of the film-type. The Trailblazer Hit results from one of two distinct methods of film production.

The Trailblazer Hit may be the product of a commercially promising or successful 'Pioneer Production' (see Table 1.1). Filmmakers behind Pioneer Productions, or 'Pioneers', combine pre-existing textual elements, and sometimes quite innovative material, in ways that differ radically from previous output so as to create what Donahue called 'unique pictures' (1987, p. 273). While some subjectivity is involved in conferring upon a film the status of a Pioneer Production, I consider Stanley Kubrick's sci-fi art film *2001: A Space Odyssey* (1968) and the disco gang movie *Saturday Night Fever* (1977) to be Pioneer Productions. Because it places great value on product differentiation, Pioneer Production is an incredibly high-risk business practice in which few filmmakers are willing, able, or permitted, to engage. Therefore, as it is relatively rare, it follows that Pioneer Productions generate few hits, thus limiting their capacity to initiate the widespread production of similar films and to bring about a cycle.

TABLE 1.1   Path to Trailblazer Hit of new film-type; Pioneer Production variant.

Stage One	
Pioneer Production →	Trailblazer Hit →
e.g. *Rosemary's Baby* (1968)	

A new cycle of an established film-type, and, often, the first cycle of a new film-type, begins to unfold as a result of a Trailblazer Hit that started life as what I call a 'Speculator Production' (see Table 1.2). In terms of a new film-type, the Trailblazer Hit that results from a Speculator Production may follow a commercially disappointing Pioneer Production (see Table 1.3). The filmmakers behind Speculator Productions, or 'Speculators', gamble on enjoying financial success with a film-type that either has never performed well commercially or has not generated a hit for a considerable time. The teen slasher film *Scream* (1996), like the animal comedy *American Pie* (1999), is a textbook example of a Speculator Production that became a Trailblazer Hit. Where *Scream* was made twelve years after the previous non-sequel teen slasher hit, *A Nightmare on Elm Street* (1984), *American Pie* was made fifteen years after the previous hit animal comedy, *Revenge of the Nerds* (1984). Speculating is less perilous than Pioneering as it is not so heavily reliant on product differentiation, although it is still a high-risk undertaking. However, because they are made to existing textual models, Speculator Productions are more common than Pioneer Productions and as such generate greater numbers of hits and are more likely to be the starting point of a cycle. In the event that a Pioneer Production fails commercially but a Speculator Production becomes a Trailblazer Hit, it is not uncommon for scholars and popular writers to misidentify the Speculator Production as the first example of a film-type.

TABLE 1.2   Path to Trailblazer Hit of established film-type.

Stage one	
Speculator Production →	Trailblazer Hit →
e.g. *Scream* (1996)	

TABLE 1.3   Path to Trailblazer Hit of new film-type; Speculator Production variant.

Stage One		*Stage Two*		
Pioneer Production →	Failure →	Speculator Production ›	Trailblazer Hit ›	

The first teen slasher film cycle started to unfold when a Pioneer Production that was profitable for its producers but not for its distributor, provided a template for two Speculator Productions, one of which became a Trailblazer Hit (see Table 1.4). The first stage of the cycle took place when the story-structure that later formed the basis of teen slasher filmmaking emerged when the Pioneer Production *Black Christmas* opened in 1974. In contrast to later teen slasher filmmakers, Bob Clark, the producer-director of *Black Christmas,* has stressed that he endeavored to 'break new ground' with the content of the film, stating consistently 'I wanted to do something that I didn't think had been done before' (interviewed in 'Going to pieces', 2006). The second stage of the teen slasher cycle occurred when the first film to have been modeled on *Black Christmas* enjoyed some success at the American box-office. That film, *Halloween* (1978), was, with *Silent Scream* (1979), one of two teen slasher Speculator Productions made in late 1977.

TABLE 1.4   Path to Trailblazer Hit of first teen slasher film cycle.

Stage One		*Stage Two*	
Pioneer Production →	Failure →	Speculator Production →	Trailblazer Hit →
Black Christmas (1974)		*Halloween* (1978)	*Halloween*
		Silent Scream (1979)	

The roles that Pioneers and, often, Speculators play in the development of a film cycle can only be gauged fully through a consideration of events that have unfolded after the films have been released. The retroactive appreciation of the contributions made by Pioneers and Speculators explains why industry-watchers did not discuss either *Black Christmas* or

Halloween as teen slasher films (or one of the synonyms that soon entered into circulation). As Jancovich has suggested, neither the label nor the blueprint, to use Altman's terms, had been established when either film was produced and distributed. '[Director John] Carpenter could not have seen *Halloween* as a [teen] slasher movie', explains Jancovich, 'because there was no such category at the time' (2002, p. 8) — a point that also applies to the makers of *Black Christmas*. Thus, it is the adoption of its distinct features by other filmmakers that, as Jancovich indicates, confer upon a film like *Black Christmas* the status of the first example of its type, and that confer upon *Halloween* the status of the first hit of its type (ibid.). In contrast, subsequent stages of a cycle reflect the production strategies of filmmakers, which are usually so transparent as to be highlighted routinely by industry-watchers.

The Trailblazer Hit — whether resulting from a Pioneer Production or a Speculator Production — lays the foundation upon which a film cycle is built. And, while not always leading to the development of a cycle, a Trailblazer Hit usually initiates the production of what I call Cash-ins, which are films modeled closely, systematically, and calculatedly on a previous film in an attempt to capitalize on its commercial achievements. Although, the makers of Cash-ins draw material from other contemporaneous hits and/or commercially viable film-types, their efforts tend to be disparagingly described as 'imitations', 'copies', 'clones' or 'rip-offs' by scholars, critics, fans, and casual movie watchers because they are recognized as having been self-consciously patterned after a high-profile commercial success. A cycle is the cumulative effect of a Trailblazer Hit being followed in rapid succession by two chronologically distinct phases of Cash-in production operations, comprised of 'Prospector Cash-ins' and 'Carpetbagger Cash-ins' respectively.[5] Therefore, if a cycle initiated by a Trailblazer Hit that began life as a Pioneer Production, or if the cycle is the second, third (and so on) cycle of an established film-type, 'Prospector Cash-ins' constitute the second stage and 'Carpetbagger Cash-ins' constitute the third stage (see Table 1.5). If, however, the cycle is of a new film-type and the Trailblazer Hit was provided by a Speculator Production that followed a Pioneer Production, 'Prospector Cash-ins' constitute the third stage and 'Carpetbagger Cash-ins' constitute the fourth stage (see Table 1.6).

TABLE 1.5 First cycle of new film-type Pioneer Production-Trailblazer Hit variant and new cycle of established film-type.

	Stage One	Stage Two	Stage Three
New Film-type	Pioneer Production →		
		Trailblazer Prospector Carpetbagger	
		Hit →	Cash-ins → Cash-ins
New Cycle of Established Film-type	Speculator Production →		

TABLE 1.6 First cycle of new film-type Pioneer Production-failure/Speculator Production-Trailblazer Hit variant.

Stage One		Stage Two		Stage Three	Stage Four
Pioneer Production → →	Failure	Speculator Production →	Trailblazer Hit →	Prospector Cash-ins →	Carpetbagger Cash-ins

Prospector Cash-ins are produced soon after the Trailblazer Hit has signaled anew, or for the first time, the financial viability of a film-type. Prospecting is a surprisingly risky undertaking because 'Prospectors' attempt to capitalize on a hit, for which a tested and commercially proven model of evocation/differentiation has yet to be confirmed by subsequent hits. Prospectors therefore risk re-using features of the Trailblazer Hit that are not appealing to their target markets, be they distributors, exhibitors, or audiences. The risks of Prospector Cash-in production are, however, offset by the potential gains. If filmmakers are fortunate or shrewd enough to replicate elements of the hit that attracted or resonated with their target market, they usually stand to face little competition from likeminded entrepreneurs. As a high-risk/high-gain practice, Prospector Cash-in production is undertaken by relatively few filmmakers.

The third stage of the first teen slasher film cycle came about with the production of three Prospector Productions: *Friday the 13th*, *Prom Night*, and *Terror Train* (all 1980). The Prospectors behind the films were acutely aware that they were attempting to emulate the financial achievements of a Trailblazer Hit by modeling their films on *Halloween*. For instance, Daniel Grodnik, writer-producer of *Terror Train*, described his film as '"Halloween" on a train' (quoted in Knoedelseder Jr., 1980a, p. N3), and Victor Miller, co-writer of *Friday the 13th*, stated: 'I went to school basically on the movie *Halloween*' (interviewed in 'Return to Crystal Lake', 2003).

Moreover, industry-watchers clearly recognized that the makers of the three films had adopted the same textual model and employed the same commercial logic. So, where *Friday the 13th*, the first of the films to open theatrically, was compared routinely to *Halloween* (C. Hicks, 1980, p. C7; Step., 1980, p. 14), *Prom Night*, the second of the trio to be released, was described as, among other things, '[an] obvious attempt to cash in on the success of "Halloween"' (Dresser, 1980, p. 2), and *Terror Train*, the last of the trio to reach movie screens, was referred to as 'another (. . .) imitation of *Halloween*' (J. Scott, 1980b) and as 'another "Halloween" rip-off' (Anon., 1980n, p. 12). As these final comments intimate, *Friday the 13th*, *Prom Night*, and *Terror Train* where often compared to each other. For example, writing in the *Montreal Gazette*, Bruce Bailey remarked of *Terror Train*, 'it's a slickly-filmed tale from the '"knock 'em off one-by-one" school of suspense — an institution whose graduates include *Prom Night* [and] *Friday the 13th*' (1980, p. 70).

The development of a film cycle hinges on the potential shown by the Trailblazer Hit being confirmed by at least one of the Prospector Cash-ins becoming a commercial success, or a 'Reinforcing Hit'. If Prospector Cash-ins are considered to have disappointed financially, production of the film-type ends or drops to base level, leaving a cluster like the roller-disco movies mentioned above (see Table 1.7, Table 1.8, and Table 1.9). However, a different pattern unfolds when at least one of the Prospector Cash-ins approaches, emulates or surpasses the achievements of the Trailblazer Hit. By galvanizing perceptions of the commercial viability of a nascent or re-emergent film-type and by signaling a seemingly lucrative approach to balancing textual evocation and differentiation, Reinforcing Hit(s) trigger a second, and usually much larger, wave of Cash-in production operations.

TABLE 1.7   Film cluster of new film-type Pioneer Production-Trailblazer Hit variant and film cluster of established film-type.

	Stage One		*Stage Two*	
New Film-type	Pioneer Production →			
		Trailblazer Hit →	Prospector Cash-ins →	Failures
Established Film-type	Speculator Production →			

TABLE 1.8   Film cluster of new film-type Pioneer Production-failure/Speculator Production-Trailblazer Hit variant.

Stage One		Stage Two		Stage Three	
Pioneer	Failure	Speculator	Trailblazer	Prospector	Failures
Production →	→	Production →	Hit →	Cash-ins →	

TABLE 1.9   New film-type film cluster, the roller-disco movie.

Stage One	Stage Two		
Pioneer Production →	Trailblazer Hit →	Prospector Cash-ins →	Failures
Saturday Night Fever (1977)	*Roller Boogie* (1979)		
	Skatetown U.S.A (1979)		
	Xanadu (1980)		

The final stage of a film cycle's development takes place with the production and distribution of Carpetbagger Cash-ins. Carpetbagging may appear to be a financially conservative mode of film production, considering that Carpetbaggers employ a textual model associated with recent and consistent commercial success, however, even though they may feel that they stand a reasonable chance of matching the financial success of the Trailblazer Hit and Reinforcing Hit(s), Carpetbaggers invariably face considerable competition from likeminded opportunists who, having drawn similar conclusions about a film-type's commercial viability, have all produced similar films at the same time. Production tends to reach such levels that market saturation occurs. The result can be that distribution deals become tougher to secure if the films were produced independently, and that ticket sales are spread thinly across several similar films opened around the same time as each other. The situation can be exacerbated if audience interest is waning as a consequence of the intensive release of films made to the same model.

The fourth and therefore final stage of the first teen slasher film cycle took place with the production in the second half of 1980, and the distribution across 1981 and early 1982, of large numbers of Carpetbagger Cash-ins. The 'group of eleven' teen slashers, as I call them, consisted of: *Final Exam, Friday the 13th Part II, Happy Birthday to Me, Hell Night, Graduation Day, Just Before Dawn, Madman, My Bloody Valentine, The Burning, The Dorm that Dripped Blood,* and *The Prowler* (all 1981). Comments made by the Rabbi Herb Freed, writer-producer-director of *Graduation Day*, indicate that Carpetbaggers are under no illusions of the nature of their conduct. 'We went to see *Halloween* and *Friday the 13th*', recalled the retired filmmaker, 'and we just saw how these things were constructed' (interviewed in 'Going to pieces', 2006). Again, industry-watchers recognized that the group of eleven had been made to fulfill the same commercial objectives, was distinguished as a coherent body of films, and had been modeled primarily on the same hits. Thus, the relationships between Carpetbagger Cash-ins and the Trailblazer Hit were spotlighted by writers including Jay Scott of Toronto's *Globe and Mail*, who described *My Bloody Valentine* as 'a clone of John Carpenter's *Halloween*' (1981a), and Gene Siskel of the *Chicago Tribune* who used the term '"Halloween" rip-off' in reference to *The Burning* (1981a, p. E18). Journalists also emphasized connections between Carpetbagger Cash-ins and the Prospector Cash-ins that preceded them. Whereas Siskel dismissed *Final Exam* as 'a "*Friday the 13th*" imitation' (1981c, p. A6), Edward Jones, writing in the *Free Lance-Star*, observed the 'splashes of "Friday the 13th" and "Terror Train"' evident in *Hell Night* (1981, p. 17), and the *New York Times*' Vincent Canby noted that '"Happy Birthday to Me" looks like a comparatively expensive ripoff of (. . .) "Friday the 13th" and "Prom Night"' (1981a, p. C13). Similarly, comments in the vein of '"The Burning" appears to be part of an endless string of "Friday the 13th" clones', written by William Beamon of the *Evening Independent* (1981, p. 17), or the comparisons Patrick Goldstein of the *Los Angeles Times* made between *Graduation Day* and *Happy Birthday to Me* (1981, p. L7), reveal that individuals with their fingers on the pulse of the American movie business viewed the individual Carpetbagger Cash-ins as members of a larger group of films.

Although Carpetbagger Cash-ins often disappoint commercially, if hits keep coming, as was the case with the CGI adventure films mentioned above, new films are produced and a film-type that had been the subject of a cycle will develop into a staple. Yet, as scholars including Neale (2000 and Balio (1993) have shown, American film history is dominated more by cycles and clusters (as per my definitions) than staples, and a string of hits will invariably end sooner rather than later causing production of a film-type to drop to base level.

The commercial failure of the group of eleven Carpetbagger Cash-ins ensured that teen slasher production dropped to base level. New Speculators concluded that the absence of large numbers of similar films had opened up an opportunity for them to realize the economic rewards of producing Trailblazer Hits, resulting in four new films, *The Final Terror*, *Friday the 13th Part 3: 3D*, *The House on Sorority Row*, and *The Slumber Party Massacre* being made for release in 1982, and two new films, *Death Screams* and *Sleepaway Camp*, being made for release in 1983. This drop in output followed the release of sixteen teen slashers in under three-and-a-half years, leaving a widely recognized film cycle (see Table 1.10), but ensuring that the teen slasher did not become a staple at this point in time, although production levels in the late 2000s suggest that it may now be on the verge of becoming a staple of American moviemaking.

In sum, the first teen slasher film cycle unfolded in four stages. The makers of a Pioneer Production, *Black Christmas*, recombined existing textual elements to form a model that differed from previous output. The makers of a second film, a Speculator Production called *Halloween*, later employed the model, enjoying some financial success when it became a Trailblazer Hit. Thereafter, the commercial achievements of Prospector Cash-ins cemented the economic viability of the model. As Reinforcing Hits, these films initiated a second, larger wave of Cash-in production operations. These Carpetbagger Cash-ins saturated the American film market, performed poorly, and caused production of the film-type to drop to base level until such time as another Speculator Production became a Trailblazer Hit and the process of film cycle development started all over again.

Conclusion

Rather than being only a discursive category, the teen slasher film, although known by a series of other labels, was recognized contemporaneously across all levels of North American film culture as a new film-type characterized by a distinct story-structure that concerned a shadowy blade-wielding maniac stalking and killing a group of fun-loving young people in an everyday non-urban setting. Building from this position, it has been possible to identify the three-part seven-point story-structure that enabled industry-professionals to fashion movies that promised not only to horrify, as is commonly assumed, but to thrill, intrigue, and amuse audiences. That model was employed as a basic 'blueprint' by independent filmmakers not to make showcases of misogynist violence destined for the male patrons of grind-houses as is often claimed, but to secure lucrative distribution deals from MPAA-members by offering R-rated films that were marketable to young people of both sexes based on similarities to recent blockbuster hits and youth-oriented hits. While teen slasher film content was impacted by the films' respective makers employing the same narrative model and implementing the same production strategies so as to realize the same commercial objectives, product differentiation (a notion not usually ascribed to teen slashers),

TABLE 1.10 The first teen slasher film cycle

Stage One	Stage Two	Stage Three	Stage Four
Pioneer Production → Speculator Productions → Trailblazer Hit → Prospector Cash-ins → Reinforcing Hits → Carpetbagger Cash-ins			
Black Christmas (1974)	Halloween (1978) Silent Scream (1979)	Halloween	Friday the 13th Prom Night	Friday the 13th Prom Night Terror Train (all 1980)	Dorm/Dripped Blood Friday the 13th Part II Final Exam Happy Birthday to Me Hell Night Graduation Day Just Before Dawn Madman My Bloody Valentine The Burning The Prowler (all 1981)

was ensured, to varying degrees, by the point in time at which the films were made, due to the undulating commercial viability of the films and film-types from which content was drawn. By breaking up the first teen slasher fim cycle into temporally distinct phases of production, each governed by different commercial objectives, a framework has been put in place to facilitate the cross-cyclic industrial analysis implemented across subsequent chapters. The first of those chapters focuses on the period 1974 to early 1979, during which the teen slasher film's distinct story-structure emerged and during which the teen slasher enjoyed its first taste of success at the US box-office. Rather than resulting from radical breaks of convention in American horror filmmaking, as is typically claimed, the emergence and early development of the teen slasher was the product of calculated commercial logic, as shrewd businesspeople based on both sides of the North American border looked to break into the big time by taking Hollywood on a slay ride to small-town USA.

Chapter 2

A Slay-Ride to Small-Town, USA

The advent of the teen slasher film,
Black Christmas *(1974) and* Halloween *(1978)*

Terry 'The Toad' Fields (Charlie Martin Smith) waits nervously in a lover's lane. His date has just described to him the latest crimes of a mysterious slasher said to prey on young people in the secluded make-out spots of southern California. Two teenage victims were discovered nearby, she explained, and they both had been marked with the mad-man's ghoulish trademark, the severed head of a goat. His date has vanished, the 'goat killer' is at large, and, as dawn begins to break, young Terry hears the ominous thud of approaching footsteps. However, Terry is not about to become the latest casualty of an American psycho. The goat killer probably does not even exist outside the over-active imaginations of fun-seeking youths and those frightful footsteps are revealed to be nothing more sinister than Terry's friend Steve. Terry's date reappears grinning mischievously. Terry is shaken, but the episode will be forgotten. The night is still young and rich with possibilities.

This sequence from the 1973 blockbuster hit *American Graffiti* drama-tizes young Americans consuming stories about characters of a similar age encountering blade-wielding killers as they undertake leisure activ-ities in everyday locations.[1] In doing so, it uncannily foreshadowed a significant development in youth-oriented filmmaking that unfolded across the remainder of the 1970s and early 1980s: the advent, develop-ment, decline, and establishment of a new film-type, the teen slasher film. By focusing primarily on 1974–1979, during which time the first teen slasher was made and during which time a teen slasher enjoyed some success at American box-office for the first time, this chapter out-lines the industrial conditions that led North American independent filmmakers to produce films about groups of young people encountering maniacs, not unlike the mythical 'goat killer'.

Providing a radically different account of the teen slasher film's advent than those published to date, which tend solely to focus on the films' status as horror movies, this chapter emphasizes the crucial role that target markets played in respect to the production and content of the teen slasher's earliest incarnations. By acknowledging the fact that teen slashers were made not just simply to frighten audiences, but to permit independent filmmakers to enable major studios to market the films to young people, to the exclusion of other demographics, this chapter moves beyond a pre-history of the film-type constructed exclusively around canonized American horror films that featured a maniac, so as to recognize the influence of other film-types, particularly those that allowed the majors to enjoy considerable economic success and those thought to attract young people. Whereas standard histories of the teen slasher's rise to prominence in the mid-to-late 1970s emphasize artistic vision and creative breaks from convention, this chapter shows that the content of the new film-type reflected established trends in block-buster filmmaking and high-earning youth-oriented films. The chapter also distances itself from great men/great film aspects of established histories, placing instead, at the heart of the film-type's emergence, the contributions of different individuals, companies, and institutions operating across the North American film industry, all of which had a vested interest in seeing tales of young adults being menaced by shadowy maniacs perform strongly at the US box office. In doing so, the chapter shows that examinations of the advent of new film-types should not be restricted to high-profile or high-earning films, and that a new film-type is just as likely to be the product of recombining pre-existing elements of content in a new way than the product of radical breaks from convention.

'A made-in-Canada blockbuster': *Black Christmas*, a Pioneer Production

Written in the early 1980s by American journalists and popular writers, before being restated by film scholars, early attempts to chart the histor-ical trajectory of teen slasher film production usually began either with *Psycho* (1960) or *The Texas Chainsaw Massacre* (1974), two American films that exhibited only tangential similarities to teen slashers and which did not influence teen slasher film production or content in any meaning-ful way. In terms of content, neither film featured a blade-wielding killer who, appearing to operate alone, stalks a group of fun-loving young people which, as chapter one showed, was identified consistently by industry-watchers, industry-professionals, and audiences as distinguish-ing teen slasher film content from that of other films. Thus, where adults with no common bonds fall victim to a knife-wielding madman in *Psycho*, the *Texas Chainsaw Massacre* featured a family of slaughterhouse workers, one of whom was a masked behemoth, terrorizing a group of characters that, while played by twenty-something actors, were not portrayed as youthful. The selection of the two films could be justified to some extent as illustrating the emergence of the sort of killer that was bound to the teen slasher story, were it not for the fact that this character-type featured in countless other films made between 1960 and 1974, including German 'Krimi filme', Italian-made 'giallo' whodunits, and American productions like Herschell Gordon Lewis' 1960s exploitation pictures. Linking *Psycho* and *The Texas Chainsaw Massacre* to the production of teen slasher films can also be challenged on several grounds. For one, although *Psycho* was a big hit, it is, as Robert E. Kapsis intimates (1992, p. 159), implausible to think that large numbers of filmmakers attempted to capitalize on its financial achievements almost two decades later with product that contained negligible similarities. Conversely, little incentive existed to produce films like *The Texas Chainsaw Massacre* in the late 1970s and early 1980s because the film, as Suzanne Mary Donahue details, performed only moderately well in the mid 1970s, performed badly at decade's end, and had for legal reasons been withdrawn from distribution from 1979 to mid 1981, before earning most of its revenue in late 1981 and 1982, only after the teen slasher production boom was over (1987, pp. 234–235). The canonization of *Psycho* and *The Texas Chainsaw Massacre* as forerunners to the teen slasher film was, however, far from arbitrary. It took place, I feel, because, when the history of what Gregory A. Waller (1987, pp. 1–12) called 'the modern era of horror' (horror films made after *Rosemary's Baby* and *Night of the Living Dead* (both 1968)) was being written, *Psycho* and *The Texas Chainsaw Massacre* were high-profile and, relative to horror, prestigious films that fitted neatly into ascendant narratives of American cinematic progress and enabled writers to position themselves in relation to debates on teen slashers.

Events in 1980 and 1981 catapulted *Psycho* and *The Texas Chainsaw Massacre* to the center of US film culture and initiated a widespread reevaluation of their respective merits and locations within the cultural hierarchies of American cinema. With the death of Alfred Hitchcock in April 1980, came countless retrospectives which, as Kapsis shows (1992), cemented Hitchcock's position as one of the most important directors in US history, particularly in respect to thrillers and horror films, with *Psycho* firmly anchored as a milestone in American filmmaking (see Schoell, 1985, pp. 7–37). Concurrently, with the cultural profile of *The Texas Chainsaw Massacre* at an all-time high due

to its commercially successful re-release in late 1981 and with media
attention focused on legal battles involving its financiers, makers, and
distributors (Farley and Knoedelseder, 1982, p. U3), several American
journalists began to reevaluate the film (Canby, 1981b, p. 19). *Psycho*
and *The Texas Chainsaw Massacre* were discussed as breaking radically from earlier horror films. *Psycho* was celebrated for locating the
source of horror within the borders of the United States and within the
confines of the American family when most of its contemporaries featured threats emanating from overseas or outer-space, while *The Texas
Chainsaw Massacre* was lauded for critiquing American institutions,
particularly the family again, when glossy horror films like *The Exorcist*
(1973) and *The Omen* (1976) were seen to endorse them (Wood and
Lippel, 1979). Both films were also attractive because they positioned
horror as a keystone film-type in a grand narrative of American cinematic evolution, which framed the 1960s as a transitional period linking
Hollywood's classical era to the taboo-breaking and stylistic innovation
said to characterize the 'Hollywood Renaissance' of the late 1960s and
early 1970s, the passing of which gave way to a 'New' Hollywood noted for
thematically conservative mass-audience product (see Krämer, 2005).

    Charting the emergence of the teen slasher across what had become
high-profile, well-regarded horror films like *Psycho* and *The Texas Chainsaw
Massacre* enabled writers, irrespective of whether they were hostile, sympathetic or apathetic to teen slashers, to justify focusing on the film-type
when horror films generally, and particularly those that featured maniacal killers, were coming under attack from cultural and media elites.
Pro-slasher writers such as John McCarty (1984) and William Schoell
(1985), as well as detached observers like William K. Knoedelseder Jr.
(1980a), were able to invest their work and themselves with a degree of
prestige or 'cultural capital' by invoking a history of visionary American
filmmakers who, it was claimed, had fashioned highly individual and
thematically sophisticated works. These distinctions also provided writers who lamented the proliferation of teen slashers a springboard from
which to mount against the film-type mournful, bemused or outraged
assaults (Canby, 1981b, p. 19), enabling writers including Vincent
Canby and Roger Ebert to place the films in binary opposition to the
teen slashers, which were framed as unaccomplished and thematically
impoverished products of soulless commercial opportunism. Ebert, an
ardent critic of teen slashers, hailed *Psycho* but lambasted *Friday the 13th*
(quoted in Unger, 1980, p. 19). Similarly, Canby, more bewildered than
outraged by the teen slasher's proliferation, declared in 1981 that *The
Texas Chainsaw Massacre* 'demonstrates the art that can very rarely be

found in horror-film sleaze', suggesting that it 'displays the kind of Grand Guignol sense of humor that effectively separates this film from those of today' before concluding that 'I'm truly baffled by the popularity of today's horror pictures, which seem to have forgotten how to scare us and instead show us (. . .) how to skewer a victim on his own shish kebab ("Happy Birthday to Me")' (1981b, p. 19). Thus, the commercial imperatives that had governed the production and distribution of *Psycho* and *The Texas Chainsaw Massacre* were largely side-stepped (ironic, given the fact that it was partly commercial achievements that made them accessible reference points) and the supposedly remarkable levels of artistry and intelligence invested in the films were spotlighted. These discourses were imported into much of the academic writing on teen slashers that started to be published in the mid-to-late 1980s, and, while the distinctions that had circulated, and which had continued to circulate, in popular media channels sometimes underpinned scholarly examinations of the teen slasher, the 'Psycho-Chainsaw' pre-history was usually restated simply to provide historical context for academic readers, who, it was presumed, were largely unfamiliar with teen slashers. Irrespective of motivation, this oft-cited version of events has given the misleading impression that the teen slasher film was the culmination point of textual and thematic shifts that unfolded gradually across landmarks in American horror, and that innovative moviemaking with something important to say about American society was transformed by the machinery of advanced capitalism into formulaic, vacuous schlock. Within the narrative of the rise and fall of the visionary and progressive American horror film existed little room for outsiders, particularly the products of other national film industries and films which could not easily be framed as milestones in post-classical Hollywood history.

Among the films excluded from the canon of modern horror was a film that was, soon after *The Texas Chainsaw Massacre* debuted, reviewed (Adil., 1974, p. 16; Siskel, 1974, p. B6; Weiler, 1975, p. 45), and, on some occasions, enjoyed (K. Thomas, 1975, p. F12), by most leading American film journalists. That film was not American, it was not deemed to be artistically important, and it was not a hit. It was Canadian and it was the product of a complex network of transnational industrial shifts that had been unfolding in the late 1960s and early 1970s involving the Canadian government, the Hollywood majors, America's theater-going youths, and independent filmmakers from around the world. That film influenced profoundly — more than *Psycho* and *The Texas Chainsaw Massacre* ever did — the output of the American film industry by setting in a motion a series of events that resulted in the first teen slasher film cycle unfolding.

It was a Pioneer Production and its name was *Black Christmas.*

In early 1974, the female-centered politically engaged whodunit *Black Christmas* was among the first Canadian films to be produced primarily to break in to the American market. Indeed, as the only film being shot in Canada at the time, it was seen by Canadian film industry-insiders to represent perhaps the final opportunity for that nation to produce its first blockbuster hit (Anon., 1973c, p. 19; Anon., 1974j, p. 26.). This was a time of great uncertainty in the Canadian film industry. For five years, the hopes of producers and financiers had been dashed, and there was a growing feeling that the country's attempts to establish an internationally recognized film industry would end in inglorious and premature failure (Anon., 1973c, pp. 19, 32; Anon., 1973d, pp. 19, 32).

The project to initiate a self-sustaining indigenous film industry began in 1968 when the Canadian government founded a federal body to distribute funding subsidies to the nation's filmmakers (Gasher, 2002, p. 52.). The Canadian Film Development Corporation (CFDC), as it was called, typically provided 30–50 per cent of a film's production budget if its script reflected the organization's mandate (Anon., 1973d, p. 19). These loans were repaid with a little interest once a film started to generate ticket sales (ibid.). The only problem was that the productions to which the CFDC channeled capital were all box-office failures, at least those films that actually made it into theaters. By prioritizing projects that 'contribute[d] to the articulation of a Canadian cultural identity' (Magder, 1993, p. 131), the organization had underestimated the fiercely competitive nature of international film distribution. Unsurprisingly, then, many of the bleak and idiosyncratic films made in Canada during the first half-decade of CFDC operations, proved to be incapable of securing any form of distribution domestically or abroad (Anon., 1973d, p. 19). By 1973, the CFDC had squandered its five-year CAD10m budget and was required to adopt more fiscally responsible, which is to say, more commercially oriented, strategies.

The relatively small population of Canada, around 23 million people in 1973, meant that domestically only the tiniest profit could be generated by the most widely seen micro-budget films. Thus, central to the CFDC's new strategy was its belated acceptance that a sustainable indigenous industry was tied to Canadian films securing distribution south of the border from a member of the Motion Picture Association of America (MPAA) (Anon., 1973b, p. 26). 'Canada wants to take its place in the international film market', declared Harold Greenburg, President of the country's largest production company, Astral Bellevue Pathé (quoted in Anon., 1973f, p. 26). 'Since the United States and

Canada are the two closest countries in matters of geography, language and customs in the western hemisphere', hc continued, 'we feel it is only good business sense to consummate mutually beneficial (. . .) agreements' (ibid.). Greenburg's views were shared by his peers. 'There's no point making a feature film in Canada unless it has a story line that will get it into international distribution', contended F. W. 'Budge' Crawley, president of Crawley Films (quoted in Anon., 1973b, p. 26). These sentiments were also shared by the CFDC's executive director Michael Spencer. 'We are banking on more returns', Spencer told *Variety*, 'there is no doubt that the Canadian industry is more conscious of box-office. At the beginning nobody really cared' (quoted in Anon., 1973c, p. 19). However, a significant gulf existed between the ambitions of Canada's commercially focused filmmakers and the fruits of their labor. As *Variety* reported in February 1974, the Canadian film industry was 'depend[ent] on American distributors whose criteria for a film's commercial success is substantially different most of the time, from what is being offered by Canadian producers' (ibid.).

Frustration had been sweeping the Canadian film industry with filmmakers increasingly disaffected by the CFDC's inability to comprehend what they felt was at stake (Anon., 1974k, p. 4). 'The whole English track Canadian film industry is at stake', lamented writer-director-producer George Kaczender, (quoted in Anon., 1973c, p. 19). '[1974] is the year of the question: is the industry going anywhere?' (Ibid.). A Canadian-made hit was seen by many Canadian industry-insiders as essential to the short-, medium-, and long-term prospects of their industry. 'Never has Canada's feature industry worked and hoped so hard', wrote *Variety*, 'to deliver its first Made-in-Canada blockbuster' (ibid.). A Canadian film that emulated the achievements of the US productions being trumpeted in *Variety* at the time — *American Graffiti* (Universal Pictures, 1974, p. 13), *The Exorcist* (Warner Bros. Pictures, 1974a, pp. 14–15), *Magnum Force* (Warner Bros. Pictures, 1974b, p. 12–13), *The Way We Were* (Columbia Pictures, 1974a, p. 11) and others — would signal to Hollywood that the Canadian film industry could be taken seriously. By erasing the image of Canadian-based producers as commercially naive amateurs or 'bush leaguers' (Anon., 1973c, p. 19), it was thought that such a hit would increase the chances of subsequent films to reap the immediate financial rewards of MPAA-member pickup deals. In early 1974, a script for a 'psychological thriller' entitled 'Stop Me', but soon renamed *Black Christmas*, was seen by CFDC executives to be capable of providing Canada with its first genuine US box-office success (Anon., 1974j, p. 26).

So confident was the CFDC in *Black Christmas*'s appeal to MPAA-members that it contributed an unprecedented CAD200,000 to the CAD400,000 that had already been provided by a consortium of Canadian production companies and Canada's largest theater chain, Famous Players, to make the film the most costly state-subsidized production in Canadian history (Anon., 1974l, p. 46). If this commitment demonstrated that the will and the means to target MPAA-members existed north of the border, then developments that had been unfolding south of the border suggested that the opportunity existed there too.

Shifts in the business strategies of the MPAA-members led the Pioneers behind *Black Christmas* to anchor their drive for MPAA-member distribution to the film's capacity to be marketable to American youths. This strategy appeared to be commercially viable because, when *Black Christmas* started production, youth was seen by MPAA-members as America's prime theatergoing demographic. The MPAA-members' recognition that the economic health of the industry was determined by the actions of young people had followed the unexpected box-office achievements of two of the biggest hits of the late 1960s. *Bonnie and Clyde* and *The Graduate* (both 1967) became big hits thanks largely to having secured the attendance of college-educated youths (Hall, 1998, p. 17), with one audience survey discovering 96 per cent of tickets for *The Graduate* had been purchased by theatergoers under 30 years of age, and that 72 per cent of tickets had been sold to people under the age of 24 (Alpert cited in Monaco, 2001, p. 184). The achievements of these films, along with a survey conducted in 1968 by Yankelovich and Associates at the behest of the MPAA that had concluded that 16–24-year-olds comprised 48 per cent of US admissions (Anon., 1968b, pp. 1, 78), prompted Hollywood to recalibrate a significant portion of its output to ensure the continued attendance of the demographic (Hall, 1998, p. 17). The strategy was galvanized by the subsequent commercial success of another 'youth-cult' film, as David A. Cook has called them (2000, pp. 162–172). The enormous returns Columbia Pictures generated from its $375,000-budgeted pickup *Easy Rider* (1969),[2] argues Cook, 'convinced producers that inexpensive films could be made specifically for the youth-market and that they could become blockbusters overnight' (1994, p. 14). This incentive prompted the production of tales of rebellion featuring characters in their twenties including *Five Easy Pieces, MASH,* and *Zabriskie Point* (all 1970), and coming-of-age stories such as *Loving* (1970) and *Summer of '42* (1971) (Cook, 2000, pp. 163–172). In addition to spotlighting the power of the youth-market, developments that occurred in the American film industry across the half-decade that preceded *Black Christmas* also suggested that independently produced films had a better chance of being picked up than hithertofore.

Independent filmmakers' confidence in their abilities to tap into the all-powerful youth-market grew rapidly as a result of the MPAA-members' decision to reduce their production budgets and the number of films they financed and released after they incurred huge losses in the late 1960s when several big-budget epics and musicals, including *Hello, Dolly!* (1969) and *Tora! Tora! Tora!* (1970) failed to attract large enough audiences to generate a profit (Hall, 1998, p. 17). In 1976, *Variety*'s industry analyst A. D. Murphy reflected on some of the implications of the financial crisis, reporting that independent production had surged in the US from 244 films in 1972 to 357 in 1974 as the number of projects financed by MPAA-members dropped by 40 per cent from 250 to 150 (1976b, p. 32). The MPAA-members' output, explained Murphy, had been insufficient to keep exhibitors supplied with product, particularly in the slower spring and autumn seasons (1976a, p. 34). About 10% of the independent productions had been bought by MPAA-members, which, suggested Murphy, 'nowadays need some outside pix [pictures] to fill out sharply reduced releasing schedules' (1976b, p. 32). In addition to the lucky few that secured a distribution deal from an MPAA-member, Murphy reported that independent productions had eagerly been acquired by established independent distributors like New World Pictures and Crown International Pictures so as to alleviate what had come to be known as the 'film famine' (ibid.).

The enormous cost-to-profit ratio of *Easy Rider* had demonstrated to the American independent sector that it was possible to make financially successful youth-oriented films on the kinds of low budgets that independents could secure (Wyatt, 1994a, p. 67), and perceptions of the commercial viability of independently produced youth-market product increased further when several of the counter-culture films that followed in 1970 were awarded MPAA-member distribution deals. With MGM acquiring *Brewster McCloud* and *The Magic Garden of Stanley Sweetheart*, United Artists (UA) picking up *The Revolutionary*, and Columbia purchasing *R.P.M.*, it appeared as though a ready-made market existed for inexpensive independently produced youth-oriented films that were, or at least appeared to be, of American origin. The potential of the American youth-market was underscored by the findings of an American Film Institute report published shortly before *Black Christmas* went into production, which showed that 73 per cent of US tickets had been sold to theatergoers that were between the ages of 12 and 29 years (Murphy, 1975a, pp. 3, 74; Murphy, 1975b, pp. 3, 34).

The recession that shook the American film industry in the late 1960s and early 1970s also had presented opportunities to producers based abroad. Canadian filmmakers were emboldened by the fact that MPAA-members were purchasing films that had not been made on American soil. The relative financial success of imports like *Blowup* (1966) and *I am Curious (Yellow)* (1967)[3] had indicated that American audiences were receptive to the products of other national film industries (ibid. pp. 71–72), and, in the early 1970s, MPAA-members had distributed several non-US productions. Many of these international pickups, as Frances Gateward notes (2007, pp. 106–107), were martial arts films from Hong Kong, including *Hei Lu*, released by MGM as *Deadly China Doll*, and *Tian Xia Di Yi Quan* (1972), which Warner Bros. re-titled *Five Fingers of Death* for the American market. Italian horror films also appeared with some regularity on the distribution rosters of MPAA-members (Cook, 2000, pp. 234–235). For example, Dario Argento's giallo film *Quattro Mosche di Vellotu Grigio* (1971) was released by Paramount as *Four Flies on Grey Velvet* and MGM had issued *La Tarantola dal Venre Nero* (1971) as *The Black Belly of the Tarantula*. With MPAA-members purchasing product from as far flung places as Italy and Hong Kong, frustration was growing and ambitions were burning in equal measures among their neighbors in the Canadian film industry.

Developments that unfolded on both sides of the North American border thus pointed to the commercial potential of a Canadian film that offered American distributors an opportunity to target young people. The box-office achievements of *Bonnie and Clyde*, *The Graduate*, and *Easy Rider* had prompted Hollywood to cultivate the youth-market, which it had recently identified as its prime audience. The financial crisis of 1969–1972 had also prompted the MPAA-members to reduce the number of films they financed which in turn had opened up opportunities for independent producers to secure distribution for their films. At the same time, the Canadian film industry was re-evaluating its objectives. The belief that the economic failure of downbeat films that focused on Canadian diversity was seen to have impeded the development of the industry in that country, in conjunction with the negative pickup deals that MPAA-members had arranged with filmmakers in countries such as Italy and Hong Kong, encouraged Canadian producers and the nation's state-managed film funding body, the CFDC, to seek to alleviate Hollywood's film famine by crafting films to appeal to the MPAA-members. In early 1974, the ambitious entrepreneurs behind *Black Christmas* stood at the forefront of a minor revolution in Canadian filmmaking as they combined the distinguishing elements of content from four red-hot American film-types in such a way that *Black Christmas* differed significantly from previous films.

In the Pioneer Production *Black Christmas*, the holiday period offers the sisters of an American sorority few reasons to be merry. It is not a time of good cheer for sharp-witted Barb (Margot Kidder), who drinks heavily to forget that family troubles mean she will not be going home for the holidays. Life is even more complicated for ambitious go-getter Jess (Olivia Hussey), whose decision to terminate her pregnancy in favor of pursuing her studies has caused partner Peter (Keir Dullea) to act in an erratic and threatening fashion. It is left to good-humored Phyl (Andrea Martin) to pick up the pieces. If all that was not bad enough, the sorority house is being plagued by sinister phone calls from a man claiming to be called 'Billy' who rants incoherently about having attacked his baby sister when he was a boy. The police cannot locate the caller, and one of the sorority sisters, Clare (Lynne Griffin), has, unbeknown to her friends, fallen victim to a shadowy prowler holed up in the attic. As the holidays progress, the calls continue and, one after another, Barb, Phyl, a cop, the house mother, and a local girl all perish at the hands of the mysterious attic dweller. When the police finally trace the source of the phone calls to the sorority house itself, Jess makes a last ditch bid to flee only to be cornered in the cellar. She kills an intruder who, it turns out, is Peter. It seems as though Jess' ordeal is over, she is administered a sedative by medics and put to bed. But what took place in the cellar with Peter was a tragic misunderstanding and, with Jess alone in the house and unable to defend herself, somebody slips quietly from the attic and heads in her direction. *Black Christmas* employs the teen slasher story-structure outlined in chapter one (see Figure 2.1).

Part One: Setup

1. Trigger: As a boy, Billy develops homicidal impulses after he attacks his infant sister.
2. Threat: Years later, Billy hides in the attic of a university sorority house.

Part Two: Disruption

3. Leisure: The inhabitants of the sorority house socialize and hold Christmas parties.
4. Stalking: Billy makes threatening phone calls to the sorority sisters.
5. Murders: Billy kills several members of the sorority.

Part Three: Resolution

6. Confrontation: Jess, the last living sorority sister, kills an intruder.
7. Neutralization: Billy appears to have been dispatched.

FIGURE 2.1   The teen slasher film story-structure in *Black Christmas*.

To increase their chances of becoming the first Canadian-based film-makers to craft a hit on the US market, the makers of *Black Christmas* combined elements from four film-types that had provided MPAA-members with huge returns. The enormous financial potential of horror films, group-centered youth-oriented films, romantic dramas, and violent police-procedurals, had been signaled by blockbuster hits of the preceding half-decade — *Rosemary's Baby* (1968), *MASH*, *Love Story* (both 1970), and *Dirty Harry* (1971)[4] — and was being underscored by the exceptionally strong openings of four films that had been released in the months leading up to production of *Black Christmas*: *The Exorcist* (Warner Bros. Pictures, 1974a, pp. 14–15); *American Graffiti* (Universal Pictures, 1974, pp. 13); *The Way We Were* (Columbia Pictures, 1974a, p. 11); and *Magnum Force* (Warner Bros. Pictures, 1974b, p. 12–13). Drawing content from these film-types appeared to offer independent filmmakers a way of demonstrating the commercial viability of their product.

Without *The Exorcist*, it is unlikely that *Black Christmas* would have been made at all. In early 1974, director William Friedkin's tale of a young girl's demonic possession dominated the trade press more than any other film (see for example Anon., 1974d, p. 5; Anon., 1974e, p. 7; Anon., 1974i, p. 5; Anon., 1974h, p. 3). *The Exorcist* had built upon the box-office achievements of *Rosemary's Baby* to cement perceptions of the unprecedented financial viability of horror films that situated human monsters within everyday American settings. While, as Mark Jancovich has suggested, the location of a horrifying threat within the borders of the United States had a rich and long tradition in North American cinema (2002, p. 4), the magnitude of *The Exorcist*'s achievements served notice to filmmakers of its immediate box-office potential. *Black Christmas* borrows minimally from Friedkin's film. Although both films take place in opulent nineteenth-century residence and the makers of *Black Christmas* used a cacophony of adult and juvenile voices during Billy's telephonic rants in much the same way as Friedkin had done to convey a child's possession, the significance of *The Exorcist* was not really in textual details. Rather, *The Exorcist* was important because it re-energized the commercial viability of horror, a film-type which had been missing from the top 20 of the annual rentals chart in the half-decade since the release of *Rosemary's Baby*.

The manner in which *Black Christmas* articulates threat and the vision of normality that is placed in jeopardy combined elements of *Magnum Force*, *American Graffiti*, and *The Way We Were*. While the depiction of the teen slasher killer is invariably described as having been influenced directly by *Psycho* and *The Texas Chainsaw Massacre* (Clover, 1992, pp. 26–30), the manner in which the makers of *Black Christmas* presented their killer actually owes more to *Magnum Force*, a film in which a group of 'killers dressed as cops', as its trailer described them, are positioned largely beyond the borders of the frame or are represented by subjective shots as they knock off various underworld figures. 'From the beginning I wanted to see if we could get away with a film', *Black Christmas*' producer-director Bob Clark has recalled, '[in which] you never saw the killer' (interviewed in 'Bob Clark unabridged', 2002). As a consequence of echoing the enigmatic assassins of *Magnum Force*, *Black Christmas*' rendition of a stalker who uses everyday objects to dispatch victims, has also led some scholars to draw parallels to the gory 'giallo' whodunits that, as Mikel J. Koven shows (2006, p. 4), had become a staple of Italian cinema in the wake of the box-office achievements in Italy and other international markets of *The Bird with the Crystal Plumage*, and to which, as noted above, North American audiences and filmmakers had been introduced during the film-famine of the early 1970s. The Cash-ins that had followed Argento's film invariably replicated the use of moving subjective shots to conceal a killer's identity while displaying his/her attacks (Koven, 2006, pp. 102–104, 146–148). By pairing the moving subjective shots that had first been used in Michael Powell's 1960 thriller *Peeping Tom* (Schneider, 2003b, p. 176) with the arresting site of the shadowy slasher that had come to prominence in *Psycho*, Argento and his imitators had, much like the makers of the German Krimi Filme of the 1960s, discovered a cost-effective way of infusing thrills and horror into a whodunit plot. But, crucially, *Magnum Force* had indicated that depicting serial murders in this way appealed not only to MPAA-members but also to American theatergoers. Whereas giallo filmmakers had depicted mysterious maniacs threatening middle-aged bourgeois Italians (Koven, 2006, pp. 45–59), and the producers of *Magnum Force* had portrayed stealthy madmen slaying adult lawbreakers, the Pioneers behind *Black Christmas* ensured that their killer's targets exhibited, in the words of Vera Dika, 'the greatest degree of likeness to the members of the film-viewing audience or, at least, to their mythical ideal' (1990, p. 59).

To demonstrate to MPAA-members that their film could be angled to young people, the Pioneers behind *Black Christmas* turned to *American Graffiti*'s group of middle-class youths. '[The] episodic structure and use of multiple protagonists was certainly not unique to *American Graffiti*', suggested Frances Gateward (2007, p. 102). 'Neither', she continues, 'was the idea of characters who would be introduced and then occupy their own little narrative segments' (ibid.). Indeed, the mobilization of young protagonists that occupy a single location but do not always interact characterized many teen films of the 1950s and early 1960s (Doherty, 2002, pp. 54–186), leading William Paul to observe that '*American Graffiti* is essentially an American International teenybopper pic with a lot more spit and polish' (1994, p. 92). These antecedents notwithstanding, the makers of *American Graffiti*, as Paul explains, had recalibrated the textual model used for the 1970 blockbuster hit *MASH* (ibid. pp. 90–110).[5] In the context of the earlier success of *MASH*, the financial achievements of *American Graffiti*, which were being trumpeted loudly in early 1974 by distributor Universal Pictures, indicated that depictions of fractured groups of young friends and acquaintances appealed to young audiences and stood to provide independent filmmakers important leverage in the battle over MPAA-member distribution deals.

By positioning a group of young adults at the centre of a horror film, the Pioneers behind *Black Christmas* brought together two of the distinguishing aspects of youth-oriented films of previous decades in ways that reflected lucrative contemporaneous trends. Representing college-age characters in this way, also permitted them to avoided portraying the male 'anti-heroes' that had dominated youth-oriented product in the wake of *Easy Rider* but which had been hit and miss with the youth-market (Monaco, 2001, p. 188), and which, as Aniko Bodroghkozy shows, had come to be viewed with suspicion by MPAA-members following the hostile reception of America's influential underground and campus press (2002, pp. 38–58). In addition to drawing content from *American Graffiti* — the biggest youth-oriented hit of its time — the makers of *Black Christmas* mined a second film-type that had focused heavily on young people but which had, unlike most of the counter-culture films, generated huge ticket sales consistently.

To show that their film was marketable to teenage girls and young women, the filmmakers behind *Black Christmas* looked to the most commercially viable film-type of its era to focus heavily on female youths: romantic dramas. It is commonly argued that at the time *Black Christmas* was in production, MPAA-members had become less interested in targeting female audiences than in previous decades. 'By 1972', writes Peter Krämer, 'there were numerous indications that Hollywood had re-oriented itself towards a new target audience of men, particularly young men' (Krämer, 1999, p. 96). However, some films clearly bucked this trend, including some of Hollywood's most prestigious and commercially successful projects. Three years after *Love Story* had topped the annual film rentals chart in 1970 by chronicling an ill-fated romance between two Harvard University students, *The Way We Were* signaled the continued financial viability of romantic dramas when audiences flocked to see Robert Redford and Barbara Streisand fall for each other at college and drift apart across their twenties and thirties. Despite the film's fairly epic scope, studio perceptions of the strength of *The Way We Were* were encapsulated in a full-page announcement that its distributor, Columbia Pictures (1974, p. 11), placed in *Variety*. Embossed across a large dollar sign were the Redford and Streisand characters in their college days, walking arm in arm and looking very much in love, he dressed in the unofficial uniform of the preppy Ivy League student (drain pipe trousers and a pale roll neck sweater), she sporting an oversized letterman cardigan. *The Way We Were* had, according to the spread, grossed a staggering $31.5m in three months (ibid.). Columbia was clearly linking the box-office achievements of *The Way We Were* to its youth-centered romantic content, and in doing so, was inviting industry-insiders to draw parallels between the film and *Love Story* (if only to stimulate the interest of exhibitors). The links between the two films were fairly obvious. *The Way We Were*, like *Love Story*, depicted lovers who start out as college students and deal with the pressures that a clash of political views exerts upon their relationship. In *Love Story* these forces emanated from outsiders (the father of one of the lovers), while *The Way We Were* dramatized conflicts that arose when the partners themselves held opposing positions on serious political questions. The financial achievements of both films had elevated the commercial viability of young love to levels that would not be matched until the release of *Titanic* (1997), almost a quarter of a century later.

To secure the patronage of young women, the Pioneers behind *Black Christmas* reworked *Love Story* and *The Way We Were* to portray a relationship imploding under the enormous weight of a young student's decision to abort her unborn child. On 24 January 1973, less than a year before *Black Christmas* started production, a US supreme court decision had guaranteed a woman's right to an abortion (Roe v. Wade, 410 U.S. 113, 1973). As has been well documented, this decision would remain one of the most divisive issues in US politics, culture, and public opinion (Schulman, 2000, p. 168). The dramatization of serious social issues has been highlighted by producer-director Bob Clark as one of his primary objectives, in respect to *Black Christmas*. 'I didn't want to do anymore beach blanket bikini movies', he recalled, 'I wanted them to be real college students' (interviewed in 'Bob Clark unabridged', 2002). The conflict is played out in ways that present *Black Christmas'* pregnant heroine Jess as sympathetic, level-headed, and responsible, in contrast to her partner Peter who is depicted as a volatile psychotic that, for most of the plot, appears to be the killer. The liberal position that the film offers on a hot-button social issue reflected Clark's work in most of his films and culminated in a critique of anti-Semitism in his 1981 hit *Porky's* (see Paul, 1994, pp. 99–100). In Clark's previous film, the bitingly satirical *Death Dream* (1972), for example, a teenage Vietnam veteran returned to a small US town as a tragic zombie who, to survive, must feed on the blood of his nearest and dearest. Over half a decade before the release of Vietnam war-themed films like *Coming Home* and *The Deer Hunter* (both 1978), Clark served up a devastating critique on the damage done to young people, those they leave behind, and those to whom they return, by what was seen by liberals at the time as a pointless and unjust conflict. Where a deeply unpopular aspect of US foreign policy provided the backdrop to Clark's previous film, with *Black Christmas*, the filmmaker located his tale of threat and horror against the backdrop of socio-political developments that were unfolding on American soil. By portraying a likeable college girl dealing with an unwanted pregnancy, a life-changing decision, an erratic boyfriend, and career opportunities, Clark provided distributors with a way of targeting *Black Christmas* both to politically engaged female youths and those who had contributed to the success of *Love Story* and *The Way We Were*.

In addition to dramatizing a pressing socio-political issue that resonated deeply with the demographic, the Pioneers behind *Black Christmas* aimed to make their film marketable to female youth by featuring young women as protagonists. Although early teen slasher films often have been accused of offering female audiences few positive female characters, such accusations cannot be leveled with any real credibility at *Black Christmas*. For one, at a point in time when youth-oriented films tended to be male-centered (Powers et al., 1996, p. 154), *Black Christmas* featured a witty, intelligent, and irreverent young woman called Barb who, in a number of standout sequences, mocks characters holding positions of authority. In one such scene, Barb exposes the ignorance of a police officer, convincing him, much to his colleagues' amusement, that the telephone number of the sorority house is Fellatio 20880 — 'a new exchange', she explains. The importance that Clark and his collaborators placed in making *Black Christmas* marketable to college-age female theatergoers was, however, reflected most clearly in the top-billing given to rising star Olivia Hussey, in what one American journalist described as 'her most important role since "Romeo and Juliet"' (Stalling, 1975, C6, C9). It is telling that the filmmakers cast as Jess the star of Franco Zeffirelli's 1968 blockbuster hit,[6] the financial success of which, as Justin Wyatt explains, was down largely to distributor, Paramount Pictures, promoting Hussey in magazines aimed at teenage girls such as *Seventeen* (1994a, p. 66). The transformation of Hussey from flag-bearer of star-crossed adolescent femininity in Zeffirelli's late 1960s film into driven careerist who rejects the roles of wife and mother five years later, represented another calculated attempt on the part of the producers of *Black Christmas* to make their film marketable to a generation of politically-informed female patrons that were perceived to subscribe to the central tenets of second-wave feminism as they entered adulthood in the early 1970s.

It was not as economically suspect as it may seem for commercially focused filmmakers to make a horror film that could be angled to young women with feminist sympathies. In fact, there were strong suggestions that this approach would neither alienate the male youths that the industry considered to be the core audience for horror films nor, for that matter, MPAA-members. As Krämer has detailed, numerous opinion polls taken at the time revealed that male youths, particularly high school graduates and those pursuing tertiary education, were sympathetic to feminist views (2005, p. 76). MPAA-members had also positioned dynamic female characters in film-types associated with male audiences. The most high-profile example of this nascent trend, which, as I show below and in later chapters, became more prominent as the decade wore on, had been the horror blockbusters *Rosemary's Baby,* which had focused on the emotional turmoil suffered by a pregnant woman (Mia Farrow), and *The Exorcist,* which, despite its title, had dealt predominantly with the turbulent relationship of a lone mother (Ellen Burstyn) and her adolescent daughter (Linda Blair). And, shortly before *Black Christmas* went into production, Warner Bros. had replaced the trigger-happy male vigilantes, gangsters, and private-eyes of moderately successful 'blaxploitation' films like *Shaft* (1971) and *Superfly* (1972) with an equally violent heroine in its 1973 production *Cleopatra Jones* (Gateward, 2007, pp. 108–109).[7] While produced primarily for urban black audiences, the 'blaxploitation' films had also attracted educated white youths. In addition to attempting to appeal to the US MPAA-members by combining content drawn from economically successful trends, the makers of *Black Christmas* also took steps to ensure that their film would not be rejected by the heavyweights of the American movie business because it received an X-rating.

The Pioneers behind *Black Christmas* employed considerable restraint in respect to violent content because the American film industry was turning its back on the X-rating. In the months leading up to the shooting of *Black Christmas,* the trade press had focused heavily on controversy surrounding X-rated films. As Jon Lewis shows, coverage had centered on legal attempts to limit the exhibition of hardcore pornography, which occupied increasingly visible locations in US cities following, perhaps the biggest sleeper hit in history, 1972's *Deep Throat* (Lewis, 2002, pp. 265–275).[8] By late 1973 and early 1974, however, the trade press was reporting regularly that the producers of non-pornographic films were avoiding the X-rating. 'No one wants that X anymore', screamed a *Variety* headline (Anon., 1974g, p. 3). A few weeks earlier, it had been reported that Paramount was re-editing its supernatural thriller *Don't Look Now* (1973) to secure an R-rating (Anon., 1973e, p. 6), and that powerful independent producer Dino De Laurentiis had announced that his films would eschew violence and gore (Anon., 1973g, p. 5). A heated debate was also unfolding over whether *The Exorcist* should have been given an X rather than an R (Anon., 1974c, p. 5; Anon., 1974f, p. 23). Given that concerns over the X-rating were being voiced by MPAA-members and top independent producers, and that their concerns were being articulated in relation to horror films, it was preferable for *Black Christmas* to feature little on-screen violence. To secure an R-rating, none of the six deaths that took place in *Black Christmas* were preceded by a chase, only one followed a brief struggle, only half showed momentary victim horror, and the blows that killed victims were positioned off-screen (see Table 2.1). Gore featured in only two of the murders, with fleeting shots of a bloodied weapon and post-mortem corporeal damage appearing on one occasion respectively (see Table 2.2).

TABLE 2.1   Pre-death features of murders in *Black Christmas*.

Victim		Features			
Gender	Type	None	Fear	Chase	Struggle
Female	Youth		✓		✓
Female	Adult		✓		
Female	Youth		✓		
Female	Youth	✓			
Male	Adult	✓			
Male	Youth	✓			

Key: '✓' denotes presence of feature

TABLE 2.2   Features of murders in *Black Christmas*.

Victim		Death-blow		Effects			
Gender	Type	Single	Multiple	Off-screen	Fear	Gore	Pain
Female	Youth			✓	✓		
Female	Adult			✓	✓		
Female	Youth	✓		✓		✓	
Female	Youth			✓			
Male	Adult			✓		✓	
Male	Youth			✓			

Key: '✓' denotes presence of feature

Thus, to attract an MPAA-member distributor in the US, the Canadian makers of *Black Christmas* had fashioned an R-rated female-centered politically engaged whodunit. In doing so, they developed what would become a new film-type. To make their film marketable to male and female youth, the entrepreneurs behind *Black Christmas* had combined content drawn from film-types that boasted a strong record of success at the American box-office in the early 1970s, positioning the strong young heroine of romantic dramas, the young adult groups of teen films, and the shadowy serial killers of police procedurals into the horror film. These strategies may have been implemented to give *Black Christmas* the best possible chance of becoming the first 'made-in-Canada-Blockbuster', but to realize that objective, the film needed not only to secure a top US distributor, but a sizable segment of the American youth-market.

The box-office success enjoyed by *Black Christmas* in Canada alerted an MPAA-member to the film's commercial potential. In August 1974, the Canadian company Ambassador Film Distributors had opened *Black Christmas* in nine theaters around Toronto where it grossed $143,000 in two weeks (Anon., 1974m, p. 32). This was an impressive achievement by the standards of the Canadian theatrical market and had prompted the CFDC to predict that *Black Christmas* would go on to gross $1.3m and thus set a new record as the highest grossing Canadian production in the history of the Canadian market (ibid.). The promise that *Black Christmas* showed in Canada resulted in Warner Bros. purchasing the US distribution rights to the film. Like the CFDC, Warner Bros. executives had high hopes for *Black Christmas*, estimating that it would generate at least $7m in US theatrical rentals (Anon., 1975f, p.8). This sum, in combination with its anticipated Canadian returns (ibid.), would have positioned the film in the top 20 of the annual rentals chart for the previous year, 1973. The confidence that Warner Bros. placed in its acquisition was therefore such that it expected *Black Christmas* to become one of the most commercially successful youth-centered films ever.

The odds of *Black Christmas* becoming the first 'made-in-Canada blockbuster' had been slashed, but its first US theatrical release was an unqualified disaster. Warner Bros. released its pickup, under the title *Silent Night, Evil Night*,[9] days before Christmas 1974, and in doing so, had thrust the film into the most fiercely contested period of the year for the American box-office dollar (Donahue, 1987, p. 128). The flagship product of the Canadian film industry was unable to compete for theatergoers' attentions with the two presold properties that also debuted in American theaters on 20 December that year, the calculated blockbuster *The Godfather Part II* and the new Bond film, *The Man with the Golden Gun*.[10] The situation was exacerbated by the presence on the market of other calculated blockbusters and sleeper hits including *The Towering Inferno* and *Young Frankenstein* (both 1974).[11] Under the name *Silent Night, Evil Night*, *Black Christmas* grossed a feeble $284,345 (Anon., 1975d, pp. 133–135). This sum meant that, in terms of gross revenue, *Black Christmas* ranked 214th of the 335 films (including hardcore pornography and reissues) that played theatrically in the US that year. Unsurprisingly, Warner Bros. cut its losses and pulled the film from theaters.

Despite its initial failure at the American box-office, *Black Christmas* was given a second chance to deliver Canada its first blockbuster hit after continuing to draw audiences to Canadian theaters. By August 1975, *Black Christmas* had almost fulfilled the CFDC's predictions by grossing $1.2m to become the second-highest grossing Canadian film in the history of the domestic market (Anon., 1976b, p. 44). In light of these achievements, Warner Bros. buckled under pressure being exerted from the film's producers and in summer 1975 re-released *Black Christmas*, this time under the title *Black Christmas* (Anon., 1975e, p. 26; Warner Bros. Pictures, 1975a, pp. 34–37).

Although the initial re-release of *Black Christmas* in Los Angeles in August 1975 caught the attention of the theatergoing public, it was not a sign of things to come. That month, a *Variety* spread announced that in one week *Black Christmas* had generated $86,340 at three of the city's theatres (Warner Bros. Pictures, 1975b, pp. 17–18). These ticket sales equated to an average of $4111 per theater per day. In comparison, the year's biggest hit, *Jaws* (1975), had generated $7.06m on 464 screens in its opening three days, a sum that equated to an average of $5071 per screen per day — a difference of less than 20 per cent. As a result of *Black Christmas'* extremely strong performance, Warner Bros. expanded its Los Angeles run to 19 locations and opened the film at Chicago's Roosevelt Theatre in October 1975. In LA, *Black Christmas* grossed $70,500, an average of $3710 per theater, in one week (Anon., 1975g, p. 9). These strong returns were bettered in Chicago, where *Black Christmas* generated $21,000 in seven days at the Roosevelt (Anon., 1975h, p. 10). A significant audience appeared to exist for the film so Warner Bros. expanded *Black Christmas'* release to 70 theaters to coincide with Halloween. At this point *Black Christmas* failed to sustain early ticket sales. From those 70 sites, the pioneering teen slasher generated in one week the paltry sum of $354,990 or, on average, around $700 per theater per day (Anon., 1975i, p. 9). In response, 58 of the theaters cancelled bookings immediately (Anon., 1975j, p. 9). Other theaters followed suit shortly thereafter and, by December of 1975, *Black Christmas* had been withdrawn from circulation (Anon., 1975k, p. 15; Anon., 1975l, p. 9; Anon., 1975m, p. 9). *Black Christmas* did not break into *Variety*'s 'Big Rental Films' chart for 1975, or for any other year, indicating that it failed to returned the $1m in rentals needed to make those lists.

Although unsuccessful commercially, the release of *Black Christmas* represented a moment at which a new textual model was added to the plethora of options that, in theory at least, were available to filmmakers — the story of young people being menaced by a shadowy blade-wielding killer. Yet, despite having secured a pickup deal from an MPAA-member, and despite having generated a profit for its makers (impressive feats for a low-budget Canadian film), *Black Christmas* provided few incentives for Cash-in production and the new textual model that it offered industry-insiders went, in practice, largely unnoticed. Due to overwhelming competition from calculated blockbusters in late 1974 and its inability to sustain ticket sales during a 1975 re-release, *Black Christmas* did not reach large numbers of American theatergoers and, as a result, it had failed to fulfill its American distributor's expectations. As Martin Rubin, the first scholar to acknowledge in writing *Black Christmas'* status as the first 'bona fide' teen slasher film, noted '[*Black Christmas'*] commercial success and critical recognition were limited, and it did not register enough impact to ignite the [teen slasher] cycle' (Rubin, 1999, p. 162).

Thus, where the emergence of the film-type that came to be known as the teen slasher film is often linked to canonized yet tangentially similar American horror films, which are celebrated as highly innovative and idiosyncratic, the teen slasher's distinct story of young people being picked off one-by-one by a shadowy killer actually emerged in Canada when a group of entrepreneurial filmmakers tried, and failed, to deliver the country's first blockbuster hit by combining, in what was a truly unique way, elements of several contemporaneous Hollywood hits. The teen slasher film emerged not with the release of auteur director Alfred Hitchcock's 1960 adult-centered blockbuster hit *Psycho* or when much-vaunted horror filmmaker Tobe Hooper fashioned *The Texas Chainsaw Massacre*, a minor drive-in hit rich in avant-garde aesthetics about twenty-somethings being menaced by a family of deranged abattoir workers, but rather, when a group of little-known Canadian-based entrepreneurs attempted to break in to Hollywood with the story of an unidentified psychotic stalking and killing the inhabitants of a college sorority house one Christmas. The case of the teen slasher film's emergence provides a timely reminder that, if scholars are better to understand the industrial implementation of film-types, more fruitful avenues of investigation may involve focusing not just on canonical films and those that reached a large audience. Rather than solely selecting films based on their capacity to electrify box-office cash-registers and/or the extent to which they attracted popular media attention, it is also necessary to consider the impact of films which, despite the best efforts of those involved, did not generate strong ticket sales, did not become hot topics for journalists, and were not seen by many viewers.

Although the first teen slasher, *Black Christmas*, was not viewed by a significant number of theatergoers in 1974 or 1975, the film's co-writer-producer-director Bob Clark has gone on record on a number of occasions to describe discussions he held with a young filmmaker while in negotiations with Warner Bros. in 1977 to helm a film that the young man had scripted called 'The Prey', described as '*Deliverance* meets *The Texas Chainsaw Massacre* with women' (Boulenger, 2001, pp. 28, 93). Their alleged conversation regarded an idea for a sequel to *Black Christmas*. 'I said what I thought I'd do is I would make it the following fall', recalled Clark, 'the killer had been caught and he had been institutionalized and I would have him escape one night' (interviewed in 'Bob Clark unabridged', 2002). The name of that inquisitive young filmmaker was John Carpenter. Clark concluded by saying: 'I was going to call it "Halloween"' (ibid.).

'A pedestrian box-office smash':
Halloween, from Speculator Production to Trailblazer Hit

Two years after the Canadian Pioneer Production *Black Christmas* was pulled from US theaters, two groups of American independent film-makers re-used its story-structure. In each case, it seems they felt *Black Christmas*' textual model exhibited significant commercial potential and that the film's US box-office failure had been a result of poor judgment by distributor, Warner Bros. One of the Speculator Productions, made in 1977, was called *Silent Scream* (1979). Lengthy re-shoots and a delayed release meant that *Silent Scream* exerted minimal influence on teen slasher film content and production. Because *Silent Scream*'s influence on industry conduct was restricted to distribution decisions in the first half of 1980, it is examined at appropriate points in subsequent chapters. In contrast to *Silent Scream*, the second teen slasher Speculator Production made in 1977, *Halloween*, contributed significantly to establishing the teen slasher as part of the American film industry's repertoire of youth-market product — although not in the ways that have been claimed to date.

Halloween is usually positioned by popular writers and film scholars as both the first bona fide teen slasher film and as another high point in innovation on the trajectory of great modern American horror movie-making that began with *Psycho* and continued with *The Texas Chainsaw Massacre*. Time after time, *Halloween* has been distinguished from other teen slashers based on the misconception that it was the first 'true' example of the film-type and based on the supposedly high levels of art-istry invested in the film by writer-director John Carpenter. Much like they had done with *Psycho* and *The Texas Chainsaw Massacre*, these two points of distinction fed into one another during *Halloween*'s contempor-aneous popular reception, as Robert E. Kapsis work in this area indicates (1992, pp. 160–163), and have, as Matt Hills pointed out, underpinned scholarly discussions of *Halloween* and its position with respect to the teen slasher film-type (2007, pp. 219–239). It is, for Hills, notions of 'repetition over originality, and commerce over art' that led scholars, like journalists before them, to draw a clear distinction between the teen slasher as a film-type and *Halloween* as an exceptional teen slasher film (ibid., p. 228). Where the previous section demonstrated that *Halloween*'s status as the first teen slasher — its 'originality' — needs to be revised, this section shows that prevailing notions of matters of 'art' outweigh-ing matters of 'commerce' in terms of the production and the content of *Halloween* are also highly questionable. The makers of *Halloween*, like the makers of *Black Christmas* before them, and like the makers of the teen slashers that followed, implemented the same production strategies designed to maximize the commercial potential of their film, as they attempted, like their peers, to secure an MPAA-member distribution deal with an R-rated film that promised to be marketable to young males and females because it shared content with some of the most lucrative trends in youth-oriented and blockbuster filmmaking of its day.

Halloween started production in late 1977 when an Oscar-winning film school graduate, the brother of a former president of Paramount Pictures, and a wealthy Syrian financier teamed up to craft a female-centered small-town-set horror film that would fulfill the promise that the pioneering teen slasher, *Black Christmas*, had shown early in its second US theatrical run. Those men — John Carpenter, Irwin Yablans, and Moustapha Akkad — made *Halloween* when, as Ed Lowry explains, the confidence of independent producers and distributors was at an all-time high as a result of shifts in the MPAA-members' business strategies (2005, pp. 48–49). As I showed above, MPAA-members had responded to the huge financial losses they incurred in the late 1960s and early 1970s by reducing their production budgets and the number of films they financed and released. By channeling less capital to fewer films, MPAA-members initiated a product shortage which caused great consternation and concern among exhibitors who felt that they had broken a 'gentlemen's agreement' to keep theaters stocked the whole year round (ibid.). With most MPAA-member releases booked for the summer and Christmas seasons, exhibitors were growing worried that they would have insufficient new films to show in spring and fall (Pollock, 1978b, pp. 5, 26). Some independent producers, as the previous section showed, responded in the early 1970s by making films cheaply to encourage distributors to purchase them in negative pickup deals — a practice that continued across the decade. However, the film famine also provided independent distributors, as Cook has suggested, with an opportunity to 'fill the vacuum created by the majors' partial abandonment of the field' (2000, p. 19) While established independent distributors like AIP and New World Pictures increased the number of films they handled to keep theaters supplied with product (Hillier, 1994, p. 40; Cook, 2000, pp. 322–324, 328–329), entrepreneurs also set up new companies, like Dimension Pictures, to satisfy exhibitors' needs (Lowry, 2005, pp. 42–43). As *Variety* reported in January 1978, another firm that sprang up to capitalize on the product shortage was Compass International Films (Anon., 1978c, p. 33).

Compass International, the company behind *Halloween*, was essentially a merger of The Irwin Yablans Co., a tiny US distributor, and the Patty Corp., a small production house owned by financier and film-maker Moustapha Akkad (Anon., 1978d, p. 28). The company initially announced it would be producing and distributing the unlikely com-bination of 'big-budget items in the $15,000,000 to $20,000,000 range and low-budget horror, sci-fi and car crash films' (ibid.). This ambitious, if not idiosyncratic, plan was, however, swiftly put on ice when Akkad's *Mohammed, Messenger of God* (1976), a $17m three-hour epic chronicling the birth of the Islamic faith, failed to secure a major distributor and performed wretchedly on international markets (Anon., 1978c, p. 33). Compass was forced to bring its corporate operations in line with those of most other independents and focus on the production and distribution of modestly budgeted youth-oriented projects. It would be a mistake to think that Compass International was not interested in securing negative pickup deals from MPAA-members simply because it possessed the means by which to distribute its own films. While independents were enjoying some degree of financial prosperity in the mid-to-late 1970s, they still operated on a fiercely competitive market with only 15 per cent of US theatrical ticket sales up for grabs (Murphy, 1976b, p. 32). Accordingly, Compass recognized that it, like other independent production com-panies, could generate instant profit without the risks of distributing films itself and this is precisely what Yablans hoped to achieve with one of Compass International's first offerings, *Halloween*.

Halloween began production in late 1977 when Irwin Yablans approached 29-year-old writer-director John Carpenter with a project called 'The Babysitter Murders' (Muir, 2000, pp. 12–13). Yablans wanted a film that was marketable to youth. 'I made "Halloween" [because] I was looking for an inexpensive film that would find a market', Yablans explained to the *Hollywood Reporter*, 'I wanted to do something that would scare me like I used to be scared as a kid when I went to the movies' (quoted in V. Scott, 1981). Yablans and Carpenter thrashed out a deal whereby Carpenter would write, direct, and score the film in return for the right to decide upon its final cut (the version of the film screened in theaters). After lengthy negotiations, Akkad agreed to put up the film's $320,000 production budget (Muir, 2000, p. 13), based on its potential to appeal to the youth market. 'Every kid in America', Akkad has since suggested, 'knows what a babysitter is' (interviewed in '*Halloween*: a cut above the rest', 2003). With complete creative control, Carpenter wrote the screenplay with producer and then-partner Debra Hill, before shoot-ing the film in April 1978 (Muir, 2000, p. 13).

In *Halloween*, a young boy called Michael Myers is incarcerated in a psychiatric institution for slashing his sister to death on Halloween night in 1963. Exactly fifteen years later he escapes and returns to the site of the murder, the small picturesque Midwestern town of Haddonfield, Illinois. Michael's psychiatrist Dr Loomis (Donald Pleasence) is convinced that his most dangerous patient will continue where he left off as a child and attempts to warn local law enforcement that 'the evil is coming'. A decade and a half of treatment has failed to rehabilitate Michael Myers. At the age of six he was a murderer, but as an adult he has become a relentless, emotionless, unstoppable killing machine. In the leafy streets of Haddonfield, Michael begins to track the movements of three high school friends: shy bookworm Laurie (Janie Lee Curtis), fun-loving Lynda (P. J. Soles), and self-confident Annie (Nancy Loomis). On Halloween night 1978, he murders two of the girls and their boyfriends as they party. Finally, Michael attacks Laurie when she is babysitting in one of the town's opulent residences. Laurie repels Michael's assaults valiantly and, just as it seems that she is about to become his latest victim, Dr Loomis arrives and sends his former patient crashing through a second-storey window in a hail of gunfire. Despite being shot several times, Michael is nowhere to be seen. 'Was that the bogeyman?' asks a near-traumatized Laurie. 'As a matter of fact', replies Loomis, 'it was'. *Halloween* employs the teen slasher story-structure outlined in chapter one (see Figure 2.2).

Where the Pioneers behind *Black Christmas* had concluded in 1974 that a female-centered politically engaged whodunit would inspire the

Part One: Setup

1. Trigger: As a boy, Michael Myers kills his sister on Halloween night of 1963.
2. Threat: Fifteen years later Michael escapes from the asylum in which he has been imprisoned and returns to his home town.

Part Two: Disruption

3. Leisure: Three high school friends, Laurie, Annie, and Lynda, plan a night of fun.
4. Stalking: Michael tracks the movements of the girls.
5. Murders: Michael kills Annie, Lynda, and their boyfriends.

Part Three: Resolution

6. Confrontation: Laurie battles with Michael.
7. Neutralization: Michael is shot by his psychiatrist Dr. Loomis.

FIGURE 2.2   The teen slasher film story-structure in *Halloween*

confidence of MPAA-members, by late 1977, several shifts had taken place in the content of blockbuster and youth-oriented hits leading the Speculators that made *Halloween* to target the same companies with a female-centered small-town-set horror film that balanced mobilization of *Black Christmas'* story-structure with four significant textual differences concerning plot structure, the killer, the youth group, and the setting.

Several commercial and creative decisions probably underpinned the decision not to render 'The Babysitter Murders' as a whodunit. It may have appeared somewhat naive to reveal the killer's identity swiftly given that the whodunits *Murder on the Orient Express* (1974) and *Murder by Death* (1976) had performed very strongly in previous years,[12] and given that, as *Halloween* was in production, Columbia was preparing to release two additional murder-mysteries, including a giallo film called *Eyes of Laura Mars* (1978) that Carpenter had penned (Boulenger, 2001, pp. 82–83). However, it seems, that Carpenter did not re-use *Black Christmas'* who-dunit plot so as to off-set the numerous textual elements that already were shared by *Halloween* and *Eyes of Laura Mars* — both films intro-duced potentially supernatural elements into contemporary US settings and featured blade-wielding killers that preyed on female characters. Thus, if *Eyes of Laura Mars* proved to be financially successful, *Halloween* already exhibited sufficient textual similarities to be deemed capable of capitalizing on the film. It therefore appears likely that Carpenter, while maintaining some textual similarities, wished to demonstrate a degree of versatility to the Hollywood executives for whom he had expressed a desire to work (ibid.), especially as he recently had completed shooting another murder-mystery *Someone's Watching Me!* (1978) (ibid., p. 28). If *Halloween's* plot-structure was fashioned with an eye on subsequent events, the version of normality threatened in the film was crafted to reflect earlier developments.

To enable distributors to target teenage girls and young women, the makers of *Halloween* built their film around three small-town high school girlfriends (see Figure 2.3). Annie, Lynda, and Laurie are, as Vincent Canby of the *New York Times* observed, 'fun-loving gum-chewing no-better-than-they-should-be baby-sitters' (1979, pp. D13, D18). Much of *Halloween* depicted the trio bonding, discussing homo-social and het-erosexual interaction, and musing over the minor personal problems that arose from their comfortable middle-class existences: having or not having a prom-date; balancing schoolwork, babysitting, and boyfriends; not being caught smoking pot. This content was deemed so important to *Halloween's* commercial prospects that the film's 27-year-old co-producer Debra Hill wrote the girls' dialogue because writer/director Carpenter felt that he, as an adult male, could not depict female youth convincingly. Hill later confirmed that the girlfriends' conversations were tailored to make *Halloween* marketable to young females. 'Here was a movie', explained Hill, 'that they could go and see, and see themselves' (interviewed in 'Filmmakers' commentary', 2003).

The transformation of *Halloween's* youth group from the careerist university students that had featured in *Black Christmas* to small-town teenage girls preoccupied with their social lives echoed two intertwined shifts that had taken place in the content of high-earning youth-oriented films in the years that had followed the release of *Black Christmas*. The first shift reflected attempts to make films that would appeal equally to young males and young females through the positioning of groups of high school or college-age characters of one sex within film-types considered to appeal more to the other sex. The second shift represented an attempt to stimulate attendance by increasing the number of similarities between on-screen protagonists and prime target audience, if not in terms of behavior then in terms of demographic characteristics, by locating young people within, what Dika described as, 'fictionalized American town[s] that can be everywhere and nowhere, a place "just like" the film viewer's home (as an American ideal, if not a lived fact)' (1990, p. 36). The commercial promise of combining these two elements had been indicated by a drive-in hit of 1976 before being fulfilled by the most financially successful youth-centered film since 1973's *American Graffiti*. Those two films, Crown International's *The Pom Pom Girls* and UA's pickup *Carrie*, ensured that, when *Halloween* was in production between fall 1977 and late spring 1978, the commercial success of horror films and youth-centered films appeared to be tied to female youth — on the screen and in front of it.

FIGURE 2.3   *Halloween's* small-town female high school students.

The Pom Pom Girls — less a narrative film than a ninety-minute montage of summer-time youth leisure — exerted a profound and far-reaching influence on the production and the content of the youth-centered films that followed, including *Halloween*. More so than any other film, *The Pom Pom Girls* initiated the widespread production of youth-centered date-movies across the late 1970s and early 1980s, a development which, despite being among the most important shifts in industry output during the period, has, in the context of the attention paid to contemporaneous 'New' Hollywood blockbusters (Schatz, 1993, Hall, 1998, Krämer, 2005), drawn little scholarly attention. *The Pom Pom Girls*, itself a Speculator Production designed to tap into the solid if unspectacular audience of a textually similar film called *The Cheerleaders* (1973), was tailor-made for young drive-in patrons of both sexes whose attention, at least in the popular imagination, drifted from what was taking place in the movie to what was happening in their vehicles (Horton, 1977, pp. 233–244). The content of the film, and its organization on-screen, drew from American youth cinema's past and pointed to its future. As a light-hearted sun-soaked teen film, replete with a smattering of sex and partial nudity, *The Pom Pom Girls* was in one sense a slightly more salacious update of AIP's beach movies (see Morris, 1993, pp. 2–11), a point recognized by Kevin Thomas of the *New York Times*, who wrote that the film, like its predecessors, 'succeeds as an evocation of freedom that youth symbolizes but practically no one, today or in the past, ever really gets to enjoy' (1976, p. F16). However, by emphasizing, over cause-and-effect storytelling, short sequences in which pop music accompanied young people enjoying themselves, *The Pom Pom Girls* was also an immediate precursor to the 'high-concept' look that Justin Wyatt showed was later embraced by MPAA-members (1994, pp. 23–60). 'The picture was of basic exploitation quality with minimal plot', notes Donahue, '(. . .) a collection of scenes containing sex, vandalism and a total disregard of authority' (1987, p. 268). While these qualities may have been reminiscent of *American Graffiti*, what made *The Pom Pom Girls* stand out from its contemporaries was the amount of time that had been given over to images of female friendship and rebellion, especially at the level of promotion.

The Pom Pom Girls was the brain-child of a 34-year-old woman who believed that the commercial success of her product hinged on its ability to attract small-town female youths — Marilyn Tenser, a high-ranking production executive at Crown International and 'a trend setter (. . .) with a keen sense of what will sell to the youth (18 to 28) exploitation market' (Gross, 1978, p. 34). Tenser spoke openly about her reasons for targeting her films to young females. 'Women influence our box office', she explained in 1978, '[t]hey're the ones that decide what movie a couple is going to see' (quoted in ibid.). Tenser also strove to reflect on-screen something of the conditions of existence of her target audience. 'We shoot in and around Los Angeles, not in Hollywood, mostly on locations because they give us the look we want (. . .) small-town U.S.A', she revealed, adding: 'The performers in these movies are like the kids the audience go to school with. We go for a natural look' (ibid.). When it came to mobilizing film content to attract the teenage girls and young women that called small-town America home, Tenser implemented an approach used by many independent producer-distributors (Donahue, 1987, p. 89), first fashioning the film's marketing campaign and then instructing creative personnel to ensure that content chimed with the promotional materials. 'The advertising — and therefore, ultimately the film itself', noted Linda Gross of the *Los Angeles Times*, 'is drawn up with women in mind' (1978, p. 34). In the case of *The Pom Pom Girls*, Tenser and her collaborators, as Gross' colleague Gregg Kilday recognized, 'sidestepped the routine raunchiness inherent in both the movie's title and its R-rating and instead produced a rather good-spirited send up of youth in Southern California' (1976, p. E8). The accommodation of female youth address enabled Crown to promote *The Pom Pom Girls* as a new kind of date-movie.

To attract young people of both sexes to its R-rated youth-oriented features, Crown employed a marketing strategy that it dubbed 'Crownsmanship', which presented films as mildly titillating and dreamily romantic depictions of all-American youngsters enjoying themselves and each other. Crown had angled *The Pom Pom Girls* to male youth by implying various high school locker-room scenes and teenage fumbling involving a group of cheerleaders, and had targeted female youth with (slightly exaggerated) suggestions that the film would foreground young females, their friendship, and their horseplay. Posters combined taglines that addressed teenage boys and young men directly by declaring 'They were the girls of our dreams . . .', and used imagery that conveyed courtship, sisterhood, and sexual confidence to appeal to their female peers (see Figure 2.4). To emphasize that *The Pom Pom Girls* was a 'female-friendly' film, Crown even used a soft-spoken actress to narrate trailers and TV-spots, a rarely used technique which has only recently been appropriated to sell female-audience-films like *Sex and the City* (2008) and *Bride Wars* (2009). Recalibrating *American Graffiti*'s youth group so as to place emphasis on high school girls enabled Crown to enjoy its biggest hit ever (Anon., 1977b, p. 49), transforming the company from a minor player into a thriving business, one that could lay claim to the National

Association of Theatre Owners' Independent Distributor of the Year Award for 1976 (Schreger, 1977, p. 28), and boast, convincingly although inaccurately, 'the biggest grossing independent feature of '76!' (Crown International Pictures, 1976, pp. 18–19).

The $4.3m in rentals generated by *The Pom Pom Girls* may have paled in comparison to the $60–120m returned by mid 1970s blockbuster hits,[13] but they were significant because they had been earned by a small company operating in a fiercely competitive market. Films released by modest outfits like Crown rarely broke into the annual film rentals chart. 'The film would be considered a hit', Cook points out, 'if it earned four or five times its negative cost' (2007, p. 132). Given that Crown's films cost $750,000–$1m to bring to the screen (Anon., 1977b, p. 49), *The Pom Pom Girls* was seen to have been a hit, and, as early as September 1976, the American popular press had begun to report that its financial achievements had 'not gone unnoticed by other producers looking to cash in on the youth-market' (Kilday, 1976, p. E8).

FIGURE 2.4   A drive-in date-movie: *The Pom Pom Girls*.

Crown's success story with *The Pom Pom Girls* had served notice to the American film industry, which remarkably had not followed up on the success of *American Graffiti*, that youth-centered date-movies could be incredibly lucrative commodities, and it was not long before producers were provided with an all-important Reinforcing Hit, when, Crown's follow-up, the Prospector Cash-in *The Van*, became the company's top earner of 1977.[14] Thus, as often happens on such occasions, film companies, from the wealthy majors down to cash-strapped independents, moved to capitalize on a trend that had been established by the achievements of two independently distributed minor hits. The hedonism and high-jinx of small-town female youths continued to be showcased in youth-oriented films emerging from the American independent sector as Crown contributed *Coach* and *Malibu High* (both 1978) and other Carpetbaggers responded with Cash-ins of their own like *Cheering Section* and *Cherry Hill High* (both 1977). The filmmakers behind *Halloween* were intimately familiar with the influence that *The Pom Pom Girls* was exerting on the American independent sector because Debra Hill, the producer and co-writer of *Halloween*, had recently completed script-supervising duties on *Satan's Cheerleaders* (1977), a drive-in date-movie that injected light-hearted supernatural goings-on into the high school milieu of *The Pom Pom Girls*. Productions of this sort had become so rampant that *The Pom Pom Girls* was becoming a byword in industry circles for, what filmmakers such as Martin Davidson, the director of Universal's contribution *Almost Summer* (1978), were calling, 'those dumb high school movies' (quoted in B. Thomas, 1977, p. A6). Presumably sensing that the American film market was on the verge of becoming saturated with films of this type, MPAA-members responded to the success of *The Pom Pom Girls* in different ways (Donahue, 1987, p. 35). While producing films in which characters of one sex were positioned within types of film that were traditionally considered to appeal to the other sex (much like Tenser and her collaborators on *The Pom Pom Girls* had done), MPAA-members, particularly Paramount, tended to reverse the gender dynamics that characterized *The Pom Pom Girls*. This approach had led to two medium-budget films in which gangs of hyper-masculine young men were situated in narratives that focused on music, dance, and romance — content considered to appeal principally to female audiences. By the time *Halloween* was in production, the first of those films, *Saturday Night Fever* (1977), had been playing US theaters and was on its way to becoming one of the biggest hits in history.[15] The second of the films, *Grease* (1978), was also expected to perform strongly. However, MPAA-members had also concluded that, with higher production values, more intensive marketing campaigns, and wider releases, youth-oriented films that replicated Crown International's use of small-town female protagonists in film-types that were thought to be male-oriented could become big hits. The most influential of these projects was the female-teen-centered horror film *Carrie*.

Carrie provided a watershed moment in American horror film production. Whereas *The Pom Pom Girls* had signaled the box-office promise of positioning small-town female youths in film-types thought to appeal primarily to young males, *Carrie* had demonstrated that the horror film provided a genuinely lucrative way of implementing that model.[16] In doing so, *Carrie* seemed also to offer filmmakers a commercially viable and cost-effective solution to adult-centered horror films, the ticket sales and profit margins of which had, with the exception of *The Omen*, dropped significantly in 1976 as a result of flops like *Burnt Offerings* and *The Premonition*.[17] Indeed, it was in response to this development that UA had gambled on angling *Carrie*, the last important horror release of 1977, to young people.

Carrie, director Brian De Palma's adaptation of Stephen King's best-selling novel, was a modern-day fairytale about a timid high school student named Carrie White (Sissy Spacek), 'the girl no one likes and everyone makes fun of', as the film's trailer described her. Carrie is brutalized by her mother (Piper Laurie), bullied by a clique of 'popular girls', terrified by her own emerging telekinetic powers, and besotted with a handsome male student. When her election as prom queen is revealed to have been a vicious hoax staged by her spiteful peers, and ends in her being doused in pig's blood, Carrie exacts a bloody revenge. UA believed that, as a result of its youth-centered content, *Carrie*'s box-office appeal was likely to be limited in comparison to that of horror films with cross-demographic appeal like *The Omen* (Arnold, 1976b, p. 141). However, to turn a profit, *Carrie*, as a low-budget pickup, needed to sell considerably fewer tickets than prestige horror films. UA had therefore been able to reduce its target audience while still standing to make money from distributing the film. *Carrie* lent itself ideally to a youth-oriented marketing campaign. Unlike contemporaneous horror films, which usually unfolded in opulent mansions occupied by middle-aged adults and their small children, *Carrie* was set in a teenage world consisting of high school classrooms and gyms, small-town streets, and white picket-fenced homes. UA could also target *Carrie* to teenage girls and young women not only because it was a female youth-centered film but, as Paul shows, because it addressed subjects of specific relevance to young females, including the emotional turmoil of burgeoning female sexuality, the heartache of adolescent crushes, and the cruelty of female youth interaction (1994, p. 362). With its promotion of *Carrie* in late 1976, UA introduced 'Crownsmanship' to horror.

As a scary movie sold to young people of both sexes, to the exclusion of other demographics, *Carrie* marked the advent of the 'New' Hollywood horror date-movie. UA's approach was encapsulated in the film's promotional poster, on which Carrie White appears as a blood-drenched specter and a radiant prom queen. The poster featured two taglines, which addressed male and female youth separately. 'If you've got a taste for terror', it advised young males, 'take Carrie to the prom'. The second tagline — 'if only they knew she had the power' — addressed their female peers by speaking as much to their own perceptions of social power dynamics as the film's content (see Figure 2.5). UA's trailer expanded the approach. Before gesturing to Carrie's vengeance, it spotlighted her transformation from unhappy outcast to blissful young

FIGURE 2.5 The horror date-movie: *Carrie*.

woman who slow-dances with the apple of her eye, is crowned prom queen, and, or so it seems, wins the acceptance of her classmates. By mid 1977, *Carrie* had become that rarest of phenomena: a commercially and critically successful teen horror film.

Strong ticket sales, Academy Award nominations, and volumes of popular press coverage made *Carrie* one of the most high-profile films of its time. Kapsis' study of the film's critical reception shows the extent to which *Carrie* was embraced by journalists (1992, pp. 199–200). 'Regardless of whether critics were writing for prestigious or esoteric publications', wrote Kapsis, 'the reviews ranged from favorable to wildly enthusiastic' (ibid., p. 199). Journalists heaped praise on De Palma as much for portraying female youth sensitively as for crafting an effective chiller. Richard Schickel of *Time* magazine (1976), for example, described a sequence in which Carrie is bullied as 'the most terrifying demonstration of the adolescent capacity for mass cruelty ever filmed', and, as chapter four shows, the depiction of young love, told from the perspective of a lonely female misfit, garnered the richest accolades of all (see Arnold, 1976a, pp. D1, D7). Given this high-profile coverage, few industry-insiders could have failed to recognize that *Carrie* had demonstrated the commercial potential of orienting horror to female youth, and so it was that the influence of the film's box-office performance and UA's forward-thinking marketing campaign was felt quickly as MPAA-members began to emphasize female youths in horror films and their marketing campaigns.

The commercial viability of placing female youths in horror films appeared to be confirmed when, between mid 1977 and spring 1978, the period before *Halloween* was shot, horror films sold on the presence of teenage girls generated significantly stronger ticket sales than horror films that were not advertised on the presence of teenage girls. Whereas the adult-centered *Audrey Rose* and *The Sentinel* (both 1977), attracted miniscule numbers of theatergoers, *Exorcist II: The Heretic* (1977), the poster art for which played down middle-aged stars Richard Burton and Louise Fletcher while emphasizing 18-year-old actress Linda Blair, and *The Fury* (1978), the poster art for which spotlighted a minor character played by Amy Irving, a young actress who also had appeared in *Carrie*, both secured large audiences, albeit not large enough to generate much profit given high production costs.[18] Much like their intimate knowledge of the impact of *The Pom Pom Girls*, the filmmakers behind *Halloween* were acutely aware of these shifts because producer Irwin Yablans' brother Frank had produced *The Fury*. Solid ticket sales for *Carrie, Exorcist II: The Heretic*, and *The Fury* had confirmed that the American horror film market was changing. Horror audiences no longer appeared large enough to support costly projects and female youth seemed to hold the key to turning modestly budgeted films into lucrative ventures.

Carrie exerted a huge influence on the way the makers of *Halloween* depicted the targets of the film's masked maniac and the location in which that action took place. Like Carrie, *Halloween* is set to what Kevin Thomas of the *Los Angeles Times* described as 'a tree-shaded small-town American setting' (1978, p. F22). Moreover, as Gary Arnold of the *Washington Post* noted, the killer menaces 'potential victims derived from Brian De Palma's "Carrie"' (1978, p. B5). Writing for Toronto's *Mail and Globe* newspaper, Jay Scott elucidated Arnold's observation noting: 'Carpenter [sic], in common with De Palma in "Carrie", is a sharp observer of suburban adolescent sociology' (1979a). To spotlight the connections between *Carrie* and *Halloween* explicitly, Carpenter cast as one of the film's babysitters P. J. Soles, who had played one of the schoolgirls that ruined prom night for Carrie White. 'I was cast because John [Carpenter] adored "Carrie"', the actress revealed in an interview (quoted in Greenberger, 1981, p. 18). Depicting small-town female youth thus enabled the Speculators behind *Halloween* to bolster the commercial viability of their horror film by mobilizing content that, after having driven the success of a breakthrough drive-in hit (*The Pom Pom Girls*), had, as *Carrie* had demonstrated, appealed to an MPAA-member and a healthy number of young theatergoers.

Where *Halloween*'s youth group reflected the content of youth-market hits, its killer reflected the distinguishing features of some of the American film industry's biggest blockbuster hits. As several scholars have recognized, the depiction of Michael Myers, first as murderous child, and then as emotionless killing machine, combined traits of the monsters from *Jaws* (1975) and *The Omen* (1976). From the makers of *Jaws*, *Halloween* borrowed a relentless and seemingly unstoppable monster that prowls a familiar location during a date of cultural significance — 4 July in the case of *Jaws*. Indeed, as Rubin observed, *Jaws*' opening and, arguably, most memorable, sequence had — by combining an everyday location (a beach), a group of fun-seeking young people, and a threatening entity represented by subjective shots — contained 'a number of ingredients that would be crucial to the upcoming [teen slasher] film' (1999, p. 60). The voice-over to the film's trailer had even described the shark in similar ways to later descriptions of *Halloween*'s killer, including that written by Rubin himself. Thus, whereas Rubin described the teen slasher killer as 'more animal than human, more machinelike than animal, more an abstract force than a physical form' (ibid., p. 164), a grave narrator had informed viewers of *Jaws'* trailer that '[w]ithout passion . . . without logic . . . it lives to kill, it will attack and devour anything . . . it is, as if God created the devil'. While *Jaws* featured a creature whose relentless malevolence invited comparisons to the devil, *The Omen* depicted a small boy as the Anti-Christ itself. It is the concept of child as Other, as Paul recognized (1994, pp. 319–330), that the filmmakers behind *Halloween* adopted from *The Omen* and presented in their film's opening sequence. There were strong economic grounds for extracting content from *The Omen* and *Jaws*.

The Omen and *Jaws* had been the two highest-earning horror films on the US theatrical market since *The Exorcist* blazed its trail across the American box-office in late 1973 and 1974.[19] In the four years that had followed the staggering returns of *The Exorcist, Jaws* and *The Omen* were the only horror films that could have been legitimately described as blockbuster hits. In 1975, *Jaws* had eclipsed the achievements of *The Exorcist* to return the highest rentals in the history of the American movie business. While *The Omen* was not quite as successful as Friedkin's or Spielberg's hits, it still had performed well enough to break into the top five of the annual rentals chart for 1976, to join *The Exorcist* and *Jaws* as the only horror films to have achieved that feat since 1960. With big-budget sequels to *Jaws* and *The Omen* being shot and promoted in the trade press when *Halloween* was in production, MPAA-members had demonstrated their continued confidence in the content of the original films. For these reasons, the commercial logic of locating content from *Jaws* and *The Omen* in an independent production that would be offered to MPAA-members seemed sound.

The traits of *Halloween*'s killer, drawn from top Hollywood blockbuster hits, were packaged in the 'marketing-friendly' figure of the masked maniac so as to reflect a trend that, after having been employed with some success to promote independently distributed horror films in the years that had passed since *Black Christmas* was made, had been used shortly before *Halloween* was produced to market a film that was accumulating the highest rentals in the history of the American film industry (see Figure 2.6). The icon of the masked madman had dominated the posters used to advertise two independently distributed horror films that had, by non-MPAA-member standards, performed relatively well at the US box-office, 1974's *The Texas Chainsaw Massacre* and *The Town that Dreaded Sundown* (1976) (see Figure 2.7). With rental sums as low as $1.1m being reported by the film's mob-affiliated distributor (Anon., 1975c, p. 75), and with gross returns as high as $50m being cited by disgruntled filmmakers who had not seen a cent of ticket sales (Tobe Hooper cited in

Farley, 1977, p. O1), the exact US theatrical performance of *The Texas Chainsaw Massacre* will probably never be known. Nevertheless, the $6m rentals cited by Donahue represent a realistic figure for a well-attended film released on about only 200 prints (1987, pp. 234–235), and is perhaps the most accurate estimation available. There were no doubts, however, that *The Town that Dreaded Sundown* had done well for AIP, when it became one of the top five independently distributed films of 1976 and the only independently distributed horror film to generate rentals of $5m or more that year (Anon., 1977a, p. 21). These sums were, however, peanuts in comparison to the revenue generated by the next distributor to spotlight in print advertising a film's masked villain. With the arresting site of a shiny black visor and helmet dominating promotional posters, Twentieth Century Fox was enjoying its biggest hit ever with *Star Wars* (1977).[20] Although the makers of *Halloween* aimed to negotiate a negative pickup with an MPAA-member by drawing content from blockbuster hits, their efforts, as chapter one explained, amounted to nothing if their film was unable to secure an R-rating.

The incentive to avoid the X-rating became particularly pronounced at the time of *Halloween*'s production because the fears that some filmmakers had expressed earlier in the decade about controversy shifting from hardcore pornography to horror films had begun to be realized. Much of that controversy had centered on one film, *Snuff* (1976), and had indicated that sexual, graphic, and sadistic violence was likely to attract the kind of attention that would alienate MPAA-members. *Snuff* was an ultra-low-budget production that had been filmed in 1971 but

Figure 2.6   *Halloween*'s masked maniac

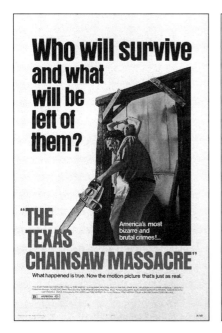

FIGURE 2.7   Masked maniacs as marketing hooks: *The Texas Chainsaw Massacre* and *The Town that Dreaded Sundown*

had remained unreleased for several years (Johnson and Schaefer, 1993, p. 43–44). A small company called Monarch Releasing, the owner of the film, shot additional footage in a documentary style that showed a film crew raping, torturing, and murdering a starlet, added it to the end of the film and deployed what was arguably the most distasteful marketing campaign of the 1970s or any other decade (ibid.). *Snuff*, as the title suggests, was promoted on the presence of what was purported to be an actual murder committed solely for commercial purposes. While not drawing significant numbers of theatergoers, the film attracted vociferous pickets, the watchful eye of the FBI, and significant coverage in *Variety* (Anon., 1976c, p. 36; Anon., 1976d, p. 26; Anon., 1976e, p. 5; Anon., 1976f, p. 36; Cedrone, 1976, p. 4). The swift revelation of the hoax did little to silence protests, with the controversy surrounding *Snuff* reaching its peak in spring 1976. Two years later, in the weeks leading up to the production of *Halloween*, coverage resumed amid new attempts to prosecute exhibitors of *Snuff* on charges of obscenity (Anon., 1978e, p. 7).

The *Snuff* controversy, as Linda Williams argues, '[produced] generic confusion between horror and hardcore' (1999, p. 193). In doing so, the response to, and reception of, the tasteless ballyhoo exercise that accompanied the film's release reinforced many independent producers' and distributors' reticence to deal in product that would struggle to secure a G, PG or an R-rating. 'Independent producers', wrote Don Carle Gillette in *Variety*, 'are missing the boat, losing thousands of available playdates because of their emphasis on "sexploitation" [and] gruesome violence' (1976, pp. 5, 40). Within little over a year, the trade paper had observed 'a quiet shift from (. . .) "sex" and "violence" exploitation films' (Tusher, 1977, pp. 5, 46), reporting that New World was moving into the production of more prestigious films such as a $6m adaptation of the Broadway musical *A Little Night Music* (1977) (Anon., 1977d, pp. 4, 28), that Crown International was trimming nudity from *The Pom Pom Girls* in preparation for its re-release as a PG-rated film (Tusher 1977, p. 46), and that even soft-core auteur Russ Meyer had announced that he would be reducing the violent and sexual content of his films to secure R-ratings (Verrill, 1976, p. 27). *Halloween*'s producer Irwin Yablans was part of the sea-change sweeping the American independent sector, with *Variety* reporting in July 1977 that Yablans had reneged on a deal to distribute a sex comedy called *Captain Lust* (1977). 'Although we feel that the box-office [sic] potential is great', Yablans had said, 'this kind of film is just not conducive to our [The Irwin Yablans Co.] image' (quoted in Anon., 1977c, p. 4). The Speculators behind *Halloween* responded to outcries over sexually violent films, much like their predecessors had done with *Black Christmas*, by tightly policing sequences of violence and horror.

The makers of *Halloween*, as both Steve Neale and Sheldon Hall have shown, emphasized thrills and minimized horror (1981, pp. 25–29; 2002, pp. 66–77). The views of Neale and of Hall echo those expressed by journalists on the film's release. 'It is a beautifully made thriller more shocking than bloody', wrote Gene Siskel of the *Chicago Tribune* (1978a, p. B7). 'There is almost no blood in "Halloween" and the murders themselves are anti-climactic', wrote Jay Scott in Toronto's *Globe and Mail* (1979a). Similarly, a *Variety* reviewer noted that 'Carpenter has a good feel for timing the thrills' (Hege., 1978, p. 20), and even the *Washington Post*'s Gary Arnold, who disliked *Halloween* immensely, acknowledged that its makers had attempted to stress thrills over horror. 'Carpenter imagines he's building up spinetingling [sic] anticipation', lamented Arnold, 'but his techniques are so transparent and laborious that the result is attenuation rather than tension' (1978, p. B5). *Halloween* thus featured only five murders. All but one of these killings was preceded by a brief struggle in which only fleeting shots of the victim's fear were displayed. Each death blow was located outside of the frame, and, with the exception of the opening murder, a single blow sufficed to bring about the victim's death. These deaths were each a silent, clean affair, with victims dying instantaneously and without fear or body-horror being shown (see Table 2.3 and Table 2.4).

TABLE 2.3 Pre-death features of murders in *Halloween*.

Victim		Features			
Gender	Type	None	Fear	Chase	Struggle
Female	Youth		✓		✓
Male	Adult	✓			
Female	Youth		✓		✓
Male	Youth		✓		✓
Female	Youth		✓		✓

Key: '✓' denotes presence of feature

TABLE 2.4 Features of murders in *Halloween*.

Victim		Death-blow			Effects		
Gender	Type	Single	Multiple	Off-screen	Fear	Gore	Pain
Female	Youth		✓	✓		✓	✓
Male	Adult			✓			
Female	Youth	✓		✓			
Male	Youth	✓		✓			
Female	Youth			✓			

Key: '✓' denotes presence of feature

Despite having been tailored to appeal to MPAA-members, *Halloween* was, in the summer of 1978, viewed and rejected by every major studio in Hollywood (Anon., 1979g, p. 6). The heavyweights of American film distribution clearly had deemed the premise of small-town female youth menaced by a masked maniac to exhibit some commercial potential otherwise they would not have screened it for busy executives. Those executives were, however, evidently not convinced that the finished product would find an audience. John Carpenter has stated that the film was screened without its soundtrack, which explains their apathy (interviewed in '*Halloween*: a cut above the rest', 2003). The blanket rejection of the film by all of the MPAA-members amounted to nothing short of a worst case scenario for Compass International. Rather than simply cashing a check and counting the profits, Yablans was forced to take the perilous route of self-distribution, which, as chapter one showed, threw up countless obstacles to profit-making. Without the instant profits of an MPAA-member pickup deal, Compass' profit-margin was to be determined by ticket sales.

In the absence of an MPAA-member distributor, *Halloween*'s chances of emulating the box-office achievements of *Carrie* or even *The Pom Pom Girls* appeared to be incredibly slim. *Variety*'s 1978 records of film rentals showed that in the previous three years only one independently distributed film had generated more than the $14.3m in rentals returned by *Carrie*, and that film, *In Search of Noah's Ark* (1977), had, as Frederick Wasser has shown, bypassed conventional distribution to be unspooled to rural Americans (1991, pp. 51–65). In fact, from 1975 to 1978, only one other independent release had returned more than $10m in rentals, and the vast majority of non-MPAA-member releases that had beaten the returns of *The Pom Pom Girls*, 12 out of 14 to be precise, had been handled by the most heavily capitalized independent companies of the period: AIP, Allied Artists Pictures, New World Pictures, and Film Ventures International (See Table 2.5). Based on the 320 films distributed theatrically in the United States by non-MPAA-members across this three year period, *Halloween* stood a 0.6% chance of generating the $4.3m in rentals, which would reward the company with a low six-figure profit after production, marketing, and distribution overheads had been covered, exhibitors had taken their share, and the IRS had received its cut. In short, when opening *Halloween* theatrically in the US on 25 October 1978, Compass International faced odds in excess of 100–1 on making a profit.

TABLE 2.5   Top rental independently distributed films, 1975–1977.

Film	Distributor	Year	Rentals $m
In Search of Noah's Ark	Sunn Classic	1977	23
Part II Walking Tall	American International	1975	11.5
Reincarnation of Peter Proud	American International	1975	7.5
Walking Tall Final Chapter	American International	1977	7.5

(continued)

Film	Distributor	Year	Rentals $m
Grizzly	Film Ventures	1975	7.2
Beyond the Door	Film Ventures	1975	7
The Man Who Would be King	Allied Artists	1975	6.6
Eat My Dust	New World	1976	5.5
Death Race 2000	New World	1975	5.2
Monty Python and the Holy Grail	Cinema 5	1975	5.1
The Town that Dreaded Sundown	American International	1976	5
Futureworld	American International	1976	5
Great Scott and Cathouse Thursday	American International	1976	4.8
Twighlight's Last Gleaming	Allied Artists	1977	4.5
Tunnelvision	World Wide Film	1976	4.3
The Pom Pom Girls	Crown International	1976	4.3

(Source: Anon., 1978a, p. 88)

Compass International attempted to offset the economic risks of self-distribution by mobilizing a sophisticated marketing campaign which framed *Halloween* as a film that shared content with the MPAA-members' blockbuster horror and youth-centered blockbuster hits rather than contemporaneous independently distributed horror films. The poster that Compass used to promote *Halloween*, an image that combined the segments of a menacing jack-o-lantern and a hand clutching a large knife (see Figure 2.7), had been tailored by design company B. D. Fox Independent to evoke the posters of the biggest horror blockbusters of the 1970s iconographically and compositionally and had been rendered in the style that had been employed to advertise several youth-oriented hits. By evoking different film-types associated with different pleasures, Compass was seeking to expand attendance by appealing simultaneously to different taste formations, which as Barbara Klinger (1989, pp. 3–19), Rick Altman (1999, p. 54), and Lisa Kernan (2004) have argued, characterizes most film marketing. The location of a single image against a black background, a highly visible example of the 'high concept' marketing that Wyatt shows was associated with MPAA-member releases of the period (1994b, pp. 24–25, 112–133), had been employed in the artwork of both *The Exorcist* and *The Omen* and MPAA-members had continued to show faith in this approach in the twelve months before *Halloween* was released by commissioning similar posters to accompany most of their costly horror releases of 1977–1978 — the Carpenter-scripted giallo *Eyes of Laura Mars*, and the calculated blockbuster sequels *Exorcist II: The Heretic* and *Damien: Omen II* (1978). The designers of these films' posters had used color sparingly to create near-monochromatic images that were fairly realistic and quite somber in tone (see Figure 2.8). The central icon of *Halloween*'s poster was, however, rendered in the bright colors and presented in the comic book style that MPAA-members had used consistently in posters for light-hearted youth-oriented films (see Figure 2.9), many of which, including *American Graffiti, Grease, Animal House,* and *Up in Smoke* (both 1978), had become huge commercial successes, particularly in the months leading up to the release of *Halloween*.[21] By imitating the artwork of Hollywood films that shared the general textual orientation of *Halloween*, Compass encouraged potential theatergoers to anticipate a film with equally high production values, which in turn distanced *Halloween* from contemporaneous independently produced and distributed horror films. Thus, where posters promoting ultra-violent drive-in releases like the aforementioned *Snuff* or *Torso* (1976) tended to feature photographs or roughly sketched images that linked violence and female sexuality (see Figure 2.10), *Halloween*'s poster eschewed direct references to victimization, blending instead suggestions of threat (a raised hand brandishing a knife) and youthful recreation (the jack-o-lantern) so as to frame *Halloween* as a film that, rather than offering eroticized suffering, delivered mild horror in the context of a fun experience, in short 'recreational terror' (Pinedo, 1997).

Compass International's blockbuster-esque marketing campaign probably did much to attract the early audiences whose positive word-of-mouth was identified as enabling *Halloween* to accumulate over an extended period small weekly returns to the point that, almost five months after it opened theatrically, the film was being discussed in some quarters as a hit. Although standard practice among scholars and popular writers, it is somewhat misleading to describe *Halloween* as a blockbuster or as the highest grossing independent film ever. Matters of accuracy notwithstanding, such claims do not reflect the fact that the vast majority of *Halloween*'s US rentals, estimated to have been $18.5m (Cook, 2000, p. 502), were accumulated across several re-releases, beginning in late 1979 and continuing throughout the early 1980s — thus providing a timely reminder that perceptions of commercial viability, whether it be in respect to a film-type or to individual elements of content, can only be gauged with a degree of accuracy when contemporaneous financial data is distinguished from monies generated at a later date. For eighteen weeks, *Halloween*'s weekly grosses had in fact been so unspectacular that the film had slipped beneath the radars of industrially-oriented film writers until the middle of March 1979 when *Variety* reported that its predictions (Hege., 1978, p. 20) had come true and that strong word-of-mouth was aiding ticket sales (Anon., 1979g, p. 6), and when, four days later, Sam Allis of the *Washington Post* described *Halloween*, somewhat hyperbolically, as 'a pedestrian box-office smash' (1979a, pp. H1, H6). In the late 1970s, eighteen weeks was usually sufficient time to get a strong, if not a conclusive, idea about a film's box-office prowess. With gross revenue standing, according to Allis, at \$12m (ibid.), *Halloween*, against-all-odds, had just surpassed the rental sums earned by Crown International's drive-in hits *The Pom Pom Girls* and *The Van*, and, if Irwin Yablans' forecasts proved to be accurate and *Halloween* did continue to defy standard rental patterns by selling an additional \$8m worth of tickets (quoted in Anon., 1979g, p. 6), the film was, in March of 1979, on-track to emulate the relative commercial success of AIP's top earners of the period and, in doing so, return its distributor around \$8m in

FIGURE 2.8 *Halloween*'s promotional poster.

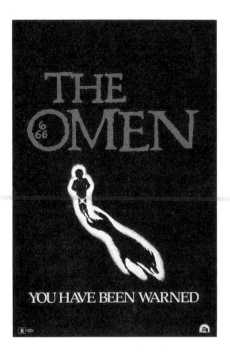

FIGURE 2.9   The near-monochromatic artwork of 'prestige horror' *The Omen* and
                  Eyes of Laura Mars.

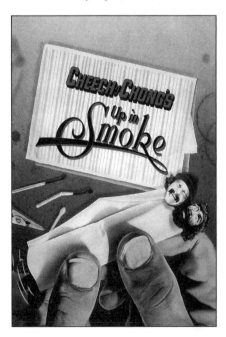
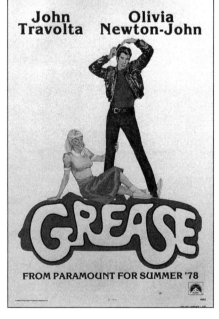

FIGURE 2.10   The comic-book style of light-hearted youth-oriented hits *Up in Smoke*
                   and *Grease.*

rentals. *Halloween*'s chances of matching the performance of *Carrie*, however, appeared at this stage, to be unlikely, even by Yablans' optimistic standards. By overlooking the fact that the film was only just being recognized as a moderate financial success by the spring of 1979, almost half a year into its theatrical run, scholars have tended to over-state *Halloween*'s impact on film production, film content, and the development of the first teen slasher film cycle.

What can be surmised from the relatively strong ticket sales that the Speculator Production *Halloween* amassed under highly unfavorable conditions of distribution is that, in March 1979 a sizable American youth audience appeared to exist for films about shadowy blade-wielding killers menacing young people. This is, however, not to say that the film would invariably initiate Prospector Cash-in operations — unsurprisingly no similar films went into production during *Halloween*'s fist eighteen weeks in circulation. The only concrete sign of *Halloween*'s impact on the American film industry to be discussed publicly was the belief that the film's solid ticket sales had once again shown that low-budget youth-centered horror films could be lucrative ventures based on their appeal to large numbers of teenagers and young adults, a notion that had been circulating since the release of *Carrie*. In a small article printed next to *Variety*'s report on *Halloween*'s earnings, Robert Rehme, vice-president of Avco Embassy, revealed that *Halloween*'s box-office performance suggested his company could expect a small windfall from *Phantasm* (1979), a $1m pickup concerning a small-town teenager's encounter with a sinister mortician (Anon., 1979f, p. 6). Although the existence of a fairly large consumer base may, at first glance, appear to have provided an enormous financial incentive for other independent filmmakers to produce similar films, *Halloween*'s inability to secure an MPAA-member distribution deal provided an equally imposing deterrent in much the same way as box-office failure had ostensibly cancelled out MPAA-member distribution of the Pioneer Production *Black Christmas*. With every major studio distributor having passed up *Halloween*, independent filmmakers who could not release films themselves needed to consider whether their Cash-ins would be given the opportunity to tap into audience interest and thus provide them with the instant financial rewards made possible by MPAA-member negative pickup deals or whether they too would be overlooked by the majors. These developments sent mixed messages to filmmakers weighing up the commercial prospects of *Halloween* Cash-in production. In early 1979, it remained to be seen whether *Halloween*'s textual model would be adopted by other filmmakers. Only time would tell if *Halloween* became an anomalous commercial success or whether

FIGURE 2.11 Combining violence and female sexuality to promote exploitation horror *Torso*.

it would generate Cash-in productions. One thing, however, was certain at that time: *Halloween* was on the verge of becoming a Trailblazer Hit.

In sum, where *Halloween* is typically framed as a highly innovative piece of filmmaking and the first bona fide teen slasher, the film was actually a Speculator Production that had been fashioned in ways that counterbalanced its replication of *Black Christmas'* story-structure with content drawn from a range of commercially viable trends in youth-oriented and horror filmmaking. Moreover, *Halloween's* financial achievements have been overstated, and its capacity to instantaneously transform the production of films about young people being menaced by knife-wielding maniacs has been exaggerated. In fact, *Halloween* initially performed only moderately well, thanks in large part to strong word-of-mouth and a shrewd marketing strategy that evoked big-budget horror and youth-oriented hits, and, after eighteen weeks on release, its capacity to initiate any independently produced Cash-ins remained inconclusive because it had been turned down by the companies with which most independents aimed to do business.

Conclusion

The teen slasher's distinct story-structure emerged in Canada in 1974 when the filmmakers behind *Black Christmas* aimed to capitalize on the MPAA-members' reduction in production/financing operations by offering them a female-centered politically-engaged whodunit that combined elements drawn from several blockbuster film-types: horror films, violent police procedurals, romantic dramas, and group-centered teen films. In attempting to produce Canada's first and much-wanted blockbuster hit, these filmmakers fashioned a pioneering story that placed a group of youths in jeopardy from a shadowy killer. After performing strongly in Canada, *Black Christmas* secured US distribution from Warner Bros. The film was, however, muscled out of the market by several winter blockbusters in December 1974 before being re-released the following year. Despite remarkably high grosses in Los Angeles and Chicago, *Black Christmas* was unable to sustain strong ticket sales and was pulled from circulation. While it had managed to secure MPAA-member distribution and had provided filmmakers with a new textual model, this Pioneer Production did not become a Trailblazer Hit, and as a consequence exerted little influence on production patterns.

One film that was heavily influenced by *Black Christmas* was *Halloween*, a Speculator Production that reshaped *Black Christmas* into a female-centered small-town-set horror film. By placing a group of fun-loving small-town female youths in the cross hairs of a maniacal sanatorium absconder, its makers balanced *Black Christmas'* story-structure with content drawn from established trends in blockbuster and youth-oriented filmmaking. Despite failing to secure MPAA-member distribution, this low-budget independent production was fast becoming a sleeper hit in early 1979 on the back of a highly sophisticated marketing campaign that distanced the film from independently distributed horror and that evoked Hollywood's horror blockbusters and youth-oriented hits.

The short-to-medium-term implications of *Halloween*'s relative financial achievements will be taken up in chapters three and four. The fourth chapter returns to Canada and shows how developments in that country's film industry intersected with shifts occurring south of the border to result in the production of *Prom Night* (1980). Before that, however, the focus of chapter three remains on the American independent sector to show that *Halloween*'s impact in the US was quite surprising.

Chapter 3

'They were warned . . . they are doomed'

The United States, the development of the teen slasher film,
and Friday the 13th *(1980)*

A Hollywood warehouse manager works into the night; behind him hangs a famous movie poster featuring a menacing jack-o-lantern and a raised butcher's knife. Suddenly, a bandaged arm rips through the poster and throttles him. Seconds later, the man is confronted by the bedraggled figure of a mummy. He runs, but there is no escape. The man clutches at his chest, a heart attack strikes him, and he falls to the floor. The mummy cackles, the man lies dead, and the screen fades to black.

Soon after *Halloween* enjoyed some box-office success in early 1979, producer Irwin Yablans bankrolled a second youth-centered horror film called *Fade to Black* (1980), which told the story of teenage movie-buff Eric Binford (Dennis Christopher) who is pushed to breaking point by the cruelty of those around him, and who takes revenge on his tormentors by adopting the roles of characters from his favorite pictures. Yablans used one of *Fade to Black*'s set-piece killings to make a bold statement about *Halloween*. The presence of the film's poster frames *Halloween* as part of a long and glorious tradition of American horror that stretched back to a time when the Egyptian undead rose from their crypts in pictures like *The Mummy* (1932), and suggests that *Halloween* occupied a preeminent position in both American youth culture and the American film industry. *Halloween* is presented in *Fade to Black* as a landmark film, the influence of which was being felt on American youth-oriented horror as early as 1979.

This chapter and chapter four examine *Halloween*'s actual influence on production patterns and content in the eighteen months that followed its theatrical debut, by each presenting a case-study of one of the teen slasher Prospector Cash-ins that were swiftly produced to capitalize on the relative commercial success of *Halloween*. While the Canadian film industry's response is examined in chapter four, this chapter focuses on *Friday the 13th* to illuminate *Halloween*'s impact on the American film industry. By examining the American response to what was becoming a hit film, this chapter shows that late-1970s independent producers were considerably more cautious vis-à-vis the types of film they made than previously thought. In doing so, it reveals that, rather than jumping immediately onto new trends, most American independents actually preferred to follow trends that boasted more established track records and that those who did adopt new textual models did so only under exceptional circumstances and went to extraordinary lengths to mitigate the perceived risks of their conduct. Similarly, by examining the distribution of *Friday the 13th*, this chapter suggests that the members of the Motion Picture Association of America (MPAA) also approached new film-types with considerable caution.

'Some movies start trends . . .':
Horror and Youth-oriented Films After *Halloween*

The first teen slasher film cycle is typically considered to have unfolded as a direct result of the box-office achievements of *Halloween* (Clover, 1992, p. 24; Dika, 1990, p. 86; Kapsis, 1992, pp. 161–162; Rockoff, 2002, p. 62). Robert E. Kapsis, for example, asserts that '[f]ilm companies — first the minors and then the majors, were quick to cash in on *Halloween*'s commercial success' (Kapsis, 1992, p. 161). Yet, John Carpenter's film did not impact production patterns or film content significantly in the eighteen months that followed its release. By July 1980, only three films had been produced to capitalize on *Halloween*: *Friday the 13th*, *Prom Night*, and *Terror Train* (all 1980), and only one of those films, *Friday the 13th*, was American. As chapter five shows, that number almost quadrupled a year later.

Genre theorists Rick Altman (1999, pp. 30–50) and Steve Neale (2000, pp. 231–255) and industry historians like Peter Krämer (2005) have shown that film cycles unfold when several groups of entrepreneurial filmmakers respond to a film's commercial success with the production of similar films. As Krämer accurately suggests, 'it is to be expected (. . .) that every big hit sparks off a wide range of imitations and combinations' (2005, p. 10). It is indeed to be expected but it does not always happen. Despite the annual chart-topping rentals of *Psycho* (1960), for example, few horror films featuring human monsters were produced in the early 1960s. Similarly, in more recent times, the phenomenal US theatrical returns of *The Blair Witch Project* (1999) and *The Passion of the Christ* (2004) did not initiate cycles of 'realist' horror or violent biblical epics respectively. This section addresses an oft-overlooked aspect of film history, examining the case of *Halloween* to illuminate the conditions that prevented what is commonly seen as a hit film from sparking the production of significant numbers of Cash-ins. In doing so, the section shows that the production of film-types often hinges on industry-insiders' perceptions of the relative commercial viability of other film-types that have the same target audience and that share content.

Two issues must be addressed before examining the network of industrial factors that restricted the production of teen slasher Prospector Cash-ins in the United States to a single film. First, one must consider whether American filmmakers shied away from the production of Cash-ins to *Halloween* because the film had slipped beneath their 'research and development' radars. Second, one must consider whether, rather than reusing *Halloween*'s story-structure, filmmakers employed other textual models to capitalize on the film.

It is inconceivable to think American independent filmmakers were oblivious to the existence of *Halloween*. It is, however, likely that, in the eight months that followed its theatrical debut, many independent filmmakers did not associate the film with huge ticket sales. For most of this period, press coverage of *Halloween* was dominated by issues of style and quality (see Allen, 1978, pp. 67, 70; Ansen, 1978, p. 116; Canby, 1979, p. D13), with the economics of *Halloween* barely addressed beyond brief discussions in the March 1979 issues of the *Washington Post* and *Variety*, discussed in chapter two (see Allis, 1979a, pp. H1, H6; Anon., 1979g, p. 6). When compared to the $320,000 that the film had cost to make, the $12m gross cited by journalists may have sounded impressive to casual readers, but industry-insiders would have understood what that figure meant in real terms for the film's producers. Even though its cost-to-gross ratio was enormous, at this stage, with all costs, overheads, and taxes still to be deducted, *Halloween* would probably have returned distributor Compass International Films just shy of $5m, a similar amount to that which Crown International Pictures had received from *The Pom Pom Girls* (1976).[1] Moreover, the fact that *Halloween* had taken eighteen weeks to accumulate these monies was not necessarily a sign of its continued longevity at the box-office. In fact, four months was usually long enough for films to generate most of their box-office revenue. Although circa $5m in rentals, generated in eighteen weeks, provided a modest company like Compass a once-in-a-lifetime pre-tax windfall of around $2m, it was hardly a sum of money that changed the conduct of large numbers of industry-professionals. Thus, in spring 1979, all that was clear was that *Halloween* had been a lucrative undertaking for its small producer-distributor and was guaranteed to be at least the fortieth or fiftieth highest-earning non-MPAA-member release of the 1970s (Donahue, 1987, pp. 292–298).

In late 1979, commercial achievements slowly took centre-stage in public discourses around *Halloween*. Previously, industry-watchers had noted in passing that *Halloween* was a minor hit, albeit one that had demonstrated remarkable durability. For example, *Newsweek*, in a lengthy cover-story entitled 'Hollywood's Scary Summer', drew a cursory comparison between *Halloween*'s relative box-office accomplishments and those of another minor hit, Avco Embassy's *Phantasm* (1979), before concentrating on the economics of Fox's calculated blockbuster *Alien* (1979) (Ansen and Kasindorf, 1979, p. 54). In fact, as late as August 1979, Samuel Z. Arkoff, head of American International Pictures (AIP), was able to use *Halloween*, almost as if it was insider-knowledge, to correct *Washington Post* journalist Samuel Allis' suggestion that the days of the independently released hit were over. 'It can still be done, but it's tougher', snapped Arkoff, '[t]here's a movie out called "Halloween" which John Carpenter made for under half a million dollars with no names, and it's making a lot of money' (quoted in Allis, 1979b, p. G1). The turning point came in October 1979 when the *New York Times*' usually reliable industry analyst Aljean Harmetz reported inaccurately that *Halloween* had become 'the most successful independent motion picture ever made' (1979b, p. C21). Notwithstanding the fact that the investment–return ratio of *Deep Throat* (1972) had been significantly greater than that of *Halloween*, or that non-MPAA releases including *Papillon* (1973) and *In Search of Noah's Ark* (1977) had generated considerably higher rentals than *Halloween*,[2] Harmetz's declaration was too great a gift-horse for *Halloween*'s distributor to look in the mouth and it was plastered across marketing materials. Harmetz's authority ensured that the phrase soon became a standard suffix attached to the title of Carpenter's film in journalistic circles.

Exaggerations notwithstanding, confirmation of *Halloween*'s commercial achievements began to circulate regularly in the public sphere in early 1980 when Avco Embassy was publicizing *The Fog*, John Carpenter's follow-up to *Halloween*. Thus, it was across January, February, and March 1980, close to a year and a half after *Halloween* had opened, that writers for the news agency Associated Press and mass-circulation newspapers like the *Christian Science Monitor* and the *Washington Post* 'broke the story' of *Halloween*'s exceptionally long road to genuine box-office success (B. Thomas, 1980; Sterritt, 1980, p. 18; Turan, 1980, p. G1). As detailed below, subsequent developments ensured that the American film industry's perceptions of the commercial viability of films about shadowy blade-wielding maniacs menacing young people were already changing in the fifteen months that it took for *Halloween* to be recognized publicly as a bona fide hit.

The fairly lengthy period of time that it took for *Halloween* to accrue profits capable of arresting the gaze of industry-insiders, and the delay in that information being proliferated in the public domain, not only contributed to the near-absence of American productions that reused *Halloween*'s story-structure but played a part in the fact that American filmmakers did not adopt other approaches to attempt to capitalize on *Halloween*. Those films released in 1979 which exhibited similarities to Carpenter's film had in fact all been made before *Halloween* hit US screens, suggesting that their makers had drawn content from the same films as Carpenter and his collaborators. *Phantasm*, the story of a teenage boy investigating strange goings-on in small-town America, which at least one critic dubbed a '"Halloween" clone' (J. Scott, 1979b), *When a Stranger Calls*, a film that opened with a babysitter being stalked, which the same critic suggested also had been influenced by *Halloween* (J. Scott, 1979c), and the second teen slasher Speculator Cash-in, *Silent Scream* (often compared to *Halloween*), had all been completed by the end of summer 1978, at least three months before *Halloween* was released. Moreover, the films made in 1979 about serial killers attacking adults, as is elucidated below, were part of other distinct production trends. In one respect, the absence of a variety of markedly different types of *Halloween* Cash-in is quite surprising given that, as Altman has argued (1999, pp. 44–48), and as scholars including James Russell have demonstrated (2009, pp. 142–158), a hit often initiates a range of textually different Cash-ins because filmmakers tend to draw different conclusions as to what content has attracted audiences, thus emphasizing, downplaying, and/or omitting different elements of the hit, and counterbalancing the content they replicate with material drawn from a variety of different filmic sources. However, in another respect, it is not entirely surprising that *Halloween* failed to inspire a spectrum of markedly different films or that filmmakers looking to capitalize on *Halloween* re-used its story-structure en masse. The way the content of *Halloween* was discussed and categorized critically factored into the narrow range of Cash-in approaches applied by Prospectors in 1979.

Halloween was received largely in terms of its story-structure, despite the fact that it was modeled structurally on *Black Christmas* and had been fashioned to invite comparisons to Crown International's drive-in hits and top-earning horror films like *Carrie* (1976). This 'reading'

— supported by the conduct of the filmmakers who made teen slashers in 1979 — is borne out by the language American journalists used
to describe the film upon its original release. Writers described, with
uncanny uniformity, the manner in which the film's story brought
together a specific sort of monster, a specific vision of normalcy, a specific setting, and a specific timescale. Thus, the unusually detailed plot
synopses that dominated early reviews (Siskel, 1978a, p. B7; K. Thomas,
1978, p. F22; Arnold, 1978, p. B5), gave way to brief summaries including
'a maniacal killer with a knife stalks young women on a *Halloween* night
in a small Illinois town' (Ansen, 1978, p. 116) and '[a] homicidal maniac
returns to a small Illinois town and terrorizes three teen-age girls during
one very long night' (Siskel, 1979, p. D3). *Halloween*'s story-structure,
one which had been used on only one occasion before, was seen to be so
striking as to overshadow other content and similarities to other horror
and youth-oriented films.

Although its pattern of distribution and its US reception prevented
Halloween from exerting all but a bare minimum of influence on
American independent production in the eighteen months that followed its theatrical debut, the widespread absence of Prospector Cash-in
productions in that period was down primarily to parallel industrial
developments. The confidence independent producers placed in other
types of youth-oriented and horror film, concerns about securing MPAA-
member distribution for product based on a film that has been turned
down by the majors, and concerns over how to identify a commercially
viable way of engaging creatively with a new type of film contributed to
the near absence of *Halloween* Cash-ins.

The confidence that independent filmmakers placed in non-horror
youth-oriented films, more so than any other factor, eclipsed the appeal
of *Halloween* Cash-in production. 'The late 1970s', wrote Timothy Shary,
'suggested the trends to come' (2002a, p. 7). In late 1978 and 1979,
American independents (and MPAA-members) concentrated on four
types of youth-market film.[3] The production of gang movies, animal comedies, roller-disco movies, and female-centered coming-of-age dramas
was a response to the release in the previous year of the three most financially successful youth-centered pictures in the history of the American
film industry: *Saturday Night Fever* (1977), *Grease*, and *Animal House* (both
1978).[4] This trio of modestly priced hits clearly signaled the huge commercial potential of non-horror youth-oriented films and, in contrast to
effects-driven chart-toppers like *Star Wars* (1977) and *Superman* (1978),
provided independent filmmakers with production/textual models that
they could afford to replicate.[5] The box-office performances of *Saturday*

Night Fever, Grease, and *Animal House* tempered the immediate impact of *Halloween,* sparking considerable activity among independent producers (Cook, 2000, pp. 51–60; Krämer, 2005, pp. 22–25; Schatz, 1993, pp. 89–104).

In 1979, comedies that focused on groups of self-indulgent young men — 'animal comedies' as William Paul (1994) has since called them — appeared to offer independent filmmakers the best opportunity of securing an MPAA-member distribution deal. This development was a direct result of the box-office achievements of *Animal House.* Paul (1994, pp. 90–94) has argued that *Animal House* underscored the financial potential of group-centered youth-oriented films that had been indicated earlier in the decade by the 1973 hit *American Graffiti.* This view was also held by industry-watchers in 1978. 'Loosely speaking', remarked Tim Taylor of the *Washington Post,* '"Animal House"' aspires to be a sort of new "American Graffiti", four years older and four rungs lower' (1978, p. 17). However, *Animal House* was quite different to George Lucas' breakthrough film. 'Where *American Graffiti* was about creating a complete teenage world', observed Peter Lev, '*Animal House* is about having fun' (2000, p. 98). Financed and distributed by Universal Pictures, the company behind *American Graffiti, Animal House* was among the first attempts by an MPAA-member to realize the commercial promise of portrayals of youthful high-jinx, signaled by Crown International's films *The Pom Pom Girls* and *The Van* (1977). However, unlike these independently distributed drive-in hits, *Animal House* focused almost exclusively on the horseplay of young men. The commercial viability of portrayals of frivolous, fun-loving males was supported by another male-centered sleeper hit of 1978, *Up in Smoke.*[6] While *Up in Smoke* had not been produced to capitalize on *Animal House,* the hedonistic and irresponsible behavior of likeable twenty-something stoners Cheech and Chong was similar to that of the madcap fraternity in *Animal House,* enabling its strong box-office returns to function like a Reinforcing Hit. With the financial potential of animal comedy underscored by two hits, both MPAA-members and independents produced Cash-ins, with MPAA-members financing *Caddyshack, The Hollywood Knights,* and *Up the Academy* (all 1980) and independents contributing films like *King Frat, Squeeze Play,* and *H.O.T.S* (all 1979). Industry-watchers clearly recognized that these films had been made because of, and to evoke, *Animal House.* For example, fresh from the set of *H.O.T.S,* Karen Stabiner of the *New York Times* reported that she had been privy to the implementation of a commonplace filmmaking strategy, namely the production of a film that was 'markedly similar to already proved commercial successes', before identifying *Animal House* as the commercial success in question (1979, p. D15). Similarly, reviews would describe *Caddyshack* as both 'the newest "Animal House" spinoff' (Canby, 1980a, p. C8) and '[t]he latest misbegotten spawn of "National Lampoon's Animal House"' (Arnold, 1980a, p. C3). While *Animal House* triggered the production of films that exhibited similarities to each other, a second youth-oriented blockbuster hit initiated two distinct types of Cash-in.

Described by Thomas Schatz as being 'as important a New Hollywood Blockbuster' as *Star Wars* (1993, p. 23), *Saturday Night Fever* had been crafted to appeal to young people of both sexes through the positioning of a group of hyper-masculine young misogynists in a narrative that emphasized 'traditionally female' interests: romance, dance, and music. Accordingly, Prospectors sought to capitalize on *Saturday Night Fever* by producing upbeat roller-disco movies and projects that focused on groups of violent, disenfranchised male youths, with the latter emerging as the dominant trend due perhaps to its high-profile in previous decades (Shary, 2005, pp. 20–26).

Producing gang movies to tap into audience interest in *Saturday Night Fever* was not as bizarre as it may seem today. Although it is often overlooked, *Saturday Night Fever*'s depiction of male youth was not far removed from that of *A Clockwork Orange* (1971). Indeed, it would not have been entirely misleading to have modified the tagline used to promote Kubrick's brutal opus and have advertised *Saturday Night Fever* as 'being the adventures of young men whose principal interests are rape, ultra-violence and [disco remixes of] Beethoven'. In fact, on its original release, *Saturday Night Fever* was received in some quarters as a gang movie. 'The characters become cruel and volatile beneath the strobe lights', wrote Frank Rich of *Time*, 'and it seems that "Saturday Night Fever" has an authentic statement to make about America's newest crop of alienated youth' (1977). In a contemporaneous article, Gary Arnold suggested that the commercial success of *Saturday Night Fever* was behind the surge in gang movie production. 'The subject of juvenile delinquency, a going concern in the '50s and always available for updates, has reemerged', observed Arnold, 'as a result of the rumble sequences in "Saturday Night Fever"' (1979b, p. K1). In the wake of the film's impressive rentals, MPAA-members financed gang movies like *Boulevard Nights*, *Walk Proud*, *The Wanderers*, and *The Warriors* (all 1979), and American independent producers contributed *Sunnyside*, (1979), and, the film that Shary described as 'one of the most extreme teen fantasies ever made', *Over the Edge* (1979) (2002a, p. 28). In addition to these gritty tales of youth angst, light-hearted musical films were also produced to capitalize on *Saturday Night Fever*.

In a roundup of production patterns, *New York Times* film industry analyst Aljean Harmetz spotlighted 'movies about disco roller skating' as a new film-type about to be unleashed on the American youth-market (1979a, p. D5). Vernon Scott, writing in the *Sarasota Herald Tribune*, summarized the development fully. 'Now some movies start trends, like the disco boom that exploded after Saturday Night Fever', he began, 'but the less creative souls follow trends (. . .) [a]nd so we have a new type of motion picture: the roller-disco movie' (1979, p. 24). From Irwin Yablans' low-cost follow-up to *Halloween, Roller Boogie* (1979), and Rastar Pictures' $3m production for Columbia of *Skatetown, U.S.A* (1979) to Universal's extravagant effort *Xanadu* (1980), music-laden teen films occupied a highly visible position in the American film industry in 1979.[7] 'By next October no fewer than two films about the latest California craze, roller-disco, will be in the theatres', Charles Schreger had written in early July, '[a]nd word is that there are at least another half dozen roller-disco feature scripts floating around Hollywood' (1979c, p. D6). While roller-disco movie content was influenced heavily by *Saturday Night Fever*, production of the new film-type, almost eighteen months after *Saturday Night Fever* became a hit, was catalyzed by *Grease*, the highest-grossing film of 1978, and by Columbia's sleeper hit *Ice Castles* (1978), a teenage love story set in the world of competitive figure skating, both of which confirmed the box-office potential of films centered on young love, dance, and music.[8]

Where some filmmakers took the success of *Grease* and *Ice Castles* to be confirmation of the commercial viability of *Saturday Night Fever*'s world of dance-floors, eye-catching costumes, and disco tracks, other opportunists concluded that the two hits had signaled the financial potential of a film-type in which the box-office strength of music and dance paled in comparison to that of the sexual, emotional, and romantic travails of teenage girls. This logic generated several female-centered coming-of-age dramas — 'films (. . .) preoccupied with the precocious sex lives of teenieboppers', to use *Washington Post* critic Gary Arnold's description (quoted in Arnold et al., 1980, p. F1) — that included director Randal Kleiser's follow-up to *Grease, The Blue Lagoon* (financed by Columbia), and the independent productions *Foxes, Little Darlings*, and *Times Square* (all 1980) (see Kleinhans, 2002, pp. 73–90).

Some filmmakers inevitably sought to capitalize simultaneously on more than one of the high-profile youth-oriented film-types being made in 1979. For example, New World produced the provocative musical *Rock 'n' Roll High School* (1979), a film that combined elements of *Grease* and *Animal House* with what Thomas Doherty's described as 'a slick catalogue of teenpic influences' (2002, p. 196). As shown below and in subsequent chapters, the makers of teen slashers drew content from many of the youth-oriented film-types in production at this time, particularly animal comedies and female-centered coming-of-age dramas.

The appeal of producing a *Halloween* Cash-in was therefore over-shadowed by the confidence filmmakers placed in several non-horror youth-oriented film-types. Animal comedies, gang movies, roller-disco movies, and female-centered coming-of-age dramas were all crafted to capitalize on films that had performed significantly better at the US box-office than *Halloween*. In addition to being produced for the youth-market, *Halloween* was of course, a horror film, which meant that decisions over whether or not to capitalize on Carpenter's film were also informed heavily by perceptions of the relative commercial viability of other types of horror film. In early 1979 horror production was at a cross-roads, with independent filmmakers caught between established horror film-types, particularly those that had enjoyed considerable commercial success earlier in the decade, and a series of potentially high-grossing, but ostensibly untested, textual models.

Established horror film-types continued to be produced across late 1978 and 1979. In the years before *Halloween* hit theaters, several horror films had generated significantly higher rentals than Carpenter's teen slasher. The box-office credentials of demonic child, city vs. country, and revenge-of-nature films had been cemented by a Trailblazer Hit of blockbuster proportions and at least one Reinforcing Hit and, despite subsequent drops in returns, independent producers continued to use these textual models at decade's end. The appeal of demonic child films, as Kapsis (1992, p. 159) suggests, was signaled by the 1973 Trailblazer Hit *The Exorcist* and reinforced by the 1976 Prospector Cash-in *The Omen*.[9] This pair of hits continued to inspire Cash-ins such as *The Brood* and *The Orphan* (both 1979). Similarly, the makers of *Up from the Depths* (1979) and *Blood Beach* (1980) interpreted strong ticket sales for *The Deep* (1977) and *Jaws 2* (1978) as confirmation of the economic viability of revenge-of-nature films that had been trumpeted across 1975 by *Jaws* (Cook, 2000, pp. 255–256).[10] Meanwhile, city vs. country tales like *Tourist Trap, Survival Run* (both 1979), and *Motel Hell* (1980) continued to be produced in the hope of emulating the returns of *Deliverance* (1972) and *Race with the Devil*, a similar film with which Twentieth Century Fox had enjoyed some commercial success in 1975.[11] American independent filmmakers' reluctance to invest in *Halloween* Cash-in production was also impacted by the return to prominence of one of the American film industry's oldest horror film-types.

A surprising number of filmmakers were making vampire films in early 1979. This trend had been gaining momentum across 1977 and early 1978 with independent productions like *Martin* (1977) and *Dracula's Dog* (1978) and by the summer of 1978 had reached such proportions that *Variety* had published an article entitled 'Hollywood Hemorrhaging [sic] Dracula Films' (Pollock, 1978a, p. 6). These projects included Universal's *Dracula* (1979) and Fox's German pickup *Nosferatu the Vampyre* (1979). It was also reported that Paramount was developing an adaptation of Anne Rice's bestselling novel *Interview with the Vampire* (ibid.). Not only did MPAA-members invest in films about bloodsuckers, independent producers also contributed to the boom. *Love at First Bite* (1979) was a horror-comedy from AIP and some of the profits that Compass International made from *Halloween* went into *Nocturna* (1979), a picture about a lady vampire in New York's disco scene. What made this trend so surprising was the fact that not a single vampire film had been a hit for over a decade. One factor driving the film-type's remarkable comeback was suggested by *Variety*'s Dale Pollock to have been the commercial success on Broadway of the play *Dracula* (ibid). However, an equally important catalyst was Paramount's 1976 *King Kong* remake. Although *King Kong*'s huge budget prevented it from generating distributor Paramount Pictures much in the way of profits, ticket sales had been very strong (Cook, 2000, p. 44).[12] The film's healthy returns therefore indicated that the audience for remakes of classical-era horror films was large, although perhaps not large enough to support a production in the $20m range, thus opening up a potentially lucrative opportunity for the makers of less-costly versions. As much as it was a product of filmmakers' attempts to recapture old glories, independent filmmakers' reticence to model films on *Halloween* was also informed by cutting-edge developments in horror film production.

In early 1979, the American film industry was eagerly awaiting the release of two MPAA-member horror films that were tipped to become blockbuster hits. If the considerable commercial potential of *Alien* (1979) and *The Shining* (1980) was realized, it promised to open up new Cash-in opportunities for independent filmmakers. As a lengthy article in *Newsweek* explained, several factors made *Alien* and *The Shining* genuine Trailblazer Hit contenders (Ansen and Kasindorf, 1979, p. 54). For a start, the films' respective distributors, Warner Bros. and Fox, were planning to stimulate attendance with wide releases or 'saturation bookings' and intensive cross-media marketing campaigns. To this could be added the fact that both films were calculated blockbusters made on significantly bigger production budgets than the $5m average for US feature films in 1979 (Prince, 2000 p. 20), with *Alien* having cost $11m and estimates for *The Shining* ranging from $12m to $18m (Cook, 2000, pp. 60–61, 79). These substantial sums of money had been used to make the films marketable to a wide-range of audience demographics and taste formations. Where Warner Bros. could highlight the presence of auteur filmmaker Stanley Kubrick and bankable star Jack Nicholson when promoting *The Shining*, Fox's marketing of *Alien* could spotlight state-of-the-art special-effects, extravagant sets, and cutting-edge crea- tures designed by Swiss artist H. R. Giger.

Alongside high-profile films like *The Shining* and *Alien*, a series of different types of film about serial killers were being produced in small numbers, underscoring further the transitional character of the horror production scene of 1979. In addition to the teen slasher Prospector Cash-ins *Friday the 13th*, *Prom Night*, and *Terror Train*, another approach pitted shadowy blade-wielding maniacs against adults of various ages who had no common bonds. These inexpensive films, which included *Schizoid* and *He Knows You're Alone* (both 1980), had much in common with AIP's minor hit *The Town that Dreaded Sundown* (1976).[13] Concurrently, a third group of killer-thrillers replicated the urban nihilism of *Taxi Driver* (1976) with depictions of tortured psychotics terrorizing city dwellers. Among these desperately bleak character studies were *Don't Answer the Phone*, *Don't Go in the House*, and *Maniac* (all 1980).[14] And, a fourth new trend consisted of glossy adult-centered murder-mysteries such as *Dressed to Kill* and *Cruising* (both 1980) that, like the Carpenter-scripted *Eyes of Laura Mars* (1978), relocated the grisly murder-mysteries of Dario Argento and his contemporaries from urban Italian locations to the upper-middle-class neighborhoods of New York City.[15] If any of the serial killer films was best positioned to generate sizable rentals, it was these American giallo films, as I call them. In terms of their box-office poten- tial, *Dressed to Kill* and *Cruising* were closer to *Alien* and *The Shining* than the low-budget teen slashers or cut-price efforts like *Schizoid* and *Maniac*. With stellar casts, high-profile directors, and up-market settings, the American gialli promised to be marketable to mature audiences as well as to the youth-market. The $7.5m entry *Dressed to Kill* starred bankable actor Michael Caine and was directed by Brian De Palma (Anon., 1979m, p. 3), Hollywood's new 'master of the macabre' as he had been described in trailers for his previous film, *The Fury* (1978). Similarly, *Cruising*, which transplanted, at a cost of $7m (Pollock, 1979, p. 6), the tale of an inno- cent's descent into a violent, sexually permissive drug-fuelled nocturnal underworld, pioneered in the minor hit *Looking for Mr. Goodbar* (1977),[16] to the bars and clubs of New York's gay S&M scene, was headlined by

A-lister Al Pacino and helmed by William Friedkin, the director of the blockbuster cop thriller *The French Connection* (1971) and the most financially successful horror film ever made, *The Exorcist.*[17] Much therefore had been done to give the American gialli the best possible chance of box-office glory.

While heavily informed by parallel industrial developments, widespread reluctance to produce *Halloween* Cash-ins also resulted from concerns about the commercial viability of producing *Halloween* Cash-ins. The first concern was the fact that *Halloween*, as reported in the trade and popular press, had been turned down by every major studio in Hollywood (Allis, 1979a, pp. H1, H6; Anon., 1979g, p. 6). This news served as a significant deterrent to modeling a film on Carpenter's Trailblazer Hit in-the-making because, across the 1970s, the MPAA-members had proven themselves wholly unwilling to release independently produced Cash-ins to high-earning independently released horror. For example, less than two years earlier, Wes Craven's city vs. country horror film *The Hills Have Eyes* (1977) had been ignored by MPAA-members despite having been tailored to evoke *Race with the Devil*. It therefore seemed fairly likely that films modeled on *Halloween* would struggle to attract the MPAA-member distribution deals upon which independent filmmakers relied to generate swift profits. The second factor that made *Halloween* Cash-in production appear somewhat perilous was the fact that *Halloween* had not been followed by a Reinforcing Hit. With the Speculator Production *Silent Scream* (1979) still awaiting release, *Halloween* was, by 1979, the only solidly performing film to feature a lone blade-wielding maniac stalking and killing a group of hedonistic young people. The absence of a Reinforcing Hit also obscured a financially viable method of modeling a film on *Halloween*, suggesting that filmmakers risked replicating elements of the film that had not driven its relative commercial success. Despite the comparatively low cost of financing a film that was similar to *Halloween*, an investment of around $0.5m–$2m represented a considerable wager for most independent producers and, as a consequence, the majority of filmmakers waited for their competitors to confront the risks of producing Prospector Cash-ins.

In sum, contrary to most accounts, *Halloween* did not initiate significant numbers of Cash-in productions. While *Halloween* had taken a considerable amount of time to suggest that it would become a genuine Trailblazer Hit, this inactivity was largely a result of parallel industrial developments. Three youth-oriented blockbuster hits had exerted a greater influence upon independent filmmakers than *Halloween*. *Saturday Night Fever*, *Grease*, and *Animal House* prompted the production of gang movies, roller-disco movies, female-centered coming-of-age dramas, and animal comedies. Horror, on the other hand, was in a state of transition. Some independents turned to established film-types, resulting in the continued production of demonic child, city vs. country, revenge-of-nature, and vampire films. However, other filmmakers waited to see if two big-budget films with blockbuster potential, *Alien* and *The Shining*, became hits and thus suggested new textual models. Despite its profitability, *Halloween* contributed to the uncertainty. Whereas the film's inability to secure an MPAA-member distribution deal raised doubts over whether Prospector Cash-ins would appeal to MPAA-members, the absence of a Reinforcing Hit raised doubts about how to capitalize on Carpenter's film textually. With caution pervading the American independent sector in 1979, the next section examines how the filmmakers behind *Friday the 13th* confronted the apparent risks of producing a teen slasher Prospector Cash-in.

'Like a summer-time Pepsi-Cola commercial': *Friday the 13th*, a Prospector Cash-in

Within little over three months of the US trade and popular press reporting that *Halloween* was becoming a Trailblazer Hit, one American filmmaker ventured where his compatriots were unwilling to tread and attempted to capitalize on the film's box-office achievements with the production of a Prospector Cash-in. In the 4 July 1979 issue of *Variety*, a full-page advertisement showed the words 'Friday the 13th' shattering a pane of glass (see Figure 3.1). 'From the producer of *Last House on the Left*', it screamed, 'comes the most terrifying film ever made' (Cunningham, 1979, p. 23). This was not an invitation to distributors to purchase a completed film, although it was designed to appear that way. Rather, on the final Independence Day of the 1970s, principal photography had not started on 'the most terrifying film ever made' and the project had yet to be financed, scripted or cast (Buckley, 1981, p. C8). Yet, from this announcement, Sean S. Cunningham, an independent filmmaker without a profitable picture to his name for almost a decade, secured sufficient capital to produce the only American-made teen slasher Prospector Cash-in, *Friday the 13th* (ibid).

In terms of aesthetics and economics, *Friday the 13th* is usually contrasted to *Halloween*. Where *Halloween* is held up as an exemplar of the vision, intelligence, and innovation said to characterize the 'independent spirit' of non-Hollywood filmmaking, *Friday the 13th*, as Matt Hills

FIGURE 3.1   The *Friday the 13th Variety* advertisement.

has argued, is dismissed routinely as a supremely cynical, crass, and imitative exercise in exploitation (2007, pp. 227–234). Underpinning such notions, he suggests, are wildly differing images of the creative personnel responsible for bringing the two films to the screen. Thus, behind the image of the cineaste auteur that is *Halloween*'s writer-director John Carpenter is said to lurk the specter of *Friday the 13th*'s producer-director Sean S. Cunningham, the mercenary hack who shamelessly ripped off Carpenter's stylish exercise in suspense and drenched it in blood (ibid. p. 321). As previously demonstrated, *Halloween* was the product as much of calculated entrepreneurialism as it was any great artistic vision, and the production of *Halloween* Cash-ins was seen in 1979 to be anything but a surefire route to financial prosperity. And, as this section shows, the production of *Friday the 13th* involved a more complex set of commercial strategies than simply re-making *Halloween* with unprecedented levels of violence and gore. Rather, the Prospectors behind *Friday the 13th* sought to offset the apparent risks of modeling a film on *Halloween* by drawing content from some of the most commercially robust trends in American moviemaking.

As was fairly standard practice, Sean S. Cunningham had commissioned the *Variety* advertisement to determine whether financiers would be receptive to an alluring film title. '[I] bet if I was trying to do something called "Friday the 13th," and advertised it as "the scariest movie ever made"', explained Cunningham to the *New York Times*, 'it would sell' (quoted in Chase, 1981a, p. C8). In the 1970s, as in previous decades, independent filmmakers valued the names of their films hugely (Hillier, 1994, pp. 40–41; Schaefer, 1999, pp. 58–60). 'Sixty to seventy per cent of an exploiter's initial [business]', estimated Frank Moreno, sales manager of New World Pictures, 'lies in the title and the campaign' (quoted in Hillier, 1994, p. 40). In particular, a film called *Friday the 13th* evoked *Halloween*, with both films' titles, as Vera Dika has suggested, referencing 'recurring occasion[s] of sinister significance' which 'call up an earlier, more primitive form of thinking' (1990, p. 66). These similarities secured Cunningham the financial backing he needed.

When a small company called Hallmark Releasing Corporation responded enthusiastically to the *Variety* advertisement with an offer of $500,000 to finance the project (Bracke, 2005, pp. 18–19), Sean S. Cunningham was provided not only the capital with which to produce *Friday the 13th* but a safety net if MPAA-members did not find the film appealing. Hallmark was the production arm of Esquire Theatres of America, a small exhibitor that owned drive-ins and multiplexes around Boston. Cunningham had been one of the first filmmakers with whom Hallmark had dealt after being set up in 1969 to supply Esquire low-cost productions and pickups after the MPAA-members had started to demand a larger percentage of box-office revenue during the industry-wide recession of 1969–1972 (Cook, 2000, p. 17). Cunningham's sex documentary *Together* (1971), as Eric Schaefer notes (2007, p. 35), did strong business when Hallmark marketed it to couples — 'Finally, an X-rated movie your wife or girlfriend can enjoy', read its poster — and, on the back of its moderate success, the company had awarded Cunningham $90,000 to make a horror picture that, under various titles, including *Last House on the Left* (1971), performed well on the exploitation circuit (Szulkin, 2000, p. 32). On the back of these achievements, Hallmark was willing to overlook the fact that Cunningham's latest ventures *Manny's Orphans* and *Here Come the Tigers* (both 1978) had failed miserably to capitalize on the box-office achievements of the 1976 children's film *The Bad News Bears* (Buckley, 1981, p. C8). With the backing of a company that possessed the means with which to distribute and exhibit films, *Friday the 13th* was guaranteed a route into American theaters and it was these privileged conditions — unavailable to most independent producers — that enabled the makers of *Friday the 13th* to confront the perceived risks of Prospector Cash-in production.

With Hallmark's financial guarantees, Cunningham and his collaborators went about off-setting the high-risk/high-gain strategy of modeling a film on *Halloween*. Production of *Friday the 13th* began in earnest when Cunningham instructed screenwriter Victor Miller to model a script on Carpenter's film. '[Cunningham] called me up', Miller revealed, 'and said, "*Halloween* is making a lot of money at the box-office, why don't we rip it off?"' (interviewed in 'Return to Crystal Lake: making Friday the 13th', 2003). Because American independent filmmakers thought it a considerable gamble to base a film on *Halloween,* the Prospectors behind *Friday the 13th,* while reusing *Halloween*'s story-structure, ensured that differences, in respect to their film's plot structure, its setting, the characters that fall victim to the killer and the one character that survives, and, perhaps most importantly, its killings, reflected commercially robust trends in which MPAA-members had placed their confidence. This approach resulted in the production of a relatively gory animal comedy-infused murder-mystery.

In *Friday the 13th,* a secluded summer camp on the outskirts of the rural town of Crystal Lake is closed in 1958 following two murders and a string of unexplained incidents. Despite warnings from local residents, Camp Crystal Lake reopens for business 22 years later. A mixed-sex group of hedonistic young people finish renovating the camp in preparation for the arrival of a new generation of campers, oblivious to the fact that one of their colleagues has already fallen victim to a mysterious slasher. This is the first in a series of murders that takes place at Camp Crystal Lake on the night of Friday the 13th of June 1980. As the counselors engage in diverse leisure activities, a shadowy prowler tracks their movements, picking them off one by one with a variety of sharp weapons. The final counselor to remain alive is a teenage tomboy called Alice (Adrienne King). She is confronted by Mrs Vorhees (Betsy Palmer), a middle-aged woman who worked at the camp in the late 1950s. Mrs Vorhees reveals that she has been killing the counselors because their predecessors had failed to supervise her son, Jason, back in 1958. She claims that this neglect resulted in the boy drowning. After a prolonged struggle Alice decapitates Mrs. Vorhees before being attacked by Jason. Although the final assault is revealed to have been a dream, the sole survivor of the campsite massacre is convinced that the boy is lurking in the woods. *Friday the 13th* employs the teen slasher story-structure outlined in chapter one (see Figure 3.2).

A murder-mystery plot provided the makers of *Friday the 13th* with

Part One: Setup

1. Trigger: In 1958, Mrs Vorhees blames summer camp counselors for her son's death.
2. Threat: Her vengeance is reignited when the camp reopens in 1980.

Part Two: Disruption

3. Leisure: A mixed-sex group of counselors engage in various recreational activities.
4. Stalking: Mrs Vorhees tracks the movements of the unsuspecting youths.
5. Murders: Mrs Vorhees kills most of the counselors with sharp weapons.

Part Three: Resolution

6. Confrontation: Alice, the sole remaining counselor, battles with Mrs Vorhees.
7. Neutralization: Alice decapitates Mrs Vorhees.

FIGURE 3.2   The teen slasher film story-structure in *Friday the 13th*.

a low-cost way of evoking well-attended horror films. The confidence that teen slasher Prospectors — including those behind *Prom Night* and *Terror Train* — placed in this strategy was fuelled by the fairly strong box-office performance of the American giallo *Eyes of Laura Mars*. An $8m production budget may have erased the film's $8.3m domestic rentals, but *Eyes of Laura Mars,* by grossing approximately $17–18m, indicated that a large enough audience existed at the time for horror-whodunits to enable a less-expensive production to turn a significant profit, much like AIP's *The Town that Dreaded Sundown* had done in 1976.[18] Equally significant was the fact that the healthy rentals of *Eyes of Laura Mars* had been generated in lieu of any significant on-screen presence of the crucial 15–25-year-old demographic, which suggested that a similar film focusing on young people and thus reflecting the industry's perceptions of actual audience composition would be easier to market to, and more likely to attract large numbers of, America's theatergoing youths (Watkins, 1980, p. 33). Where a shadowy prowler had preyed on the residents of some of New York City's most exclusive streets in *Eyes of Laura Mars*, *Friday the 13th* featured a serial killer who operated in a place that had been frequented by, or was at least familiar to, a much broader cross-section of the film's American youth target audience.

By relocating *Halloween*'s story to a summer camp, the Prospectors behind *Friday the 13th* mobilized an element of content that had shown considerable box-office prowess in 1979. In the months leading up to the production of *Friday the 13th*, youth-oriented films set at summer camps had, relative to their conditions of distribution, generated strong ticket sales, first for independent distributors and then, crucially, for an MPAA-member. The new fad began when *Piranha* (1978), a light-hearted revenge-of-nature film made by New World to capitalize on under-water horror hits like *Jaws 2* (Hillier, 1994, pp. 41–45), and an animal comedy called, inevitably, *Summer Camp* (1979), were reported to be performing well by the standards of independent releases (Seymour Borde & Associates, 1979, p. 31). Whereas the solid earnings of *Summer Camp* and *Piranha* signaled youth audience interest in summer camp-set films, a couple of months later a third picture demonstrated that an MPAA-member had placed its faith in independent productions that employed the location, that that faith was paying off handsomely, and that, as a consequence, MPAA-member interest in subsequent summer camp-set films appeared a distinct possibility.

Just as *Friday the 13th* was being scripted, Paramount's low-budget Canadian-made animal comedy pickup *Meatballs* (1979) was becoming a genuine sleeper hit on a scale of which the makers of *Halloween* could only dream (Adilman, 1979, pp. 3, 40). By having delivered the Canadian Film Development Corporation its long-awaited 'made-in-Canada blockbuster' (Anon., 1979k, p. 448), *Meatballs* was the focus of considerable attention from the trade and popular press, ensuring that few industry-insiders could have been oblivious to the fact that the film's producers had enjoyed the rewards of an MPAA-member distribution deal thanks to a youth-oriented film set at a summer camp. The impact on Cunningham and his collaborators of the 'summer camp fad' was certainly not lost on Jim Moorhead of the *St. Petersburg Independent* who routinely discussed *Friday the 13th* as one of the spate of summer camp-set films (1980a, p. 22; 1980c, p. 3), nor was it lost on Tom Allen of the *Village Voice* who described *Friday the 13th* as a combination of *Halloween* and *Meatballs* (1980a, p. 21). *Meatballs*, like its contemporary *Summer Camp*, and like *Gorp!* and *Caddyshack* — two more summer camp-set projects in production at the same time as *Friday the 13th* — were part of the larger boom in films about groups of pleasure-seeking middle-class youths that were being made primarily to capitalize on Universal's blockbuster hit *Animal House*.

The makers of *Friday the 13th* looked to take advantage of the high-profile surge in animal comedy by allocating significant screen-time to a large mixed-sex group of young people whose principal interests are interactive leisure pursuits. Textual and structural similarities between

Halloween and animal comedies enabled the Prospectors behind *Friday the 13th* to imbed seamlessly into *Halloween*'s story-structure sequences of youths chatting, flirting, and sunbathing, and playing pranks, games, and sports. With Carpenter's film having shared animal comedies' 'emphasis on groups of people brought together by some common activity or location' (Paul, 1994, p. 89), it was clear that *Friday the 13th* could transition from sequences of youth leisure to moments of threat and horror without altering *Halloween*'s distinct narrative model. This conduct was also made easier by the fact that *Friday the 13th*'s co-writer Ron Kurz had just scripted for Hallmark *King Frat* (Grove, 2005, p. 18), a film that he had modeled closely on *Animal House* and which Bruce Bailey of the *Montreal Gazette* had dubbed 'a witless, scatological and adolescent attempt to copy "Animal House"' (1981, p. 34). Kurz and his collaborators also aimed to evoke hit animal comedies by emphasizing what William Paul recognizes as the film-type's primary thematic concern. Animal comedies, argues Paul, critique institutions of power by depicting conflicts over 'liberation from social constraints' (ibid., p. 102), between, on one side, likeable groups of hedonists and, on the other side, unsympathetic characters that occupy positions of power within the self-contained worlds of the university, the police academy or the summer camp (ibid., pp. 85–112, 122). The makers of *Friday the 13th* deployed scenes that critiqued law enforcement, the only institution of control in its parentless, teacher-less, milieu. For example, in one memorable sequence, a male youth is confronted by a police officer who is so fixated on the possibility that the boy's high-spirits are fuelled by cannabis that he is oblivious to the fact that a genuine threat exists in the form of an active serial killer lurking in nearby woods (see Figure 3.3). The presence of animal comedy material in *Friday the 13th* did not go unnoticed by journalists. 'Except for the portions that earned the picture's R-rating', noted Joseph McLellan in the *Washington Times*, 'the content of *Friday the 13th* looks and sounds remarkably like a summertime Pepsi-Cola commercial' (1980a, p. B3). A similar point was made by Janet Maslin of the *New York Times*'. 'More interesting than the bloodshed, somehow, is the middle-class ordinariness with which Mr. Cunningham invests the characters' conversations', observed Maslin, 'they seem to be inciting the killer's fury by chatting about vitamins and playing monopoly' (1980a, p. 14). The 'middle-class ordinariness' and mildly transgressive behavior of the camp counselors was thus used to encourage distributors and audiences to draw comparisons between *Friday the 13th* and animal comedy by replicating the 'generalized desire for liberation' of a group of young people aligned to an institution that Paul identifies as one of the defining features of the film-type (1994, pp. 85–113).

The commercial potential of imbedding into a tale of sustained homicidal threat extended sequences of groups of aimless young people enjoying the outdoor summer life had been showcased by one of the biggest hits of 1978. The makers of *Jaws 2* had taken the scenes of youth leisure that opened the first film and scattered them throughout their sequel. Thus, where sequences of dynamic adults had taken up most of Spielberg's original blockbuster hit, its big-budget follow-up featured scene after scene of attractive young people enjoying the sun, the sand, the sea, and each other. Although *Jaws 2* was not a hit on the scale of the first film, it nonetheless generated over $50m in rentals, about the same as *Animal House*, to become the fifth highest-earning film of its year.[19] The presence in *Friday the 13th* of material extracted from animal comedies came at the cost of dispensing with content that the filmmakers behind *Halloween* had used to make their teen slasher marketable to teenage girls and young women, material such as central female protagonists and sequences of female-bonding. To ensure that their film also could be targeted to this key audience segment, the Prospectors behind *Friday*

FIGURE 3.3 'Middle-class ordinariness' meets failed institutional power in *Friday the 13th*. (Source: *Crystal Lake Memories*).

the 13th portrayed a type of heroine that, in the summer of 1979, had featured in a big-budget MPAA-member horror film for the very first time.

From the 'middle-class ordinariness' of *Friday the 13th*'s youth group
emerged the film's heroine, Alice, a tomboy who wears little make-up,
sports clothing that is barely distinguishable from that worn by her male
friends, and bests the killer singlehandedly. Carol J. Clover famously
called this sort of masculine heroine 'the Final Girl' (1992, pp. 35–41),
arguing that she was geared largely to a young male audience (ibid.,
p. 51). While I have no grounds to dispute Clover's suggestion that the
character-type was employed to generate the sympathy of male spectators, there are, however, several economic factors that point to the
figure of the dynamic and heroic female being mobilized to appeal also
to female youth — a notion that chapter one showed was highlighted
by the writers of the teen slasher Speculator Production *Silent Scream*
(1979). Across the 1970s, MPAA-members and ambitious independents
had mobilized female protagonists in horror films routinely, with a view
to expanding their potential audience and thus enhancing their films'
prospects at the box-office. Previous chapters detailed that the rewards
of emphasizing female protagonists in horror films had been trumpeted
by a string of blockbuster hits that focused heavily on thirty-something
middle-class mothers, including *Rosemary's Baby* (1968), *The Exorcist*
(1973), and *The Omen* (1976), and that the next wave of well-attended
horror films — *Carrie* (1976), *Exorcist II: The Heretic* (1977) and *The Fury*
(1978) — all had emphasized female youth. The mobilization of a boyish
teenage heroine reflected a high-profile shift in the female protagonists
of MPAA-member horror that took place in the weeks leading up to the
production of *Friday the 13th*.

Where earlier MPAA-member horror hits had stopped short of showing women or teenage girls dispatching monsters themselves (unlike
some independent contemporaneous releases), Fox's much-hyped sci-
fi/horror film *Alien* had featured a masculine heroine who confronted
and overcame the titular extra-terrestrial alone. Here was evidence of
an MPAA-member placing such confidence in this character-type that
she had been employed in a calculated blockbuster. *Alien* had cost a
staggering $27m to bring to the screen ($11m to make and $16m to
advertise) and was expected to emulate the commercial success of *Star
Wars* (Cook, 2000, pp. 60–61). Simply recouping this huge outlay, never
mind emulating the biggest hit in history, required *Alien* to generate
around $68m in ticket sales, which necessitated cross-demographic
appeal. The film's tough heroine, a feature that had been spotlighted
in audiovisual marketing materials, was the only element of content that

appeared to have been employed solely to resonate with, and thus to secure, the attendance of, the female theatergoers that were needed to prevent *Alien* from being a costly mistake. Thus, shifts to younger and to more heroic female horror protagonists suggested that it was commercially viable for the filmmakers behind *Friday the 13th* to counterbalance the male bias of the film's youth group by transforming *Halloween*'s last-girl-standing from a traumatized wreck rescued by a valiant male into a self-sufficient young woman who disposes of the killer single-handedly. The profound influence that was exerted by big-budget MPAA-member horror extended to another of the elements used in *Friday the 13th* to offset the risk of evoking solely *Halloween*.

Innovative Hollywood horror and an apparent sea-change in the reception of filmic violence provided the backdrop against which the Prospectors behind *Friday the 13th* fashioned a series of elaborate set-piece murders. These carefully choreographed sequences of spectacle, like those discussed in reference to Italian horror by Donato Totaro (2003, p. 162), ran considerably longer than needed to advance the plot. So important were *Friday the 13th*'s murders that Cunningham paid $20,000, twice the sum that had been given to the film's best paid actor, to secure the services of one of the industry's leading liquid latex artists (Grove, 2005, p. 19). 'The film's real attraction', noted Joseph McLellan of the *Washington Post*, 'is the work of special effects expert Tom Savini' (1980a, p. B3). Savini knew how to supply spectacular murder scenes but he also knew that his work could be the difference between a film's receipt of an X or an R rating, and that it therefore had to be regulated accordingly. Indeed, it had been Savini's contributions that had resulted in his previous project, George A. Romero's independently distributed zombie film *Dawn of the Dead* (1978), being rated X (Anon., 1979i, p. 37). Even attempting this sort of conduct, which, a couple of years earlier would have been unthinkable for an independent production being angled at MPAA-members, was made possible by the controversy that had surrounded X-rated films and cinematic bloodshed across the 1970s having quieted considerably — albeit temporarily (Sandler, 2002, p. 215).

In summer 1979, the furor that had surrounded X-rated films for almost a decade seemed to have run its course with controversies over filmic content barely having been seen in the trade or popular press for over a year. The exhibition of hardcore pornography had been restricted tightly (Lewis, 2002, pp. 265–266), the majors, as Kevin S. Sandler notes, had released only G-, PG-, and R-rated films (2002, p. 215), and, in the wake of the *Snuff* scandal of 1976, the majority of independents had self-regulated violent and sexual material to avoid the X-rating. Indeed,

the only negative publicity related to film content had been reports
of skirmishes breaking out during screenings of two gang movies, *The
Warriors* and *Boulevard Nights* (Anon., 1979e, pp. 3, 26; Anon., 1979h,
p. 24; Klain, 1979, p. 24). In contrast, some high-profile horror films
and violent thrillers like *The Omen, Eyes of Laura Mars*, and *Halloween*
had avoided controversy while others, such as *Carrie* and *Looking for Mr.
Goodbar*, had been applauded critically and had even received Academy
Award nominations. As chapter five shows, this period of relative calm
did not last long, but, in the summer of 1979, several filmmakers clearly
interpreted these developments as evidence that a shift was taking place
in the priorities of the American popular press and the Classification
and Ratings Administration (CARA). In the absence of prominent ratings scandals, and in the context of the favorable reception of some
violent films, several filmmakers, including those behind *Cruising, Dressed
to Kill* and, indeed, *Friday the 13th*, saw an opportunity to highlight the
depiction of bloodshed. There were precedents to suggest that MPAA-
members would not be alienated by this content.

At points in time at which controversy over violent content was low,
MPAA-members had been willing to handle films that featured over-the-
top deaths. On the back of Dario Argento's 1969 international hit *The
Bird with a Crystal Plumage*, MPAA-members had imported Italian giallo
films into the US to alleviate the product shortage of the early 1970s
(Cook, 2000, pp. 234–235). As Mikel J. Koven argued, set-piece killings
distinguished these gory whodunits from most other murder-mysteries
(2006, pp. 61, 123–138). The giallo films were not hits in the US, but
the production of American versions, discussed above, suggests that they
resonated deeply with some American filmmakers. But more influential
than the giallo films were two horror blockbuster hits that had mobilized
the kind of excessive and outlandish death scenes that had featured in
the films of Argento, Mario Bava, and other Italian directors; both films
had been produced and distributed by Twentieth Century Fox.

In Fox's *The Omen* (1976) and *Damien: Omen II* (1978) characters died
swiftly and painlessly but in a variety of dazzling and improbable ways.[20]
As John McCarty observed, the *Omen* films 'succeeded in introducing a
new concept to the (. . .) mainstream (. . .) the device of the "creative
death"' (1984, p. 106). 'The only thing that separates them', he continued, 'is the individual sense of showmanship exhibited by each film's
writer and director in coming up with new and more creative ways of lur-
ing [Antichrist] Damian's enemies to their deaths' (ibid. pp. 106–107).
In the first *Omen* film, a priest is pierced to the ground by the falling
spire of his church, and a young woman who jumps from a roof during

a child's birthday party is jerked spectacularly through a window by the noose that she has tied around her neck. Fittingly, the most outlandish death was reserved for the streets of Rome as an unlikely sequence of events leads to a man being decapitated when a sheet of glass slides from the back of a truck. Fox's big-budget sequel upped the ante. In *Damien: Omen II* a journalist has her eyes pecked out by a raven before being run down by a speeding juggernaut. Later in the film, a scientist is cut in two by a flailing elevator cable. Most filmmakers viewed the box-office achievements of *The Omen* films as having underscored the potential of demonic child films, but for some industry-professionals they signaled a method of emphasizing killings in ways that were eye-catching but which did not prolong suffering, fear, and violence. Crucially, *The Omen* and its first sequel had indicated that an MPAA-member was willing to attach its name to films that featured these kinds of set-piece deaths on not one but two occasions, and that CARA was prepared to award such films R-ratings.

The set-piece deaths of *The Omen* films provided the filmmakers behind *Friday the 13th* with a way of tailoring murders to appeal to MPAA-members. Thus, *Friday the 13th*'s killings showcased a wide range of weapons and little-seen contexts. For example, a youth is discovered pinned to a target board by several arrows, another slumps to the floor with a hatchet buried in her face, and a young man, lying on a bunk, has an arrow pushed through his throat from underneath the bed. *Friday the 13th* featured ten killings, twice as many as *Halloween*. This content was, however, tightly policed to avoid an X-rating. Accordingly, four of *Friday the 13th*'s murders omitted thrilling sequences of stalking altogether. Of the six murders that were preceded by thrills, only two featured chases and only the killer's demise followed an extended struggle. Similarly, each of the six murders that were preceded by thrills showed only brief victim-horror immediately prior to death (see Table 3.1). Producer-director Sean S. Cunningham was quick to explain to journalists that he had been eager to limit violence and gore in *Friday the 13th*. 'Most scary movies aren't scary', revealed Cunningham, '[t]hey're just disgusting. A face hacked into four pieces isn't scarier than a face hacked into two pieces, it's just more disgusting' (quoted in Chase, 1981a, p. C8). Consequently, whereas three murders (including the only victim to die from multiple injuries) occurred outside of the frame, ellipses eliminated the impact of the weapons during four of the seven on-screen murders with the victims of each on-screen killing dying immediately after the impact of the initial violent blow. Brief displays of victim-horror and pain featured during only one attack respectively, while both responses featured together in only two murders. While the blood and/

or superficial wounds of eight victims were shown, five instances were restricted to displays of post-mortem damage (see Table 3.2). Instead of focusing on pain, suffering, and extended displays of damaged bodies, the makers of *Friday the 13th* had aimed to avoid the alienation of their preferred distributors by spotlighting what *Variety* described as 'one Grand Guignol close-up of each atrocity' (Step., 1980, p. 14).

TABLE 3.1   Pre-death features of murders in *Friday the 13th*.

Victim		Features			
Gender	Type	None	Fear	Chase	Struggle
Male	Youth		✓		
Female	Youth		✓	✓	
Female	Youth		✓	✓	
Male	Youth	✓			
Male	Youth	✓			
Female	Youth		✓		
Female	Youth		✓		
Male	Adult	✓			
Male	Youth	✓			
Female	Killer		✓		✓

Key: '✓' denotes presence of feature

TABLE 3.2   Features of murders in *Friday the 13th*.

Victim		Death-blow		Effects			
Gender	Type	Single	Multiple	Off-screen	Fear	Gore	Pain
Male	Youth	✓		✓	✓	✓	✓
Female	Youth			✓			
Female	Youth	✓			✓	✓	✓
Male	Youth			✓		✓	
Male	Youth	✓			✓	✓	
Female	Youth	✓		✓		✓	

(continued on next page)

Victim		Death-blow		Effects			
Gender	Type	Single	Multiple	Off-screen	Fear	Gore	Pain
Female	Youth			✓		✓	
Male	Youth	✓		✓			✓
Male	Youth		✓	✓		✓	
Female	Killer	✓				✓	

Key: '✓' denotes presence of feature

In sum, *Friday the 13th* was the first American film to be made to capitalize on the relative commercial achievements of *Halloween*. Where most of the country's independent filmmakers were too cautious to employ a textual model that had not also been used by a Reinforcing Hit, the makers of *Friday the 13th* were able to confront the apparent risks of Prospector Cash-in production because they had been provided a safety net if an MPAA-member did not buy the film by the theater circuit owned by their financiers' parent company. With a direct route into theaters, Sean S. Cunningham and his team aimed to offset the risk of modeling a film on *Halloween*. By combining content from commercially attractive trends that emerged after *Halloween* had been shot, the Prospectors behind *Friday the 13th* crafted a relatively gory animal comedy-infused murder-mystery in which the paths of a mixed-sex group of hedonistic camp counselors and a mysterious slasher crossed at a rural summer camp. They also emphasized a series of set-piece murders that downplayed representations of pain, fear, and body-horror so as to avoid an X-rating, and offered a tough heroine so as to make their film marketable to female youth.

Budgeted at $500,000 and produced by a filmmaker who had not made a profitable movie for almost a decade, *Friday the 13th* appeared to be an unlikely candidate to convince MPAA-members that they could tap into audience interest in *Halloween*. Particularly, considering that most independents, including the producer of *Halloween*, had shied away from capitalizing on Carpenter's film in the first place. However, not even the leading lights of the American independent production sector could anticipate how intervening developments would shape Hollywood's response to a nascent teen slasher film.

'A yeoman's selling job': *Friday the 13th*, a Reinforcing Hit

'They were warned . . . they are doomed', screamed the tagline on *Friday the 13th*'s promotional poster. This prophetic reference to the fate that awaited a group of summer camp workers in the film echoed the pessimism expressed in the trade press about the box-office prospects of the film. *Variety* had gloomily forecast that *Friday the 13th*'s distributor would 'have to do a yeoman's selling job to squeeze major cash from the sprockets of this sporadically gory but utterly suspenseless [sic] pickup' (ibid.). By focusing on the distribution of *Friday the 13th*, this section examines the MPAA-members response to a nascent film type, showing that, like independent producers, MPAA-member distributors also required market-conditions and consistent commercial success to suggest not only that a film-type itself is commercially viable, but that it offers a more reliable investment than other product.

The pessimism of industry-watchers was not shared by industry-insiders. Believing that their Prospector Cash-in was capable of securing an MPAA-member distribution deal, the financiers of *Friday the 13th* had arranged for the film to be screened for several MPAA-members (Bracke, 2005, p. 38). In early 1980, their confidence proved not to have been misplaced when a bidding-war over the film erupted between Paramount, Warner Bros. and UA (Buckley, 1981, p. C8). Paramount secured the domestic rights to *Friday the 13th*, Warner Bros. had to settle for the right to distribute the film internationally, and UA was left empty-handed. 'The minute we saw "Friday the 13th"', explained Frank Mancuso Sr., Paramount's vice-president of marketing and distribution, 'we knew we had a hit' (quoted in Morrisroe, 1980, p. 101). The studio paid $1.5m for the film and set aside $4.5m for marketing and publicity (Anon., 1980i, p. 25; Harmetz, 1980a, p. C14; Harmetz, 1980d, p. C15). While it can be reduced to 'a major studio knocking off the genre success of an independent production' (Heffernan, 2004, p. 203), the MPAA-members' interest in *Friday the 13th* was underpinned by a more complex network of motives, concerning low purchase costs, dwindling profits of once lucrative film-types, similarities to ascendant film-types, and suitability for target markets.

Friday the 13th was a low-risk investment for an MPAA-member. Whereas most independent filmmakers had been unwilling to stake $0.5m–$2m on the production of a largely untested textual model, the $2–6m that was required to bring a completed film like *Friday the 13th* to the big screen represented a minor gamble for the wealthy MPAA-members, compared to the average $13m cost of producing and promoting a major studio film in 1980 (Prince, 2000 p. 20). The relatively minor cost of purchasing, marketing, and distributing a low-budget production like *Friday the 13th* meant that a smaller number of tickets had to be sold to generate profit. Thus, although Hollywood's biggest earners have historically been expensive projects, such expenditure carried with it 'substantially higher risks of commercial failure than medium or low-budget movies' (Stokes and Maltby, 1999, p. 2), for, as Sheldon Hall points out, about 40 per cent of big-budget productions failed to break even during the late 1970s (1998, p. 22). In the event that *Friday the 13th* failed to attract theatergoers, the extent of the financial loss would be tolerable for a company the size of Warner Bros., Paramount or UA. If, however, the film's rentals were to approach those that *Halloween* had accumulated by early 1980, its distributor stood to generate significant profits.

Underwriting this logic were two intertwined developments that traversed the independent production, and the MPAA-member distribution, of horror films. In the mid 1970s, the spectacular box-office performances of the 'quality horror' blockbusters *The Exorcist, Jaws,* and *The Omen* had permitted the majors to dismiss independently distributed hits like *The Town that Dreaded Sundown,* as they focused on producing Cash-ins to their own hits. Several of the demonic child and revenge-of-nature films that followed were expensive prestige projects that required annual chart-topping rentals to break even. However, almost all of the Cash-ins had failed to fulfill industry expectations. 'By fall 1978', notes Kapsis, 'the popularity of [demonic child] films had already peaked' (1992, p. 159). Similarly, Cook views the revenge-of-nature opus *The Swarm* (1977) as a 'virtual textbook example of how the industry (. . .) [runs] winning formulas into the ground' (2000, p. 256). From 1977 to 1979, declining ticket sales and big budgets wiped out the high rentals of Paramount's calculated blockbuster *King Kong,* erased the underwhelming returns of Warner Bros.' much-hyped sequel *Exorcist II: The Heretic,* and caused the same company to incur huge financial losses on *The Swarm.*[21] This shift indicated that the audience for horror films was no longer large enough to sustain lavish productions but was big enough to enable modestly priced films to generate sizable profits. As a consequence, the MPAA-members were forced to re-evaluate their relationship to independent producers of low-budget horror films.

The financial achievements of *Halloween,* which had been confirmed when *Friday the 13th* was offered to distributors, in conjunction with those of AIP's haunted house film *The Amityville Horror* (1979), indicated firmly that some low-budget independent productions were capable of filling the void left by the demise of 'quality horror'.[22] Moreover, the widespread commercial failure of lower-budget demonic child and revenge-of-nature Cash-ins,[23] including those distributed by MGM/UA and Paramount,[24] also signaled that the economic potential of horror pickups was tied to up-to-the-minute textual models. Such candidates were, of course, films that had been closely patterned after a recent Trailblazer Hit — i.e. Prospector Cash-ins like *Friday the 13th*. Although too little time had passed for producers to model films on *The Amityville Horror*, sufficient time had passed to make films that were similar to *Halloween* and, crucially, while *Friday the 13th* was in still production, two developments at the American box-office had suggested that significant audience demand existed for films about youths being menaced by shadowy maniacs.

The first development took place across the fall of 1979 when Columbia Pictures' low-budget pickup *When a Stranger Calls* performed strongly at the American box-office (Harmetz, 1979b, p. C21). *When a Stranger Calls* was not a teen slasher film. It was in fact a downbeat character study about an emotionally scarred psychotic struggling to reintegrate into society and an equally unstable cop seeking to make him pay for his past crimes. The film had, however, featured a sequence in which the killer makes threatening phone calls to a teenage babysitter — which only Canadian journalist Jay Scott seemed to recognize had been lifted from *Black Christmas* (1979c). And it was on these sequences — and these sequences alone — that Columbia's promotion and publicity campaigns had focused. By misleading audiences into anticipating a film that bore close similarities to *Halloween*, an MPAA-member had scored the most profitable horror film of the year. By generating a very respectable $10.1m in rentals,[25] *When a Stranger Calls* (in the context of its somewhat deceptive marketing) suggested that *Halloween* had not been an anomalous hit and that a similar film would provide an MPAA-member a low-cost investment with genuine sleeper hit credentials. Confirmation came soon after.

Any lingering doubts that *Halloween* had been a one of a kind event in American box-office history were erased in early 1980 when American Cinema Releasing began to enjoy considerable commercial success, by the modest standards of independent distributors, with the teen slasher Speculator Production *Silent Scream*, a 'Saturday afternoon type of chiller aimed at young adults' (Walentis, 1980, p. 72) that combined 'Hollywood style knife slayings' (Paseman, 1980, p. 2C) and 'very sweet love scenes' (Gross, 1980a, p. F8). *Silent Scream* — much like the Prospector Cash-in *Terror Train* — was a teen slasher film that, on account of the timing of its production and release, exerted little influence on the content of subsequent teen slashers and is therefore discussed only briefly in this book. The distribution of *Silent Scream*, again like that of *Terror Train*, did, however, impact perceptions of the commercial viability of the teen slasher film and thus influenced the industry's conduct in relation to the film-type significantly. Despite having been shot before *Halloween* was released, *Silent Scream* was the first teen slasher to be offered to distributors after *Halloween* became a hit. American Cinema Releasing purchased the rights to *Silent Scream* and, after it performed well during trial run in November 1979 (American Cinema Releasing, 1979, pp. 14–15), the company opened the film in 131 California theaters the following January. In the first seven days of its re-release, *Silent Scream* grossed $1.67m, a sum that was paraded across *Variety* (American Cinema Releasing, 1980, pp. 18–19). Opening week ticket sales of this sort indicated that *Silent Scream* would become one of the most commercially successful independently distributed horror films of the 1970s — a feat that it went on to achieve after continuing to attract theatergoers.[26]

The box-office achievements of *Silent Scream*, a film that was compared time and again to *Halloween* (Walentis, 1980 p. 72; Paseman, 1980, p. C2), and was even described by one journalist as 'this year's "Halloween"' (Anon., 1980c, p. 2C), had underscored the financial potential of teen slasher film distribution for MPAA-members. In the space of little over a year, two small companies — Compass International Films and American Cinema Releasing — had generated huge profits from the new film-type despite only being able to open their films on small numbers of screens on a region-by-region basis and without the benefit of multi-million dollar marketing budgets. Given that the MPAA-members were in a position to reach a larger audience by investing heavily in advertising and by delivering their films to well over a thousand screens nationwide, they could expect to generate even bigger profits than Compass International and American Cinema had done.

MPAA-members also placed huge confidence in *Friday the 13th* because it featured non-horror content that had appealed to youth audiences. Kapsis' examination of the production of the low-budget supernatural horror film *Fear No Evil* (1981), mentioned in chapter one, reveals much about the logic of MPAA-members at the time (1992, pp. 163–164), with director Robert LaLoggia explaining to Kapsis that Avco Embassy, 'found the high school setting the most appealing aspect of the picture' (quoted in ibid., p. 164). As detailed above, the filmmakers behind *Friday the 13th* had set their film at a summer camp and, by spring 1980, this setting had been used in the two most commercially successful films to have been targeted exclusively to youth audiences since the release of *Grease* and

Animal House. By virtue of its setting, *Friday the 13th* boasted the textual element that most palpably connected Paramount's animal comedy pickup *Meatballs* to the studio's next independently produced acquisition, the female-centered coming-of-age drama *Little Darlings*. Both films were big sleeper hits. *Meatballs* had placed among the top twenty earners of its year, 1979, and it seemed likely that *Little Darlings* would emulate this feat.[27] Due to the commercial success of the two films, Paramount was prepared to fight more fiercely and pay a higher price for *Friday the 13th* than its competitors. The influence of these factors was gestured to by Frank Mancuso Sr. 'The attraction of acquiring *Friday the 13th* for a studio like us', Mancuso explained, 'was that it served a natural, frequent movie-going demographic [and] it was the right subject matter' (quoted in Bracke, 2005, p. 41).

Relative to Paramount's investment, *Friday the 13th* became a solid commercial success. Following a $5.8m opening three-day gross, the film rapidly earned the majority of the $16.5m that it would generate by year's end to place twentieth in the annual rentals chart.[28] Of the seventeen films that Paramount distributed in 1980, only two, *Urban Cowboy* and *Airplane!*, returned the company more in rentals than *Friday the 13th*.[29] Indeed, the achievements of *Friday the 13th* are underscored when compared to other releases that shared content and/or target audience. That year, *The Shining* was the solitary horror film to generate higher rentals than *Friday the 13th* (see Table 3.3) and *Friday the 13th*'s rentals were bettered by only five of the 20 films that MPAA-members angled primarily or exclusively to youth (see Table 3.4). *Friday the 13th* went from being a Prospector Cash-in to a Reinforcing Hit.

TABLE 3.3   Top rental horror films, 1980.

Film	Release	Distributor	Rentals ($m)	Position
The Shining	05/23/80	Warner Bros.	30.2	10th/1980
Friday the 13th	05/09/80	Paramount	16.5	20th/1980
Dressed to Kill	06/23/80	Filmways	15	23rd/1980
The Fog	02/01/80	Avco Embassy	11	29th/1980

(Source: Anon., 1981a, p. 29)

TABLE 3.4   Top rental youth-oriented films, 1980.

Film	Release	Distributor	Rentals ($m)	Position
The Blues Brothers	06/20/80	Universal	31	8th/1980
The Blue Lagoon	07/05/80	Columbia	20.2	11th/1980
Cheech & Chong's Next Movie	07/18/80	Universal	21	15th/1980
Caddyshack	07/25/80	Orion/Warner Bros.	20	17th/1980
Little Darlings	03/21/80	Paramount	16.7	19th/1980
Friday the 13th	05/09/80	Paramount	16.5	20th/1980

(Source: Anon., 1981a, p. 29).

The commercial performance of *Friday the 13th* was made possible by the groundbreaking marketing and distribution strategies employed by Paramount. When musing over the film's bleak chances at the US box-office, *Variety* had declared that '*Friday the 13th* has nothing to exploit but its title and whatever oomph Par[amount] puts into its [marketing] campaign' (Step., 1980, p. 14). That marketing campaign was tailored, much like the film itself, to 'lure the profitable *Halloween* audience' (ibid). 'What we [Paramount] started doing with a picture like *Friday the 13th* was target marketing', revealed Frank Mancuso Sr., 'I never believed we would have a demographic spill-over for the film beyond (. . .) someone in their early twenties' (quoted in Bracke, 2005, p. 41). To target youth, the studio promoted *Friday the 13th* as, what I would call, an illicit event picture. The governing principle of this approach was Paramount's location of its pickup within canons of major studio blockbusters and independently distributed horror. This strategy invited theatergoers to anticipate a film with similarities to *Halloween*, fun-toned teenpics, 'prestige' horror films, and grisly drive-in hits.

The poster that Alex Ebel of the design company Spiros Associates fashioned to promote *Friday the 13th* encapsulated Paramount's marketing approach perfectly (Spiros Associates, 1980, pp. 14–15). By suggesting that the film was similar to several types of youth-oriented product, the poster permitted multiple audiences to be addressed simultaneously. *Friday the 13th*'s artwork echoed compositionally, stylistically, and iconographically the poster that had heralded the release of *Halloween* eighteen months earlier. The hand-painted image of an unidentifiable blade-wielding maniac set against a solid black background invited potential theatergoers to draw parallels between both films' posters and, by implication, the content of both films (see Figure 3.4). The remobilization of the individual components that comprised *Halloween*'s artwork also enabled *Friday the 13th*'s poster to import similar meanings. The image itself projected the thrills and horror associated with an incongruous threat while its concealment of the perpetrator's identity signaled an intriguing murder-mystery.

While the mobilization of a shadowy figure brandishing a huge bladed-weapon echoed iconographically the marketing of such notorious 1970s product as *I Spit on Your Grave* (1977), other elements distanced the piece from these releases (see Figure 3.5). Again, the comic book style of the poster, in stark contrast to the garish photography employed in the posters of much of the period's exploitation, counterbalanced the violent connotations of the image's content. This quality was augmented by the artwork's inter-textual relationships to the posters of contemporaneous light-hearted youth-oriented comedies such as *Animal House*. Indeed, the presence of youths and a woodland cabin in the image invited parallels to Paramount's own animal comedy hit *Meatballs* (see Figure 3.6). Similarly, the combination of a striking image and a black background served to further distance *Friday the 13th* from independently distributed releases by recalling the striking artwork of 'prestige horror' films like *The Exorcist* (see Figure 3.7).

FIGURE 3.4   Evoking *Halloween* to promote *Friday the 13th*.

FIGURE 3.5 Using comic-book style to distance *Friday the 13th* from exploitation: *I Spit on Your Grave.*

FIGURE 3.6 Evoking *Meatballs* to promote *Friday the 13th.*

FIGURE 3.7   Evoking *The Exorcist* to promote *Friday the 13th.*

Friday the 13th's trailer and TV spot built upon the themes of its poster to trumpet the film's status as an illicit event picture. Both audiovisual marketing tools intercut thirteen instances of youth placed in jeopardy from an unidentified blade-wielding killer and an onscreen numerical record. The montage concluded with a severe baritone announcing: 'Friday the 13th, you may only see it once, but that will be enough'. This tagline, as Lisa Kernan suggests, served as an overt challenge to theatergoers to test their nerves by attending a screening of the film — at least once (2004, pp. 49–50). The direct address to the audience to confront and overcome supposedly horrifying content characterized much exploitation marketing of the 1970s. The most famous, and oft-plundered, example being the mantra 'to avoid fainting keep repeating "it's only a movie"' which had been employed by Hallmark to promote Cunningham's own micro-budget hit *The Last House on the Left.* The recycling of rhetoric associated with the trailers of illicit unrated drive-in fare was, however, contrasted by the high-profile status that Paramount's sizable marketing budget provided its pickup.

Paramount's $4.5m marketing budget afforded *Friday the 13th* a highly visible position on the American market. This figure was almost double the average $2.5m advertising costs for US releases in 1979 and approached the $6m that was typically allocated to calculated blockbusters at the time (Cook, 2000, pp. 15, 517n. 27). Indeed, the high levels of audience awareness that were generated by the prevalence of the film's promotional materials prompted Hy Smith, vice-president of UA, to declare enviously that '*Friday the 13th* was *made* on television' (quoted in Harmetz, 1980b, p. C15 [emphasis in original]). The kind of massive television advertising blitz that had catapulted blockbusters like *Jaws* 'from the level of film to national media event' framed Paramount's *Halloween* Cash-in as a 'must-see event' picture of the summer of 1980 for young theatergoers (Cook, 2000, p. 15). The structure of the film's trailer reflected this strategy, the rapid escalation of its individual moments of threat towards the film's title creating a sense of urgency designed both to mirror and to catalyze viewers' longing to see the film.

Paramount's distribution strategy underscored its attempt to portray *Friday the 13th* as an unmissable event for youth audiences. Whereas *Halloween*'s inability to attract an MPAA-member distributor had necessitated a region-by-region roll-out, Paramount's vast capital resources ensured that *Friday the 13th* was granted a pattern of release usually reserved for calculated blockbusters. In combination with intensive cross-media marketing campaigns, saturation booking — or the simultaneous release of a film on large numbers of screens in different regions and/or territories — remains the primary vehicle employed by the majors to increase the visibility of their films (ibid.). As Hall explains, saturation booking was not always employed in the distribution of calculated blockbusters (Hall, 1998, pp. 11–26). Rather, during the 'road-show era' of the 1950s and 1960s, high-cost productions were typically opened 'on a limited or exclusive basis in a major metropolitan centre for an extended or indefinite run at "advanced" (raised) prices' (ibid.). Yet, by the late 1970s, saturation booking was becoming Hollywood's standard release strategy for big-budget productions. By the middle of the decade, major studios had adopted this strategy from exploitation distributors and UA, and expanded its scope, first to the national level and later to near-global proportions.[30] While used in Southern California to propel the low-budget film *Billy Jack* (1971) to sleeper hit status, Hollywood's confidence in the approach was galvanized by *Jaws* which was opened by Universal at 409 US theaters and which generated what were the highest rentals of all-time.[31] Thereafter, *King Kong* opened on 961 screens, *Saturday Night Fever* on 726, and *Grease* on 902 (Doherty, 2002, p. 139). One drawback of saturation booking is the increased importance that it places on a film's ticket sales in its first week of release (Schatz, 1993, p. 19). However, as Schatz suggests, the advantages of the strategy are that it 'maximize[s] a movie's event status while diminishing the potential damage done to weak pictures by negative reviews and poor word-of-mouth' (ibid.). These benefits, as Cook notes, lend themselves ideally to a horror film like *Friday the 13th* (2000, p. 16).

On 9 May 1980, *Friday the 13th* premiered simultaneously on 1127 screens, at the time one of the widest openings in the history of the industry.[32] This number was surpassed by only three films that year — *Any Which Way You Can* (1541), *Bronco Billy* (1321), and *Smokey and the Bandit II* (1196).[33] The release of *Friday the 13th* on this enormous number of screens ensured that the film occupied a highly visible location on the American market. To avoid potentially negative reviews impacting attendance, Paramount refused to screen the film for the press (Pollock, 1980, p. G11). In addition, the timing of *Friday the 13th*'s release catalyzed its box-office achievements. As chapter two demonstrated, a film's commercial performance is partly determined by the competition it faces from releases that have the same target audience. Whereas the pioneering teen slasher *Black Christmas* initially suffered from opening during the fiercely contested Christmas blockbuster period, *Friday the 13th* benefited from its release at a moment of particularly low competition for youth audiences (Donahue, 1987, p. 128). The only other MPAA-member film that opened on 9 May 1980 was Universal's *The Nude Bomb*, a spy film parody that posed little threat to *Friday the 13th*'s share of the youth-market. *Friday the 13th* also circumvented competition from every other MPAA-member film that shared its target audience and/or general textual orientation. The theatrical runs of four horror films — *The Fog, Cruising, Death Ship, Inferno* — like that of the female-centered coming-of-age drama *Foxes* had all but ended, and most other youth-oriented films were slated for release later in the summer. The animal comedy *Up the Academy* and the boisterous musical *The Blues Brothers* were both going to debut in June of that year and at least two months separated *Friday the 13th* from an additional quintet of horror and/or youth-oriented films: the American giallo *Dressed to Kill*, the female-centered coming-of-age drama *The Blue Lagoon*, the roller-disco movie *Xanadu*, and two comedies *Cheech & Chong's Next Movie* and *Caddyshack*. Paramount also ensured that *Friday the 13th* avoided clashes with three calculated blockbusters, *The Empire Strikes Back*, *Smokey and the Bandit II*, and *Urban Cowboy*. The only film therefore that posed a threat to *Friday the 13th* was *The Shining*. Yet, in the context of saturation booking and the low expenditure that had been required to bring *Friday the 13th* to the screen, the two weeks that separated the release of the two horror films, provided ample time for *Friday the 13th* to gather momentum and generate significant revenue.

As a Reinforcing Hit, *Friday the 13th* sent a clear message to the American independent sector. *Halloween* may have indicated that a sizable youth audience existed for films about young people being menaced by shadowy maniacs, but the MPAA-members' blanket rejection of the film had fostered concerns among would-be Prospectors that similar independent productions would struggle to tap into that audience fully and would therefore find it difficult to turn a profit. However, the revenue that *Friday the 13th* generated at the US box-office for Paramount Pictures suggested that MPAA-member distribution deals, and, as a consequence, swift profits, irrespective of box-office performance, were a distinct possibility for the producers of new teen slashers.

In sum, *Friday the 13th* demonstrated the box-office potential of the teen slasher under privileged conditions. By spring 1980, the caution about the teen slasher that had pervaded the American independent sector proved not to be shared by the MPAA-members. With the high costs of prestige productions decimating the sizable rentals of films like *King Kong* and *The Swarm*, inexpensive independent productions provided MPAA-members a more financially viable method of capitalizing on continued audience interest in horror. *Friday the 13th* was also attractive because it replicated some of the content of non-horror youth-oriented hits like *Meatballs*. To capitalize on these trends, Paramount promoted *Friday the 13th* as an illicit event picture, positioning the film in marketing materials as one similar to *Halloween*, independently distributed horror films, horror blockbusters, and non-horror youth-market hits. This innovative campaign was backed by a well-timed blockbuster-style distribution strategy which saw *Friday the 13th* open simultaneously on a near-record number of screens. Released at a time of minimal competition for youth audiences, the Prospector Cash-in *Friday the 13th* emulated, within weeks, rental sums that the Trailblazer Hit *Halloween* had accumulated gradually over almost two years.

Conclusion

Contrary to standard thinking, *Halloween* did not inspire significant numbers of American-made Cash-ins. Most independent producers based in the United States were reluctant to try to capitalize on a Trailblazer Hit in the making that had failed to secure MPAA-member distribution and which had yet to be followed by a Reinforcing Hit. American independents were in fact more cautious than has commonly been suggested, choosing instead to target MPAA-members with gang movies, animal comedies, roller-disco movies, and female-centered coming-of-age dramas that had been patterned after MPAA-members' own blockbuster hits, or with established types of horror film, or they waited to see if horror films with huge box-office potential became Trailblazer Hits and in doing so provided new financially viable textual models. Within the context of such widespread and justifiable caution, the production of *Friday the 13th* — the solitary *Halloween* Prospector Cash-in to have been made in the USA — can be viewed in a new light. Rather than being an act of risk-free profiteering, it can be seen as a calculated gamble against fairly long odds, one only made possible by the fact that *Friday the 13th*, like *Halloween*, was financed by a company with the means by which to release the film itself in the event that an MPAA-member distribution deal was not forthcoming. Rather than tailoring their film for the exploitation circuit, the Prospectors that made *Friday the 13th* aimed to increase their chances of negotiating a pickup deal with an MPAA-member by counterbalancing their use of *Halloween*'s story-structure with bankable elements drawn from prestige horror films such as *Alien*, *Eyes of Laura Mars*, and *The Omen*, and youth-oriented hits like *Meatballs* and *Animal House*. These highly sophisticated commercial strategies resulted in the production of a relatively gory animal comedy-infused murder-mystery that boasted a series of 'painless' set-piece deaths, a summer-camp setting, a group of hedonistic youths, and a tough heroine. The surprising levels of enterprise and audacity displayed by Sean S. Cunningham and his collaborators paid dividends when, with big-budget productions unable to support the continued, albeit diminished, audience interest in horror, and with the teen slasher film *Silent Scream* having demonstrated that *Halloween* had not been a one-of-a-kind hit, *Friday the 13th* proved highly appealing to MPAA-members. Paramount Pictures purchased the film, going on to score a hit in summer 1980 by marketing *Friday the 13th* to young people as an illicit event picture and by employing saturation booking at a time of low competition for its target audience.

Several industrial developments had made *Halloween* Prospector Cash-in production a risky undertaking that no other American filmmakers were willing to confront, thus challenging the notion that *Friday the 13th* was made because it was expected to be a surefire hit. This situation questions the validity of the distinctions that have been drawn between *Friday the 13th* and *Halloween*. The commercial logic and strategies that governed the production and content of *Friday the 13th* were in fact remarkably similar to those that underwrote *Halloween*; both teams of filmmakers balanced their replication of a story-structure that had been used in an earlier film with sites of textual differentiation drawn from a range of contemporaneous hits in order to offer MPAA-members commercially viable youth-market product. Again, the manner in which both films were distributed (if not the size of the companies that released them) shared important commonalities. Both Compass and Paramount went to great lengths to ensure that their respective properties were given the greatest chance of financial success, opening the films on as many screens as budgets allowed and using marketing materials to present them to America's prime-theater-going demographic as light-hearted horror films that had much in common with blockbuster hits and youth-oriented hits.

Sean S. Cunningham and his team may have been the only Americans to confront the apparent risks of producing a Prospector Cash-in to *Halloween*, but they were not the only filmmakers willing to do so. The next chapter focuses on a group of Canadian Prospectors who also believed that the nascent teen slasher provided the ideal instrument with which to appeal to the MPAA-members. Where *Friday the 13th* had warned of impending doom, *Prom Night* promised American youths, particularly teenage girls, a night to die for.

Chapter 4

Murder on the Dance-floor

Canada, the development of the teen slasher film,
and Prom Night *(1980)*

All-American teenagers huddle around a bonfire as a summer camp counselor tells them a story. A young couple speed from a nearby lovers' lane, he explains, after hearing a radio news bulletin warning that a hook-handed killer has just escaped from a local asylum, only to discover, when they return home, a large, bloody, stainless-steel hook embedded in their car door. Female teens tremble under blankets as they hear that the madman was never apprehended despite a huge manhunt. 'Some people say he is still up here in the woods waiting for the chance to kill again', proclaims the counselor. 'And I', he continues, 'I say, they're right'. The girls recoil as he reveals a gleaming hook, only to burst into laughter when they realize that they are victims of nothing more malicious than a good-humored prank.

This sequence, shot in late 1978, presents a tale of youth being menaced by a shadowy maniac as a recreational activity for young Americans and, while the diegetic audience is mixed-sex in composition, it is girls that are emphasized. It suggests that at the end of the 1970s, filmmakers considered young female Americans to be a key audience for horror narratives in which blade-wielding killers preyed on their fictional peers. And, even though it combines two elements that would have been familiar to most US teenagers, a summer camp and an urban legend known as 'The Tale of the Hook' (Koven, 2008, pp. 113–114), this depiction of American youth leisure does not feature in an American film. It is in fact from the Canadian teen comedy *Meatballs* (1979). *Meatballs* proved to be remarkably prophetic in terms of anticipating the Canadian film industry's response to the relative commercial success of *Halloween* (1978), a film, which, not unlike this campfire tale, entertained American youths with a rendition of a murderous sanatorium absconder threatening young people.

This chapter uses a case study of the teen slasher Prospector Cash-in

Prom Night to examine the Canadian film industry's oft-overlooked contribution to the development of the first teen slasher film cycle, focusing on the conditions that resulted in Canadian-based filmmakers attempting to capitalize on *Halloween* at a time when almost all of their American counterparts were unwilling to do so, and examining the logic and the strategies that led to the production of teen slashers that masked their Canadian production origins and which were designed to be angled primarily to young women.[1] By showing that the female youth-orientation of *Prom Night* was bound to its status as an example of Canadian transnational filmmaking, this chapter reveals the extent to which film cycles associated with the American film industry, in terms of production and content, are impacted by developments taking place outside the American film industry, while, at the same time, revealing the extraordinary lengths to which the producers and promoters of a horror film-type that is widely seen as misogynistic went to make their films attractive to female youth.

'The clone capital of North America': Canada and Commercial Film Production in the 1970s

In 1979, few filmmakers had been prepared or equipped to confront the perceived financial perils of *Halloween* Cash-in production. Those that did adopt the high-risk/high-gain strategy of attempting to capitalize on a commercially promising film that had been rejected by every member-studio of the Motion Picture Association of America (MPAA), each took advantage of fairly exceptional circumstances. Where the makers of the American independent production *Friday the 13th* (1980) were able to rely on their financiers' theater-chain if an MPAA-member distribution deal did not materialize, the Canadian-based filmmakers behind *Prom Night* — like their compatriots who made *Terror Train* (1980) — also occupied a relatively privileged position among North American independent producers. These teams of Prospectors were able to take advantage of a series of initiatives that had been introduced by the Canadian government to assist the nation's filmmakers and were able to employ a new production/textual model that promised Canadian films entry into the US market.

During the 1970s, the content of Canadian films was impacted by the shifting funding criteria of the state financing body, the Canadian Film Development Corporation (CFDC). The CFDC's prioritization of specific textual approaches prompted entrepreneurial filmmakers to tailor the content of their films to increase their chances of securing production subsidies. Indeed, even if a film did not receive CFDC funding, the organization still influenced content indirectly. To ensure that the CFDC would consider funding applications for subsequent films, Canadian producers sought to avoid the alienation of the state financier at all cost. Therefore, even though *Prom Night* did not receive state funding, the film was influenced profoundly by the political and economic strategies of the CFDC. Five phases of funding strategies followed the establishment of the organization in 1968, each of which overlapped slightly due to the delay between a film's production and release, were bookended by relative success and failure, and were dominated by a particular approach to film content: 'National Cinema' (1968–73), 'Balanced Output' (1973–1974), 'Established Film-types' (1974–1976), 'Carpetbagger Cash-ins' (1976–1979), and 'Youth-oriented Cash-ins' (1979–1983), as I call them. Shifts in strategies across these five phases culminated in the production in 1979 of two primarily female youth-oriented teen slasher films.

Phase one (1968–73), as chapter two indicated, was characterized by the funding of 'national cinema'. In its earliest years, the CFDC, even though it had been founded in part to initiate an internationally recognized film industry (Marshall, 2001, p. 54), had tended to distribute its CAD10m budget (Gasher, 2002, p. 52) among filmmakers that examined the diversity of Canada and Canadians (Magder, 1993, p. 131). Unsurprisingly, the limited box-office potential of films like the racial drama *Red* and the lesbian romance *Love in a 4 Letter World* (both 1970) resulted in the CFDC exhausting its budget by 1971, having recouped only CAD600,000 or 9 per cent of its investments.[2] The CFDC's prioritization of projects with limited commercial viability, as Jim Leach has argued, severely undermined the domestic and international appeal of its films and impeded the development of the industry (2004, p. 3). With powerful industry-insiders voicing frustration with the organization following the commercial failure of 'national cinema' (Gittings, 2002, pp. 95–96), and with Avco Embassy's US distribution of the privately funded drama *Wedding in White* (1972) highlighting the economic potential of seeking to alleviate the product shortage south of the border through the production of films that appealed to American distributors, the CFDC balanced its cultural mandate with greater levels of fiscal responsibility, bringing about an end to phase one.

Phase two (1973–1974) was characterized by the implementation of increasingly commercially oriented funding and production strategies. The sustainability of the Canadian industry, as chapter two showed, was seen widely to be tied to US distribution from the member-studios of the MPAA. Between 1973 and 1974, the CFDC divided subsidies between 'national cinema' projects and films that seemed capable of securing MPAA-member distribution deals, irrespective of how they represented Canada or Canadians. To assist this ambitious expansion, the Canadian government increased the CFDC's budget to CAD20m,[3] a move that permitted the organization to invest in ultra-low-budget 'Quebecois national cinema' such as *La Mort d'un Bûcheron* (1973) and to support more costly Anglophone films like *Black Christmas* and *The Apprenticeship of Duddy Kravitz* (both 1974), which, although commercially oriented, were quite distinct from established American models. Yet, during phase two, only *Black Christmas* and *The Apprenticeship of Duddy Kravitz* — along with a privately financed disaster film called *The Neptune Factor* (1973) — secured MPAA-member distribution. While performing poorly at the US box-office,[4] the duo generated profits for their producers and the CFDC, and, in doing so, underscored the economic potential of projects crafted, first and foremost, to appeal to the MPAA-members.

Phase three (1974–1976) was distinguished by a reduction in 'national cinema' and the channeling of funds to 'established film-types' (Clandfield, 1987, pp. 87–88). The Canadian government took a drastic step to increase the competitiveness of the nation's film industry in 1974. By increasing the capital cost allowance for Canadian-produced feature films from 60 per cent to 100 per cent, it abolished the taxation of film-makers' profits (Anon., 1975a, p. 7; Gasher, 2002, p. 53). This measure was designed to enable filmmakers to sell their films to US distributors at lower prices than their tax-paying American competitors. Where the short-term effectiveness of the tax shelter was determined by the ability of Canadian films to secure MPAA-member distribution in the first place (Marshall, 2001, pp. 133–134), its medium- to long-term effectiveness was dependent on those films capturing large American audiences and thus ensuring continued relations between Canadian producers and MPAA-members. In response, the CFDC funded bigger budgeted projects that relocated to Canadian settings film-types that Hollywood had been making for decades (Clandfield, 1987, p. 88), including the romantic comedy *Love at First Sight* (1977), a mystery called *Full Circle* (1977), and four horror films: *Shivers* (1975) *The Keeper, Death Weekend* (both 1976), and *Rabid* (1977). Due perhaps to the similarities these films exhibited to American product, they failed to attract MPAA-member distributors. During phase three, the only CFDC-financed film to be picked up by an MPAA-member was *Breaking Point* (1976), an organized-crime thriller set in Philadelphia that emulated prominent elements of the blockbuster hit *The French Connection* (1971) and subsequent films about underworld activity like *The Sting* (1973).[5] While failing at the American box-office,[6] *Breaking Point* signaled that MPAA-members were more receptive to films that obscured their Canadian origins and evoked contemporaneous hits.[7] In the context of the inability of the Canadian-set established film-types to secure MPAA-member distribution, *Breaking Point*, despite failing to capture a large audience, prompted the funding strategy that characterized phase four.

Phase four (1976–1979) was distinguished by the CFDC financing films that featured non-Canadian settings and which imitated new trends in blockbuster filmmaking. This shift to Carpetbagging operations ushered in a period during which, as Tom Allen of *The Village Voice* remarked, Toronto became the 'clone capital of North America' (Allen, 1980b, p. 40). To support bigger-budgeted product, the Canadian government increased the CFDC's annual budget to CAD25m (Anon., 1979s, p. 36).[8] This injection of capital made possible the production of the US-set sports dramas *Running* and *Title Shot* (both 1979), which were produced to capitalize on the achievements of *The Longest Yard* (1974) and *Rocky* (1976), and the 'placeless' drag racing film *Fast Company* (1979), which aped scenes of automotive leisure that had featured in *American Graffiti* (1973) and *Smokey and the Bandit* (1977).[9] It also made possible the aquatic thriller *Bear Island* (1979), which invited comparisons to *The Poseidon Adventure* (1972), *The Deep*, and *The Spy Who Loved Me* (both 1977), as well as *City on Fire* (1979), a US-set urban disaster film modeled on blockbusters like *The Towering Inferno* and *Earthquake* (both 1974).[10] Independently produced Carpetbagger Cash-ins, as chapter one explained, often face fierce competition for MPAA-member distribution deals from similar films. This turn of events befell the phase four films, with only *Running* being picked up by a major, Twentieth Century Fox (Anon., 1979c, pp. 5, 41). *Running*'s $2.72m rentals — a sum bettered by 90 other films in 1979 — proved to be the high-point in yet another period of disappointment for the Canadian film industry.[11]

For a decade a man called Michael Spencer had overseen the operations of the state-funding body. Under his management, the Canadian film industry had developed from one that produced a handful of micro-budget box-office failures to one that produced a handful of medium-budget box-office failures. But things were set to change for 'Hollywood North'.

In 1978, a change of leadership took place at the CFDC (Anon., 1979k, pp. 448, 460) and incoming executive director, Michael McCabe, brought with him new strategies designed to increase the profile and profitability of Canadian films. 'McCabe took over the job last June and from the first day', noted *Variety* in May 1979, '[he] has been egging producers to a more professional marketing stance and to deliver commercial international product' (Anon., 1979j, p. 460). McCabe's impact was swift and dramatic. Although the CFDC continued to bankroll Cash-ins to US hits during phase five (1979–1983), under McCabe's leadership, considerations of target audiences were incorporated into the organization's financing strategies.[12] Whereas the makers of the Carpetbagger Cash-ins had anchored their drive for MPAA-member distribution solely to textual models employed in blockbuster hits, phase five funding strategy was distinguished by the prioritization of films that were thought to be marketable to America's prime theatergoing audience. The shift to 'youth-oriented Cash-ins' was galvanized by the financial achievements of one of the first films subsidized by McCabe.

Meatballs was the first CFDC-financed film to secure a major US studio distribution deal and to prove successful commercially. Shortly before *Prom Night* started production, Paramount had purchased the US distribution rights to *Meatballs*, which had cost only $1.4m to produce, for $3.8m (Anon., 1979j, p. 448). MPAA-member distribution deals had been grounds for celebration for Canadian filmmakers. That Paramount had placed its confidence in the film only added to the excitement surrounding *Meatballs* because, in the late 1970s, Paramount had demonstrated an uncanny ability to recognize the commercial potential of youth-oriented films. In the sixteen months that preceded its purchase of *Meatballs*, the company had generated more revenue from youth-market product than every other US distributor combined. From *Saturday Night Fever* (1977), *Grease*, and *Up in Smoke* (both 1978) Paramount could boast three of the four most commercially successful youth-centered films released from late 1977 to early 1979.

Meatballs finally provided the Canadian film industry with the 'made-in-Canada' blockbuster that filmmakers had been attempting to deliver for six years (Anon., 1973c, p. 19). Released in the US on 26 June, the film had opened strongly and, by the time *Prom Night* was in production, the low-budget animal comedy had generated most of the $19.6m in rentals that it amassed in 1979 (Anon., 1980b, p. 21) — a sum bettered by only fifteen of the 189 new films that opened in the US that year (Cook, 2000, p. 492). *Meatballs* also performed strongly at home, first dislodging *Black Christmas* as the second most commercially successful Canadian film in the history of the Canadian market, and then dethroning *The Apprenticeship of Duddy Kravitz* to become Canada's biggest ever domestic hit.[13] 'Producers have taken a quantum leap', enthused McCabe, 'here is proof that Canadian producers can crack the U.S market' (quoted in Anon., 1979j, p. 460). Other Canadian films also secured MPAA-member distribution at this time, but it was the achievements of *Meatballs* that industry-watchers singled out. 'Heading the list of milestones', announced *Variety*, 'was "Meatballs"' (Grigsby, 1979, p. 50). '"*Meatballs*" did it for Canada this year', stressed the trade paper in another report (Anon., 1979q, p. 46). Against the backdrop of a decade of evolving strategies, failed attempts to attract MPAA-member distributors, and wretched US box-office returns, the commercial success of *Meatballs* did more than simply inject confidence into the Canadian film industry; it provided filmmakers with a new production/textual model that had proven to be attractive both to the American youth-market leader and to American theatergoers.

The combination of three elements that characterized the '*Meatballs* model' was ingenious in its simplicity. First, *Meatballs* highlighted the potential of producing a Prospector Cash-in to a contemporaneous youth-oriented Trailblazer Hit.[14] As the trade press recognized, '[*Meatballs* was] a little summer film designed to cash in on the success of "National Lampoon's Animal House"' (Grigsby, 1979, p. 50). Second, *Meatballs*' box-office accomplishments reinforced the commercial viability of masking a film's Canadian origins — the film had featured a largely American cast and had been shot at what Geoff Pevere has called 'place-less' Ontario locations (Pevere, 1995, pp. 9, 22). Third, *Meatballs* signaled the financial rewards available to the makers of a Cash-in that expanded its target audience to include a demographic that had been less important to the film upon which it was based. The makers of *Meatballs*, as several journalists observed, had omitted scenes of alcohol and drug consumption, violence, and sex that had been central to *Animal House* so as to secure a PG-rating and thus the attendance of the unaccompanied under-17s that had contributed to the success of a film with which it shared several similarities, *The Bad News Bears* (1976).[15] As K. C. Summers of the *Washington Post* explained, '"Meatballs" is a cleaned up version of "National Lampoon's Animal House" for the grade-school set' (1979, p. W24). The *Meatballs* model therefore refined textual evocation to a youth-oriented Trailblazer Hit and textual differentiation to elements that enabled the expansion of a film's target audience.

Meatballs exerted an immediate influence on the content of Canadian films in two ways. As the film was a Reinforcing Hit that had confirmed the financial viability of *Animal House*, it unsurprisingly initiated Carpetbagging operations. Thus, the filmmakers behind *Hog Wild* and *Pinball Summer* (both 1980) patterned their films closely after *Meatballs* and *Animal House*. '"Pinball" [Summer] is billed as (what other) (. . .) [a] fast-paced high school comedy', *Variety* noted with a hint of sarcasm (Anon., 1979n, p. 55). *Meatballs* also prompted more ambitious filmmakers to re-use its production model and thus aim to beat their American competitors to the punch by being the first filmmakers to capitalize on a different youth-oriented Trailblazer Hit through the production of a Prospector Cash-in that masked its Canadian production origins and which expanded the target audience of the original hit.

In spring 1979, youth-oriented hits that had not already sparked significant quantities of Cash-in productions were in short supply. However, two articles published side-by-side in the *Washington Post* had spotlighted two films that were attracting a sizable segment of the American youth-market. Under the headline 'Two movie "sleepers" that woke up fast', Sam Allis was, as discussed earlier, chronicling the long road to box-office success being trodden by *Halloween* (1979a, pp. H1, H6), and Gary Arnold detailed the swifter achievements of *The Warriors* (1979) (1979a, pp. H1, H6). One of the films lent itself to the application of the *Meatballs* model and that film was not *The Warriors*. Walter Hill's tale of violent youth, as chapter three explained, was one of many gang films produced in the wake of *Saturday Night Fever* (1977). If the *Meatballs* model stressed moving quickly to avoid competition from likeminded entrepreneurs that had produced similar Cash-ins, then that time had truly passed when it came to gang movies. As Don Shirley of the *Washington Post* had reported back in October 1978 'an unusually large chunk of next year's market has been set aside for the hitherto marginal genre of stories focusing on youth crime' (1978, L1, L2). Six months later and Warner Bros. was preparing to open *Boulevard Nights* (1979) and the studio's subsidiary, Orion Pictures, had scheduled a 4 July release for *The Wanderers* (1979). The situation with *Halloween* was quite different. The *Washington Post*'s article, along with a similar piece that had appeared in *Variety* the same week (Anon., 1979g, p. 6), was, as chapters two and three explained, the first report on the film's box-office achievements. Filmmakers had had little time to model films on *Halloween*, suggesting that low numbers of Prospector Cash-ins would be competing for MPAA-member distribution deals in early 1980. With *Halloween* the only youth-orientated film in mid 1979 that seemed destined to become a Trailblazer Hit but which had not already initiated significant quantities of Prospector Cash-in productions, two groups of Canadian filmmakers recognized the commercial potential of applying the *Meatballs* model to Carpenter's film. In addition to the makers of *Prom Night*, Canada's largest production company, Astral Bellevue Pathé, had started production on its own *Halloween* Cash-in, a

$3.5m teen slasher called 'Train to Terror' (later re-titled *Terror Train*) that had secured CFDC subsidies.

The Prospectors behind *Prom Night* (and *Terror Train*) amplified *Halloween*'s already prominent address to young women because expansion of target audiences had been a cornerstone of the *Meatballs* model. Yet, recalibrating content to make a film marketable to younger children, like the producers of *Meatballs* had done, was not unfeasible for horror filmmakers in 1979. As Gregory A. Waller has argued, in 1970s America, horror movies invariably received an R-rating that, in theory at least, excluded under 17s from screenings unless they were chaperoned by an adult (1987, p. 5). At the time there was no PG-13 rating and the advent of 'PG-13 horror' like *The Ring* (2003) was three decades away.[16] Moreover, the possibilities that existed to expand audience address for youth-centered horror films were fairly limited. Expanding the address of horror films to include ethnic minority youth was 'out of fashion' in 1979. As John Corry of the *New York Times* noted on reflection, 'blacks and Hispanic people seldom suffer[ed] in the new horror films' (1981, p. 51).[17] The reluctance to spotlight non-whites was the product of two developments that occurred in the mid 1970s and one that was unfolding in 1979. After some minor successes, low-budget 'blaxploitation' films had failed consistently to draw significant quantities of African-Americans to US theaters in the mid 1970s (Cook, 2000, pp. 263–265). Around this time, the trade press had also reported that blacks had embraced the horror blockbuster *The Exorcist* — a film that featured an all-white cast (cited in Guerrero, 1993, p. 105). It appears therefore that filmmakers presumed young ethnic minority audiences would attend horror films irrespective of whether the characters on-screen were the same race as them. In 1979, MPAA-member attempts to target young Hispanic audiences were backfiring badly as Warner Bros.' gang movie *Boulevard Nights* came under attack from prominent Chicano groups, who argued that its depiction of Hispanics was racially insensitive (L. Grant, 1979, G19). Demonstrations against the film outside theaters had caused Warner Bros. to cancel bookings and had led Universal Pictures to pull its gang movie *Walk Proud* (1979) — which also focused on young Hispanics — from several potentially lucrative urban markets that were home to large numbers of Chicanos (Schreger, 1979b, E12). At a time when the producers of horror films seemed disinterested in targeting young gays and lesbians, female youth was the only youth-market sub-demographic that remained open to accommodation.

In sum, shifts in state film subsidization strategies and filmmaking practice culminated in the production of Canadian-made *Halloween* Cash-ins that could be angled heavily to young female American audiences. By 1979, the Canadian government had put in place several measures to assist the nation's filmmakers — founding an organization which allocated production subsidies, and increasing the capital gains allowance to 100 per cent so that Canadian filmmakers did not have to pay tax on their profits and could thus sell their films to distributors at lower prices than their taxpaying American competitors. The appointment in 1978 of Michael McCabe as head of that organization had also ensured that the CFDC was run by a man who bankrolled projects that seemed likely to appeal to MPAA-members and, after a considerable period of trial and error, Canadian filmmakers and the CFDC had finally hit upon a production/textual model that had secured MPAA-distribution and a large American audience. The box-office achievements of *Meatballs* highlighted the commercial potential of producing Prospector Cash-ins to youth-oriented hits, concealing the film's Canadian production origins, and expanding audience address.

In March 1979, the trade and popular press had published reports about a low-budget tale of a masked slasher stalking a group of youths that was drawing young people to American theaters. As the only youth-oriented film that seemed destined to become a Trailblazer Hit but which had not sparked significant quantities of Cash-in productions, *Halloween* lent itself ideally to the application of the *Meatballs* model. Two groups of Canadian-based filmmakers sought to capitalize on *Halloween* by amplifying the film's representation of, and address to, female youth. The delayed release of one of those Prospector Cash-ins, *Terror Train*, rendered minimal its contribution to the development of the first teen slasher film cycle, but the other Canadian-made Prospector Cash-in exerted a profound influence upon teen slasher film production and content, and it is to that film, *Prom Night*, that the next section turns.

'A slumber party-scare story': *Prom Night*, a Prospector Cash-in

Although *Halloween* did not exert an immediate or a profound influence on American independent production patterns, the film's relative commercial success had transformed the profile of its producer-distributor, Irwin Yablans. Before the release of *Halloween* Yablans had been a minor player, required to negotiate with a wealthy business partner to secure funding for low-budget projects. But, as the producer-distributor of a film that was becoming a sleeper hit, Yablans and his company, Compass

International Films, became an early port of call for independent film-makers hoping to acquire production capital. One of the first filmmakers who sought to take advantage of Compass International's newfound resources was Paul Lynch, a 33-year-old former advertising executive working at the margins of the Canadian film industry (Rockoff, 2002, p. 85). 'I had seen *Halloween* and quite liked it', Lynch revealed, 'and I thought "there has got be potential here for some kind of interesting movie"' (interviewed in 'Going to pieces', 2006).

During a meeting with Yablans in spring 1979, Lynch had tried to make the case that his latest concept 'Don't See the Doctor' was capable of emulating the box-office achievements of *Halloween* (Rockoff, 2002, p. 85). The head of Compass International instantly dismissed the idea of a psychotic gynecologist as too distasteful and urged Lynch to come up with a project that, like *Halloween*, combined horror and an event of cultural significance for young Americans (Paul Lynch interviewed in 'Going to pieces', 2006). This advice resonated with Lynch, who, a couple of months later, pitched a new idea to Peter R. Simpson, head of a small Canadian production company called Simcom (Rockoff, 2002, p. 85), which, despite having only recently entered into film production, had capital to invest after selling its debut feature, a family adventure film called *Sea Gypsies* (1978), to American television network NBC.[18] 'Lynch brought me a piece of art', recalled Simpson, 'it was a knife in a heart with blood dripping out of the heart. And it said 'Prom Night''' (quoted at 'Terror Trap').[19] Lynch was quite open about the commercial imperatives that underwrote his conduct. 'I did *Prom Night* because I was washed up in the industry', he told the *Ottawa Citizen*, '(. . .) [o]ne does *Prom Night* to survive' (quoted in Anon., 1980l, p. 35). Simpson agreed to produce the film.

The low budget on which *Halloween* had been fashioned indicated that a modest outfit like Simcom was capable of financing a Prospector Cash-in, irrespective of whether it secured CFDC subsidies. Moreover, as a youth-oriented Trailblazer Hit in the making that had not gener-ated significant numbers of Cash-in productions, *Halloween* enabled the application of the *Meatballs* model. To mask their film's Canadian production origins and to make their film marketable to female youth, the Prospectors behind *Prom Night* reshaped *Halloween*'s story-structure into a female-centered disco-infused whodunit that unfolded in an unnamed Midwestern American state. This approach, which reorganized *Halloween*'s plot, elaborated on *Halloween*'s depiction of the youth-group, and which substituted much 'stalk and slash' action for 'female-friendly' sequences of spectacle, generated a film that Vincent Canby of the *New*

York Times described as 'a comparatively genteel hybrid, part shock melo-drama, like "Halloween", and part mystery' (1980b, p. 11).

In *Prom Night*, a children's game ends in tragedy when a ten-year-old girl named Robin Hammond plummets to her death from a second-storey window. The youngsters involved — Wendy, Nick, Kelly, and Jude — agree to a vow of silence in fear of the repercussions. A local man, Leonard Murch, is wrongly imprisoned for what has been treated by the police as a sex-crime. Six years later and all, it seems, has been forgotten. Then, on the anniversary of Robin's death, the children, as they are about to graduate high school, each receive a threatening phone call. Meanwhile, Murch has escaped from a secure psychiatric facility and the police are hot on his trail. A group of students that includes Robin's elder sister Kim (Jamie Lee Curtis) and the now-teenaged bullies are preparing for Hamilton High's senior prom. On the night of the graduation dance, the police capture Murch, but a mysterious figure stills prowls the school halls. The shadowy stalker picks off the students whose thoughtlessness led to Robin's death. His final target is Kim's boyfriend, Nick (Casey Stevens). A confrontation ensues on the deserted dance-floor and after a brief struggle Kim delivers an ax blow to the masked maniac. It is at this moment that she realizes that the killer is her younger brother, and Robin's twin, Alex (Michael Tough). Heartbroken, Kim cradles her dying brother in her arms. With his final words Alex explains that he had seen Robin's fatal plunge and the cruelty that preceded it. *Prom Night* employs the teen slasher story-structure outlined in chapter one (see Figure 4.1).

Part One: Setup

1. Trigger: Alex Hammond holds four classmates responsible for his sister Robin's death.
2. Threat: The sixth anniversary of Robin's death ignites Alex's rage.

Part Two: Disruption

3. Leisure: Robin's former classmates engage in prom-related activities.
4. Stalking: Alex makes threatening phone calls to Robin's classmates.
5. Murders: Alex kills several of the youths that caused her death.

Part Three: Resolution

6. Confrontation: Alex battles his elder sister Kim and her boyfriend Nick.
7. Neutralization: Kim kills Alex.

FIGURE 4.1   The teen slasher film story-structure in *Prom Night*.

The Prospectors behind *Prom Night*, like the makers of each of the teen slasher Cash-ins produced in 1979, rearranged *Halloween*'s story-structure into a whodunit. This approach, as chapter three suggested, balanced textual evocation of *Halloween* with difference in ways that evoked *Eyes of Laura Mars* (1978). Waller, writing in the mid 1980s, drew distinctions between *Friday the 13th* and *Prom Night*, based on the latter film's resemblance to what he called a 'classical whodunit' (1987, p. 10). Waller's observation highlights the emphasis placed on *Prom Night*'s murder-mystery plot, a degree of emphasis that led Mikel J. Koven to suggest that *Prom Night* is representative of a 'slasher sub-type' that he called 'North American gialli' (2006, pp. 162–168).

Prom Night's makers presented an investigator and a quartet of suspects in ways that veiled the film's Canadian origins by calling forth American cultural reference points, particularly hit US films. Brooding, no-nonsense lawman Lt. McBride (George Touliatos) evoked the protagonists of several 1970s US police procedurals that, in the words of Mia Mask, 'took masculine heroics to new heights of violence and cruelty' (2007, p. 57), including *Dirty Harry* (1971) and its increasingly successful sequels *Magnum Force* (1973) and *The Enforcer* (1976).[20] *Prom Night*'s red-herrings are school bully Lou (David Mucci), a pothead called Slick (Sheldon Rybowski), Hamilton High's creepy janitor Sykes (Robert Silverman), and the shadowy asylum escapee Leonard Murch. Lou is the kind of Italian-American thug that made John Travolta a star. He is, as Koven suggests, '"in the tradition of" Billy Nolan' (2006, p. 165), the young tyrant played by Travolta who ruined prom night in *Carrie* (1976). Slick is a laidback stoner modeled closely on the marijuana smokers Cheech & Chong from the sleeper hit *Up in Smoke*.[21] And, where mental institution absconder Murch evoked the madmen from *Halloween* and 'The Tale of the Hook' urban legend, which, as noted above, was told to campers in Canada's biggest ever hit, *Meatballs*, Sykes echoed the rural American psychopath character-type that, as Carol J. Clover details (1992, pp. 114–137), had risen to prominence in the 1970s — his hunched posture, filthy denims, and band-aid-repaired spectacles recalling the backwoods maniacs that menaced city folk in *Deliverance* (1972) and *Race with the Devil* (1975) (see Figure 4.2).[22] *Prom Night*'s murder-mystery plot, the characters enriching it and, thus, its capacity to provoke fairly intense intrigue, provided an important way of making the film marketable to male youth, which was important because the filmmakers behind *Prom Night*, in stark contrast to the American independents that had crafted *Friday the 13th*, played down thrills and horror. This quite different approach to the depiction of stalking and killing was a result of developments that had unfolded in Canada but which had not affected American filmmakers.

While the controversies that had surrounded violent and sexual material across the 1970s had quieted in the US by 1979, albeit temporarily, the Canadian film industry was still reeling from its first high-profile scandal over this sort of content. With film production in Canada underwritten by a state-owned funding body, the country's media and political elites inevitably found an angle that permitted their intervention. The film that had excited this high-level response was David Cronenberg's *Shivers*, a horror movie subsidized by the CFDC in 1975. *Shivers* centered on the residents of an apartment complex who are transformed into violent and lascivious zombies after contracting a sexually transmitted disease. The film was, in the words of Robin Wood, 'premised on and motivated by sexual disgust' (1984, 164–200). A large segment of the Canadian cineaste elite had anticipated Wood's rhetoric when Cronenberg's 'most infamous and talked about' film was released theatrically in late 1975, as Ernest Mathijs' reception study has shown (2003, p. 109). Widespread critical outrage directed at *Shivers* triggered a series of parliamentary debates in 1976 which focused on whether it was acceptable for 'taxpayers' money' to bankroll horror films generally and, in particular, those that combined sex and violence (ibid., p. 113). '*Shivers* [was] disapproved of', suggests Mathijs, 'because it is a horror film, and [did] not fit the framework of Canadian film' (ibid., p. 114). The '*Shivers* scandal' linked depictions of brutality and sexuality to 'un-Canadian-ness' and misappropriation of government money and in doing so served notice to Canadian-based filmmakers, particularly those lacking Cronenberg's emerging 'auteur' status, that content of this nature ought to be omitted from their films if they wished to secure CFDC funding. Yet, by singling out *Shivers*, Canadian media and political elites had inadvertently spotlighted types of horror film that were more politically viable.

FIGURE 4.2   Using red herrings to evoke American films in *Prom Night*.

Controversy had, after all, not overshadowed the release in Canada of the other high-profile horror production that received CFDC subsidies, the pioneering teen slasher film *Black Christmas*. Although Canadian-based filmmakers had returned to the production of horror by 1979, the *Shivers* scandal clearly had left its mark as the makers of *Terror Train, The Changeling* (1980), and *Prom Night* jettisoned the sexual themes, explicit violence, and gore that had made Cronenberg's film so contentious in Canada.

On the back of such high-profile controversy, it was advisable for the filmmakers behind *Prom Night* to eschew the kind of set-pieces killings with which the producers of *Friday the 13th* had sought to attract an MPAA-member distributor. Paul Lynch and his collaborators therefore depicted stalking in ways designed to numb audience thrills — showing the killer making threatening phone calls as well as depositing photographs and shards of glass in targets' lockers. Journalists recognized that the physical distance that existed between the killer and potential victims diminished the intensity of thrills. '"Prom Night" is a scary enough suspenser [sic]', noted *Variety*, '[but the filmmakers spend] too much time setting up each murder, thus eliminating much suspense' (Berg., 1980, p. 20). The impact of such sequences was undermined further by having the killer's targets fail to respond to calls, dismissing the caller as a harmless prankster, and being unable to determine the significance of the pictures that have been left in their lockers. When the killer and a potential victim finally met face-to-face, low intensity thrills were provoked by fleeting shots that established the killer's advantageous position, and when they finally interacted, only brief shots of fear were shown, physical struggles were omitted, and a prolonged game of cat-and-mouse was restricted to a sequence involving a highly unsympathetic youth (see Table 4.1). The filmmakers behind *Prom Night* also downplayed the film's murder sequences by delaying the killing of five youths until the final third of the plot, showing brief fear in only two of the deaths, restricting displays of corporeal damage to fleeting shots of the post-mortem injuries of four casualties, and locating the impact of the murder weapon outside of the frame or blocking it with objects (see Table 4.2). The effects of this conduct were acknowledged by critics on the film's release. '"Prom Night"', noted Kevin Thomas in the *Los Angeles Times*, 'lets you complete its grislier moments in your imagination' (1980a, p. G4). '[Director Paul] Lynch chooses to underplay the bloody spectacle', observed the *New York Times*' Vincent Canby, 'more often than not, the camera cuts away, or the screen goes discreetly gray' (1980b, p. 11). Even Gene Siskel of the *Chicago Tribune*, a man who, as chapter five shows, would go to great lengths to purge teen slasher films from the American market, opened his review of *Prom Night* by acknowledging the restraint that its makers had shown. 'The film is not as violent as one might expect', wrote Siskel (1980c, p. A6). The attempts of Paul Lynch and his collaborators to minimize thrills and horror, and the emphasis they placed on provoking intrigue, gesture to the principal commercial imperative that governed the content of *Prom Night* — to provide American distributors ample material with which to angle the film to teenage girls and young women.

TABLE 4.1   Pre-death features of murders in *Prom Night*.

Victim		Features			
Gender	Type	None	Fear	Chase	Struggle
Female	Youth	✓			
Female	Youth		✓		
Male	Youth		✓		
Female	Youth		✓	✓	
Male	Youth	✓			
Male	Killer				✓

Key: '✓' denotes presence of feature

TABLE 4.2   Features of murders in *Prom Night*.

Victim		Death-blow		Effects			
Gender	Type	Single	Multiple	Off-screen	Fear	Gore	Pain
Female	Youth	✓		✓	✓	✓	
Female	Youth		✓	✓	✓	✓	
Male	Youth			✓			
Female	Youth		✓	✓		✓	
Male	Youth	✓					
Male	Killer	✓			✓	✓	✓

Key: '✓' denotes presence of feature

To demonstrate marketability to young American females, much of *Prom Night* was given over to three high school girlfriends in the build up to, and on the day of, their senior prom. The stress placed on female youth-oriented content was recognized by several reviewers, one of whom went as far as to suggest that *Prom Night* 'is basically a slumber party-scare story brought to the screen' (K. Scott, 1980, p. 3D). Depictions of the preparations and celebrations associated with this specifically American social ritual were also used to obscure *Prom Night*'s Canadian origins and thus to make it more attractive to American distributors. In the late 1970s, the profile of prom was at an all-time high in the US. As cultural historian Amy L. Best has argued, after its appeal had diminished in the 1960s and early 1970s, prom rebounded in the latter part of the decade as 'an iconic event in American culture (. . .) one of the most important experiences in high school, perhaps even of all adolescence' (2000, p. 2). The cultural profile of the event had also increased for young Americans as a result of proms and similar high school dances having appeared in several of the period's biggest youth-centered hits: *American Graffiti* (1973), *Carrie*, and *Grease*.

In *Prom Night*, an American prom is presented as a rite-of-passage for female youth. Director Paul Lynch has since gone on record to explain that this was his intention. 'We know the prom to be a wonderful event in teenagers' lives', he stated: 'that girls (. . .) look back on like they do their [wedding day]' (interviewed in 'Going to pieces', 2006). Through Kim, Jude (Joy Thomson) and, Kelly (Marybeth Rubens), the makers of *Prom Night* enacted a range of scenarios designed to enable distributors to market the film to young female theatergoers, including several sequences in which issues arising from heterosexual courtship are presented from the girls' perspectives, with the teenage characters who filled out the youth group (Slick, Lou, and others) serving to catalyze the girls' negotiation of these social challenges (see Figure 4.3). While male–female interaction in early teen slashers is mischaracterized as amounting to nothing more than an endless procession of promiscuous singles pursuing casual sexual liaisons (Shary, 2002a, p. 148–149; Wood, 1987), it was in fact the case that teen slasher filmmakers often went to great lengths to paint sex as an emotionally-wrought rite-of-passage for the uninitiated or for love-struck young people. Nowhere is this type of conduct more apparent than in *Prom Night* in which, as Kelly Scott of the *St. Petersburg Times* noted, 'much attention is devoted to the problem of when the girls will lose their virginity' (1980, p. D3). Jude worries about getting a date for the prom before falling in love with Slick. Lovelorn Kelly, on the other hand, is being pressurized by boyfriend Drew to

FIGURE 4.3   *Prom Night*'s youth group.

surrender her virginity at prom. The depiction of their sexual experiences during prom is contrasted and, in both cases, it is the emotional impact of the female participants upon which the makers of *Prom Night* lingered. Jude loses her virginity to Slick. The aftermath is presented as a shared moment of contentment and intimacy. In Slick's van, warm lighting shrouds post-coital Jude as she reclines blissfully in a cloud of cannabis smoke. The same cannot be said of the awkward and swiftly aborted fumbling of Kelly and Drew (Jeff Wincott). When she rejects Drew's advances, Kelly is abandoned unceremoniously, cutting a pitiful figure in a deserted locker-room as her feelings of rejection and humiliation are reflected in the blue-lighting that swathes the tiled walls around her (see Figure 4.4).

The third member of the group is Kim who, as the film's principal protagonist, played an important role in showing distributors that *Prom Night* could be targeted to female youth. The prioritization of the young female audience is encapsulated in the characterization of Kim and the actress chosen to play her. Kim is played by Jamie Lee Curtis who had starred as *Halloween*'s timid babysitter Laurie. In Carpenter's film, the Curtis character was a shy bookworm who had enjoyed the pleasures

FIGURE 4.4   Contrasting female experiences of sex in *Prom Night*.

of the opposite sex by proxy — through constant discussions with her sexually active friends. In *Prom Night*, however, Curtis' character is transformed into the popular pretty girl who wears the most stylish clothing, is the best dancer in the school, dates the most eligible boy in her class, and is elected prom queen. It should be noted that scholars have thus far tended to over-emphasize the presence in teen slashers of masculine heroines like *Friday the 13th*'s Alice (Clover, 1992, pp. 35–42), when boyish 'Final Girls' were actually closer to the exception than the rule. As the next chapter shows, the female protagonists that featured in subsequent teen slashers owed much to *Prom Night*'s last girl standing. For the duration of the plot, Kim is presented as an ambassador of varnished femininity. It is only when she is forced to save her boyfriend from the killer that Kim is shown to adopt, albeit momentarily, a 'traditionally masculine' trait. Even then, Kim is depicted as responding in a 'conventionally feminine' way. Kim fatally wounds the killer with an ax before her eyes meet those of the masked madman and she recognizes that he is her beloved brother, Alex. Kim cradles Alex in her arms, removing his mask gently, wiping the tears from his face, and comforting him in his final moments. A poignant ballad, entitled fittingly 'Fade to Black', plays on the soundtrack as a single tear and a steely look indicate the prom queen's feelings of sadness, loss, and resignation (see Figure 4.5). There were several economic factors driving the selection of female youth-oriented material.

Films that combined teenage girls and romance, as chapter three showed, were considered to possess significant box-office potential in 1979. This potential was largely a result of *Grease*, a musical tale of 'summer lovin'' at a California high school that had transferred successfully from stage to screen to become the number one film of 1978 and the highest earning teen-centered film in history.[23] Soon after, the commercial viability of tales of teenaged paramours had been underscored

FIGURE 4.5 *Prom Night*'s 'conventionally' feminine heroine.

firmly by the ice-skating drama *Ice Castles*, a moderate sleeper hit that had been angled to female youths on the presence of dance, romance, and Robby Benson, one of the biggest teen heartthrobs of the period.[24] By mid 1979, the production of youth-centered love stories was gaining momentum with films that focused much attention on adolescent courtship, such as *Little Darlings*, *Foxes*, and *The Blue Lagoon* (all 1980) all being produced at the same time as *Prom Night*. The American film industry's renewed confidence in teen romance dovetailed with high-profile shifts taking place in the content of MPAA-member horror hits.

With *Rosemary's Baby* (1968) and *The Exorcist* (1973), two films that focused on motherhood, having demonstrated that stressing important events in women's lives, as well as their emotions, could launch horror towards the top of the annual rentals chart, it was only a matter of time before romance re-emerged in MPAA-member horror films.[25] For over half a century, Hollywood had been spotlighting heterosexual courtship in films and their marketing campaigns to attract women to theaters (Altman, 1999). Romantic horror was therefore nothing new. The production of romantic horror often surged when it was felt that women were attending theaters in unusually large numbers. Hence the prevalence of love stories in scary movies during the classical era (Berenstein, 1996, pp. 70–87) when it was misreported widely that females dominated theatrical attendance, despite attendance having been split roughly fifty-fifty between the sexes (Stokes, 1999, pp. 43–45). Similarly, the shift to big-budget glossy horror in the early 1990s, with films like the 1992 remake of *Dracula* (Austin, 2002, pp. 298–299), took place after two sleeper hits of blockbuster proportions, *Pretty Woman* and *Ghost* (both 1990), had re-alerted Hollywood to the enormous commercial potential of targeting films primarily at women (Krämer, 1999, pp. 99–103). The rewards of courting female audiences were also seen to be high when *Prom Night* started production. Hot on the heels of female-oriented blockbuster hits like *Funny Lady* (1975), *A Star is Born* (1976), and *The Goodbye Girl* (1977), Columbia had spotlighted a love story subplot in the promotion of its American giallo *Eyes of Laura Mars*, Fox had billed *Magic* (1978) as 'A terrifying love story', and Universal had sold *Dracula* (1979) on the tagline: 'Throughout the ages he has filled the hearts of men with terror . . . and the hearts of women with <u>desire</u>' [emphasis in original].[26] Solid ticket sales for these films indicated that romance-inflected horror could secure sufficient numbers of theatergoers to make MPAA-member distribution deals for independent productions a distinct possibility. The film that more than any other had initiated the late-seventies shift to romantic horror, and one which profoundly influenced the content of *Prom Night*, was UA's commercially and critically successful pickup *Carrie*, which, as Paul shows, had been crafted to address female youth (1994, p. 362).[27]

A romantic subplot had been mobilized by the makers of *Carrie* to demonstrate that the film could be angled to teenage girls and young women. It had also been spotlighted in the film's marketing campaign and had figured heavily in the critical reception of the film. 'Before people are electrocuted and stabbed to death in "Carrie"', wrote Gene Siskel of the *Chicago Tribune*, 'it's not a bad little love story' (1976, p. A7). Siskel was referring to a significant narrative thread running through *Carrie* in which a teenage girl arranges for her boyfriend to take the eponymous high school outcast to the graduation dance. Following this warm-hearted if misguided gesture, a touching love story unfolds in which timid, unpopular, unhappy Carrie White and the 'best-looking boy in the senior calls', as UA's trailer described him, begin to fall for one another. Towards the end of the film, the subplot reaches a crescendo at the aptly titled 'love amongst the stars' prom where, as a bitter-sweet ballad plays on the soundtrack, the unlikely couple approach the dance-floor nervously, begin to slow-dance, and finally, after much hesitation, they kiss. Gary Arnold of the *Washington Post* encapsulated the feelings of much of the US cineaste elite when he described the scene as 'far and away the most romantic interlude achieved in American movies in years' (1976a, pp. D1, D7). As chapter two showed, no other horror picture influenced teen slasher film content in the late 1970s more than *Carrie* because *Carrie* had demonstrated that combining horror and depictions of female youth appealed to an MPAA-member and a sizable number of young theatergoers. *Carrie*'s impact on *Prom Night* was not lost on journalists with *Variety* accusing *Prom Night*'s makers of 'borrowing shamelessly from "Carrie"' (Berg., 1980, p. 20), and Gene Siskel of the *Chicago Tribune* describing the Canadian teen slasher as 'a watered-down cross between "Halloween" and "Carrie"' (1980c, p. A6). In addition to employing a tried-and-tested method of making horror marketable to female audiences, Paul Lynch and his collaborators also adopted a strategy that had emerged in the months leading up to the production of *Prom Night*.

To enable prospective distributors to sell *Prom Night* to young females, the film's makers emphasized sequences of disco dancing and used a disco music soundtrack. When *Prom Night* started production in the second half of 1979, the representation of disco, as chapter three showed, was seen by some MPAA-members and powerful independents as a lucrative trend, with Universal investing a staggering $20m in *Xanadu* (1980), Rastar Pictures, the company behind hits like *Smokey and the Bandit*, producing

Skatetown U.S.A (1979), and Compass International plowing some of the profits from *Halloween* into *Roller Boogie* (1979). When *Prom Night* was about to be shot, the confidence American industry-insiders placed in disco seemed to have increased even further when UA paid Compass International $3.5m for *Roller Boogie* and cable TV company HBO spent $600,000 on the film's US broadcast rights — despite having seen only a fragment of rough footage (Schreger, 1979a, p. 16). Furthermore, by this time, *Saturday Night Fever* (1977) had been catapulted from blockbuster hit to bona fide cultural phenomenon, not on account of its gang movie content, but on the back of its female youth-oriented content: music and dance. As social historian Bruce J. Schulman argues, '[t]he Bee Gees' falsetto vocals, Travolta's white leisure suits [and the final] dance contest proved more enduring mementos of seventies America than the film's dark subject matter' (2000, pp. 144–145). As *Prom Night* went before the cameras, the commercial viability of celluloid disco was at an unprecedented and never-to-be repeated high. Joseph McLellan of the *Washington Post* was not alone in recognizing the influence of the content of *Saturday Night Fever* on the makers of *Prom Night* (von Maurer, 1980, p. 4B; K Scott, 1980, p. 3D), when he declared that, in the film, '"Friday the 13th" meets "Saturday Night Fever"' (1980b, p. D2).

The commercial logic underwriting the combination of disco and horror was not as skewed as it may seem today. *Prom Night* was not even the first female-centered disco-infused whodunit of the late 1970s. That honor went to the aforementioned American giallo *Eyes of Laura Mars*, producer Jon Peters' follow-up to *A Star is Born*. Peters, as Justin Wyatt details, was among a small vanguard of producers spearheading the 'pre-marketing' of films through their soundtracks (1994b, pp. 133–138). In the weeks before Columbia opened *Eyes of Laura Mars* theatrically, its soundtrack was released and songs from the film were played extensively by radio stations (ibid., pp. 136, 138). That soundtrack was dominated by disco tracks, including 'Boogie Nights' by Heatwave and Odyssey's 'Native New Yorker'. The focus on disco music extended to the film's audiovisual marketing materials, which opened, not with superstar Barbara Streisand's power-ballad theme song 'Prisoner', but with 'Let's all Chant', a disco anthem from the little-known Michael Zagar Band. Although *Eyes of Laura Mars* was not a blockbuster hit on the scale of *A Star is Born*, its $8.3m rentals indicated that using disco in a horror-murder-mystery could draw enough theatergoers to generate a sizable profit for a less expensive production, like *Prom Night*. In fact, the Prospectors behind *Prom Night* were not the only independent filmmakers to have recognized the economic promise of this approach, as *Variety* announced on 9 May 1979 the production of a film called 'Murder at Disco Down', the promotional artwork for which featured a pair of menacing eyes looking down onto a chalk outline of a body etched across a checkerboard dance-floor (Steinberg, 1979, p. 253). Industrial developments thus signaled that disco would be commercially viable material to imbed into *Halloween*'s story-structure.

Disco occupied a prominent location in *Prom Night*. A lingering close-up of spinning lights and a thumping drum beat herald Hamilton High's 'disco madness' prom, a four-minute dance number follows, and disco music plays on the soundtrack for the next 37 minutes. The names of the tracks — 'Love Me 'til I Die', 'Dancing in the Moonlight', 'It's Time to Turn around', 'Changes' and, of course, 'Prom Night' — are repeated continuously in the songs' choruses and reflect the principal elements of the film's content. Much like the killings in *Friday the 13th*, *Prom Night*'s dance sequences were significantly longer than strictly required to advance the narrative. The depiction of disco dancing was crucial to attracting young female theatergoers because, as feminist scholar Angela McRobbie has argued, 'for women and girls, dance has always offered a channel, albeit a limited one, for bodily self-expression and control, it has also been a source of pleasure and sensuality' (1984b, pp. 132–133). 'Even though it has often been directed towards men', she continued, 'the spectacle of women dancing has been linked unambiguously with female pleasure' (ibid.). However, the emphasis that the producers of *Prom Night* placed on this female-oriented material risked the alienation of male youth. Where the producers of the contemporaneous music-centered blockbusters *Grease* and *Saturday Night Fever* had counterbalanced displays of gyrating male hips and thrusting male pelvises with portrayals of misogynistic hyper-masculine groups of young men, *Prom Night*'s makers employed a different strategy to ensure that their film also could be angled to male youth. By inverting the gender dynamics of *Saturday Night Fever*, the Prospectors behind *Prom Night* substituted what Jeff Ynac described as the 'eroticized spectacle' of John Travolta with the highly sexualized dance performances of actress Jamie Lee Curtis (1996, pp. 39–53). Curtis, sporting a low-cut dress, is shown pirouetting, twirling, and high-kicking in a manner designed to invite a (heterosexual) male gaze (see Figure 4.6). In *Prom Night*, it really was murder on the dance-floor.

Writing in Toronto's *Globe and Mail* shortly after *Prom Night* hit theaters, Jay Scott, widely regarded as Canada's most respected and influential film critic, and an astute observer of film industry conduct, turned his attention to the efforts exerted to make the Canadian Prospector

FIGURE 4.6 Set-piece disco dancing in *Prom Night.*

Cash-in commercially viable (1980a). While he was well aware that *Prom Night* delivered just enough thrills and horror to give 'teen females the opportunity to scream and teen males the opportunity to manfully squeeze their not-really-all-that-scared dates' (ibid.), Scott highlighted the presence of additional non-horror content that 'must be present if the picture, directed at teen-agers of all ages, is to become a hit' (ibid). 'The high school heroine is attractive and self-possessed', he began: '[t]here is an attempt to capitalize on teen music'; 'A teen performs in some fashion — sings and/or dances'; 'The red herring villain is old and/or retarded and/or a former inmate of an insane asylum'; 'actual villains are twisted teens and/or villainous adults' (ibid.). Scott's list of what he called 'Clichés of Success' captured many of the ways in which his compatriots had drawn material from American hits to fashion a *Halloween* Cash-in that promised both to be an attractive proposition to MPAA-members and an appealing movie-going experience for American youths, particularly teenage girls and young women.

In sum, as a team of American independent filmmakers was attempting to capitalize on *Halloween* with a relatively gory animal comedy-infused murder-mystery called *Friday the 13th,* another group of Prospectors started production on a *Halloween* Cash-in. The inexperienced Canadian-based filmmakers behind *Prom Night* applied the *Meatballs* model to *Halloween*, reshaping the story-structure of Carpenter's Trailblazer Hit in the making into a female-centered disco-infused whodunit that took place in a Midwestern American high school. This approach, combining elements of content drawn from the youth-oriented hits *Carrie, Saturday Night Fever*, and *Grease*, not only veiled *Prom Night*'s Canadian production origins, but offered distributors the opportunity to expand attendance by angling the film to female youth. To make their Cash-in marketable to young female theatergoers, the filmmakers behind *Prom Night* downplayed thrills and horror (which also enabled them to circumvent domestic hostility), focusing instead on the romantic travails of a group of high school girls, and emphasizing disco music and dance.

Prom Night, as Jay Scott recognized on the film's release, had been fashioned to offer American distributors the oxymoronic prospect of a calculated sleeper hit. Yet, as *Friday the 13th* had indicated, it was nigh on impossible for independent filmmakers to predict, with any real accuracy, industrial developments that would take place once their film had gone into production, and it was incredibly difficult to forecast the behavior of MPAA-members and America's theatergoing youths. The next section shows that is precisely what Paul Lynch and his collaborators on *Prom Night* were about to discover.

'To watch them dance, to see them fall in love, to see them die': *Prom Night*, a Reinforcing Hit

Shots of young couples dancing at a graduation party were the first images that introduced American youth to *Prom Night* in the summer of 1980. The opening frames of the film's trailer were almost an exact replica of those that had opened *Carrie*'s trailer and a narrator reinforced connections between the Canadian teen slasher and Brian De Palma's female youth-centered horror hit. The same baritone that had summarized the tragic tale of high school scapegoat Carrie White informed young Americans that 'there's a special night in the lives of all of us, a night to be beautiful; to be desirable . . .'. *Prom Night*'s trailer demonstrated that the film's distributor shared the convictions of its producers: *Prom Night*'s prospects at the US box-office would be driven by its ability to attract young female theatergoers.

Although it is commonly assumed that early teen slashers were 'unambiguously advertised as horror movies' (Waller, 1987, p. 10), an examination of Avco Embassy's US release of *Prom Night* reveals that extent to which the films were framed differently for young females. In doing so, this section reveals that distributors looked to enhance the commercial viability of horror by evoking additional film-types for specific audience segments, thus inviting a reconsideration of the relationships between American distribution companies, scary movies, and teenage girls.

The strategy upon which a group of inexperienced Canadian filmmakers had banked so much, had secured *Prom Night* a foothold in the American market but, despite being tailored to appeal to a major studio, *Prom Night* had been picked up by mini-major Avco Embassy, a recent addition to the MPAA. The bidding-war that had taken place over *Friday the 13th* in spring 1980 had not been repeated for the right to distribute *Prom Night*. Instead, the Canadian teen slasher was a last-minute addition to Avco Embassy's list of summer releases after being purchased at the Cannes film market of May 1980 (Anon., 1980e, p. 27). *Prom Night*'s inability to secure major studio distribution was the result of three unforeseeable developments. First, re-shoots ordered by producer Peter Simpson delayed completion of the film by several months (Peter Simpson interviewed at 'Terror Trap'), in which time the majors had each already taken steps to capitalize on the commercial potential of youth-oriented horror films. Paramount had of course emerged victorious from the bidding-war over the domestic rights to *Friday the 13th* while Warner Bros. had secured the international rights to the film. Similarly, MGM/UA had picked up two youth-oriented horror productions, *He Knows You're Alone* and *Motel Hell* (both 1980), a fourth major, Twentieth Century Fox, had purchased the other Canadian-made teen slasher Prospector Cash-in, *Terror Train*, and Universal was producing its own teen horror film, *The Funhouse* (1981). Second, most of the major studios did not need to purchase an independently produced youth-oriented film like *Prom Night* because they had financed their own youth-market films for release in summer 1980: Warner Bros. had, via its subsidiary Orion Pictures, bankrolled the animal comedies *Up the Academy* and *Caddyshack*; Universal had produced the roller-disco movie *Xanadu* and the comedy sequel *Cheech & Chong's Next Movie*; and Columbia had financed the animal comedy *The Hollywood Knights* as well as *The Blue Lagoon*, a female-centered coming-of-age drama. It is also highly likely that *Prom Night*'s focus on disco music and dancing actually had alienated the majors. As *Variety* noted, 'the emphasis on the prom's discotheque look (. . .) seems to have dated the film before its release' (Berg., 1980, p. 20). Things move fast in Hollywood. In summer and early fall 1979, disco had been identified as a commercially viable trend by several film producers, many of whom had been responsible for bona fide hits. Yet, within the space of a year, disco had lost its shine completely. Columbia had put *Skatetown, U.S.A* into theaters as quickly as possible, but it had bombed.[28] In June of 1979, Irwin Yablans had billed *Roller Boogie* as 'the hot new musical movie that will take America by storm' (Compass International Films, 1979, p. 27). On the eve of *Roller Boogie*'s release, Yablans had even dismissed the commercial failure of *Skatetown U.S.A* as the result of a marketing miscalculation on the part of its distributor. '[T]he film was rushed too quickly into release', Yablans told *Variety*, 'and thus there was insufficient lead time to prepare a substantial advertising campaign' (quoted in Anon., 1979t, p. 23). Yablans may have been correct, but *Roller Boogie* did not 'take America by storm'. The film's disappointing box-office performance demonstrated that a large enough segment of the American youth-market did not exist to make roller-disco movies hits.[29] This view appears also to have been held by marketing executives at Universal, who, to the amusement of industry-watchers, went to great lengths in summer 1980 to conceal the wealth of content that *Xanadu* shared with the increasingly unpopular craze (Harmetz, 1980b, p. C15). '*Xanadu* (. . .) was born a disco-roller movie', wrote Richard Labonté, 'but when that fad died onscreen (witness the flops of *Skatetown, U.S.A.* and *Roller Boogie*) it was remoulded as a dance extravaganza, with a few numbers by veteran hoofer Gene Kelly blown out of all proportion in promotion for the feature' (1980a, p. 38). Despite this desperate effort to re-brand its property, Universal could not prevent *Xanadu* from being seen alongside Michael Cimino's Western *Heaven's Gate* as the biggest box-office failure of 1980 (Cook, 2000, p. 220). Disco was dead.

With the majors fully stocked with youth-oriented films, the door was left ajar for the smallest and least-capitalized MPAA-member to pick up the most commercially viable independent productions. In 1980, Avco Embassy stood unchallenged at the zenith of the second tier of the US film distribution hierarchy. A vanguard of small companies had competed with the majors in the youth-market during the 1970s, but by 1980, Allied Artists and Associated Film Distributors were financially crippled, AIP was fiscally wounded and in merger negotiations with Filmways (ibid., pp. 322–334), and many of the smaller independent distributors were struggling badly (Anon., 1979d, pp. 5, 40). Crown International Pictures had been unable to replicate the relative commercial success that it had enjoyed in previous years with films like *The Pom Pom Girls* (1976) and *The Van* (1977), and things were much worse for Dimension Pictures, which, as Ed Lowry details, stood on the verge of bankruptcy due to costly lawsuits initiated by disgruntled filmmakers (2005, p. 49). Its competitors' troubles, as Suzanne Mary Donahue points out (1987, p. 275), enabled Avco Embassy to briefly thrive by purchasing the distribution rights to independently produced youth-oriented films.

The emphasis that Avco Embassy placed on independently produced youth-market product was sparked by the precarious financial position in which it had found itself in the mid-to-late 1970s. The company became, as Cook explains, 'a briefly major force in the industry' in the late 1960s on the back of the 1967 blockbuster hit *The Graduate* (2000, pp. 322–334).[30] Avco Embassy had, however, fared badly in the mid 1970s as a consequence of the commercial failure of expensive films aimed at mature audiences such as 1973's *The Day of the Dolphin* (ibid., pp. 322–334). As a result of these flops, parent company Avco had slashed its film studio's in-house production budget, leaving management no other choice than to scour the market for completed films (Harmetz, 1981, p. C13). The downward spiral in which Avco Embassy had been thrust concluded for most industry analysts with the appointment in 1978 of an ambitious new vice-president of marketing (ibid.). That year, the company had head-hunted from New World Pictures, the most successful independent distributor of the decade, Robert Rehme. Under Rehme, Avco Embassy regrouped, consolidating its distribution operations with a back-to-basics strategy that re-channeled capital to the type of product that had catalyzed its brief flirtation with major status — films aimed at American youths.

In mid 1980, Avco Embassy placed enormous confidence in the box-office potential of youth-centered horror films. For example, that summer, as Robert E. Kapsis details, the company insisted that the independent producers of *Fear No Evil* (1981), to whom it had advanced some capital, emphasize the representation of teenagers (1993, pp. 163–164). Rehme had identified the financial viability of this kind of content when it emerged that *Halloween* was performing well, relative to its conditions of distribution (Anon., 1979f, p. 6) and the first film Avco Embassy released after *Halloween*, *Phantasm* (1979), underscored the potential of youth-centered horror when it became a minor hit and the company's highest earner of the year.[31] Rehme had then sought to build upon this achievement by securing the services of *Halloween*'s writer-director John Carpenter for a subsequent project, *The Fog* (1980). But with few youth-centered horror films having been produced in 1979, Avco Embassy was forced initially to purchase films that featured youth and horror separately.[32] As films of these types could be acquired for lower prices from Canadian producers than from their American competitors, the company looked north of the border consistently for commercially viable product. Thus, in 1980, three of Avco Embassy's ten releases were Canadian pickups: *Prom Night*, the animal comedy *Hog Wild*, and the adult-centered horror film *Death Ship* (Anon., 1980f, pp. 7, 36).

Avco Embassy's comeback as a distributor of youth-oriented product, with a discernible accent on horror, garnered mixed results in the spring of 1980. Despite being marketed to broaden attendance by conveying textual similarities to adventure films and disaster films, *Death Ship* had sunk without a trace.[33] The box-office performance of the company's second aquatic shocker was also disappointing, if not quite as catastrophic as *Death Ship*. Backed by horror-centered promotion, *The Fog*, while drifting into respectable profitability, had fallen considerably short of expectations.[34] The disappointing amount of revenue that Avco Embassy had generated from targeting *Death Ship* and *The Fog* almost exclusively to male audiences most likely played a role in the company's decision to angle *Prom Night* to female youth. The commercial viability of this approach had also been indicated to some extent by marketing materials used for the teen slasher hits of 1978 and 1980.

Displays of content thought to appeal specifically to teenage girls and young women had occupied an important, albeit secondary, position in marketing materials used in the promotion of *Halloween*, *Silent Scream*, and *Friday the 13th*. Although *Halloween* and *Friday the 13th* had primarily been sold in ways that invited parallels to horror blockbusters and to youth-oriented hits, their respective distributors had also taken steps to communicate the fact that the films had been produced for female as well as male youth. For example, Compass International had demonstrated that *Halloween* featured sequences of female-bonding by including the film's trio of high school girlfriends in its trailer and lobby cards. Lobby cards were also chosen by Paramount to suggest that *Friday the 13th* had been made with a young female audience in mind. The company used these photographs to emphasize, over *Friday the 13th*'s moments of horror, romance and active female protagonists, an approach that was encapsulated in an image that reversed the gender dynamics of a clichéd sexist joke by depicting the film's heroine showing a befuddled young man how to change a light-bulb (a shot that did not appear in the film). An even more overt bid for the attentions of young female theatergoers had been made by the distributor of *Silent Scream*, American Cinema Releasing. The majority of the company's theatrical trailer consisted of footage of a female youth investigating a dilapidated attic among which was interspersed shots of a young couple caressing tenderly and a young woman checking mysterious noises in a cellar. 'Are you afraid of the dark? Of being alone?', asked a narrator, 'or are you willing to explore the unknown — holding back your fear, allowing your natural curiosity to guide you?'. The voiceover provided a commentary of on-screen events while simultaneously issuing a challenge to a particular audience segment to overcome its fear and attend the film. Given that, in American culture, the prevailing image of fear of horror films is young and female, and that the act of overcoming fear was being performed in this horror film by young female characters, the object of address, and by extension the group being encouraged to purchase tickets, was evidently young and evidently female. The box-office achievements of *Halloween*, *Friday the 13th*, and *Silent Scream* had suggested that the commercial logic of angling teen slasher film promotion to teenage girls and young women was sound, and MPAA-members began to respond accordingly.

About a month before the release of *Prom Night*, one of the majors finally revealed publicly that it believed the financial prospects of films which featured shadowy maniacs and young people hinged on their capacity to garner the attendance of female youths. As was reported widely in the American press, MGM/UA had announced that, '[p]articular emphasis will be paid to the 15–21-year-old female audience' (Anon., 1980h, p. 15), when it came to promoting *He Knows You're Alone*, an independently produced serial killer film, featuring some twenty-something female characters, that the company had purchased after failing to secure *Friday the 13th*. The fact that *He Knows You're Alone* was not a teen slasher was largely irrelevant — early descriptions of the film made it clear that its content was fairly similar to that of *Prom Night*. What made this development particularly significant was the fact that the strategy was being employed, not by an inexperienced independent outfit, but by the distributor that had used similarly innovative marketing tactics to transform *Carrie* from a long shot with limited box-office potential into the highest earning youth-centred horror film in the history of the American market (Arnold, 1976b, p.141). If any distributor knew about the potential of selling horror to female youth it was MGM/UA and if any company was aware of developments in film marketing it was Avco Embassy, which, as Donahue explains, commonly invested up to six times as much in advertising its products than in producing or purchasing them (1987, p. 79). With *He Knows You're Alone* scheduled to hit American theaters later that fall, the opportunity presented itself for Avco Embassy to be the first company to distinguish its film in the marketplace with what promised to be a lucrative approach to horror marketing.

Avco Embassy's marketing campaign for *Prom Night* placed more emphasis on female youth-oriented material than that of any other horror film since *Carrie*. The company targeted *Prom Night* squarely to young females while taking steps to avoid the alienation of the male youths that were considered to dominate horror film attendance. The film's promotional poster sought to invite comparisons to *Halloween* and to appeal to young females. The artwork used to advertise Carpenter's Trailblazer Hit was evoked iconographically, compositionally, and stylistically by the location, against a dark background, of a menacing face, a hand, and a bladed-weapon (see Figure 4.7). However, the taglines used on the two posters indicated that *Prom Night*'s distributor had employed fairly overt tactics to attract female youth. Where the tagline 'The Night *He* Came Home' had stressed male narrative centrality in *Halloween*, *Prom Night*'s poster's tagline — 'If you're not back by midnight . . . you won't be coming home' — addressed teenage girls directly by pairing the clichéd lexicon of the overbearing patriarch and a reference to Cinderella. *Prom Night*'s poster hinted at the more elaborate techniques Avco Embassy employed in audiovisual marketing materials.

Prom Night's theatrical trailer and TV spots presented elements that were primarily designed to appeal to female youth in ways that would not alienate young males, while elements used to attract male youth

FIGURE 4.7 Evoking *Halloween* and addressing female youth to promote *Prom Night*.

were selected so as not to put off young females. A film's marketing materials, as both Altman (1999, p. 54) and Lisa Kernan (2004, p. 167) demonstrated, have historically been constructed in such ways as to target different audience segments by implying the diverse attractions that are offered by an individual film. These scholars show that, rather than each frame exhibiting a sense of cross-demographic appeal, the montages which comprise most trailers incorporate components or 'hooks' that have been selected specifically to resonate with different audience segments.[35] In the case of *Prom Night*, audiovisual marketing materials were fashioned to target young females immediately by beginning with montages dominated by female youth-oriented hooks. Once the film was presented as offering pleasures to young women, the trailer and TV spots concluded with 'female-friendly' depictions of attractions that were considered to appeal more strongly to male youth. These sections were bookended with different title logos. The first, reminiscent of *Saturday Night Fever*'s logo, was shown during the female youth-oriented section to highlight the fact that *Prom Night* shared features with roller-disco movies (see Figure 4.8). The second logo, in red with blood dripping from each letter, concluded the male youth-oriented sections and signaled the presence of horror-related content (see Figure 4.9).

The female youth-oriented sections of *Prom Night*'s trailer and TV spots highlighted dance, romance, and female beauty rituals in ways that showed male spectators the pleasures afforded by the eroticized female body. In this respect, these sections mirrored the steps taken by Columbia and UA to avoid the alienation of male youth when promoting their respective roller-disco movies, *Skatetown, U.S.A* and *Roller Boogie*. While *Skatetown, U.S.A* and *Roller Boogie* had performed poorly at the US box-office, it appears that Avco Embassy felt that the evocation of roller-disco movies still had the capacity to increase attendance by securing some young female theatergoers. This approach is shown clearly in *Prom*

FIGURE 4.8 Marking *Prom Night* as a disco movie.

FIGURE 4.9 Marking *Prom Night* as a horror film.

Night's TV spots. 'These are the girls of Hamilton High, and tonight they will be more beautiful than ever before in their lives', declared a male narrator over a montage of beauty rituals. The statement was much like Columbia's invitation to male youth to admire 'the most beautiful girls' in *Skatetown, U.S.A.* The voice-over that opened *Prom Night*'s other TV spot and its theatrical trailer, also employed this dual mode of address. As noted above, the narrator proclaimed, '[t]here's a special night in the lives of all of us, a night to be beautiful; to be desirable; a night when we can break all the rules and make our own'. While the 'us' testified to its direct address to female youth, the close-ups of pouting female lips, pulsating breasts, and quivering denim-clad buttocks that accompanied the declaration, presented a performance of femininity designed to satisfy a heterosexual male gaze.

The emphasis that Avco Embassy placed on addressing male and female youth shifted in the second halves of *Prom Night*'s audiovisual marketing tools. In these montages, the company attempted to assure young men that they too could enjoy *Prom Night* without alienating the young women whom it already had endeavored to attract. Avco Embassy's approach was, however, slightly different than in the first halves of the TV spots and trailer. Rather than selecting images which were likely to appeal to both audience segments simultaneously, the company combined shots from the film that communicated *Prom Night*'s capacity to horrify, thrill, and intrigue the audience with shots of romantic action and dance. It seems two factors informed this approach. First, because female-oriented hooks had already been established within the 'traditionally male' domain of the horror film, it became necessary to establish the presence of material that would appeal to male youth. Second, where images of conventionally attractive female teens lent themselves to the perceived desires of male youth, shots of a shadowy maniac prowling school halls were framed less easily in ways that would, in theory at least, resonate with young women. Thus, the second half of one of *Prom Night*'s TV spots consisted of nine shots which established the film to be an intriguing whodunit by showing a mysterious ax-wielding figure lurking in the shadows. These shots were followed swiftly by two shots of a young couple disco dancing. The approach was repeated when a close-up of the killer's weapon was followed by two shots of young couples. In the first, the girl is shown resting her head on her partner's shoulder. In the second, a different young woman appears to have initiated a passionate embrace. From there, the TV spot established *Prom Night*'s capacity to provoke thrills and horror. In quick succession, two shots showed a female youth recognizing that the killer was about to strike and then screaming. The TV spot concluded with the blood-dripping logo. Throughout this fleeting montage a narrator had reinforced the coexistence of romance with horror, thrills, and intrigue in the film. 'For some it's the end of innocence', he proclaimed, 'for others it's the end'. A comparable collection of images comprised the second half of *Prom Night*'s other TV spot and its voice-over expressed similar sentiments. 'Someone will come to the prom alone', we hear, 'just to watch them dance, to see them fall in love, to see them die'.

Backed by Avco Embassy's sophisticated marketing campaign, *Prom Night* appeared well positioned to emulate the healthy box-office returns of *Friday the 13th*. Ten weeks had passed since *Variety* predicted that *Friday the 13th* would perform abysmally at American theaters (Step., 1980, p. 14). Of course, that prediction had been wide of the mark. In the wake of *Friday the 13th*, *Variety* sounded a more optimistic note when it forecast *Prom Night*'s financial prospects. 'Nice initial boxoffice [sic] action for distrib[utor] Avco Embassy', noted the trade paper on the eve of the film's US release (Berg., 1980, p. 20). However, *Prom Night* generated only $6m in rentals (Anon., 1981a, p. 29). This figure was bettered by 52 of the 192 new films that were released in 1980 (Anon., 1981a, p. 29; Cook, 2000, p. 492). Indeed, *Prom Night*'s rentals were surpassed easily by each of the film's nine immediate competitors and represented little more than a third of the sum that had been generated by *Friday the 13th*.[36] On the surface, then, *Prom Night* seemed to have been a considerable box-office disappointment. Yet, the conditions under which *Prom Night* was distributed suggest something quite different, and it is only through an examination of the film's conditions of distribution that the true significance of *Prom Night*'s commercial performance can be appreciated.

Despite placing considerable value on the youth-market, Avco Embassy seriously misjudged the timing of *Prom Night*'s release. In contrast to Paramount's distribution of *Friday the 13th*, at a moment of low competition for youth-oriented films and horror movies, on 18 July 1980, 195 prints of *Prom Night* were thrust into the most fiercely contested period of the year for the attentions of young audiences (Avco Embassy Pictures, 1980, p. 24). Not only was *Prom Night* required to compete with *Cheech & Chong's Next Movie* during its all-important opening weekend, but its appeal to male and female youth was undermined by a plethora of major studio-distributed films. The hit comedies *Airplane!* and *The Blues Brothers* continued to draw audiences, and Columbia's teen romance *The Blue Lagoon*, like Fox's youth comedy *My Bodyguard*, had entered the second and third weeks of their theatrical runs. Seven days later, the American giallo *Dressed to Kill* and the animal comedy *Caddyshack* entered the fray, followed swiftly by the roller-disco movie *Xanadu* and the calculated blockbuster *Smokey and the Bandit II*. Indeed, during this whole period, the two biggest horror hits of the summer — *Friday the 13th* and *The Shining* — had still been on release in the US. Nine of these films went on to place in the top twenty of the annual rentals chart (Anon., 1981a, p. 29), while the other two, *Xanadu* and *My Bodyguard*, sold enough tickets to secure 32nd and 36th place respectively (see Table 4.3).

Relative to such highly adverse conditions of distribution, *Prom Night* was not really a commercial failure; a point that was made by Laurie Warner of the *Los Angeles Times* in a report on the financial performances of the summer's horror films. 'Now showing is "Prom Night"', wrote Warner, '[i]magine: it did a reported $1.3m in its premiere nights — in only New York and L.A. theatres' (Warner, 1980, p. R5). *Prom Night* was in fact generating more revenue per theater than *Friday the 13th*, and, of the 77 films that were not distributed by the major studios or their affiliates in 1980, only three films, *Dressed to Kill*, *The Fog*, and the Chuck Norris martial arts vehicle *The Octagon* returned more in rentals than *Prom Night* (Anon., 1981a, pp. 29, 50). The bottom line read that *Prom Night* had been profitable, despite its distributor's inability to finance a wide opening and in the face of intense competition. As such, *Prom Night*'s returns represented a considerable achievement and, although it was not readily apparent from its US theatrical rentals alone, the Canadian-made Prospector Cash-in, like its American counterpart *Friday the 13th*, had became a Reinforcing Hit.

TABLE 4.3 Top rental youth-oriented films, May–August 1980.

Film	Release	Distributor	Rentals ($m)	Position
Airplane!	07/02/80	Paramount	40.6	4th/1980
Smokey and the Bandit II	08/15/80	Universal	37.6	5th/1980
The Blues Brothers	06/20/80	Universal	31	9th/1980
The Shining	05/23/80	Warner Bros.	30.2	10th/1980
The Blue Lagoon	07/05/80	Columbia	28.4	11th/1980

(continued over page)

TABLE 4.3   (*continued*)

Film	Release	Distributor	Rentals ($m)	Position
Cheech & Chong's Next Movie	07/18/80	Universal	21	15th/1980
Caddyshack	07/25/80	Orion/Warner Bros.	20	17th/1980
Friday the 13th	05/09/80	Paramount	16.5	20th/1980
Dressed to Kill	07/25/80	Filmways	15	23rd/1980
Xanadu	08/08/80	Universal	10.2	32nd/1980
My Bodyguard	07/11/80	Fox	9.6	36th/1980
Prom Night	07/18/80	Avco Embassy	6	53rd/1980

When *Prom Night*'s box-office performance was considered alongside that of *Friday the 13th*, a clearer picture of the economic viability of teen slasher film production and distribution emerged. Ticket sales for *Prom Night* signaled to the North American movie business a commercial robustness to the teen slasher film that could not otherwise have been determined by the economic achievements of *Friday the 13th*. The rentals of *Friday the 13th* may have signaled the financial potential of teen slasher films under optimal distribution conditions — saturation booking and blitz marketing at a time of minimal competition — but *Prom Night* had indicated that the new film-type could compete in a particularly crowded market and still secure a large enough segment of the youth audience to ensure profitability when it was angled to female youth.

In sum, despite having been tailored to appeal to the US distribution elite, *Prom Night* was not purchased by a major studio. While its focus on disco likely alienated the majors, most of these companies already had made arrangements to release youth-oriented product in summer 1980 and therefore no longer needed to acquire independent productions. *Prom Night* did, however, exhibit enough commercial potential to be picked up by MPAA-member mini-major Avco Embassy — a company that concentrated on the American youth-market and often purchased Canadian films. Avco Embassy promoted *Prom Night* heavily to young females while aiming to avoid the alienation of their male peers. The company, however, mistimed the release of *Prom Night*. Overwhelming competition from several major studio-distributed blockbusters and youth-oriented films, in combination with Avco Embassy's inability to finance a wide opening, prevented *Prom Night* from emulating the box-office achievements of *Friday the 13th*. Yet, by remaining profitable, despite these adverse conditions, *Prom Night* indicated a commercial robustness to teen slasher film distribution that could not have been ascertained from *Friday the 13th*'s ticket sales due to their having been generated under exceptionally privileged conditions, and seemed to confirm that young female ticket-buyers held the key to generating profits from teen slasher film distribution.

Conclusion

Canadian-based filmmakers, particularly the Prospectors behind *Prom Night*, contributed hugely to the rise to prominence of the teen slasher film, a film-type that is usually associated solely with the American film industry. By 1979, the Canadian government had put in place several mechanisms that had increased the competitiveness of filmmakers based in Canada. Production subsidies and a tax shelter enabled filmmakers to offer films to MPAA-member distributors at lower prices than their tax-paying American competitors. The new head of the state funding body, the CFDC, had prioritized youth-oriented Cash-ins and one of these films had become a hit on the American market. In doing so, *Meatballs* had indicated a potentially lucrative new production/textual model that had appealed to a US major and American youth. Producing a US-set Prospector Cash-in to a youth-oriented Trailblazer Hit (or a film that appeared destined to become a Trailblazer Hit) and expanding address to a demographic segment that had been less important to the Trailblazer Hit appeared finally to offer Canadian filmmakers a reasonable chance of securing MPAA-member distribution south of the border. A group of novice Canadian filmmakers applied the *Meatballs* model to *Halloween*, the only youth-oriented film that seemed set to become a Trailblazer Hit and which had not already prompted significant quantities of Cash-in productions. They tailored their film to appeal to young women by amp-lifying *Halloween*'s, not insignificant, representation of, and address to, female youth. Drawing on several youth-oriented and horror hits, the Canadian Prospectors re-shaped *Halloween*'s story-structure into a female-centered disco-infused whodunit, downplaying thrilling and horrifying material so as to avoid domestic hostility. *Prom Night* demonstrated the commercial potential of the teen slasher under highly unfavorable con-ditions, when it remained profitable despite being released at arguably the most competitive period of the year for youth-oriented films. Avco Embassy's predominantly female youth-oriented marketing campaign indicated that the relative success of the film was down to its ability to secure the patronage of young women.

By the end of the summer of 1980, *Halloween* appeared to be anything but an anomalous one-off success story. The commercial potential of the Trailblazer Hit's story-structure had been underscored not by one but by two Reinforcing Hits, both of which had in quick succession secured distribution from MPAA-members and had, relative to their conditions of distribution, performed remarkably well at the US box-office. Indeed, in addition to *Friday the 13th* and *Prom Night*, the remaining Prospector Cash-in, *Terror Train*, was about to be opened by another MPAA-member, Fox, in a staggering 1000 American theaters (David Novak Associates Inc., 1980) — 250 more than first planned (Schnurmacher, 1980, p. 69). The implications of these developments are taken up in the next, and final, chapter in which it is shown that, although the teen slasher was transforming from a financially perilous undertaking into arguably the single most attractive film-type of its time, the teen slasher was about to become a victim of its own success.

Chapter 5

The Animal House on Sorority Row

Boom and bust, and the establishment of the teen slasher film,
1980–1981

A blood-curdling scream escapes a female mouth and shrieks puncture the air as water-doused sorority sisters perform for a crowd of raucous onlookers. Screams give way to drumbeats and rock music, a young couple embraces, a partygoer swigs a beer, and a boisterous mob of students descends upon a fraternity house. Finally, a triumphant bugle chorus and blazing beacons herald the passage of teen-filled cars through a darkened hillside path.

The opening shots of the trailer for the teen slasher film *Hell Night* (1981) captured shifts in industry perceptions, signaled the crystallization of a textual model, and proclaimed the return of the 'merchant of menace' (Chase, 1981b, p. C8). By combining teen romance and animal comedy with an unidentified threat, this fleeting montage encapsulated the impact of recent industry developments on teen slasher film content while, to the evocative mix of drums, bugles, and torchbearers, Irwin Yablans, the producer-distributer of *Halloween* (1978), announced his return to teen slasher filmmaking with a Cash-in that he boasted to the *Hollywood Reporter* would 'make a fortune' (quoted in V. Scott, 1981). Yet, when considered within the context of then-recent industrial developments, desperation permeated the trailer and Yablans' line-shooting seemed like blind optimism or hopeless delusion. Yablans had, after all, initially abstained from producing films modeled on *Halloween* in favor of bankrolling box-office flops like the city vs. country horror film *Tourist Trap* and the vampire comedy *Nocturna* (both 1979). As a consequence of these decisions, the independent entrepreneurs behind *Friday the 13th*, *Prom Night*, and *Terror Train* (all 1980) had capitalized swiftly on *Halloween* by selling similar films to powerful distributors. 'I could probably sue, but I won't', mocked Yablans, '"Hell Night" will be better than all of them. I've improved the formula' (quoted in ibid.). In August 1981, *Hell Night* was poised to open in 600 North American theaters (ibid.), and, according to *Variety*, the commercial prospects of Yablans' second teen slasher were bleak (Lor., 1981b, p.14). Much had changed from late 1980 to late 1981.

This chapter focuses on the short period during which the teen slasher transformed from a financially perilous undertaking into a highly attractive prospect for independent producers before confidence in the film-type evaporated almost completely, and during which the production and release of a 'group of eleven' Carpetbagger Cash-ins ensured that the teen slasher became firmly established as part of the North American film industry's repertoire of youth-market product. By demonstrating that a combination of over-production, insufficient product differentiation at the levels of film production and promotion, and market-saturation account, in large part, for the decline in teen slasher production after 1980, this chapter shows that the conditions which initiate the widespread production of a film-type tend to lead to its swift erasure from production and distribution rosters. In doing so, the chapter suggests that the short life-spans, above base level production, of most film-types, may be an inevitable consequence of film markets being unable to sustain product for which demand is invariably exceeded by supply. Or, to put it another way, once filmmakers and distributors start to act on the belief that a film-type is commercially viable, the commercial viability of the film-type plummets. This view was certainly held by one executive who claimed that as soon as one had spotted a trend in moviemaking, the chances were it was already box-office poison (Gabe Sumner cited in Donahue, 1987, p. 89). The case of the first teen slasher film cycle's boom and bust period points to a great irony in North American 'genre filmmaking'; that the greatest monetary rewards tend to be enjoyed by those who produce examples of a film-type when its commercial potential is unclear while those who embark upon production when the film-type's commercial potential seems enormous are often left out-of-pocket, a state of affairs which in turn suggests that the implementation of tried-and-tested textual models, so as to reduce the inherent risks of crafting capital-intensive product that does not reach consumers for a significant amount of time, provides less a secure safety net than a collection of frayed threads.

'It was a no-brainer':
Carpetbagger Cash-ins and the Contexts of Over-production

The Trailblazer Hit *Halloween* is positioned consistently, yet inaccurately, as having triggered the production surge that resulted in unprecedented numbers of new teen slasher films flooding American theaters in 1981. For example, Vera Dika (1990, p. 85) links the explosion in teen slashers to the low budgets required to craft films in the vein of *Halloween*. Standard thinking is represented by Carol J. Clover (1992, p. 24), Robert E. Kapsis (1992, pp. 159–169), and Stephen Prince (2000 pp. 224–225, 351–352), who all suggest that the teen slasher boom was part of a general surge in horror film production, which, they propose, was also ignited by *Halloween*. Over the next two years [1979–1980]', suggests Kapsis, 'film companies produced a large number of films so similar to the *Halloween* formula that a new subgenre of horror emerged' (1992, p. 159). These accounts are, however, complicated by the fact that most of the teen slashers — eleven out of fourteen to be precise — were produced in late 1980, almost two years after *Halloween* was released.

The failure to distinguish between the handful of Prospector Cash-ins made in 1979 to capitalize on *Halloween* and the significantly larger number of Carpetbagger Cash-ins that were, for different reasons, produced over a year later, has resulted in scholars painting a misleading picture of the conditions that led to the teen slasher film boom of 1981. Due to its status as a Trailblazer Hit that had not been followed by a Reinforcing Hit, its inability to secure distribution from a member-studio of the Motion Picture Association of America (MPPA), and the overwhelming appeal of other youth-oriented and horror films-type, *Halloween* did not initiate significant numbers of Cash-ins. Moreover, those filmmakers that confronted the perceived risks of Prospector Cash-in production had each relied on exceptional industrial/economic circumstances unavailable to most of their competitors. The extent to which *Halloween* did not influence production patterns was encapsulated in a startling statistic: fewer teen slashers were being produced in the United States in 1979 after the relative commercial success of *Halloween* became apparent than when *Halloween* was in production in late 1977. Indeed, even when the two Canadian-made Cash-ins, *Prom Night* and *Terror Train*, are taken into account, the increase in teen slasher production brought about by Carpenter's Trailblazer Hit amounted to a solitary film.

The absence of a systematic, coherent, and exhaustive account of the rapid upsurge in teen slasher production that took place in late 1980 has been highlighted by David A. Cook (2000, p. 237). Yet, ironically, the titles that Cook cites, point to the primary impediment that has restricted his, and others', ability to resolve this issue. It is unfeasible to distil to a single set of conditions the production of such diverse films as the revenge-of-nature narrative *Blood Beach*, the teen slasher sequel *Friday the 13th Part II* (both 1981), and *Maniac* (1980), a bleak character study of a New York serial killer (ibid.). Instead of searching for a single set of conditions that gave rise to several different types of film, I believe it is more fruitful to consider the relative commercial viability of the film-types available to filmmakers at a particular moment in time, in order to ascertain which of those film-types offered filmmakers a way of realizing their commercial objectives. In the case of the teen slasher film production explosion of late 1980, it is necessary to examine the ways in which the economic potential of the range of youth-oriented and horror film-types available to independent filmmakers differed between 1979 when teen slasher production was viewed with great caution and late 1980 when it was seen to be exceptionally attractive. The teen slasher film production boom of late 1980 was triggered by a network of factors relating to the relative commercial viability of teen slashers and other types of horror film and youth-oriented film.

Several obstacles to MPAA-member distribution undermined independent filmmakers' confidence in the youth-oriented and horror film-types that had appeared, eighteen months earlier, to be more commercially viable than *Halloween* Cash-ins. Back in 1979, independent youth-oriented film production had been dominated by films that were made to capitalize on the blockbuster hits *Saturday Night Fever* (1977), *Grease*, and *Animal House* (both 1978).[1] However, by summer 1980, it had become clear that MPAA-members were unlikely to offer pickup deals for gang movies, roller-disco movies, and animal comedies, and as the next section explains, uncertainties also existed as to the commercial viability of independently produced female-centered coming-of-age dramas.

Little incentive remained for independent producers to make animal comedies, 'the genre of raunchy farces spawned in the wake of "National Lampoon's Animal House" (. . .)', to use *Washington Post* writer Gary Arnold's description (1980b, p. B9). The capacity to produce *Animal House* Cash-ins on low budgets had prompted considerable activity across the North American film industry in 1979. The intensive production of the films had even prompted Stephen Harvey to write in the September/October 1980 edition of *Film Comment* that '[t]he closest thing to a fresh trend to be spotted this summer has been the spate of fart-jiggle-pratfall orgies at the high school-drive-in-golf-course inspired by the memory of those millions of adolescents who queued up for *Animal House*' (1980,

p. 49). A similar observation was made by Christopher Hicks of the *Desert News.* 'Ever Since "Animal House", bemoaned Hicks, 'we've essentially had "Animal House" goes to camp ("Gorp"); "Animal House" goes to military academy ("Up the Academy"); "Animal House" goes to Hollywood Blvd. ("The Hollywood Knights"); and "Animal House" goes golfing ("Caddyshack")' (C. Hicks, 1980, p. C7). Yet, because MPAA-members had financed and distributed their own animal comedies — *Caddyshack, The Hollywood Knights,* and *Up the Academy* (all 1980) — independent productions like *H.O.T.S, King Frat,* and *Squeeze Play* (all 1979) had been surplus to the MPAA-members' requirements.[2] Restricted to a handful of down-market theaters or left to gather dust on producers' shelves, these films, and others like them, were loss-making ventures.[3] With no news of the majors buying animal comedies for release in 1981, one of the most commercially attractive film-types of 1979 offered little to independent filmmakers in late 1980. If the conduct of industry gatekeepers had stricken animal comedy from independent production rosters, America's theatergoing youths ensured that gang movies and roller-disco movies had become a thing of the past.

When several filmmakers extracted *Saturday Night Fever*'s hypermasculine young men from their romantic and dance-floor contexts, Gregg Kilday of the *Los Angeles Times* predicted that 1979 would 'go down in the record books as the year of the gang movie' (1978, p. L23). Yet, within less than twelve months, the *New York Times*' industry analyst Aljean Harmetz was announcing that '[d]efinitely consigned to the 1980 dustbin are gang movies' (1979a, p. D5). This dramatic turnabout took place because independently produced examples like *Sunnyside* and *Over the Edge,* much like the MPAA-member versions *Walk Proud, Boulevard Nights,* and *The Wanderers* (all 1979), disappointed commercially.[4] Several of these films, including *The Warriors* (the only gang movie to make it into the black) had also triggered violence during screenings which had required distributors to pay compensation to theater-owners and to finance new — and less provocative — marketing campaigns.[5] In light of their poor ticket sales and their capacity to excite social unrest, gang movies no longer seemed the ideal instrument with which independent filmmakers could secure an MPAA-member distribution deal and production of the film-type ground to a halt. Roller-disco movies, which blended the soundtrack and dance styles of *Saturday Night Fever* with the fun-toned adolescent milieu of *Grease,* also proved unappealing to their young, and predominantly female, target audience, as chapter four showed.[6] Following the lackluster returns of *Skatetown, U.S.A* and *Roller Boogie* (both 1979), a 'threatened, er, promised cycle of roller-disco romps', that Gary Arnold had anticipated would follow the release of *Skatetown, U.S.A*, failed to materialize (1979c, pp. E1, E7).

The commercial failure of gang movies and roller-disco movies along with the MPAA-members distribution of self-financed animal comedies deterred independents from producing the youth-oriented film-types that had initially overshadowed *Halloween* Cash-in production, meaning that, by late-summer 1980, the range of commercially viable youth-market film-types available to independents had, in comparison to 1979, narrowed considerably. Industrial, as well as social, developments across 1979 and 1980 also ensured that most of the horror film-types that had appealed to independent filmmakers eighteen months earlier, no longer seemed attractive.

The confidence that independent filmmakers had placed in established horror film-types securing MPAA-member distribution deals proved misplaced. In contrast to 1979, demonic child, revenge-of-nature, and city vs. country films were no longer seen to be financially viable options. In the aftermath of the huge losses Warner Bros. incurred with *Exorcist II: The Heretic* (1977), and the underwhelming performance of similar films, MPAA-members turned their backs on demonic child films like *The Brood, The Orphan* (both 1979), and *The Changeling* (1980), all of which performed badly.[7] 'Possession films are not working right now', Robert Cort, vice-president of advertising and publicity at Fox, had warned (quoted in Harmetz, 1980d, p. C15). These sentiments were echoed by Avco Embassy's Don Borchers, who declared that '[i]f you spend $6.5m on a movie starring George C. Scott about a house that's possessed [*The Changeling*], you're not going to make money' (quoted in ibid.). Similarly, a survey of distribution rosters suggests that Hollywood executives had not considered independently produced city vs. country horror films such as *Survival Run* (1979) and *Tourist Trap* or revenge-of-nature films like *Blood Beach* to be commercially viable product. In the absence of MPAA-member pickup deals, the makers of these films and others like them had been reliant on small financially unstable distribution companies. The same situation befell the independent producers of vampire films after the MPAA-members' own contributions fell short of box-office predictions.[8] Indications that horror filmmaking was in a period of transition may have been confirmed by the decline of these once-reliable models, but, in late 1980, the shape of 1980s horror was far from certain with many of the new textual models that surfaced in 1979 having proven to be commercially disappointing.

The ability to provide replicable and cost-effective textual models of two big-budget horror films — *Alien* (1979) and *The Shining* (1980)

— remained inconclusive. While both calculated blockbusters had drawn sizeable audiences to American theaters, their impact on production patterns had been stifled by the enormous expenditure required to achieve this feat.[9] As Cook shows, despite generating the fifth-highest rentals of 1979, *Alien*, because of its massive $27m production and marketing budget, took 'almost a year to show a modest gain' of $4m (2000, p. 61). A year later, *Variety* was reporting that *The Shining* had just broken even, but only as a result of highly favorable deals Warner Bros. had negotiated with exhibitors (Cohn, 1981, pp. 7, 42). These conditions could have prompted independent filmmakers to craft cut-price imitations so as to enable the MPAA-members to capitalize on the not-inconsiderable-levels of audience interest in both films. Yet, in the absence of Reinforcing Hits, neither *Alien* nor *The Shining* was able to unambiguously communicate a commercially viable approach to balancing evocation of the hit with textual differentiation. The narrative ambiguities of *The Shining* seem to have complicated Cash-in production further. The film's 'supernatural story', observed Janet Maslin, 'knows frustratingly little rhyme or reason' (1980b, p. C8). Conversely, imitation of *Alien*'s futuristic imagery and creature effects represented arguably the most potent method of capitalizing on the film. However, such an approach required amounts of capital that were beyond the reach of most independent filmmakers. Under these conditions, producing a Cash-in to *Alien* and *The Shining* appeared an excessively risky undertaking, and neither option was pursued by significant numbers of independent filmmakers in late 1980.

Factors beyond economics chronically undermined confidence in another nascent horror film-type, the American giallo. Although box-office returns for *Cruising* and, particularly, *Dressed to Kill*, had been respectable, if unspectacular, the appeal of basing films on either of these violent murder-mysteries was tempered by high-profile controversies they had triggered. With activist organizations and factions of the American media having leveled charges of homophobia at the makers of *Cruising* and having accused *Dressed to Kill*'s writer-director Brian De Palma of misogyny (Lewis, 2002, pp. 276–280; Vaughn, 2006, pp. 59–63, 109–110), few independent producers believed MPAA-members would buy similar films.[10] I will be returning to the ways these controversies impacted the production and content of teen slashers, however, at this stage it is important to note that the furor surrounding *Cruising* and *Dressed to Kill* cemented the belief that the production of low-budget adult-centered serial killer films was no longer politically viable. With a paucity of pickup offers and woeful ticket sales already having rendered the film-types financially questionable, in late 1980 independent filmmakers all but stopped targeting MPAA-members with downbeat character studies in the vein of *Don't Go in the House* (1980) or tales of itinerant maniacs à la *Schizoid* (1980). Where a cocktail of protests, critical outrage, and commercial underachievement had rendered politically and economically problematic the majority of film-types featuring multiple murderers, one approach had largely avoided controversy and demonstrated an uncanny ability to attract MPAA-member distributors and sizable audiences.

In stark contrast to the types of film that had seemed so lucrative in 1979, the teen slasher's market value soared during summer 1980 to such heights that it was arguably the hottest production trend in American moviemaking. In mild 1980, the teen slasher film had been the only independently produced low-budget film-type to have secured MPAA-member distribution and proven to be financially successful on a consistent basis. That part of the year marked the first occasion upon which these pivotal developments had occurred in tandem. Previously, these factors in isolation had failed to spark widespread production of the film-type. As chapter two showed, woeful US theatrical returns had neutralized Warner Bros.' distribution of the Pioneering teen slasher *Black Christmas* (1974), while *Halloween*'s impressive rentals had been offset by its producer's need to self-distribute — a notoriously unpredictable method of moneymaking. The handful of filmmakers that had adopted the high-risk strategy of evoking Carpenter's film had discovered that their peers' reservations were not shared by MPAA-members. *Friday the 13th, Prom Night,* and *Terror Train* all had generated swift profits for their producers after being purchased by MPAA-members. This shift exerted a profound influence on independent filmmakers because it demonstrated that powerful distributors had placed their confidence in the film-type. The point is made clear by Gary Sales, the producer of the Carpetbagger Cash-in *Madman* (1981). '*Halloween* was distributed by Compass International, but *Friday the 13th* was distributed by Paramount', Sales explained, 'and that was the big change in the fate of films of this nature, a major studio released an independent picture' ('Filmmakers Commentary', 2001). Moreover, as chapters three and four demonstrated, *Friday the 13th* and *Prom Night*, the two teen slashers that had been released in summer 1980, had both performed admirably at the US box-office.[11] In confirming that *Halloween* was not an inexplicable anomaly, *Friday the 13th* had, in the words of Martin Rubin, 'demonstrated the bedrock commercial strength of the basic formula' (1999, p. 162). Fuelled by saturation booking at a point of limited competition for youth audiences, the film had signaled the economic potential of the teen slasher under premium distribution conditions. Conversely, by proving profitable at the most competitive period of the year for youth-oriented product, *Prom Night* had indicated the durability of the film-type.[12] The middle of 1980 was thus a pivotal period for the teen slasher film, and the popular press had been on hand to report it in ways that amplified the commercial potential of the film-type.

Journalists had ensured that by the end of summer 1980 there cannot have been many independent filmmakers in North America that were unaware of the fact that some of their own kind were enjoying the enormous financial and professional rewards of having produced hit teen slasher films. With the story of *Prom Night*'s robust ticket sales just beginning to break, attention had circulated around *Friday the 13th*. In stark contrast to their coverage of *Halloween*, the American trade and popular press had been quick to report on the box-office achievements of *Friday the 13th*, devoting endless pages to the subject, and framing the story in such a way as to imply that the principal beneficiary of the film's financial achievements was not distributor Paramount Pictures, which actually collected the lion's share of the profits, but producer-director Sean S. Cunningham and screenwriter Victor Miller. In much the same way as it had contributed to the widespread reluctance among independent entrepreneurs to model films on *Halloween* in 1979, the press served a crucial role in fuelling the surge in teen slasher film production that took place across the second half of 1980.

Where *Halloween*'s region-by-region roll out had prevented it from accumulating rentals rapidly, thus ensuring that genuine box-office success was slow to come and slow to be reported, the pattern of distribution given by Paramount to *Friday the 13th* ensured that journalists had been able to report its success story within weeks of the film's theatrical debut. Moreover, the celebratory discussions of film style and aesthetics that often overwhelmed economic matters in the reception of *Halloween* did not enter in any meaningful way into coverage of *Friday the 13th*, which was largely dismissed as a derivative and workmanlike yet highly effective exercise in commercial exploitation. Thus, while panning *Friday the 13th* as 'a truly awful movie' (Siskel, 1980a, p. A9) and as a 'silly, boring youth-geared horror movie' (Gross, 1980b, p. 17), the US press was swift, loud, and hyperbolic in trumpeting the film's box-office achievements.

The American trade press, along with newspapers spread across the United States and Canada, ran article after article in which the solid box-office performance of *Friday the 13th* was overstated to such an extent that it was compared to that of *The Empire Strikes Back* (1980), the year's only genuine 'superhit', to borrow Peter Krämer's term (2005, p. 6). The *New York Times* alone published three pieces all proclaiming *Friday the 13th* the second biggest hit of the summer (Boyles, 1980, p. D17; Harmetz, 1980a, p. C14; Harmetz, 1980c, p. C4). 'Of approximately 20 movies released during the last six weeks', wrote Aljean Harmetz, 'only "The Empire Strikes Back" and "Friday the 13th" (. . .) can be labeled hits' (1980a, p. C14). Similarly, Dale Pollock of the *Los Angeles Times* published an article on the teen slasher entitled '2nd Most Successful Film, Scary News: It's "Friday the 13th"' in which he declared that '[t]he most successful movie so far this summer is "The Empire Strikes Back", which comes as no big surprise' before asking '[a]nd the second most successful? . . . "Friday the 13th"? Who's kidding whom?' (1980, p. G11). The attention that journalists lavished on *Friday the 13th* would have been understandable had the film actually been the second biggest hit of summer 1980. But, by any measure, it was not. While genuinely impressive, *Friday the 13th*'s rentals were still similar to those generated by *Dressed to Kill* and significantly less than those accumulated by *The Shining*, both of which received considerably less coverage. In fact, ticket sales for *Friday the 13th* were almost identical — slightly weaker to be exact — to those of the other summer camp-set pickup Paramount had targeted to young people in 1980, *Little Darlings*, and *Little Darlings* had been all but ignored by American industry-watchers.[13] It is possible that industry analysts gravitated to *Friday the 13th* because of its exceptionally high budget-to-gross ratio, but when Paramount's $4.5m marketing and publicity budget is reckoned in, the profit made from the distribution of *Friday the 13th* was still likely to have been comparable to that of *Little Darlings*. The press's disproportionate coverage of *Friday the 13th*, as I have argued elsewhere, bore all the hallmarks of a publicity drive orchestrated by Paramount Pictures, one which seemed designed to protect the company from being associated with, what was seen in most quarters, as a fairly disreputable commodity (Nowell, 2011). This explanation goes a long way to accounting for why press coverage largely side-stepped Paramount's investment in the film's distribution and the fact that Paramount would bank most of the film's profits, electing instead to emphasize the ways in which *Friday the 13th* had changed the lives of individuals involved solely in the film's production.

Any independent filmmaker based in North America, who possessed even the most passing of interest in the industry of which he or she was part, would have been witness to one of the most extraordinary rags-to-riches narratives in the history of film journalism, as Sean S. Cunningham and Victor Miller were held up as the latest everymen to realize the American dream. 'What was the secret of producer-director Sean Cunningham's success?', asked Dale Pollock (1980, p. G11), during the same week as Miller was invited by two prestigious publications, the *Los Angeles Times* and the *Washington Post*, to chronicle his own 'success story' (1980a, p. K1; 1980b, p. Y6). The immediate financial rewards and the medium-term career opportunities that *Friday the 13th* had provided the duo were showcased time and again. 'I have written a blockbuster and all my dreams have come true', wrote Miller in the *Washington Post*, 'thanks to that hit I can now command six times the amount I got for it on the new script. I have gained what people in the business call "credibility," and I am told that I can bank on that' (1980b, p. Y6). Similar sentiments were expressed by Cunningham. 'Before *Friday the 13th* nobody would even listen to me', Cunningham explained to the *Montreal Gazette*, '[n]ow I've made buckets of money and everyone is coming to me with offers' (quoted in Morrisroe, 1980, p. 101). By playing down *Friday the 13th*'s status as a modest earner for a major distributor and instead spotlighting its status as a once-in-a-lifetime blessing for down-on-their luck independent filmmakers, the press had framed *Friday the 13th* in a way that was likely to resonate deeply with other independent filmmakers. Catalyzed by growing doubts over the commercial viability of other youth-oriented and/or horror models, encouraged by consistent profitability and the intervention of MPAA-member distributors, and galvanized by highly positive press reports, independent filmmakers' confidence in teen slasher film production swelled rapidly, transforming the film-type into one that provided Carpetbaggers like *Madman*'s Joe Giannone with 'a shot of going at a major distributor' ('Filmmakers commentary', 2001).

Further increasing the appeal of teen slasher film production was the fact that by late 1980 it had become clear that it was possible for almost any independent filmmaker to craft an example of the film-type. The professional backgrounds of the filmmakers behind *Halloween*, *Friday the 13th*, and *Prom Night* had been covered in detail in the trade and popular press which had demonstrated that commercially successful teen slashers could be produced by entrepreneurs with little moviemaking experience and, as Dika notes, limited amounts of capital (1990, p. 85). Experienced filmmakers, similar to those behind *Friday the 13th*, contributed the low-budget examples *Final Exam*, *Graduation Day*, *Just before Dawn*, and *The Prowler* (all 1981) while newcomers, like the makers of *Prom Night*, made *The Dorm that Dripped Blood*, *Madman*, and *The Burning* (all 1981) as 'calling card films' with which to attract the interest of industry gatekeepers. In addition to provoking activity from filmmakers working at the margins of the American movie business, perceptions of the increased commercial viability of teen slasher film production also stirred to action some of the emergent heavyweights of North American independent filmmaking.

On account of having produced earlier youth-oriented hits, the makers of four of the Carpetbagger Cash-ins were not required to scrape for capital or distribution deals. As noted above, *Hell Night* was produced by Irwin Yablans, the man behind *Halloween.* If overlooked by MPAA-members, *Hell Night* was provided a route into American theaters by Yablans' distribution company, Compass International. *Friday the 13th Part II* and *My Bloody Valentine* (both 1981) were the only teen slashers to receive MPAA-member conditional pickup offers before they went before the cameras. Shortly after *Friday the 13th*'s impressive opening, Paramount's vice-president of marketing and distribution Frank Mancuso Sr. had pledged Hallmark a distribution deal for a swiftly completed R-rated $1m sequel (Grove, 2005, pp. 65–67). 'The first film was such an immediate success that we looked to establish it on a long-term basis almost immediately', Mancuso explained, 'it was a no-brainer — when you make an acquisition like *Friday the 13th* at that kind of price the profit margin is built in' (quoted in Bracke, 2005, p. 50). Paramount offered similar terms to the producers of another of its hit pickups, *Meatballs* (1979), promising to distribute *My Bloody Valentine,* providing self-proclaimed 'Canadian Carpetbagger' John Dunning and his partner André Link completed an R-rated film in time for release around its titular celebration.[14] *Meatballs'* achievements, along with a threatened Screen Actors Guild strike placing American-based film production at risk, convinced Columbia Pictures to also award the duo a pickup deal for *Happy Birthday to Me* (1981) while the film was still being shot (Vatnsdal, 2004, p. 77). As the producers of Canada's biggest ever hit, and with the achievements of *Terror Train* and *Prom Night* trumpeting the economic viability of Canadian-made teen slashers, Dunning & Link also secured production subsidies for their new teen slashers from the Canadian Film Development Corporation (CFDC). The organization clearly shared Dunning's view that 'anybody that gets in at the beginning of the cycle (. . .) has a good chance of succeeding' (interviewed in 'Going to pieces', 2006) by absorbing some of the $3m cost of *Happy Birthday to Me* and a portion of *My Bloody Valentine*'s $2m budget.[15] The CFDC's perception of the ongoing commercial viability of teen slasher film production was spotlighted by André Lamy, Michael McCabe's replacement as CFDC head. 'I don't want to be the minister of culture,' Lamy explained to Toronto's *Globe and Mail,* 'I will continue to support "My Bloody Valentine"; like it or not, there will be movies like "My Bloody Valentine", so let's make sure they are Canadian' (quoted in

J. Scott, 1981b). Across North America, independent filmmakers raced to complete their teen slashers for release in 1981 and, in doing so, they sowed the seeds of market-saturation.

The sheer quantity of teen slasher films produced in late 1980 suggested that supply was destined to outstrip demand, and that, in stark contrast to the previous spring, the balance of power was poised to shift away from producers to distribution executives, who would be able to pick and choose which, if any, of the films they picked up, and dictate the terms of purchase. While four groups of filmmakers had ostensibly sealed distribution of one sort or another prior to completing their films, the other seven teams of Carpetbaggers set their targets on the MPAA-members. Herein lay the problem. For each of these filmmaking teams to realize their objectives, every major studio, excluding Disney's distribution arm, Buena Vista, which eschewed R-rated product anyway (Krämer, 2002), was required to purchase at least one teen slasher. And, even if the mini-major Avco Embassy and powerful independent Filmways were to join Columbia, Twentieth Century Fox, MGM/UA, Paramount, Universal, and Warner Bros., every significant distributor operating on the American market would have needed to pick up one of the Carpetbagger Cash-ins.[16] For all of the Carpetbaggers to realize their commercial objectives, almost 10 per cent of Hollywood's annual output — based on the 122 films these companies distributed the previous year (Cook, 2000, p. 492) — would have had to have been comprised of films that had been made for the same audiences and to the same story-structure. The utter implausibility of such a scenario enables the teen slasher production boom of late 1980 to be described as over-production.

In sum, by summer 1980, teen slasher film production had transformed into a highly attractive proposition for independent filmmakers. Consistent MPAA-member distribution deals twinned with relative box-office success increased confidence in the commercial viability of the film-type. Concurrently, obstacles to MPAA-member distribution eroded the appeal of the other types of horror and youth-oriented film that earlier had undermined *Halloween* Cash-in production. These conditions caused the over-production of teen slashers as eleven Carpetbagger Cash-ins went into production near-simultaneously. The likelihood of over-production of teen slasher films leading to economic disappointment for the Carpetbaggers was made even greater by the widespread implementation of a specific approach to film content that generated insufficient levels of product differentiation to permit filmmakers and distributors to achieve their commercial objectives, and it is to that approach that the next section turns.

'Teen-age-love-and-meat-cleaver films':
Schematization of Content in the Group of
Eleven Teen Slasher Carpetbagger Cash-ins

In late 1980, it was common knowledge in industry circles that a surge
in teen slasher film production was taking place across North America.
Countless 'in-production' lists in trade papers and articles in North
American newspapers ensured that industry-insiders were informed
of the development had they not heard about it on the 'Hollywood
grapevine' — a remote possibility given the movement of production
personnel, cast members, and technicians between the films. It was not
uncommon for American journalists to report that 'the hearty of spirit
are going right ahead in an attempt to twist the knife profitably before
the cyclical goose is totally cooked' (C. Williams, 1980, p. E1), or for
their Canadian colleagues to write that 'dozens of would-be directors,
capitalizing on the current trend, are stamping out pale carbon copies
of (. . .) Hallowe'en [sic]' (Morrisroe, 1980, p. 101).

Amid this activity and chatter, some leading figures in the American
independent sector had concluded that the situation spelled trouble
for the companies producing and distributing the films. Among them
was Roger Corman, head of New World Pictures, the most economically
successful independent producer-distributor of the 1970s. Corman was
concerned that theaters would be flooded with teen slashers. 'The cycle is
peaking', explained Corman, 'by spring the market will be oversaturated'
(quoted in C. Williams, 1980, p. E1). These sentiments were echoed by
leading independent horror producer Christopher Pearce. '[T]he cycle
is going to end soon', predicted Pearce, 'there are twice as many films
this time as ever before' (quoted in ibid.). With supply seeming destined
to exceed demand, Corman and Pearce suspected that ticket sales would
be spread so thinly that most of the films would lose money. For this
reason, two of the most informed men in the American movie business
elected to err on the side of caution, with Pearce backing *New Year's Evil*
(1980), a tale of a maniac speeding across America to strike at midnight
in different time-zones, and Corman suspending production of his teen
slasher, *The Slumber Party Massacre*, until the Carpetbagger Cash-ins had
finished their theatrical runs (ibid.). Equally telling was the fact that,
when it was made in 1982, *The Slumber Party Massacre* reflected none of
the textual developments that had occurred in teen slasher filmmaking
during Prospector and Carpetbagger operations. New World's tale of a
sanatorium absconder targeting a group of fun-loving small-town high
school girlfriends was an anachronism, the content of which, as Linda

Gross of the *Los Angeles Times,* recognized, came 'suspiciously close to that of "Halloween"' (Gross, 1982, p. G3).

Whereas Pearce had responded to concerns over the profitability of teen slasher film production, Corman had acted primarily because of, what he foresaw, as the looming difficulties of making money from teen slasher film distribution. Their concerns, along with their respective companies' conduct vis-à-vis the content of *New Year's Evil* and *Slumber Party Massacre,* highlight the extent to which the commercial objectives of teen slasher film producers were seen to be jeopardized by similarities between Cash-ins. In the context of what already was being viewed in some quarters as over-production, product differentiation — distinctive content that could be highlighted in marketing materials to make a film stand out from the pack — was at a premium if Carpetbaggers hoped to secure a distribution contract, particularly one from an MPAA-member. If, however, a Cash-in offered little that set it apart from other Cash-ins, its value to distributors would likely drop and the negotiation of a pickup deal would become very difficult.

While by no means a homogeneous mass of undistinguishable product, the content of the group of eleven teen slashers produced in late 1980 was, in comparison to the quite distinct content of the Prospector Cash-ins *Prom Night* and *Friday the 13th,* significantly more schematic. Although they stressed material differently and employed some innovative content, the makers of the Carpetbagger Cash-ins adopted similar strategies to realize their commercial objectives. This is, however, not to say, as has been claimed, that the new films became increasingly violent showcases for some of the most misogynistic brutality ever put on film (Prince, 2000, pp. 298, 351–352). Rather, Carpetbaggers tended to reshape the nascent film-type into female-centered animal comedy-infused murder-mysteries.[17] This approach combined features of *Friday the 13th* and *Prom Night* that had demonstrated broader audience appeal as a result of having also featured in three of 1980's most financially successful youth-oriented and/or horror films: the American giallo *Dressed to Kill,* the female-centered coming-of-age drama *Little Darlings,* and the animal comedy *Caddyshack.* The location within a murder-mystery plot of a dynamic conventionally attractive young woman and a host of frivolous male youths, while not entirely surprising given that the films had been made to the same model at the same point in time in the context of the same industrial developments, generated textual patterns across the Carpetbagger Cash-ins, increasing considerably the precarious position already occupied by a relatively large group of films that shared a story-structure, iconography, and emotional/cognitive orientation, and which had been made to appeal to a small number of distributors that would all be targeting the same audience.

Like many of the third cycle teen slasher films made after *Scream* (1996) (Koven, 2008, pp. 115–117; Rubin, 1999, pp. 163–164), the group of eleven Carpetbagger Cash-ins featured murder-mystery plots. Whereas eight of the films were whodunits, the remaining three protractedly concealed the killer's motive. Although the intense intrigue provoked by plots of this sort promised to enable filmmakers to sustain the engagement of viewers who were expected to be growing accustomed to the narrative conventions of teen slashers, important economic factors drove this conduct. While the makers of the Prospector Cash-ins had employed whodunit plots to counterbalance the replication of *Halloween*'s story-structure, the box-office achievements of *Friday the 13th* and *Prom Night* had transformed the concealment of the killer's identity and/or motive into a way of evoking hit films.

In addition to inviting parallels to the teen slashers of 1980, murder-mystery plots provided a politically anodyne way of capitalizing on the American giallo *Dressed to Kill*. In late 1980, *Dressed to Kill* — a film about a game of cat-and-mouse involving a young prostitute, a teenaged technophile, a psychologist, and a cross-dressing maniac — provided a barometer with which to measure the economic and political climate for violent R-rated cinema, because it had drawn both charges of misogyny and a large enough audience to suggest that it would place in or around the top twenty of the annual rentals chart.[18] Economically, in the context of the profitability of *Friday the 13th* and *Prom Night*, *Dressed to Kill* underscored the financial potential of murder-mysteries featuring blade-wielding killers and young people. Politically, the fact that *Dressed to Kill* had been the victim of a critical backlash, when the teen slashers largely had avoided hostility, indicated that depicting the swift executions of male and female youths rather than portraying the brutalization of exclusively female targets was more likely to chime with MPAA-members' self-styled images as purveyors of 'harmless entertainment', to use Richard Maltby's term (1983). Therefore, with controversy having seemingly rendered *Dressed to Kill* Cash-in production politically unviable for independent filmmakers hoping to secure MPAA-member distribution, murder-mystery plots enabled Carpetbaggers to evoke De Palma's film while also inviting comparisons to the teen slasher hits, *Friday the 13th* and, particularly, *Prom Night*.

Carpetbaggers invited comparisons to *Prom Night* with a range of hapless investigators and red herrings, mobilizing, in films like *Happy Birthday to Me* 'enough twists to keep teenage sleuths satisfied' (Sheffield,

1981, p. 7). Most of the Cash-ins used investigators who, while prompting the audience to ask 'who is the killer?' and sometimes 'why is s/he killing?' (Bordwell, 1985, pp. 55–56), failed to identify accurately the perpetrator so as to enable the narrative to progress. For instance, in *My Bloody Valentine*, a small-town sheriff trails a notorious serial murderer only to discover that he died years earlier. Similarly, hounding innocents in *The Prowler* and *Graduation Day* ultimately yields the culprits but only after several youths lose their lives. The diverse suspects on display in the group of eleven also echoed the characteristics of *Prom Night*'s red herrings. Along with Peeping Toms and eccentrics inspired by janitor Sykes' voyeurism and mental instability, several filmmakers drew upon school bully Lou to cast suspicion over various thugs and hot-heads. In addition, the Carpetbaggers behind Cash-ins like *My Bloody Valentine*, *Friday the 13th Part II*, *Hell Night*, and *The Burning*, built upon the suggestion that semi-mythical asylum-escapee Leonard Murch was behind *Prom Night*'s killings by reworking elements of urban legends to construct a milieu in which, as Mikel J. Koven has argued, the films' protagonists and the characters in their campfire stories seem to intermingle freely (2006, p. 165). The investment in fairly elaborate murder-mystery plots also sparked the recalibration of the look of the films' killers, who, far from being grotesque sexual deviants, as commonly is claimed (Clover, 1992, pp. 26–30), were, for the most part, highly stylized villains whose arresting images lent themselves ideally to movie marketers looking to grab the attention of potential theatergoers.

Eye-catching maniacs were gaining momentum rapidly among teen slasher filmmakers, long before receiving 'high-concept' standardization in the form of the hockey goaltender mask used to sell the later *Friday the 13th* sequels (1984–2009), and the distorted Edvard Munch 'Scream' mask used for the *Scream* trilogy (1996–2000). The employment of killers donned in extraordinary costumes distinguished most of the group of eleven from the Prospector Cash-ins released in summer 1980. In *Friday the 13th*, unreturned subjective shots and framing devices had reduced its summer camp stalker to an off-screen presence during the disruption phase of the film, and an understated black ski-mask had made *Prom Night*'s ax-wielding gatecrasher barely visible in shadow-soaked school halls, unlit classrooms, and darkened make-out spots. 'We started thinking', recalled *My Bloody Valentine*'s producer John Dunning, 'which kind of character can be a killer that can be masked?' (interviewed in 'Going to pieces', 2006). The sinister Darth Vader-like miner, to paraphrase Jay Scott of Toronto's *Globe and Mail* (1981a), upon which he settled, and which *Variety* credited with huge box-office potential (Carl., 1981a,

p. 20), epitomized the inventive methods that permitted these striking figures to remain intriguingly unidentifiable, horrifyingly incongruous, and, so it seemed, commercially viable (see Figure 5.1). Other examples included the combat fatigues and veil used to camouflage the titular character of *The Prowler*, the fencer's faceguard and jumpsuit sported by the slasher in *Graduation Day*, and the hessian sack in which the madman from *Friday the 13th Part II* is dressed to kill (see Figure 5.1).

The widespread adoption of stylized killers was probably fuelled by an advertisement that Twentieth Century Fox had taken out in an August 1980 issue of *Variety* to announce press screenings and to excite interest among exhibitors for *Terror Train*, the last teen slasher Prospector Cash-in to hit theaters (Twentieth Century Fox Film Corporation, 1980, pp. 28–29). The Groucho Marx-masked figure that dominated the spread, but, crucially, not the film itself, indicated that an MPAA-member

FIGURE 5.1 The costumed killers of *My Bloody Valentine* and *Friday the 13th Part II*.

valued an attention-grabbing killer. As the only teen slasher to open after *Prom Night* but before most of the Carpetbagger Cash-ins were completed, *Terror Train* — in terms of its content, marketing, distribution, and box-office performance — provided a unique window onto the commercial viability of the teen slasher as a film-type and onto elements of teen slasher film content, both for producers and distributors. For this reason, I return to the film and the ways in which it influenced industry logic and conduct between late summer 1980 and spring 1981. An early effect of *Terror Train*'s marketing campaign was to signal to independent filmmakers that MPAA-member distribution executives, like some independent distributors of the mid 1970s, identified striking maniacs as an important marketing hook — a development which in turn indicated that featuring similar characters in new films would give producers an edge in the battle to secure an MPAA-member distribution deal.

In addition to developing components related to the generation of intrigue, Carpetbaggers recalibrated the composition, internal dynamics and, actions of the youth group. Where the targets of early teen slasher killers are usually claimed to have been comprised of troupes of beautiful promiscuous young women that invariably perish and a virginal acquaintance who survives (Clover, 1992, p. 21; Prince, 2000, p. 351), the makers of most of the group of eleven actually re-formed the teen slasher youth group into a cell of young and mostly male hedonists, with a nucleus provided by a conventionally attractive, dynamic female youth. This version of horror film 'normalcy', to use Robin Wood's term (1984), combined elements of *Friday the 13th* and *Prom Night* that also had featured in *Caddyshack, Dressed to Kill,* and *Little Darlings*. In doing so, it promised to allow Carpetbaggers to serve the perceived requirements of MPAA-members and their youth target market, and to shield themselves from the X-rating and distributors from critical hostility.

Crafting teen slasher films that were marketable to female youth was destined to continue in earnest when, in early October 1980, shortly before most of the Carpetbagger Cash-ins were shot, industry analyst Aljean Harmetz revealed in the *New York Times* that a research study had concluded that the efforts of teen slasher producers and promoters to attract teenage girls and young women to the films had been hugely successful and that teen slashers were attracting unusually large numbers of female youths (1980d, p. C15). Harmetz explained that the document showed 45 per cent of tickets for *Halloween* and *Friday the 13th* had been sold to under-17s, 55 per cent of which had been girls (ibid.). These findings were particularly eye-opening because the American film industry believed that 15–25-year-old males dominated horror film attendance

(Watkins, 1980, p. 33). Although Harmetz did not detail how tickets sales to over-17s had been divided between the sexes, she explicitly highlighted a causal link between depictions of female youth, disproportionately high attendance among young females, and box-office success (1980d, p. C15). Harmetz's article appeared to confirm what filmmakers already had concluded: a 'female-friendly' teen slasher was more likely to become a financially successful teen slasher. The conduct of the man who had provided Harmetz with the information demonstrated that an MPAA-member distributor shared this view.

The confidence that independent filmmakers placed in positioning female youth-oriented content in teen slashers across the mid-to-late 1970s continued into the early 1980s when Robert Cort, Harmetz's source and Fox's vice-president of advertising and publicity, revised the $5m marketing campaign that his company had drawn up to promote *Terror Train* so as to emphasize the fact that *Terror Train* was a female youth-centered film. Fox had commissioned *Terror Train*'s poster art when *Friday the 13th* was demonstrating the box-office prowess of teen slasher films without its female youth-oriented content having been emphasized in marketing materials, other than lobby cards. Early poster art for *Terror Train*, which was premiered in *Variety* in August 1980, thus featured the Groucho Marx-masked killer brandishing a knife and the uninspired tagline: 'What screams in the night isn't the train. It's the terror at your throat' (Twentieth Century Fox Film Corporation, 1980, pp. 28–29). However, with *Prom Night* performing well soon after on the back of a marketing campaign that had been angled heavily to female youth, the final version of *Terror Train*'s poster art emphasized a college sorority with the addition of an illustration of students gathering around a bonfire and a new tagline: 'The boys and girls of Sigma Pi, some will live and some will die.' Lobby cards also highlighted the presence of female youths flirting with boys and spotlighted female lead Alana (Jamie Lee Curtis) instead of characters played by her male costars, Oscar-winner Ben Jonson and heartthrob Hart Bochner. Similarly, Fox's theatrical trailer marked *Terror Train* as a film that had been designed for young people of both sexes by way of the announcement 'Stay with your date', advice that, in addition to being directed at young couples on the screen, articulated the, somewhat sexist, yet widely held, belief that young female theatergoers sought 'protection' from their male partners when confronted by the frightening content of horror films like *Terror Train*. By recalibrating *Terror Train*'s marketing campaign and by his revelations in the Harmetz article, Robert Cort, a leading figure at an MPAA-member — precisely the type of person whose confidence an independent filmmaker needed to generate if s/he hoped to secure a pickup deal — had, in word and deed, sent a clear message to Carpetbaggers: a 'female-friendly' teen slasher was more likely to become an MPAA-member-distributed teen slasher. The Carpetbaggers clearly took heed and many formulated a solution which placed a new spin on an old strategy, as John Dunning, producer of *Happy Birthday to Me* and *My Bloody Valentine*, explained 'we needed a girl lead' (interviewed in 'Going to pieces', 2006).

The makers of the group of eleven tended to use heroines who were both conventionally attractive and dynamic so as to enable distributors to target the films to young people of both sexes, but particularly to females. The presence of heroines who possessed traditionally masculine and feminine traits was among the most significant innovations in content provided by the Carpetbaggers. Previously, *Halloween*'s timid babysitter Laurie and extrovert Kim from *Prom Night* (both Jamie Lee Curtis) had projected conventional, albeit different, forms of femininity and had only demonstrated some traditionally masculine attributes when they engaged with the killer directly. Alice (Adrienne King), on the other hand, had been presented throughout *Friday the 13th* as 'more boy than girl' (Dika, 1990, p. 70). While scholars have invariably highlighted the presence of female leads in first cycle teen slashers (Clover, 1987; Wood, 1987, Dika 1990), few have acknowledged the prevalence of heroines that exhibited an abundance of traditionally feminine traits, never mind glamorous examples. On the contrary, Dika's reading of the 'stalker cycle' as encapsulating the United States' transition to Reaganite bellicosity necessitates that she downplay the femininity of their female leads — 'strong, practical (. . .) essentially "masculine"' heroines clearly provide more convincing metaphors of the shift than flag-bearers of femininity like sorority sisters and prom queens (Dika, 1990, pp. 55, 133–139). Similarly, Clover describes the 'Final Girl' as 'boyish, in a word', a description to which she anchored her view that the character enabled male youths to play out sadistic and masochistic fantasies (1992, p. 51). The adoption among scholars of the term 'Final Girl', like its absorption into the vocabularies of fans and popular writers (Harper, 2004, pp. 31–39; Whitehead, 2000, pp. 15–16), bespeaks the extent to which it is assumed that first cycle teen slashers focus invariably on an asexual wallflower.[19] However, the absence from Clover's influential work of most of the group of eleven indicates that different modes of gender representation and address were in operation in the films.

The female leads that featured in the majority of the teen slasher Carpetbagger Cash-ins were younger and less varnished versions of the 'New Women heroines' that feminist scholar Elana Levine showed had risen to prominence in the high-rating TV series *Charlie's Angels* (1976–1981) and *Wonder Woman* (1976–1979), and that would become commonplace in late nineties teen television like *Buffy the Vampire Slayer* (1997–2003) (2007b, p. 168). As Levine points out, while the makers of the late 1970s action-adventure shows 'endowed their fictional New Women with conventionally masculine traits', the eponymous heroines 'were also represented as excessively feminine' (ibid.). By proposing that this combination of characteristics dramatized and contributed to contemporaneous debates concerning 'whether or not feminism required a rejection of traditional femininity', Levine illuminates the industrial logic that led American media producers to use the character-type to make product attractive to a young female audience (ibid.). Similarly, Jason Middleton (2007) has argued compellingly, in relation to their late-seventies and late-nineties incarnations, that such female protagonists also offered a powerful way of making female-centered filmed entertainment more appealing to young males. Elaborating on Yvonne Tasker's work on the heroines of female-centered fantasy films like 1985's *Red Sonja* (1993, pp. 18–21), Middleton, ironically while employing Clover's formulation of the masculine Final Girl to distinguish the 'cult heroines' heroines of *Buffy the Vampire Slayer* and similar product, concludes rightly that these characters' 'deadly capabilities' and 'excessive signifiers of femininity and sexuality' have been used to target, or at least to avoid the alienation of, teenage boys and young men because they invite 'a voyeuristic and/or fetishistic [heterosexual] male gaze' (2007, p. 162). While major US television shows of the late-seventies provided highly visible channels through which the commercial viability of tough yet traditionally feminine heroines had been broadcast to film industry-insiders, developments at the American box-office across spring and summer 1980 had suggested that this character-type also could energize ticket sales for youth-oriented films.

The financial achievements of the teen slasher Prospector Cash-ins, *Friday the 13th* and *Prom Night*, in conjunction with parallel industrial developments, communicated unambiguously the economic potential of shaping R-rated youth-oriented horror films around independent conventionally attractive young women. On the one hand, the box-office strength of *Prom Night*'s mode of gender representation and address had been supported by strong ticket sales for *Little Darlings*, a female-centered coming-of-age drama starring teen starlets Tatum O'Neil and Kristy McNichol that Paramount had released in March 1980 and that had performed even better commercially than its summer hit *Friday the 13th*.[20] Like *Prom Night*, this tale of two adolescent girls negotiating romantic, platonic, and emotional challenges during a summer camp as they race to lose their virginity stressed, as Chuck Kleinhans suggests, 'white young women bonding, expressing the situation of girls in a group or pair, and showing the world from their perspective' (2002, p. 73). The sleeper hit status of *Little Darlings* had thus demonstrated that placing traditionally feminine teenage girls at the center of an R-rated film had attracted the MPAA-member that recently had dominated the American youth-market, and had attracted a large number of young people. With the commercial failure of MGM/UA's pickup *Foxes* (1980) having raised doubts over the ability to secure MPAA-member distribution deals of subsequent female-centered coming-of-age dramas, and with the weak returns of *Times Square* (1980) supporting such assessments, the incorporation of prominent elements of *Little Darlings* into other film-types was more appealing to independent filmmakers than the production of Cash-ins — in much the same way as parallel developments had undermined the production of American gialli in the mould of *Dressed to Kill*, but had not discouraged filmmakers from embedding into other types of film some elements of De Palma's picture, particularly when content had featured in other hits.[21] In addition to underscoring the financial potential of youth-centered murder-mysteries, *Dressed to Kill*, and particularly its depiction of an enterprising female teen tracking and trapping a maniacal killer, had signaled that the achievements of *Friday the 13th* may in part have been down to the presence of tomboy heroine, Alice. Market-conditions thus led teen slasher filmmakers to place considerable confidence in female leads that unified the traditionally feminine appearance and the homo-social and heterosexual acumen of *Prom Night*'s prom queen Kim with the conventionally masculine practicality and aggression of *Friday the 13th*'s tough survivor, Alice.

The confidence that Carpetbaggers placed in the new breed of heroine was encapsulated by the manner filmmakers who had made an earlier teen slasher introduced the character in their new films. In *Hell Night*, produced by *Halloween*'s Irwin Yablans, Marti (Linda Blair) is first seen at a frat party. 'Who's she?', enquires a playboy fraternity president. 'Look who just walked in', beams another suitor. Marti contrasts dominant modes of North American teen film representation whereby, as Timothy Shary shows, female youths that excel academically or creatively, such as those in *The Breakfast Club* (1984) and *She's All That* (1999), usually require hyper-feminine makeovers to garner homo-social acceptance and heterosexual attention (2002b, pp. 235–250). Marti's visual presence was a far cry from the first glimpse the audience was given of *Halloween*'s Kim — sporting conservative clothing and little makeup. Instead, it echoed the marketing rhetoric used to describe Blair's character in Yablans' 1979 roller-disco movie *Roller Boogie*. Dressed throughout *Hell Night* in a low-cut figure-hugging ball gown, Marti is framed, much like Blair's all-dancing heartbreaker in *Roller Boogie*, as 'the hottest date in town' (see Figure 5.2). It soon emerges that, in addition to catching the eye of handsome males, Marti is an authority on politics, a capable mechanic, and a high-flying student. She is, in short, not only sexually desirable, but knowledgeable, practical, and intelligent, a point acknowledged even by Wood in his otherwise uncompromising summary of 'teenie kill-pics' (1987, p. 82). The shift in the characterization of the female leads was also trumpeted during Ginny's self confident entrance (Amy Steel) in *Friday the 13th Part II*. Where the makers of its predecessor introduced Alice as she repaired cabins while dressed in denim jeans and a shapeless lumberjack shirt, the sequel's conventionally attractive lead is established immediately as combining masculine traits with feminine attributes. Ginny exits a battered VW bug in a flowing fuchsia skirt and a low-cut t-shirt. Having arrived late for an induction meeting, she flirts her way out of a public reprimand from her boss, with whom she is involved romantically. 'Ginny, I was starting to worry about you', he mentions. 'Bullshit, Paul', she replies, before kissing him. Satisfied with her effective performance of femininity, the psychology major departs with a wry grin, returns to the car, and corrects her hair in its rear-view mirror. The recalibration of heroines from *Friday the 13th* to *Friday the 13th Part II* was not lost on James H. Burns, who observed in leading horror magazine *Fangoria* that: '[Director Steve] Miner also brought to the sequel a new female lead (. . .). Like [Adrienne] King's Alice, Ginny is an independent type, but [Amy] Steele injects her heroine with another quality: sex appeal' (1981b, p. 65). The mobilization of heroines that promised to be marketable to the perceived tastes of male as well as female youths, led to distribution companies being offered teen slasher after teen slasher that featured young women juggling investigations of suspicious goings-on and romantic escapades before contributing to the defeat of the killer.

Most of the Carpetbaggers positioned female leads in heterosexual courtship subplots. Teen slasher filmmakers, as previous chapters showed, labored to treat depictions of heterosexual interaction with considerably more sensitivity than that for which they commonly are credited, often portraying the emotional, social, and psychological pressures of burgeoning heterosexuality, particularly the experiences of female characters, in, what may seem, surprisingly thoughtful ways. Some carpetbaggers were not coy about revealing their investment in romantic content. For example, director George Mihalka, who explained to

FIGURE 5.2   *Hell Night*'s conventionally attractive female lead, Marti (Linda Blair).

Fangoria magazine that in *My Bloody Valentine* '[t]he *people* are the main storyline (. . .). We tried to deal with the characters backgrounds: their loves, lives and small town mentality [emphasis in original]' (quoted in Burns, 1981a, p. 54). Similarly, fresh from interviewing producer Irwin Yablans and star Linda Blair, Ellen Farley of the *Los Angeles Times*, described *Hell Night* as '"Halloween" with pop romance overtures' (1981, p. N22), a description that must have been fed to her by Yablans, Blair or one of their collaborators given that *Hell Night* was still being shot. Romantic subplots became so prevalent among the Carpetbagger Cash-ins that the *New York Times*' Vincent Canby later coined the term 'teen-age-love-and-meat-cleaver films' to refer to teen slashers like *Happy Birthday to Me* (1981a, p. C13), and Judith Martin at the *Washington Post* went as far as to open her review of *Happy Birthday to Me* by declaring that '[t]he difference between the teen-age love film of some years ago and the teen-age blood film now in fashion is negligible' (1981, p. W19). Canby and Martin were responding to characters like Sarah (Lori Hallier) in *My Bloody Valentine*, who called the shots with old flame T. J.

(Paul Kelman) and boyfriend Axel (Neil Affleck) during a protracted love triangle subplot, the aforementioned Ginny from *Friday the 13th Part II* (see Figure 5.3), as well as her namesake (Melissa Sue Anderson) from *Happy Birthday to Me*, and *Graduation Day*'s Anne (Patch MacKensie), both of whom command and reject numerous male admirers. To these heartbreakers were added the flirtatious female leads of *Hell Night, The Prowler*, and *Final Exam*. Whether filtered through sagas of unconsummated attraction, burgeoning romance, or stable relationships, these sexually desirable young women were shown controlling their love lives completely, suggesting that this content had been mobilized primarily to make the films marketable to female youth. Moreover, the presentation of heroines as sexual beings promised to protect distributors from having their 'good names' besmirched by accusations that the films ostensibly punished female sexuality by featuring virgins that outlasted their lascivious friends, a particularly attractive attribute given the charges of misogyny directed at the makers of *Dressed to Kill*.

The combination of traditionally masculine and feminine traits that underpinned the female leads' adoption of dominant roles during heterosexual courtship was also emphasized in their depiction outside

FIGURE 5.3   Romance in *Friday the 13th Part II* (Source: *Crystal Lake Memories*).

romantic interaction. Drawing on *Dressed to Kill*'s young sleuth Liz
Blake (Nancy Allen), teen slasher Carpetbaggers commonly rendered
sexually desirable, intelligent, and resourceful heroines probing connections between past and present-day events with what Middleton
called 'detective-like curiosity' (2007, p. 161). Significantly more alert
to changes in their environment, these characters were portrayed as
'watchful to the point of paranoia' (Clover, 1992, p. 39). The depiction
of young women who self-consciously mastered different situations by
implementing gendered modes of behavior again recalled the New
Women crime-fighters of *Charlie's Angles* and *Wonder Woman*, who, as
Levine explains, were characterized by a 'multiply-positioned identity
that sees gender as fundamentally entwined with other axes of social
experience' (2007b, p. 170). Thus, in *Graduation Day* a young naval
officer 'wearing comparatively high fashioned clothes and high heeled
shoes', as Dika points out, sets about uncovering how her sister's mysterious death connects to a spate of teen murders (1990, p. 101). Similarly,
in *The Prowler*, journalism student Pam (Vicky Dawson) forwent her
prom, although not her prom dress, to ascertain whether the links between two killings that caused the suspension of a graduation dance and
a sinister figure that has accompanied the event's revival. The traditionally masculine traits upon which these young women, and others like
them, drew in their investigatory undertakings were amplified during
the resolutions of many Carpetbagger Cash-ins.

The female leads emerged unscathed from the disruption phase usually to contribute actively to the killer's downfall. As *Friday the 13th* and
Prom Night indicated, heroines confronting and overcoming maniacs
appeared to have resonated with young females, possibly seeking portrayals of empowerment — as the *New York Times* had reported, over a quarter
of teen slasher ticket-buyers had been 12–17-year-old girls (Harmetz,
1980d, p. C15). However, such scenes, when preceded by protracted
sequences of menace and danger, risked alienating MPAA-members
and thus jeopardizing the lucrative pickup deals prized by producers,
because it was widely believed by industry-insiders that the MPAA would,
through its certification office CARA, respond to the *Dressed to Kill* controversy (examined below) by clamping down on films that showcased
victimization of female characters through the imposition of the commercially damaging X-rating. Filmmakers targeting MPAA-member
distributors with product to be aimed at female youths but which pitted
gender against gender in extended scenes of threat and violence therefore faced a problem in late 1980. Thus, whereas discussion of early
teen slashers typically focuses on the exceptional films that featured a

lone heroine vanquishing the killer singlehandedly (Clover, 1987; Dika, 1990), diverse renditions of female valor were in fact on display across the group of eleven.

Understandably, most Carpetbaggers with little or no experience of dealing with MPAA-members failed to recognize the commercial risks of crafting showdowns between female teens and killers of the opposite sex. Exploitation specialists concluded *Final Exam, Graduation Day*, and *Just Before Dawn* with sagas of male-on-female threat in which lone heroines dispatched a campus intruder, a teenage psychopath, and gargantuan twins respectively, and concluded *The Prowler* with the eleventh-hour rescue of a petrified student. The newcomers that produced *Madman* and *The Dorm that Dripped Blood* demonstrated even less comprehension of the socio-political forces shaping the segment of the industry they aimed to penetrate, by closing sequences of female-youth-in-peril with the heroines' deaths. However, Carpetbaggers who already had dealt with MPAA-members evidently recognized the complexity of the situation, showing considerable invention as they looked to preempt problems with CARA and their distributors-of-choice.

To avoid the X-rating, teen slasher filmmakers that previously had sold films to MPAA-members ensured that female valor operated in contexts that did not represent victim and victimizer along binary axes of gender. The first approach drew inspiration from *Friday the 13th* by employing an all-female confrontation. However, given that the killer's apparent femininity had not prevented *Dressed to Kill* from provoking powerful cultural arbiters, the filmmakers behind *Happy Birthday to Me* jettisoned *Friday the 13th*'s thrilling chases and struggles in favor of the prolonged revelation of the murderess's identity and motives which, as Vincent Canby of the *New York Times* noted, 'requires almost as much footage as the murders' (1981a, p. C13), before eventually showing her remarkably swift and painless death. The Carpetbaggers behind *My Bloody Valentine*, as well as the astute newcomers behind *The Burning*, Miramax, a company that became a major force in the American film industry partly by making teen slashers for teenage girls (Wee, 2005; Wyatt, 1998), were more cautious, removing female leads, and themselves, from the line of fire completely by showing young women directing the flight of traumatized targets as men confronted killers (see Figure 5.4). Other experienced filmmakers sought inspiration from *Prom Night*, which concluded with a standoff between a male and female youth and a masked assassin, during which the killer's aggression was directed against the male, thus allowing the heroine to step in at the last minute and dispatch the killer effortlessly. With *Prom Night* having signaled a method of portraying a teenage girl's valor that had not generated critical hostility, the makers of *Friday the 13th Part II* showed the film's heroine saving her lover before emerging victorious from a suspenseful game of cat-and-mouse with a pitchfork-wielding maniac, and the makers of *Hell Night* shielded themselves from accusations of misogyny by featuring a male youth besting a murderous giant and its leading lady disposing of his equally malevolent brother.

The Carpetbaggers' portrayal of female valor may have been considerably more wide-ranging than has been suggested to date, but, in the context of over-production of teen slashers, the reoccurring presence of conventionally attractive female youths acting bravely to contribute to the downfall of shadowy killers added another degree of similarity to a large group of films that, from a distributor's perspective, already bore too many similarities to be commercially viable. Similarities in content resulting from the widespread mobilization of the 'New Women' leads and depictions of their acts of valor, investigatory undertakings, and romantic escapades, were compounded by the Carpetbaggers' importation of textual and thematic material from a film-type in which, as William Paul notes, 'romantic interest always remains secondary' (1994, p. 90): the tales of youthful high-jinx that came to be known as animal comedies.

The emphasis that they placed on animal comedy sequences of youths' 'crude and deliberate transgressions of the bounds of normal everyday taste' (King, 2002, p. 63), was among the most visible, widespread, and, or so it seemed, shrewd strategies employed by Carpetbaggers to enhance the commercial potential of teen slasher films. Journalists recognized this approach contemporaneously with *New York Times* film critic Janet Maslin noting that '[*The Burning*] devotes endless time to horseplay

FIGURE 5.4 Non-violent female valor in *The Burning.*

among the campers' (1982, p. C7), Linda Gross of the *Los Angeles Times* observing that *Final Exam* 'vacillate[s] between the college-prank humor of an "Animal House" with a killer-thriller like "Prom Night"' (1981b, p. H7), and Skip Sheffield writing in the *Boca Rotan News* that 'like all cinema teenagers, the kids [in *Happy Birthday to Me*] continue to yuck it up, have fun and go about their pranks as their ranks decrease' (1981, p. 7). The logic, incentives, and market-forces that led the makers of the group of eleven to use substantially larger amounts of animal comedy material than their predecessors, were, in many respects, similar to the conditions underwriting their adoption of fairly elaborate murder-mystery plots and dynamic conventionally feminine heroines.

First and foremost, animal comedy material permitted independent filmmakers to demonstrate to distributors that their films could be marketed to young people who usually avoided horror movies, by highlighting content that had been drawn from a non-horror youth-oriented film-type which boasted a sizable consumer base but which, as a result of industrial factors that they were powerless to change, offered them little hope of securing an MPAA-member distribution deal — in this instance, MPAA-members' self-production of animal comedies had rendered independently produced examples of the film-type surplus to requirements. The commercial viability of mobilizing animal comedy content also had been signaled by its use in a financially successful teen slasher Prospector Cash-in, in this case *Friday the 13th*, and in a second well-attended film of 1980, Orion Pictures' *Caddyshack*, a tale of unruliness at an exclusive golf club that had captured a large enough segment of the youth-market to place in the top twenty of the annual rentals chart.[22] The possibility that animal comedy content had contributed to the box-office success of *Friday the 13th* had even been entertained publicly in July 1980 by David Ansen and Martin Kasindorf of *Newsweek*. 'Just what made "Friday [the 13th]" stand out from an already crowded horror market is difficult to say', they began, before adding, '[p]erhaps [it was] the summer-camp setting, [and] the smattering of teen sex that precedes the ax murders' (Ansen and Kasindorf, 1980, p. 74). The box-office performance of *Caddyshack* thus indicated that the impressive returns of *Friday the 13th* had, like *Newsweek* suggested, been generated partly because, and not in spite, of the intermittent presence of animal comedy.

Despite having used animal comedy material comparatively sparingly, the filmmakers behind *Friday the 13th* had shown that animal comedy content and the teen slasher's story-structure could be blended seamlessly. As chapter three showed, *Friday the 13th* reflected, what Paul called, 'the central project of animal comedy', which is to say that, by transporting pleasure-seeking male youths into *Halloween*'s story-structure, *Friday the 13th*, like *Animal House* and *Meatballs* before it and like *Caddyshack* after it, had depicted the rewards and consequences of testing 'how far one can go before some repressive force steps in' (1994, p. 109). In fact, *Friday the 13th* provided a high-profile demonstration that, in terms of content, the line which separated as film-types the teen slasher from the animal comedy lay in the gravity of the threat posed to groups of youthful characters whose principal aim was to interact recreationally. Where puritanical nemeses like *Animal House*'s Dean Wormer (John Vernon) and Doug Neidermeyer (Mark Matcalf) had labored to prevent the hedonism of animal comedy youths by limiting their leisure opportunities and by restricting their social, sexual, and academic mobility, the penalties were magnified to homicidal proportions in teen slashers. For those teen slasher Carpetbaggers that had failed initially to grasp either the correspondences between animal comedies and teen slashers, or the economic potential of combining elements thereof — inexperienced or unaccomplished players of what Altman called 'The Producers' Game' (1999, p. 38) — a more conspicuous point of entry into the relationships between the film-types was signaled by their shared settings. Distinguishing the teen slasher and animal comedy from the overwhelming majority of industry output, was the fact that, by summer 1980, both film-types had been set at the same locations — academic institutions in *Animal House* and *Prom Night* and summer camps in *Meatballs* and *Friday the 13th*. The mobilization of animal comedy content promised to show distributors that teen slashers could be promoted directly to one half of their target audience without alienating the other half.

By infusing teen slashers with animal comedy material, Carpetbaggers provided distributors with content that could be used to angle the films not only to male youths, but to their female peers as well. The Carpetbaggers cast conventionally attractive actors to play the types of characters that had featured heavily in animal comedy hits. This strategy enabled the male youth-orientation of animal comedy to be maintained in a manner that promised also to satisfy the fetishistic gaze of heterosexual female youths in much the same way as the new teen slasher heroines had been used to offer something appealing to both sexes and, in much the same way as Geoff King has suggested that, gross-out/romantic comedies like *American Pie* (1999) were fashioned to offer 'the prospect of the industrially attractive "date movie"' (2002, p. 73).

The Carpetbaggers recalibrated the composition of the teen slasher youth group, which had hitherto been dominated by young women, to reflect the 'male bias', as Paul describes it, of animal comedies (1994,

p. 100). While individual group members rarely exceeded the screen-time allocated to the female leads, as a collective, they occupied equally prominent locations. On display was the spectrum of white heterosexual middle-class character-types that Shary suggests have dominated North American youth-oriented filmmaking since the mid 1970s — and some that he has not: alpha-male jocks and their loyal sidekicks, detached rebels, hyper-masculine bullies, narcissistic Casanovas, timorous introverts, frustrated virgins, laidback stoners, energetic tricksters, and wisecracking jokers (2002a, pp. 26–79). These character-types were shown embarking upon quests for personal liberation which, reflecting Paul's observation that 'the real focus of [animal comedy] is finally more social than individual' (1994, p. 90), take the form of diverse interactive undertakings that promised, even if they sometimes failed to deliver, swift gratification. Against the backdrop of mildly transgressive behavior like recreational drug and alcohol consumption and less controlled leisure like team sports and dancing, the quest for recreational sex occupied a privileged position among the group of eleven. 'The victims are portrayed as being sexually active in a casual, hedonistic way', noted the *Spokesman-Review*'s Tom Sowa (1981, p. D14), providing a somewhat literal spin on Paul's suggestion that '[f]or the male animal in animal comedy sex is always a matter of life and death' (Paul, p. 100).

Most young male characters were presented, like the heroines, in ways that invited a voyeuristic heterosexual gaze. These youths, while by no means gym-cultivated Adonises, were played predominantly by athletic, tanned, bright-eyed ambassadors of Caucasian good health, like Bill Randolph who played Jeffrey in *Friday the 13th Part II* (see Figure 5.5). The presence and the purpose of these well-conditioned and conventionally attractive young men, while overlooked by male industry-watchers and reviewers, were certainly recognized by female critics, with Janet Maslin of the *New York Times* passing comment on 'a pretty-boy counselor named Todd' in *The Burning* (1982, p. C7), and the *Los Angeles Times*' Linda Gross stressing that 'sexiness' had been infused into *My Bloody Valentine* thanks to its male lead's 'bedroom eyes' (1981a, E2). The mobilization of animal comedy material also enabled Carpetbaggers to offer distributors teen slashers that could be marketed in a tried-and-tested way to youth audiences, irrespective of gender or whether they tended to avoid or gravitate to horror films.

Animal comedy content provided an amplifier through which the volume of the principal thematic current running through the teen slasher story-structure could be increased from a low-pitched hum to an ear-piercing blast. With greater emphasis being placed on depictions of

FIGURE 5.5   Conventionally attractive male youth in *Friday the 13th Part II* (Source: *Crystal Lake Memories*).

young people pushing social boundaries before their lives were brought to a premature and unjust end, came increasingly pronounced critiques of traditional forms of authority, a theme that Jon Lewis (1992) has identified as lying at the core of youth-oriented films and one which adult producers and distributors have utilized consistently to make their films appear relevant to, and thus, in theory, resonate with, their young target audience. Horror films in which youth constitute normalcy, as Steve Neale points out, 'nearly always insist on the adult status of those in authority (. . .) [and their] (. . .) culpability, irresponsibility and ignorance' (2000, p. 36). Max Alvarez of the *Milwaukee Journal* captured the amplification of such themes in the group of eleven when he remarked that '"Happy Birthday to Me" is the type of horror film in which the collegiate cast of victims doesn't heed the advice of its elders, who tell them to drink less and study more' (1981, p. 26). Although the makers of earlier teen slashers had implicated adult characters in the deaths of their young charges as a result of their ineptitude or, as both Lewis and Vivian Sobchack note (1992, pp. 66–68; 1987, p. 175), their absence, they had stopped short of delivering genuinely devastating critiques of the adult world by electing not to portray parents, teachers, and police officers as unquestionably malicious (Dika, 1999, p. 56). Tempering critiques in this way ended, however, with the widespread adoption of animal comedy material as teen slasher after teen slasher detailed abuses and betrayals perpetrated by adults.

Teen slasher Carpetbaggers, much like the makers of animal comedies, aimed to make films that would be attractive to a general youth audience by contrasting likable young characters to mendacious, hypocritical, and self-serving adults. In the group of eleven, a teacher who propositions students, a police officer who confiscates marijuana for his own consumption, and a father who abandons his emotionally distressed daughters are among the lowlifes that suggest adults are not to be trusted or admired. The insidious character of traditional adult authority in the Carpetbagger Cash-ins is captured in a scene from *Hell Night* during which police officers initially ignore, and then aggressively dismiss as a hazing prank, a youth's desperate pleas for assistance. The youth returns to help his imperiled friends and is promptly killed. The makers of many of the group of eleven enriched their critiques of traditional forms of authority by inviting the audience to draw parallels between the actions of adults and those of the killer. For instance, when it is revealed in *Graduation Day* that the subjective shots used usually to signal the presence of the killer have in fact been representing the perspective of a local sheriff, who has been spying on youths in case they are making out or getting high, a clear link is made between the two characters by virtue of the fact that they both impede the recreational interaction of young people. The links between the killer and the adult world were trumpeted in Carpetbagger Cash-ins that tied the murders to the wrongdoings of adults. Thus, in *The Burning* and *The Prowler*, killers are exposed as middle-aged males in positions of authority over youth, in *Happy Birthday to Me, Graduation Day*, and *Hell Night* the killings are sparked by the misdeeds of patriarchs, and in *Friday the 13th Part II* and *Just Before Dawn* it is suggested that feral maniacs are the products of failed social welfare systems. The parallels that are invited between adults and the killer support the arguments made by several scholars and commentators that the protracted concealment of the killer's true motive, in the context of the victims' participation in restricted behaviors, suggests that teen slasher killers act in a punitive fashion (Wood, 1987, pp. 80–82). However, where this observation has been used as a springboard from which to first conclude that early teen slashers suggested that the 'damn kids' were getting what they deserved and that, as a consequence, they were reactionary films which endorsed right-wing ideological positions (ibid.), by taking into account the sympathetic depictions of the killer's young targets, the killer's status as an agent of horror, the killer's location within a broader critique of adult authority, and the fact that millions of dollars rested on the films' capacity to appeal to teenagers and young adults, it seems that, rather than celebrating the most radical, ruthless, and criminal of responses to the pettiest of misdemeanors, teen slashers actually invited their youth target audience to recognize and to denounce this type of extreme social conservatism, in much the same way as Paul shows the animal comedies did (1994, p. 111): by pitting likeable groups of hedonists against caricatured puritanical nemeses in struggles over appropriate behaviors.

Finally, animal comedy offered a way of avoiding the X-rating. Although it is often claimed that teen slasher killers preyed almost exclusively on women, by mobilizing the groups of young men that were a defining feature of animal comedies, teen slasher filmmakers ensured that the majority of the killers' victims were in fact males (see Appendix). As Gregory A. Waller noted in the mid 1980s: 'The many horror films that picture teenagers as survivors and monsters, but predominantly as victims find their doubles in *Porky's* (. . .) and other comedies of sexual misadventure and adolescent highjinks [sic]' (1987, p. 11). The presence of large numbers of male victims was an invaluable commodity for Carpetbaggers because it had the capacity to undermine the credibility of claims-makers who suggested that the films were misogynistic. As indicated above, it would have been commercially suicidal for an independent filmmaker to target MPAA-members with a film that opened itself up to accusations of glorifying violence against women. The reason for this was quite simple. Misogynistic films were highly susceptible to the X-rating, the receipt of which would have made the negotiation of an MPAA-member distribution deal all but impossible and left the filmmakers facing the distinct prospect of incurring substantial financial losses. In addition to shielding the filmmakers from accusations of misogynistic practice by ensuring that the killers were supplied with a steady stream of young male targets, infusing the films with sequences of animal comedy served to regulate the overall tone of the Carpetbagger Cash-ins in such a way as to make the receipt of an R-rating highly likely. The deployment of scenes of adolescent summertime horseplay, and the on-screen displays of laughter and joy that ensued, generated a form of 'comic relief' that, as King argued in the context of other types of violent film, can offset quite intense moments of threat and horror (2002, pp. 170–196). Moreover, as *Carrie*, *Halloween*, and *Friday the 13th* had demonstrated, taking such steps to fashion films that produced for audiences the pleasurable 'roller-coaster' experience that Isabel Christina Pinedo called 'recreational terror' (1997, pp. 9–51), served to distinguish youth-centered horror films from downbeat, humorless horror films like *I Spit on Your Grave* (1977), whose makers often failed, or were required to make severe edits, to avoid the X-rating (Anon., 1980j, p. 33). In short, a light-hearted, sun-soaked horror film was more likely to secure an R-rating in early 1980s America than one which was gloomy, bleak, and desolate. Ironically, the very promise of a risk-free method of bolstering commercial potential being offered by animal comedy material generated a third level of similarity among the Carpetbagger Cash-ins, as filmmakers infused their teen slashers with sequences of groups of self-indulgent, conventionally attractive young men seeking swift gratification from various leisure pursuits, and devastating critiques of the social institutions that aimed to prevent them from doing so.

In sum, the 'group of eleven' Carpetbagger Cash-ins combined content from *Prom Night* and *Friday the 13th* that also had been employed in the most financially successful youth-oriented films of 1980. In combination with *Dressed to Kill*, *Little Darlings*, and *Caddyshack*, these two teen slasher Prospector Cash-ins had highlighted the commercial potential of female leads that combined traditionally masculine and feminine traits, groups of fun-seeking young males, and murder-mystery plots. The confidence that independent filmmakers placed in these features yielded an avalanche of female-centered animal comedy-infused murder-mysteries. Much like the conditions that had made the production of teen slasher films so economically appealing, the conditions that led Carpetbaggers to fashion teen slasher content in similar ways, had laid a highly infirm foundation upon which to build a bid for an MPAA-member distribution deal. The fate awaiting the Carpetbaggers is the focus of the next, and final, section, which reveals the conditions that prompted the retreat of MPAA-member distributors and audiences, and shortly thereafter the evaporation of independent filmmakers' confidence in the teen slasher.

'Killer-with-a-knife sweepstakes': the Decline of the Teen Slasher Film

'I think we will just about slip in, before the market becomes too saturated', predicted *Terror Train*'s co-producer Sandy Howard in October 1980, 'I'm afraid that before long there may be too much competition and the same thing may happen as happened with the street gang pictures last year' (quoted in Anderson, 1980, p. 21). On the eve of the release of the last teen slasher Prospector Cash-in, Howard could afford to forecast his film's box-office prospects with an unusually candid mixture of sobriety, resignation, and indifference because earlier that year

Twentieth Century Fox had purchased *Terror Train*, thus ensuring that the film returned producers a swift profit irrespective of its commercial performance. Howard's pessimism, if not his tone, was echoed by Fox's vice-president of advertising and publicity Robert Cort who had brought forward *Terror Train*'s release by four weeks due to concerns over market saturation (Harmetz, 1980d, p. C15). 'The box office for these films has been dropping recently', lamented Cort, 'we hope we can give [*Terror Train*] some breathing room between the summer glut and the end of October glut' (quoted in ibid.). Howard and Cort reflected a decline in industry confidence in the commercial viability of teen slasher films that would have been inconceivable a few weeks earlier.

Fox's distribution of *Terror Train* was a watershed moment for the teen slasher. Thereafter, MPAA-members eschewed non-franchise independently produced teen slashers until 1986 when MGM released *Killer Party* and Paramount distributed *April Fool's Day*. A torrent of new teen slashers slowed to a trickle as production plummeted to base level. Kapsis (1992, p. 159), Cook (2000, p. 237), and Prince (2000, p. 353) each suggest this decline in production was part of general drop in horror output that followed the box-office failure of a range of horror film-types in 1983. Yet, as this section shows 'the fall of the slasher film' (Rockoff, 2002) actually predated the general downturn in horror production by over two years. In doing so, this section reveals some of the conditions under which the production of a film-type drops significantly. In the case of the teen slasher, the situation was brought about by a series of interlocking factors relating to distributors' concerns and audience attendance patterns.

By the time *Hell Night* became the last high-profile Carpetbagger Cash-in to hit American theaters in August 1981, the teen slasher film had become a commercial liability for independent producers and major distributors, and, less than three months later, Janet Maslin of the *New York Times* would declare, with obvious relief, that '[t]he best news about the nameless-killer-and-his-trail-of-carnage movie is (. . .) its moment in the sun seems just about over' (1981, p. 15). The developments that first led to MPAA-members abandoning teen slasher film distribution and then to independent filmmakers all but abandoning teen slasher film production occurred across two time-periods: September 1980–March 1981 and May–August 1981.

The first of the two periods concluded with the teen slasher Carpetbagger Cash-ins that had not received conditional pickup offers prior to completion failing to secure MPAA-member distribution deals. Because *My Bloody Valentine* and *Friday the 13th Part II* were finished punctually and had received R-ratings, Paramount was legally bound to distribute both films. Similarly, Columbia had to fulfill its contractual obligations by releasing *Happy Birthday to Me*. The remaining eight Carpetbagger Cash-ins were relegated to independent distributors (see Table 5.1). Even *Hell Night*, Irwin Yablans' follow-up to *Halloween*, had been rejected by the majors (Donahue, 1987, p. 242) and two films had struggled to attract any kind of distributor. As *Fangoria* reported, *Madman* remained in distribution limbo in summer 1981 (Anon., 1981e, p. 59), and *The Dorm that Dripped Blood* did not secure distribution until early 1982 (Carlomagno and Martin, 1982, p. 22). From September 1980 to March 1981, a series of socio-political, industrial, and institutional shifts had prompted grave reservations to surface among MPAA-members concerning the commercial and political viability of teen slasher films.

TABLE 5.1 US distribution of 'group of eleven' teen slasher film Carpetbagger Cash-ins.

Film	Distributor	Status
My Bloody Valentine	Paramount	MPAA-member
Friday the 13th Part II	Paramount	MPAA-member
Graduation Day	IFI/Scope III	Independent
The Burning	Filmways	Independent
Happy Birthday to Me	Columbia	MPAA-member
Final Exam	Motion Picture Marketing	Independent
Hell Night	Compass International	Independent
The Prowler	Sandhurst	Independent
Madman	Jensen Farley	Independent
Just Before Dawn	Picturemedia	Independent
The Dorm that Dripped Blood	New Image	Independent

Doubts over the political viability of teen slashers emerged, ironically, from the reception of two films that had contributed to the surge in teen slasher production. As shown above, high-profile controversies surrounding *Dressed to Kill* and *Cruising* had initially galvanized perceptions of the commercial potential of teen slashers. By avoiding protests, the light-hearted youth-centered films had been considered by independent producers to offer a more politically anodyne horror film-type. Yet, in late 1980, teen slashers were engulfed by the controversies surrounding the adult-centered thrillers — and not the other way around, as Kapsis has suggested (1992, p. 202). The furor that greeted *Dressed to Kill* and *Cruising* ultimately led the MPAA and prominent media figures to attempt to restrict MPAA-member distribution of violent product.

By June 1980, outrage from some quarters of America's gay community over allegedly homophobic representation in *Cruising* had transformed into debates about the validity of the ratings system (Anon., 1980g, pp. 3, 37; Sandler, 2007, pp. 63–72). Due to depictions of brutal killings and niche homosexual S&M practices, powerful theater chains had cancelled bookings of *Cruising*, questioned the appropriateness of its R-rating, and imposed on the film improvised X-ratings (Prince, 2000, p. 346). As Prince suggests, the MPAA's authority and its ability to shield its members from external regulation were at stake (ibid.). 'If the ratings system were undermined or impeded', argues Prince, 'the industry would be more vulnerable to charges from outside groups that its films were unwholesome, unhealthy, or otherwise deserving of censure' (ibid.). In response to contestation of its values, policies, and jurisdiction, the MPAA began, via CARA, to reassert its power. Among the first films to encounter more stringent policing of the R and X ratings was *Dressed to Kill* (Lewis, 2002, pp. 276–280).

While brief cuts ensured *Dressed to Kill* avoided an X-rating, as Jon Lewis and Kevin S. Sandler both have detailed (2002, pp. 276–280; 2007, pp. 73–82), De Palma's film still incurred the wrath of several feminist groups. Whether picketing theaters or protesting in writing, activist organizations including Women against Violence in Pornography and Media lambasted De Palma for, what they saw, as his film's 'insidious combination of violence and sexuality' (quoted in Lyons, 1997, p. 77). While sparking one-sided protests, *Dressed to Kill* became the site of heated debate among leading lights of the American cineaste elite (Kapsis, 1992, pp. 202–208). As heavyweight cultural arbiters like Pauline Kael and Andrew Sarris sparred over 'their reputations as film critics and opinion leaders' (ibid., p. 204), less venerated, yet highly driven, reviewers looked to forge alternate niches in which to stake their own claims to relevancy.

In a popular critical landscape being shaped by debates over cinematic violence, the charges leveled at *Dressed to Kill,* and the 'pornography of horror' rhetoric used to make them, provided a powerful arsenal for other claims-makers seeking untouched targets (Sandler, 2007, p. 77). The most prominent of these opportunists were the film critics of Chicago's *Tribune* and *Sun-Times* newspapers, Gene Siskel and Roger Ebert, who together hosted the high-rating film review show 'Sneak

Previews' (1976–1996) (Anon., 1980p, p. B2; Prince, 2000, p. 352). In September 1980, the duo embarked upon a mission to denounce what they dubbed 'women-in-danger movies' — a crusade that reached its apotheosis the following March when *American Film* published an article written by Ebert entitled 'Why the Movies aren't Safe Anymore' (Anon., 1980q, pp. 6, 30). Paradoxically, whereas Siskel and Ebert championed *Halloween* as a paradigm of 'good and scary' horror, among the culprits named by the duo were the teen slasher Prospector Cash-ins *Friday the 13th*, *Prom Night*, and *Terror Train*, as well as the Speculator Production *Silent Scream* (Siskel, 1980d, p. D6). Contradictorily, Siskel earlier had stated that *Prom Night* was not misogynistic. '[Y]ou would think that "Prom Night" was another of those hideous attacks-on-promiscuous-women pictures', he proclaimed, 'It's Not. Gender makes no difference in this routine revenge film' (Siskel 1980c, p. A6). Critical flip-flopping notwithstanding, teen slasher films had become targets of hostility.

The relatively high profile enjoyed by teen slashers, particularly *Friday the 13th*, enabled Siskel and Ebert to exaggerate the extent to which depictions of violence against women had infiltrated the cinematic mainstream, and, crucially, the shopping mall multiplexes frequented by their viewers and their viewers' children. For, as Arthur Unger of the *Christian Science Monitor* reported, the duo 'involves itself only with films everybody can see' (1980, p. 19). Siskel and Ebert did not mince their words. 'We want to warn people to be more careful about the films they pay to see and the films their children may be seeing', Siskel revealed, '[y]our children may be going to see an "innocent" film like "Prom Night" and be subjected to sick ideas and dangerous imagery' (quoted in ibid.). The framing strategies that Siskel and Ebert employed to transform films like *Prom Night* and *Friday the 13th* from critiques of misused power into 'gruesome and despicable' fantasies of a backlash against feminism were hugely influential, as a survey of subsequent scholarship indicates (Kapsis, 1992, p. 161; Clover, 1992, pp. 21–64; Cook, 2000, p. 237; Prince, 2000 p. 353), and highly misleading. For their accusations to be convincing, the duo withheld the presence of content that contradicted their claims. First, teen slasher victims were defined solely by femaleness, and not actual correlatives: youth, whiteness, heterosexuality, and middle-class belonging (Siskel, 1980d, p. D6). Echoing rhetoric employed by activist groups during contemporaneous moral panics over actual serial killers (Jenkins, 1994, pp. 86–90), the duo unsurprisingly suppressed the fact that most victims in the films were male (see Appendix). '[W]hat we are saying', explained Ebert, 'is that it is very sick when the torture and death of the woman victim is the whole point of the film' (quoted in Unger, 1980, p. 19). Second, irrespective of the motives presented in the films (personal or familial revenge, jealousy, trespass or unexplained madness), killers were said to be acting to reverse the social gains made possible by second-wave feminists. '[T]he killer gets some sort of gratification from killing women (. . .) [t]he killers are often portrayed as frustrated men who kill to gain satisfaction', added Siskel (quoted in ibid.). Finally, Siskel and Ebert needed to convince their audience that viewers of the films were encouraged, not to revile such human monsters, but to support their efforts to 'systematically demean half the human race' ('Sneak Previews', 1980). The subjective shots, sometimes used to conceal the killer's identity, were thus endowed uncomplicatedly with the ability to 'enlist sympathy' and rouse the vocal support of armies of out-of-control patrons (ibid.). '[T]he point of view of the camera encourages the audience to identify with the killer', declared Ebert, before concluding that: 'Traditionally in horror films, you are manipulated to identify with the victim — that's what made them scary. (. . .) The audience is now being trained to think of itself as the killer. That's very sad and dangerous' (quoted in Unger, 1980, p. 19). Siskel and Ebert had begun a process that would see teen slashers assimilated discursively with other film-types — particularly rape-revenge pictures like *I Spit on your Grave* and grim character studies of misogynist serial rapists and murderers such as *Don't Answer the Phone* — in spite of the fact that filmmakers had gone to great lengths to differentiate their teen slashers from these genuinely provocative films.

   Driven by the arguments of Siskel and Ebert, a convergence of distinct constellations of film content was taking place in the public sphere, much like that which Linda Williams identified as having occurred between horror and hardcore pornography during the *Snuff* scandal of 1976 (1999, p. 193). Whereas Ebert claimed to be 'appalled at the growth in popularity of the new wave of drive-in-type horror films such as "I Spit on Your Grave", "Don't Answer the Phone," (. . .) and "Friday, the Thirteenth [sic]"' (quoted in Unger, 1980, p. 19), Siskel informed 'women activists' that they 'would do better protesting the perverted films that are reaching mainstream America. [Because] [f]ilms such as "Silent Scream" and "Friday the Thirteenth" [sic] play to audiences 50 times as large as most porno features' (1980c, p. A5). Siskel and Ebert's erasure of the distinctions that, both Wood (1987, pp. 79–85) and I have shown, differentiated teen slashers from 'violence-against-women movies', went largely unnoticed by the US popular press. Some journalists, including the *Evening Independent*'s Jim Moorhead, simply reiterated unquestioningly Siskel and Ebert's conclusions by making statements like '[f]rom *Halloween* to *My Bloody Valentine*, these movies seem to reflect someone's sadistic pleasure in seeing near-helpless females fall victim to all sorts of atrocities' (1981, p. 21). Even those journalists who attacked the duo on the grounds that the supposedly rampant film-type posed no threat to theater patrons or the general public, did so only after recycling, and by extension, reinforcing Siskel and Ebert's self-serving elimination of, what once had been, clearly drawn generic boundaries between teen slashers and violence-against-women movies (see Dibsie 1980, pp. 63, 80). Nowhere was the shift more apparent than in a craze that swept American film journalism, whereby, in order to emphasize the quantity of supposedly misogynistic horror films, reviewers hyphenated as many contemporaneous horror film titles as possible. Hyphenates like 'Don't Go in the House of the Boogey Man or You'll Leave in the Hearse, Howling a Silent Scream' (ibid., p. 83), which Wood later lampooned (1987, p. 63), captured the extent to which Siskel and Ebert's deft sleight-of-hand had shaped the critical discourse of film journalists and, it was fair to assume, some of their readers. In a development that heavily influenced scholarly discussion of the film-type, the teen slasher film had been absorbed into the unsavory and, as far as MPAA-members were concerned, untouchable category of the violence-against-women movie.

Teen slasher films provided Siskel and Ebert the ideal instrument with which to place pressure on the MPAA, via CARA, to redraw the boundary that separated the R and X ratings. 'I don't understand how the R rating became so large', bemoaned Ebert, 'as to include these films that go right of the map of any kind of good taste' ('Sneak Previews', 1980). By misrepresenting teen slashers calculatedly, Siskel and Ebert looked to engineer a situation that would see teen slashers rated X, thus preventing the films from attracting MPAA-member distributors, and ultimately removing the incentives to produce new examples of the film-type. In a kind of film culture Munchausen syndrome by proxy, the duo would further their careers by slaying a monster that they themselves had created. The crusade was not without its successes.

The controversies surrounding the teen slasher Prospector Cash-ins as well as *Cruising*, and *Dressed to Kill*, re-formed the socio-political, industrial and, institutional environment for subsequent horror films. As Prince observes, the left liberal perspective of Siskel and Ebert and the groups that denounced *Dressed to Kill* and *Cruising* dovetailed neatly with the views of the right-wing fundamentalists that had been rallying against the migration of hardcore pornography into public arenas since the early 1970s (2000, pp. 356–357). In the context of such an 'unlikely alliance', as Prince called it (ibid., p. 357), slippages in ideological labeling occurred. 'The political climate in this country is shifting to the right', declared MPAA president Jack Valenti in late summer 1980, 'and that means more conservative attitudes towards sex and violence' (quoted in ibid., p. 365). The targets of stricter regulation of the R-rating soon became apparent when Richard Heffner, chairman of CARA, informed Paramount's vice-president of marketing and distribution Frank Mancuso Sr. that *Friday the 13th* had 'diminished the board's sensitivity to violence and allowed everything to build further and further on it' (quoted in Vaughn, 2006, p. 102). By suggesting that an error in judgment, rather than liberal policy, had allowed *Friday the 13th* to avoid an X-rating, Heffner, a man who Stephen Vaughn described as 'the least-known most powerful person in Hollywood' was ostensibly forewarning Mancuso that subsequent submissions would not benefit from such leniency (ibid., liner notes). Just before most of the teen slasher Carpetbagger Cash-ins were shot, news of an imminent crackdown on violent content went public, as journalists like Richard Harrington of the *Washington Post* reported that 'the Motion Picture Association of America is considering stringent new ratings for excessive violence' (1980, p. M1). As shown below, the teen slasher filmmakers who had emulated *Friday the 13th* were required to jettison much of their (usually already strictly limited) violence and body-horror to obtain R-ratings, for, as Heffner confirmed to Robert E. Kapsis (1992, pp. 269–270 n. 11), many films that would have been rated R in 1979 were deemed worthy of X-ratings in 1981.

The MPAA-members would likely have sought to weather these storms had teen slashers demonstrated a capacity to match the rentals of *Halloween*, *Friday the 13th* or even *Prom Night* and *Silent Scream* but, by March 1981, economic developments caused serious reservations about the continued financial viability of the film-type to sweep the industry. In the eight months that followed the release of the second Prospector Cash-in *Prom Night*, every MPAA-member-distributed film that paired maniacs and young people, irrespective of story-structure, tone or other content, performed wretchedly at the American box-office — a slump that affected every MPAA-member except Columbia (see Table 5.2). The unrelenting series of commercial disasters began in September 1980 with the weak returns of MGM/UA's pickup *He Knows You're Alone*. At this point *Variety* coined the phrase 'the killer-with-a-knife sweepstakes' to reflect the sense of growing uncertainty among industry-insiders (Carl., 1980, p. 20). The following month, both *Variety* and the *New York Times* were predicting that 'the terror-horror genre may have peaked in the US' (Harmetz, 1980d, p. C15; Watkins, 1980, p. 3), when MGM/UA's second acquisition, *Motel Hell*, struggled to attract its youth target audience. By November, industry-watchers were suggesting that 'with many similar movies playing across theaters simultaneously, not all of them will break even' (Williams, 1980, p. E1), and distributors were voicing their concerns publicly. For example Mick Garris, a horror expert at Avco Embassy, concluded that 'psycho-knife killer movies' had become one of the least commercially viable horror film-types (quoted in ibid.). The slump continued into 1981 when Avco Embassy's *Fear No Evil*, Universal's *The Funhouse*, and Warner Bros.' *Eyes of a Stranger* flopped at the US box-office. Industry analysts were no longer writing about sweepstakes nor were phrases like 'may have peaked' being printed. In its review of the film, *Variety* simply forecast a 'bleak outlook' for *The Funhouse* (Carl., 1981b, p. 133). Had they been immune to this general downturn, teen slasher films' market value to MPAA-members would likely have increased, but late 1980-early 1981 also witnessed a change in fortune for the teen slasher film.

TABLE 5.2   Rentals of MPAA-member-distributed films featuring maniacs and youth, September 1980–March 1981

Film	Release	Distributor	Rentals ($m)	Position
He Knows You're Alone	09/12/80	MGM/UA	1.7	104th/1980
Terror Train	10/03/80	Twentieth Century Fox	3.5	84th/1980
Motel Hell	10/18/80	United Artists	1.4	117th/1980
Fear No Evil	01/81	Avco Embassy	3	93rd/1981
My Bloody Valentine	02/11/81	Paramount	2.6	99th/1981
The Funhouse	03/13/81	Universal	3.8	89th/1981
Eyes of a Stranger	03/27/81	Warner Bros.	<1.0	<135th/1981

(Source: Anon., 1981a, pp. 29, 50; Anon, 1982a, pp. 15, 42).

The teen slasher films released between September 1980 and March 1981 failed to emulate the financial achievements of their predecessors. Just like Sandy Howard predicted, *Terror Train* managed to 'just about slip in' (quoted in Anderson, 1980, p. 21), when it generated Fox an inglorious $3.5m in rentals despite receiving a similar saturation release and generous marketing budget to those which Paramount had given *Friday the 13th* (Anon., 1981a, p. 50). Five months later, at a point in time that Avco Embassy's werewolf film *The Howling* was performing solidly thus demonstrating that audience interest in other horror film-types existed,[23] the 'loser' *My Bloody Valentine*, as the *Los Angeles Times* described it (Pollock, 1981a, p. G1), returned Paramount the derisory sum of $2.6m (Anon., 1982a, p. 42). The combined rentals of the pair amounted to barely a third of the figure that had been generated by *Friday the 13th* and only narrowly surpassed the $6m that *Prom Night* returned under considerably more adverse conditions. For MPAA-members, the box-office failure of *Terror Train* and *My Bloody Valentine* — the last Prospector Cash-in and first Carpetbagger Cash-in to hit theaters — hammered another nail in the coffin of the teen slasher film.

Weak ticket sales for *Terror Train* and *My Bloody Valentine* also indicated that the textual approach to which the makers of the group of eleven Carpetbagger Cash-ins had anchored their commercial ambitions was not attracting audiences. Promotional materials had framed both films as murder-mysteries shaped around female protagonists and jovial male youths (see Figure 5.6). The emphasis that Fox placed on animal comedy was encapsulated in the voice-over to *Terror Train*'s trailer. 'For the students onboard', intoned the narrator, 'it's going to be the one party to end them all'. Similarly, the film's poster spotlighted college students and conveyed the presence of female characters with an image of sorority sisters and its tagline: 'The Boys and Girls of Sigma Phi . . .'. Following *Terror Train*'s underwhelming returns, Paramount re-oriented these elements in what *Variety* called its 'customary shrewd' promotion of *My Bloody Valentine* (Carl., 1981a, p. 20). While the film's poster relegated animal comedy to a small image of male revelers, its title, tagline ('there's more than one way to lose your heart'), an illustration of young couples slow-dancing beneath love-hearts, and its Valentine's weekend opening, emphasized romance to angle the film squarely to young women. Confirmation of audiences' apparent rejection of films that promised to combine blade-wielding maniacs either with animal comedy content or material geared to young women had been provided by the disappointing box-office performances of *He Knows You're Alone*, which had been advertised with the tagline 'every girl is frightened the night before her wedding', and *Eyes of a Stranger*, which had been sold, somewhat misleadingly, on the tagline 'sorry your party is dead'. The teen slasher Carpetbaggers' prospects looked very bleak indeed.

Dwindling ticket sales, critical hostility, and institutional obstacles prompted MPAA-members to eschew the recently completed teen slasher Carpetbagger Cash-ins to which they had no contractual obligations. This shift in distributor conduct alerted independent producers to the distinct possibility that teen slashers did not offer a relatively secure

 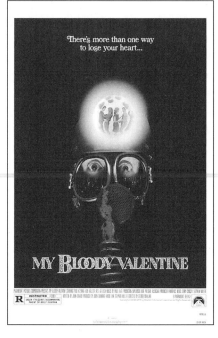

FIGURE 5.6   Selling teen slashers on whodunit plots, female characters, and animal comedy *Terror Train* and *My Bloody Valentine.*

method of obtaining lucrative MPAA-member pickup deals. *Variety* even reported that the Prospectors behind the teen slasher hits of 1980 would not be attempting to emulate their previous achievements by producing new teen slashers. *Prom Night*'s producer Peter Simpson explained that his next film, *Curtains* (1983), was 'aimed for an adult audience' because he 'got nervous about the failure of teenybopper horror films such as "Terror Train"' (quoted in Anon., 1980r, p. 36). Regarding his follow-up, a 'straight suspense picture', as he described it, called *A Stranger is Watching* (1981), *Friday the 13th*'s producer-director Sean S. Cunningham explained: 'we can have a hit in today's market (. . .) you can't do that with last year's movie' — a clear reference to *Friday the 13th* and the Cash-ins made in its wake (quoted in Cohn, 1981, pp. 6, 41). However, the continued production of teen slashers in significant numbers hinged upon the box-office performances of subsequent releases. The commercial failure of these films would justify the majors' strategies. But if the films were financially successful, the withdrawal of the heavyweights of American film distribution would have been revealed to have been a hasty over-reaction. During summer 1981, the retreat of the MPAA-members was confirmed to have been astute and well-timed.

Questions concerning the economic potential of the teen slasher film-type were answered conclusively when the five Carpetbagger Cash-ins released between May and August 1981 disappointed commercially (see Table 5.3). With the exception of *Friday the 13th Part II*, each film failed even to match *Prom Night*'s returns. The Canadian production *Happy Birthday to Me* was the least financially disastrous of these releases, generating $4.9m, 18 per cent less than its compatriot and only the 74th highest rentals of the year. Motion Picture Marketing's *Final Exam* returned a paltry $1.2m and the other independently distributed Cash-ins *Hell Night, Graduation Day*, and *The Burning* fared even worse, each accumulating less than $1m in rentals.[24] Based on publicity, prints, and other negative costs, distributors certainly lost money on this quartet of flops.[25] Although its $6.4m three day gross from 1350 North American theaters improved upon the $5.7m generated by its predecessor (Paramount Pictures, 1981, pp. 30–31; Anon., 1981d), *Friday the 13th Part II* fulfilled *Variety*'s gloomy long-term predictions. 'Enthusiasm will dampen once [audiences] recognize too many of the same old twists and turns used in the original', the trade paper had noted, 'that shouldn't hurt initial business, but could cause problems further down the line' (Lor., 1981a, p. 31). The $10m rentals that the sequel amassed were almost 40 per cent lower than the $16.5m returned by the first film (Anon., 1982a, p. 15). By means of comparison, both *Friday the 13th 3: 3D* (1982) and *Friday the 13th: The Final Chapter* (1984) matched the domestic theatrical rentals of *Friday the 13th*, when they, like the original film, faced little competition from similar product.[26] Market saturation and derivative marketing had facilitated the disappointing box-office performances of the first wave of Carpetbagger Cash-ins to hit theaters.

TABLE 5.3 Rentals of 'group of eleven' teen slasher film Carpetbagger Cash-ins.

Film	Release	Rentals ($m)	Position
My Bloody Valentine	02/11/81	2.6	99th/1981
Friday the 13th Part II	05/01/81	10	33rd/1981
Graduation Day	05/01/81	<1	>135th/1981
The Burning	05/08/81	<1	>135th/1981
Happy Birthday to Me	05/15/81	4.9	74th/1981

(continued over page)

TABLE 5.3   Rentals of 'group of eleven' teen slasher film Carpetbagger Cash-ins.
                  (*continued*)

Film	Release	Rentals ($m)	Position
Final Exam	06/05/81	1.3	120th/1981
Hell Night	08/28/81	<1	>135th/1981
The Prowler	11/06/81	<1	>135th/1981
Madman	01/82	<1	>258th/1982
Just before Dawn	03/82	<1	>258th/1982
The Dorm that Dripped Blood	04/82	<1	>258th/1982

(Source: Anon., 1982a, pp. 15, 42; Anon., 1983, pp. 13, 46, 52)

Market saturation prevented any teen slasher from emulating the commercial achievements of *Halloween* and *Friday the 13th*.[27] *Friday the 13th
Part II* and *Graduation Day* had opened simultaneously on 1 May, followed
seven days later by *The Burning*, before *Happy Birthday to Me* debuted
the following week. 'If Hollywood [sic] continues to knock off college
students at such a prolific rate pace', wrote one critic, 'there won't be
any more to patronize films like "Happy Birthday to Me"' (Alvarez, 1981,
p. 26). While the combined rentals of these films suggest that a similar
number of tickets to that sold in summer 1980 was spread across the films,
the devastating impact of this intense period of releases was reflected in
the box-office performances of the teen slasher Carpetbagger Cash-ins
that opened between June and August 1981, *Final Exam* and *Hell Night*,
both of which failed to draw sizable quantities of their youth target audience. The distribution of *Final Exam* and *Hell Night* echoed the release
of *Prom Night* twelve months earlier, with the presence on the market of
seven of the annual top ten, including the blockbuster hits *Raiders of the
Lost Ark* and *Superman 2* impeding the teen slashers' capacity to garner
infrequent theatergoers.[28] Yet, unlike *Prom Night*, the youth-oriented
films against which *Final Exam* and *Hell Night* competed proved more
appealing to young people. Instead of teen slashers, the male-centered
comedies *Stripes* and *Cheech and Chong's Nice Dreams* cruised into the top
twenty of the annual rentals chart,[29] while *Endless Love*, a male-centered
film about an emotional breakdown that Justin Wyatt has shown to have
been targeted at teenage girls on its fairly brief romantic content (Wyatt,
1994b, p. 119), and the supernatural horror film *An American Werewolf in
London*, also generated strong ticket sales.[30] Even the romance/animal

comedy *Private Lessons* returned independent distributor Jensen Farley Pictures rentals well in excess of the combined sum generated by the teen slashers released from June to August 1981.[31] By the time the last of the Carpetbagger Cash-ins had opened, a new teen slasher had been released on average once every six weeks across the previous fifteen months, which, in conjunction with solid ticket sales for other youth-oriented and horror film-types, suggested that America's theatergoing youths were tiring of tales of blade-wielding maniacs menacing their on-screen equivalents.

In the small number of public forums available to them in 1981, young Americans admitted that they were growing weary of teen slashers. These sentiments can certainly be gauged from interviews conducted by Jade Garner of the *Los Angeles Times* in respect to teenagers' views on cine-matic trends (Garner, 1981, p. L29; Caulfield and Garner, 1981, p. L22). 'I'm just not interested in things like *Meatballs* and horror movies', one youth revealed, 'I won't go to see "Happy Birthday to Me", "Prom Night", "Friday the 13th" and stuff like that' (quoted Caulfield and Garner, 1981, p. L22). Reader comments in horror magazine *Fangoria* also suggested that some horror fans were rejecting teen slashers. Despite the editors' increasing focus on special effects, (what were adjudged to be) excessive amounts of gore had in fact alienated some of the magazine's readership. One contributor, who described himself as 'not a fan of the "blood-and-guts" type film', explained that viewing *Friday the 13th* had been 'more like punishment than entertainment' (Evans, 1981, pp. 6–7). Another reader, who professed to have enjoyed *Friday the 13th*, was moved to air his dissatisfaction at 'depressing gore' on display in *My Bloody Valentine* (D. Hicks, 1981, p. 7). That reader also voiced his frustration at what he saw as insufficient levels of textual difference between teen slashers. 'I just got back from wasting more money on another cheap *Halloween* rip-off, *My Bloody Valentine*', he lamented, before announcing: 'Here's to abolishing the slasher image forever' (ibid.). As attested to by the pen-ultimate remark, these disenchanted horror fans already had paid to see teen slashers, and were in no mood to repeat that mistake. Ensuring that they, and others like them, recognized precisely which films to avoid were the promotional materials that accompanied the teen slashers of summer 1981.

Distributors' derivative marketing campaigns exacerbated market saturation by making teen slasher films clearly distinguishable from other film-types. In response to the box-office failure of the teen slashers advertised on female protagonists, animal comedy, and murder-mystery plots (*Terror Train* and *My Bloody Valentine*), distributors played down product differentiation in favor of echoing the advertising of *Friday the 13th* so as to imply similarities to the film. This damage-limitation strategy was most apparent in Paramount's promotion of *Friday the 13th Part II*, which was tailored to evoke exclusively its predecessor. After showing that sequel marketing tends to evoke earlier installments, thus tipping heavily in the favor of evocation the balance between evoking earlier hits and spotlighting difference that Altman argues to be a central tenet of 'genre film' promotion (1999, pp. 115–121, 132–139), Lisa Kernan, in her groundbreaking study of film trailers, singled out the trailer for *Friday the 13th Part II* as an exceptional instance in which suggestions of difference are all but obliterated (2004, pp. 48–50), arguing correctly that '[t]he idea of repetition and the notion of sequel are over-determined' in the marketing of the film (ibid., p. 49). 'The trailer to *Friday the 13th Part II*', she explained, 'is a sequel to the trailer for *Friday the 13th*' (ibid.). Similarity and continuation are emphasized in the structure and address of the trailer. 'Why should Friday the 13th 1981 be any different?', asks its narrator, as an on-screen numerical record of victims commences at the exact point at which the first film's trailer had concluded. Similarly, by situating its title and tagline against a plain black background, the poster that promoted *Friday the 13th Part II* also eschewed elements that could have risked alienating the theatergoers that had propelled *Friday the 13th* into the top twenty of the annual rentals chart for 1980. To communicate that this sequel is a continuation of the previous film, Paramount labeled its product 'Part II'. The first film, it was implied, is restarted rather than explored or complemented. Continuity was cemented by the tagline. The sequel does not merely add to *Friday the 13th*'s victims, rather, as its tagline promises, in *Friday the 13th Part II* 'the body count continues . . .' (see Figure 5.7). Despite appearing at a point in time at which film sequels with numerical titles were becoming increasingly common, Paramount's marketing strategies received a surprisingly large amount of attention from industry-watchers. With reviewers of mass-circulation newspapers including the *Washington Post* lauding the company's approach and describing its tagline as a 'sassy slogan' (Arnold, 1981a, p. B6), and with the *Los Angeles Times* crediting it with stimulating the film's strong opening weekend (Pollock, 1981b, p. H1), the reception of *Friday the 13th Part II* provided the marketers of other Carpetbagger Cash-ins with an additional incentive to encourage audiences to anticipate similarities between their respective teen slashers and *Friday the 13th*, thus providing, or at least they hoped, a possible antidote to the precipitously declining box-office returns of teen slashers.

The posters used to promote the teen slashers released in summer

FIGURE 5.7 Emphasizing continuity to promote *Friday the 13th Part II*.

1981 also emphasized parallels to *Friday the 13th*. In the hand-painted art-work employed by Filmways and Motion Picture Marketing to advertise *The Burning* and *Final Exam* respectively, back-lit silhouettes of blade-wielding figures and similar contextual iconography ensured that minor compositional differences such as the parameters and content of 'cor-poreal space' were outweighed by similarities to *Friday the 13th*'s poster. *Final Exam*'s poster positions its campus setting against a night sky, billowy clouds, full moon, and trees, all of which is rendered in a palette of blues, blacks, and purples, much like the artwork that had advertised *Friday the 13th* (see Figure 5.8). Similarly, even though *The Burning*'s poster sub-stitutes moonlight for sunbeams, it, like, *Friday the 13th*'s poster, conveys the film's summer camp setting with an image of a wooden cabin that is positioned in the centre of the design and which too is shrouded by trees (see Figure 5.9). The posters advertising the remaining teen slasher Carpetbagger Cash-ins evoked *Friday the 13th* in more subtle ways. For example, *Hell Night*'s poster reproduced in a similar palette the clouds, trees, and full moon that had featured on *Friday the 13th*'s poster, and employed near-subliminal compositional similarities. On the left of *Hell Night*'s poster, metal bars and the outline formed by the heroine's body and the arm of her assailant match exactly that produced by a tree and the body of *Friday the 13th*'s killer (see Figure 5.10). Even *Happy Birthday to Me*, the promotional poster of which was least reliant on aping *Friday the 13th*'s poster art, was recognized as being advertised as a 'typical teen-age mayhem flick' (Sheffield, 1981, p. 7). Across summer 1981, it was quite simple for audiences to avoid teen slashers if they so desired.

The poster art that advertised, and framed for audiences, the Carpetbagger Cash-ins indicates that distributors were targeting the films primarily to horror fans. 'There's always a certain number of people who'll go see a horror movie', revealed Don Borchers, a top-ranking Avco Embassy executive involved in the promotion of *Prom Night* and other contemporaneous horror films, 'and if you do it right there's no limit to how many times they'll see it' (quoted in Knoedelseder, 1980a, pp. N3–4). Such damage-limitation exercises reveal that distributors considered teen slashers to be no longer capable of appealing to a cross-section of youth-market sub-demographics and taste formations. This conduct also represented a tacit acceptance that making huge profits from teen slasher film distribution was no longer likely and that instead commercial success would be measured by the extent to which financial loss was minimized.

 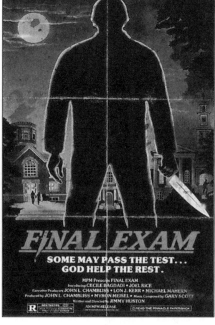

FIGURE 5.8   Evoking *Friday the 13th* to promote *Final Exam*.

FIGURE 5.9   Evoking *Friday the 13th* to promote *The Burning*.

FIGURE 5.10   Evoking *Friday the 13th* to promote *Hell Night*.

The low rentals of the teen slashers released in summer 1981 indicate that horror aficionados had also rejected the film-type. By 1981, teen slashers offered little to the audience segment seeking intense horror, thrills, and gory effects — the 'gore-tech fans' (Harrington, 1980, p. M3) being served by *Fangoria* magazine. Several filmmakers, including those behind *Hell Night* and *Happy Birthday to Me*, had telegraphed CARA's stricter policing of the R-rating and positioned violence and its grisly consequences for the most part outside the frame. The results were not lost on industry-watchers. Despite subsequent claims that violence increased across the teen slasher cycle (Prince, 2000 p. 298), several reviews noted the diminishing levels of on-screen violence and body-horror, including Kevin Thomas of the *Los Angeles Times* who acknowledged that *Hell Night* 'is rightly rated R for its grisly shock effects, but it resists (. . .) lingering morbidly' (1981, p. G13). Other Carpetbaggers had, however, emulated the producers of *Friday the 13th* by recruiting leading make-up effects artists to fashion set-piece murders. But much of Tom Savini's work for *The Burning* and *The Prowler* (see Harrington, 1980, p. M3), like that which Thomas R. Burman had contributed to *My Bloody Valentine*, had been excised before the films were submitted to CARA so as to secure R-ratings.[32] The popular press recognized the results if not the causes. For example, Linda Gross wrote in the *Los Angeles Times*' that, due to being 'less graphic (. . .) My Bloody Valentine* relies heavily on gruesome cerebral associations' (1981a, p. E2), and Gary Arnold of the *Washington Post* noted of *Friday the 13th Part II*'s director Steve Miner, '[c]omparatively speaking, he seems less bloodthirsty than the directors of "Friday the 13th", "The Exterminator" or "Mother's Day" [both 1980] to name only a few competitors of grosser gruesomeness' (1981a, B6). As Arnold intimated, 'gore-tech fans' could consume unrated independent releases like *Mother's Day* and European imports such as *Zombie* (1980) that fulfilled the promise of their promotion by showcasing protracted and detailed renditions of corporeal evisceration (Prince, 2000 p. 366). And it was these titles, along with earlier X-rated entries still in circulation like *Dawn of the Dead* (1978), which were being championed by this niche market across the readers' letters pages of *Fangoria*. Meanwhile, the makers of *An American Werewolf in London* — like the producers of *The Howling* in early 1981 — also had found a way of catering to this audience and of sidestepping CARA's crackdown: by channeling body-horror into state-of-the-art lycanthropic metamorphoses.

As the self-reflexive voice-over to *An American Werewolf in London*'s trailer insisted, the American youth-market, like the film's college-age protagonists, was 'changing, changing, changing (. . .) [into] something new, something different'. The unexpected box-office success of Jensen Farley's *Private Lessons* would lead to films about teenage boys having affairs with older women, among which were *Class, Losin' It* and, *Risky Business* (all 1983). The production of animal comedies would briefly be re-invigorated after the Canadian-made high school comedy *Porky's* (1981) was picked up by Fox and became the most commercially success-ful youth-centered film since *Animal House, Grease,* and *Saturday Night Fever,* resulting in films like *Private School* and Sean S. Cunningham's minor hit *Spring Break* (both 1983). Concurrently, the production of youth-centered horror proved less appealing with films like Paul Lynch's *Humongous* (1982) and John Carpenter's *Christine* (1983) outnumbered by violent adult-centered thrillers including *Visiting Hours* (1982), *The Dead Zone,* and *Psycho II* (both 1983). For the time being at least, the fin-ancial incentives to produce and distribute teen slashers had diminished considerably, and in place of the teen slasher film had emerged a range of more commercially attractive youth-oriented and horror film-types.

Conclusion

Like the unfortunate backpackers in John Landis' *An American Werewolf in London*, perceptions of the teen slasher's financial viability underwent a pronounced and spectacular transformation between late summer 1980 and late summer 1981. Within little over a year, the confidence MPAA-member distributors and independent producers placed in the commercial potential of teen slasher films escalated rapidly before evap-orating swiftly. Across the first half of 1980, MPAA-member distribution, relative commercial success, and the dwindling financial viability of other types of youth-oriented and horror film transformed teen slasher production from a perilous enterprise into a highly attractive venture. These conditions fuelled over-production as independent filmmakers moved to capitalize on a seemingly lucrative model. The implications of this surge in production were exacerbated by insufficient product dif-ferentiation as Carpetbaggers combined content of *Prom Night* and *Friday the 13th* that also had featured in additional youth-oriented hits of 1980 to shape the teen slasher into female-centered animal comedy-infused murder-mysteries.

When many of the Carpetbagger Cash-ins were still in production, MPAA-member confidence in teen slashers plummeted. Doubts con-cerning the commercial viability of the film-type swelled swiftly when films combining youth and human monsters, including two teen slashers that had been promoted on murder-mystery plots, animal comedy, and female protagonists, proved financially unsuccessful in late 1980 and early 1981. Concurrently, the political viability of the teen slasher was brought into question when it became embroiled in controversies over other films. In response, MPAA-members elected not to distribute teen slashers to which they had no prior contractual obligations. This decision was validated when market saturation, derivative promotion, and insufficient product differentiation contributed to the disappointing box-office performances of the teen slashers released in summer 1981. The universally weak returns of these films signaled to independent filmmakers that subsequent productions would struggle to secure MPAA-member distribution deals and by extension struggle to turn a profit. As with gang movies and roller-disco movies, and demonic child, revenge-of-nature, and city vs. country horror films, when MPAA-member distribution appeared unattainable, independent filmmakers ceased to perceive teen slasher film production as commercially viable and levels of production dropped considerably. Yet, like so many motionless killers, the teen slasher film would rise again.

Conclusion

Time after time

After several miserable failures, frustrated high school senior Edward 'Pee Wee' Morris (Dan Monahan) is about to lose his virginity. His buddies are all on hand to impart words of encouragement as their diminutive friend slopes into a parked bus. Unbeknown to the gang, somebody else is watching. Subjective shots reveal a shadowy figure scuttling through nearby undergrowth. Suddenly, the mysterious prowler makes a lunge for the gang. Ms Balbricker (Nancy Parsons), tyrannical Phys-Ed instructor and scourge of Angel Beach's hedonistic student body, wrestles one of the boys to the ground to prove, in no uncertain terms, that he is the owner of the 'tally-whacker' that was revealed several weeks earlier in the girls' showers. Amid howls of laughter, the puritanical educator is hauled away by police officers.

Filmed shortly before the group of eleven teen slasher Carpetbagger Cash-ins started to open theatrically, the climactic moments of the 1981 animal comedy *Porky's* reflected emerging perceptions of the teen slasher film. With a brief sequence that parodied affectionately teen slasher content, writer-director-producer Bob Clark gestured openly to the textual and industrial development of the film-type he had inadvertently conceived with *Black Christmas* (1974). Just over a half-decade after Clark's Pioneer Production limped through theatres, the conventions of the teen slasher had become a target of parody.

In a November 1980 interview with the *Los Angeles Times*, Jamie Lee Curtis, who, as the star of *Halloween* (1978), *Prom Night*, and *Terror Train* (both 1980) had become somewhat of a poster child for the teen slasher film, joked about a potential teen slasher parody (Knoedelseder Jr., 1980b, p. Q4). 'Gobble', she jested, would concern a farm boy who is transformed into a blade-wielding maniac when he discovers the Thanksgiving fate awaiting his beloved turkeys (cited in ibid.). Curtis teased her interviewer that she would pitch the project to Avco Embassy's resident horror expert Don Borchers as 'the "Airplane!" of horror movies' (quoted in ibid.). Within six months, the same newspaper had run a light-hearted piece that offered titles and synopses of potential cinematic 'holiday hell-raisers' as it called them (Williamson, 1981, p. L31), and a report on 'spoofs of "Friday the 13th"' that were in production at the time (Pollock, 1981b, p. H1). Shortly thereafter, Linda Gross, a film critic at the *Los Angeles Times*, asked her readers: 'what if you looped together "Friday the 13th Part I and II", "Halloween", "Prom Night", "Final Exam", "Happy Birthday to Me" and "Terror Train", among others, for laughs?' (1981c, p. G4). 'You would probably come up with "Student Bodies"', she responded, a film which Gross considered to have 'some funny moments, but is definitely not another "Airplane!"' (ibid.).

The marketing of *Student Bodies* (1981) revealed much about the reasoning behind Paramount's distribution of the first teen slasher parody. 'This motion picture is based on an actual incident', proclaimed the somber title card that opened the film's trailer, 'last year 26 horror films were released. None of them lost money'. This incongruous, yet revealing, declaration of industrial logic was followed by an equally telling insight into the studio's target audience. 'Hello', announced a voice-over narrator, 'it's me — the heavy breather from every horror film you've ever seen'. A principal commercial imperative that had underwritten *Student Bodies*, much like the trio of teen slasher parodies in production when the film debuted in August 1981, was flaunted in such a gratuitous manner as to render its candor invisible. In addition to capitalizing on its hit disaster film parody *Airplane!*, Paramount sought to attract the young theatergoers that had propelled its 1980 pickup *Friday the 13th* into the top twenty of the annual rentals chart. Underpinning this logic was the notion that the conventions of the teen slasher film had, for American youths, become firmly established because parodies, as Geoff King has argued, target individual films, production trends, and cycles that 'as a result of significant box-office success and/or cultural prominence' are familiar to a sizable segment of their own target audience (2002, p. 112). 'To become a target for parody', he suggests, 'is to have achieved a certain status' (ibid.). The emergence of the first teen slasher film parody also indicated, in line with Dan Harries' ideas, that its makers considered audiences to hold a fairly ambivalent view of the film-type, one marked by the paradoxical combination of mocking critical distance and genuine affection (2000, p.8). Indeed, if the 'equal amounts of enjoyment and hostility' emanating from the audience with which *Washington Post* film critic Gary Arnold watched *Student Bodies* was representative of the American youth-market more generally, then the logic behind the film's production appeared to have been sound (1981d, p. C10). 'The sources of the hostility also seemed to be mixed', observed Arnold, 'on one hand a rejection of the parody itself as "dumb" or unsatisfying; on the other, a curious disappointment at finding the movie making fun of horror clichés in the first place' (ibid.). As Arnold, the 'high school kids' with whom he watched the movie, and the 'wisecracking group of movie-saturated adolescents' whom he concluded sarcastically must have conceptualized the film, all recognized, *Student Bodies*, much like its contemporaries, *Class Reunion, Pandemonium,* and *Wacko!* (all 1982), utilizes the same story-structure as the teen slasher films its makers lampoon.

Blood Money has examined the conditions that informed the emergence, development, and establishment of that story-structure. By combining content analysis and industry analysis I hope to have illuminated industry logic, operations, and ambitions regarding what was a new narrative-based filmic model, shed new light on early teen slasher film content, production, marketing, and distribution, enriched understandings of the complex interaction that was conducted between the various parts of the North American independent sector and Hollywood during the mid-to-late 1970s and early 1980s, and gone some way to explaining the manner in which film cycles tend to develop both industrially and in terms of film content.

By treating film cycles as a series of chronologically distinct phases of activity, *Blood Money* has shown how production and distribution, in addition to the content of individual films and their marketing campaigns, is impacted by industrial developments, market shifts, and changing commercial imperatives. This book illuminated the ways in which the teen slasher's inauspicious advent in 1974, its rise to prominence across 1980 and 1981, and its temporary demise in late 1981, were products of perceptions of the bankability of other types of film, particularly blockbuster hits, up-market horror films, glossy thrillers and youth-market fare like animal comedies, female-centered coming-of-age dramas, gang movies, and roller-disco movies. *Blood Money* demonstrated that the teen slasher became an established part of the North American film industry's range of youth-market product as a result of a complex network of factors that included the transnational approach of commercially ambitious Canadian filmmakers and financiers, the enterprise of American independent filmmakers, industry-insiders' perceptions of gendered film consumption, and shifts in the corporate strategies of the major Hollywood studios.

The book began by outlining a story-structure used by teen slasher filmmakers not only to horrify, but also to thrill, intrigue, and amuse audiences. Where much scholarship assumes that early teen slashers showcased misogynistic violence to satisfy exploitation companies and male grind-house patrons, I argued that quite different commercial objectives governed the production and content of the film-type. From 1974 to 1981, independent filmmakers actually crafted teen slashers to appeal to the member-studios of the Motion Picture Association of America (MPAA) in order to secure a lucrative negative pickup deal, whereby they sold the films for a set fee and in doing so generated a swift profit irrespective of the film's box-office performance. This strategy allowed the films' makers to avoid unreliable, financially unstable, and unscrupulous independent distributors but hinged on MPAA-members concluding that teen slashers were cut-price product with sleeper hit potential. To achieve what *Variety* termed 'the ambitions of most independent filmmakers' (Anon. 1980i, p. 25), the producers of teen slashers went to great lengths to ensure that their pictures exhibited three qualities: similarities to contemporaneous hits, the capacity to avoid the X-rating, and marketability to male and, significantly, female youth (together the prime movie-going audience).

By making teen slashers that could be angled both to young men and young women, independent filmmakers were able to offer their preferred distributors movies that promised to be appealing to half of the American theatergoing public, a quality that, it was hoped, would excite the confidence of companies like Warner Bros. and Paramount Pictures. Downplaying violence, suffering, and gore so as to secure an R- rather than an X-rating was a prerequisite of doing business with Hollywood, because of its reticence to handle films that could not be advertised or exhibited widely. The mobilization of a range of content from blockbuster hits and top youth-oriented earners, not only masked the films' somewhat disreputable production origins, but allowed independents to demonstrate to distribution executives that the films' marketing campaigns could be tailored easily to highlight content that boasted a recent track-record of attracting the teenagers and young adults upon whom distributors relied to make money from the films they released.

Although scholars have characterized 'genre filmmaking' as balancing evocation of previous hits with differentiation, discussion of teen slasher films has invariably focused on similarities between the films and continuities across the film-type to frame teen slashers as arguably the most formulaic films in American movie history. The analysis conducted in this book has, however, revealed the surprising degree of value that teen slasher filmmakers placed upon product differentiation, and shown that these sophisticated businesspeople implemented a highly selective form of textual plundering governed by the shifts in content of commercially successful films. In doing so, *Blood Money* has shown that the textual development of different film-types, including those across the budget spectrum and from different North American production sectors, was more intricately intertwined than had previously been thought. Thus, exposing the logic and the strategies that led the makers of films about maniacal killers menacing young people to draw content from what may initially seem unlikely sources such as a blockbuster romance like *The Way We Were* (1973), a drive-in date-movie like *The Pom Pom Girls* (1976), a boisterous comedy aimed to teens and pre-teens like *Meatballs* (1979), and a female-centered coming-of-age drama like *Little Darlings* (1980).

To account for the conditions which shaped levels of teen slasher film production, this book presented and applied a new model of film cycle development. The model reflected, structurally and lexically, the temporally distinct phases of production operations which comprise film cycles, enabling for the identification of the points in time at which production of a film-type increases, remains constant, and drops. As such, time-specific developments relating to general output, hit patterns and other factors, can be pinpointed in order to facilitate a deeper and more accurate sense of the conditions which influence not only decisions of whether or not to produce an example of the film-type in question, but which are likely to impact upon the content of individual films as well.

Applying the model to teen slashers of the mid-to-late 1970s and early 1980s, as well as to other contemporaneous production patterns, shed new light on the ways in which film cycles develop. Where it has commonly been assumed that a single hit is sufficient to trigger a sizable surge in production of a film-type, it was shown that one commercially successful film tended not to initiate widespread replication. Instead, financially prudent filmmakers required confirmation of a film-type's commercial viability, and a method of capitalizing on the film textually, to be provided by at least one additional hit film. Moreover, for independent filmmakers, like those behind the teen slashers, economic concerns played an enormous role in their conduct due to their inability to spread risk, unlike MPAA-members, across a broad range of different films. Therefore, widespread production among independents was determined heavily by MPAA-members offering at least one pickup deal to the makers of an example of the film-type, by an MPAA-member pickup performing well commercially, and was swayed by their perceptions of the relative commercial viability of the other film-types they could afford to produce.

Thus, teen slasher production did not increase significantly when the first teen slasher film, a Canadian-made female-centered politically-engaged whodunit called *Black Christmas*, was released in 1974, because, even though it secured MPAA-member distribution, it was a box-office failure. Similarly, *Halloween* (1978), a female-centered small-town-set horror film and the first teen slasher film to demonstrate, through solid ticket sales, the existence of a large audience for the film-type, did not generate the large-scale production of similar films because it had been turned down for distribution by every major studio in Hollywood, thus indicating that independent filmmakers would run the risk of losing money if they too produced teen slashers. It was in fact the combination of significant box-office success and MPAA-member distribution experienced in 1980 by subsequent independently produced teen slasher films, particularly a relatively gory animal comedy-infused murder-mystery entitled *Friday the 13th*, and, to some extent, a female-centered disco-infused whodunit called *Prom Night*, that provided the incentive for large numbers of independent filmmakers to begin production of new teen slashers that brought about the production boom of late 1980, which transformed low levels of production and a minor increase in production into one of the most high-profile film cycles in the history of the American film industry. Even though most of the contributors to this production boom were doomed from the outset — due to over-production in late 1980 saturating the market with similar films across 1981 and into 1982, which in turn caused ticket-sales to be spread thinly, leading MPAA-members to stop offering distribution deals, and leading the production of new films to drop markedly — their teen slashers, like those of independent producers before them, ensured that tales of young people encountering shadowy killers in everyday locations became an established part of the North American film industry's repertoire of youth-market product. And, with the establishment of the teen slasher film, generations of entrepreneurial filmmakers were provided with a user-friendly low-cost textual model to which they could anchor their commercial and professional ambitions.

The identification of the conditions under which the first teen slasher film cycle unfolded, and the model used to identify them, also explains why some film-types do not develop into film cycles. Made around the same time as the early teen slashers, gang movies and roller-disco movies are cases in point. Gang movie production exploded in 1978 to unprecedented levels after the commercial success of *Saturday Night Fever* (1977), which was received contemporaneously as a type of gang movie itself. But production ground to a complete halt in 1979 when all of the films disappointed commercially, thus leaving what can best be described as a film cluster. Similarly, the production of roller-disco movies, which provided a different way of capitalizing on the achievements of *Saturday Night Fever*, was restricted to 1979, when they secured MPAA-member distribution but only limited audiences. While gang movies and roller-disco movies indicate the applicability of the model to other production patterns contemporaneous to the first teen slasher film cycle, the teen slasher film-type itself suggests that the model is transferable to other historical periods.

The remarkable commercial and professional success that some marginal industry-professionals enjoyed in the late 1970s and early 1980s on the back of relatively inexpensive stories of blade-wielding maniacs slaughtering young fun-seekers ensured that opportunistic filmmakers often attempted to replicate their achievements with teen slashers of their own and, at certain points in time, they fulfilled their objectives, triggering intense bursts of activity among other filmmakers which resulted in new cycles of the teen slasher film developing. So, when Wes Craven, a personal friend of *Friday the 13th*'s producer-director Sean Cunningham, scored a big sleeper hit with *A Nightmare on Elm Street* (1984), soon after the third *Friday the 13th* (1984) sequel, misleadingly subtitled *The Final Chapter*, emulated the achievements of Cunningham's original film, a second teen slasher film cycle began to unfold. And, a third teen slasher cycle started to take shape when eye-catching ticket-sales for Craven's 1996 teen slasher *Scream* were almost matched by *I Know What You Did Last Summer* (1997).

Examinations of subsequent teen slasher cycles will provide new challenges as they occurred against the backdrop of industrial landscapes that had been reshaped by conglomeration, globalization, synergy, the rapid expansion of new delivery systems such as home video and cable television, and an increased reliance upon ancillary markets (Balio, 1998, pp. 57–73). The structure and segmentation of the North American film industry was undergoing profound changes and the rise of companies such as New Line Cinema and Miramax Films significantly blurred the lines that had distinguished independents from the majors in the 1970s and early 1980s (Wyatt, 1998). These developments need to be taken into account when considering the conditions that shaped the production and content of teen slashers like *April Fool's Day* and *Killer Party* (both 1986) and *Urban Legend* (1998) and *Cherry Falls* (1999). This book has shown the extent to which Canadian teen slashers like *Black Christmas* and *Prom Night* contributed to the development of the first teen slasher film cycle, but examinations of later cycles will be required to address the impact of intervening national and transnational developments in order to account for the production of, among others, the US/Japan coproduction *Cheerleader Camp* (1987), Germany's *Swimming Pool: Der Tod Feiert Mit* (2001), and Bollywood entries like *Kucch to Hai* and *SSSSHHH* (both 2003).

Although it seemed unlikely back in 1981, when the first teen slasher film cycle ended, the teen slasher film continues to inspire confidence among filmmakers looking to use low-budgets to make a killing. Almost thirty years after a group of Canadian independents used the title, Sony Pictures' 'genre subsidiary' Screen Gems opened a $6m production called *Prom Night* (2008). The film came hot on the heels of 're-inventions' of *Black Christmas* (2006) and *Halloween* (2007) and was followed by new versions of *Friday the 13th* and *My Bloody Valentine* (both 2009), with remakes of *Friday the 13th Part II*, *Terror Train*, and *Hell Night* reportedly in the pipeline. The marketing campaign that accompanied the April 2008 release of *Prom Night* provides a gauge with which to measure contemporary industry perceptions of the teen slasher. The film's trailer depicted a new generation of young adults, another shadowy blade-wielding killer, and more 'preparations', 'anticipations', and 'celebrations' of a 'night to die for'. This content was presented by way of a sweeping inter-textual montage that catalogued almost three decades of filmic output, from animal comedies like *Fast Times at Ridgemont High* (1982) to female-centered coming-of-age dramas such as *Pretty in Pink* (1986) and *She's all That* (1999) before finally evoking the horror sleeper hit *Saw* (2004). Backed by Quietdrive's upbeat cover of a 1980s Cindy Lauper ballad, the new *Prom Night*'s trailer championed the teen slasher as a film-type that resonates with ambitious filmmakers and mixed-sex youth audiences, in the words of the songstress, time after time.

Appendix

Victim Gender in Teen Slasher Films, October 1978–April 1982

Title	Victims Including Killers			Victims Excluding Killers		
	Female	Male	Total	Female	Male	Total
1978–1980 (A)						
Halloween	3	2	5	3	2	5
Silent Scream	3	2	5	2	2	4
Friday the 13th	5	5	10	4	5	9
Prom Night	3	3	6	3	2	5
Terror Train	1	7	8	1	6	7
Subtotal A	15	19	34	13	17	30
%	44.1	55.9		43.3	56.7	
02/81–08/81 (B)						
My Bloody Valentine	5	5	10	5	5	10
Friday the 13th Part II	4	5	9	4	5	9
Graduation Day	3	4	7	3	3	6
The Burning	5	5	10	5	4	9
Happy Birthday to Me	2	6	8	1	6	7
Final Exam	2	8	10	2	8	10
Hell Night	2	6	8	2	4	6
Subtotal B	23	39	62	22	35	57
%	37.1	62.9		38.6	61.4	

Title	Victims Including Killers			Victims Excluding Killers		
	Female	*Male*	*Total*	*Female*	*Male*	*Total*
11/81–04/82 (C)						
The Prowler	4	4	8	4	3	7
The Dorm that Dripped Blood	4	4	8	4	4	8
Just Before Dawn	1	5	6	1	3	4
Madman	5	6	11	5	5	10
Subtotal C	*14*	*19*	*33*	*14*	*15*	*29*
%	42.4	57.6		48.3	51.7	
Total (A+B)	38	58	96	35	52	87
%	39.5	60.5		40.2	59.8	
Total (B+C)	37	58	95	36	50	76
%	38.9	61.1		47.4	52.6	
Grand Total (A+B+C)	*52*	*77*	*129*	*49*	*67*	*116*
%	*40.3*	*59.7*		*42.2*	*57.8*	

Notes

Introduction

[1] I refer to 'independent productions' and 'independently distributed films'. By 'independent productions' I mean films financed with capital acquired exclusively from sources other than the member-studios of the Motion Picture Association of America (MPAA). By independently distributed films I mean films that were not distributed by an MPAA-member. The distinction is important because some independent productions were distributed by MPAA-members. For the record, in 1980, the MPAA-members were the majors: Columbia Pictures, Disney/Buena Vista, MGM/UA, Paramount Pictures, Twentieth Century Fox Film Corporation, Universal Pictures, Warner Bros. Pictures, and the mini-major Avco Embassy Pictures.

[2] Although Clover uses the label 'slasher films', the films she highlights in her definition, like her use of the terms 'boys' and 'girls', indicates that she approaches films in which the victims are comprised primarily of young people.

[3] The label 'exploitation film' has been used widely by scholars, journalists, and industry personnel. The application of the label to particular films has, however, been partly determined by different national and historical contexts and by different users. It is not wholly uncommon that a particular film has also been labeled 'mainstream' product or 'art cinema'. I employ 'exploitation film' to refer to the status of group of films that were released in the US in the 1970s and early 1980s. The definition I use is based on Eric Schaefer's work on 'exploitation films' released in the US between 1919 and 1959 (1999). Like Schaefer, I consider a film to be exploitation if it fulfils five criteria concerning its production, content and/or themes, marketing, distribution, and exhibition. In the 1970s and early 1980s, exploitation films were produced independently on low budgets and distributed by non-MPAA-members. The films featured content and/or themes that were absent at the time from major studio releases due to being considered too controversial or taboo to secure an R-rating. Marketing spotlighted and often exaggerated the presence of this material. The exhibition of exploitation films was restricted to unprestigious venues that screened few if any films distributed by major studios, mainly drive-ins and urban theaters.

4   Scholarship on Roger Corman's New World Pictures (Hillier and Lipstadt, 1981, 1986; Hillier 1992) and Timothy Shary's (2002, 2005) efforts to map the general terrain of American youth-centered films of the period, are exceptions.

5   It is beyond the scope of this book to ascertain whether other teen slashers failed ever to secure any form of distribution.

6   This book follows Hall (1998) in distinguishing between 'calculated blockbusters' (films produced to be major earners) and 'blockbuster hits' (high-earning films).

7   Scholars have predominantly framed the gendered consumption of teen slashers in one of three ways. Clover (1987), and James Twitchell (1985, p. 6) presuppose that the film-type addresses and is, therefore, predominantly consumed by male youth. Others, including Tania Modleski (1986b, p. 161), conduct textual analysis almost exclusively on sequences of violence to conclude that teen slashers address male spectators exclusively. A third tendency is represented by Brigid Cherry (1999, pp. 187–204) who contends that for females to take pleasure from horror, including teen slashers, they must adopt radical viewing positions.

8   Domestic theatrical rentals (monies received by distributors from US and Canadian exhibitors) are taken from *Variety*'s year-end charts — 'Big Rental Films' ($1m and over) and 'All-time Box Office Champs' ($4m and over). Figures will be expressed in the following abbreviated form: *American Graffiti*: $10.3m (10th/1973); meaning that *American Graffiti* generated US$10.3m in rentals to rank tenth of all films in circulation in 1973. For films that accumulated significantly higher rentals after their first year of release, an 'all-time' sum is also listed relevant to the point in time at which its commercial performance is being discussed. Thus *American Graffiti*: $41.2m (14th/All-time, 1975) reflects *American Graffiti*'s having accrued, as of January 1975, $41.2m in domestic rentals so as to generate the fourteenth highest figure in the history of the North American film market.

Chapter 1

1   This approach sidesteps what Andrew Tudor called the 'empiricist's dilemma', a catch-22 situation faced by scholars looking to build a corpus of films by using criteria that can only be identified once a corpus has been built (1989, pp. 135–138).

2   For example, *Happy Birthday to Me* was described by Gary Arnold of the *Washington Post* as a 'mystery' and a 'thriller' (1981b, p. F4) but as 'horror' by the *Chicago Tribune*'s Larry Kart (1981, p. A8).

3   The teen slasher story-structure is indebted to Dika's 'plot structure of the stalker film', which, despite conflating story and plot, and despite not distinguishing between features present across all of the films in her corpus and those limited to some films, provides an invaluable template given that her corpus consists entirely of teen slashers (1990, pp. 59–60).

4   There may be a degree of cross-over between phases. For example, some films made during stage two may still be awaiting release as the production of new films

begins, or late-starters in stage three may be wrapping up production as nimble filmmakers just start production of a stage four contribution.

5 Sequels are Cash-ins par excellence. However, their impact on the development of film cycles must be considered carefully and on a case-by-case basis. A significant portion of the revenue generated by sequels results from their being pre-sold properties, of which target markets hold well-formed expectations, thus suggesting that the commercial success of a sequel usually communicates the economic viability of the franchise to which it belongs, rather than communicating unambiguously the commercial viability of the film-type.

Chapter 2

1 *American Graffiti*: $10.3m (10th/1973), $41.2m (14th/All-time, 1975) (Anon., 1974a p. 19; Anon., 1975b, p. 26).

2 *Easy Rider*: $7.2.m (11th/1969) (Anon., 1970, p. 18).

3 *Blowup*: $5.8m (14th/1967); *I am Curious Yellow*: $6.6m (12th/1969) (Anon., 1968a, p. 23; Anon., 1970, p. 15).

4 *Rosemary's Baby*: $12.3m (7th/1968), $15m (63rd/All-time, 1974); *MASH*: $22m (2nd/1970), $36.5m (12th/All-time, 1974); *Love Story*: $50m (1st/1971), $50m (4th/All-time, 1974); *Dirty Harry*: $16m (5th/1972), $16.4m (54th/All-time, 1974) (Anon., 1969, p. 18; Anon., 1971, p. 11; Anon., 1972, p. 9; Anon., 1973a, p. 7; Anon., 1974b, p. 22).

5 Although the group members in *MASH* are in their late twenties and early thirties, as Paul suggests, they were characterized as youths (1994, pp. 94–110). As Jon Lewis argues, it is not uncommon for films that are targeted primarily at youth audiences to feature slightly older characters (1992, p. 2).

6 *Romeo and Juliet*: $14.5m (5th/1969), $17.4m (48th/All-time, 1974) (Anon., 1970, p. 15; Anon., 1974b, p. 23).

7 *Shaft*: $6.1m (12th/1971); *Superfly*: $4m (33rd/1972) (Anon., 1972, p. 9; Anon., 1973a, p. 7).

8 Although *Variety* did not list rentals of hardcore pornography, Cook reports that *Deep Throat* generated $20m in US theatrical rentals — the fifth highest of any film opened in 1972 (2000, p. 498).

9 Producer Gerry Arbeid said that Warner Bros. changed the title to avoid confusion with 'blaxploitation' films (cited in Anon., 1975e, p. 26).

10 *The Godfather Part II*: $26.9m (5th/1975); *The Man with the Golden Gun*: $9.5m (15th/1975) (Anon., 1976a, p. 18).

11 *The Towering Inferno*: $55m (2nd/1975); *Young Frankenstein*: $30m (4th/1975) (Anon., 1976a, p. 18).

12 *Murder on the Orient Express*: $17.8m (8th/1975), $18.9m (86th/All-time); *Murder by Death* $18.8m (8th/1976), $22m (60th/All-time) (Anon., 1976a, p. 18; Anon., 1977a, p. 14; Anon., 1978a, p. 25).

13 *The Pom Pom Girls*: $4.3m (46th/1976) (Anon., 1977a, p. 14).

[14] *The Van*: $4.5m (54th/1977) (Anon., 1978b, p. 21).

[15] *Saturday Night Fever*: $71.4m (10th/All-time, 1979) (Anon., 1979a, p. 30).

[16] By January 1978, *Carrie* had generated $14.5m in rentals, an amount that, if it had been generated in a calendar year, would have placed the film in the annual top twenty for either 1977 or 1978. *Carrie*: $2.5m (67th/1976), $14.5m (132nd/All-time, 1978) (Anon., 1977a, p. 14; Anon., 1978a, p. 25).

[17] *The Premonition*: <$1m (>116th/1976); *Burnt Offerings*: $1.56m (95th/1976) (Anon., 1977a, pp. 14, 44).

[18] *Audrey Rose*: $2m (85th/1977); *Exorcist II: The Heretic*: $13.9m (22nd/1977); *The Sentinel*: $4m (57th/1977); *The Fury*: $10m (25th/1978) (Anon., 1978b, pp. 21, 50; Anon., 1979b, p. 19).

[19] *Jaws*: $102.2m (1st/1975), $121.3m (2nd/All-time, 1978); *The Omen*: $27.8m (3rd/1976), (37th/All-time, 1978) (Anon., 1976a, p. 18; Anon., 1977a, p. 14; Anon., 1978a, p. 25).

[20] *Star Wars*: $127m (1st/1977, 1st/All-time, 1978) (Anon., 1978b, p. 21; Anon., 1978a, p. 25).

[21] *American Graffiti*: $47.3m (13th/All-time, 1978); *Grease*: $83m (1st/1978); *Animal House*: $52.3m (3rd/1978); *Up in Smoke*: $21.2m (11th/1978) (Anon., 1978a, p. 25; Anon., 1979b, p. 17).

Chapter 3

[1] *The Pom Pom Girls*: $4.3m (46th/1976) (Anon., 1977a, p. 14).

[2] *Papillon*: $22.5m (55th/All-time, 1978); *In Search of Noah's Ark*: $23m (50th/All-time, 1978) (Anon., 1978a, p. 25).

[3] These films were produced in late 1978 and 1979 and released in 1979 and 1980.

[4] *Animal House*: $52.3m (3rd/1978, 15th/All-time, 1979); *Grease*: $83m (1st/1978, 4th/All-time, 1979); *Saturday Night Fever*: $71.4m (10th/All-time, 1979) (Anon., 1979b, p. 17; Anon., 1979a, p. 30).

[5] The earliest *Star Wars* Cash-in, a Japanese film called *Message from Space* (1978), was released in the US seventeen months after *Star Wars* debuted (Siskel, 1978b, p. A5)

[6] *Up in Smoke*: $21.2m (11th/1978, 75th/All-time, 1979) (Anon., 1979b, p. 17; Anon., 1979a, p. 29).

[7] Roller disco movies were also produced to capitalize on the commercial success of the soundtracks to *Saturday Night Fever* and *Grease*, the top-selling albums of 1978 in the US (*People*, 2000).

[8] *Ice Castles*: $9.5m (38th/1979) (Anon., 1980b, p. 21).

[9] *The Exorcist*: $66.3m (2nd/1974), $82.3m (5th/All-time, 1979); *The Omen*: $27.8m (3rd/1976, 47th/All-time, 1978) (Anon., 1975c, p. 24; Anon., 1977a, p. 14; Anon., 1979a, p. 20).

[10] *Jaws*: $102.2m (1st/1975), $121.3m (2nd/All-time, 1979); *The Deep*: $31m (6th/1977); $31.3m (38th/All-time, 1979); *Jaws 2*: $49.3m (4th/1978, 18th/

All-time, 1979) (Anon., 1976a, p. 18; Anon., 1978b, p. 21; Anon., 1979b, p. 17; Anon., 1979a, p. 20).

11 *Deliverance*: $18m (2nd/1973), $23.4m (69th/All-time, 1979); *Race with the Devil*: $6m (37th/1975) (Anon., 1974a, p. 19; Anon., 1976a, p. 18; Anon., 1979a, p. 20).

12 *King Kong*: $35.8m (5th/1977) (Anon., 1978b, p. 21).

13 *The Town that Dreaded Sundown*: $5m (52nd/1977) (Anon., 1978b, p. 21).

14 *Taxi Driver*: $11.6m (12th/1976) (Anon., 1977a, p. 14).

15 It has been pointed out that these adult-centered films are bracketed commonly with teen slashers (Dika, 1990, pp. 124–125; Wood, 1987, pp. 79–85).

16 *Looking for Mr. Goodbar*: $9m (31st/1977), $16.3m (120th/All-time, 1979) (Anon., 1978b, p. 21; Anon., 1979a, p. 34).

17 *The French Connection*: $6.1m (13th/1971), $26.3m (51st/All-time, 1979); *The Exorcist*: $66.3m (2nd/1974), $82.3m (5th/All-time, 1979) (Anon., 1972, p. 9; Anon., 1975c, p. 24; Anon., 1979a, p. 20).

18 *Eyes of Laura Mars*: $8.3m (34th/1978); *The Town that Dreaded Sundown*: $5m (52nd/1976) (Anon., 1979b, p. 17; Anon., 1977a, p. 21).

19 *Jaws 2*: $49.3m (4th/1978, 18th/All-time, 1979); *American Graffiti*: $55.8m (13th/All-time, 1979) (Anon., 1979b, p. 17; Anon., 1979a, p. 20).

20 *The Omen*: $27.8m (3rd/1976); *Damien: Omen II*: $12m (20th/1978) (Anon., 1977a, p. 14; Anon., 1979b, p. 17).

21 *King Kong*: $35.8m (5th/1977), $36.9m (35th/All-time, 1980); *Exorcist II: The Heretic*: $13.9m (22nd/1977); *The Swarm*: $7.6m (40th/1978) (Anon., 1978b, p. 21; Anon., 1979b, p. 17; Anon., 1980a, p. 24).

22 *The Amityville Horror*: $35m (5th/1979, 40th/All-Time, 1980) (Anon., 1980b, p. 21; Anon., 1980a, p. 24).

23 *The Sentinel*: $4m (57th/1977); *Tentacles*: $3m (67th/1977); *Day of the Animals*: $2.8m (72nd/1977); *Empire of the Ants*: $2.5m (74th/1977); *The Food of the Gods*: $1m (112th/1977); *The Legacy*: $4.2m (69th/1979); *Nightwing* (81st/1979) (Anon., 1978b, pp. 21, 50; Anon., 1980b, pp. 21, 70).

24 *Orca*: $9.2m (30th/1977); *Prophecy*: $10.5m (34th/1979); *Demon Seed*: $2m (84th/1977); *Audrey Rose*: $2m (85th/1977) (Anon., 1978b, pp. 21, 50; Anon., 1980b, pp. 21, 70).

25 *When a Stranger Calls*: $10.1m (35th/1979) (Anon., 1980b, p. 21).

26 *Silent Scream*: $7.9m (41st/1980) (Anon., 1981a, p. 29).

27 *Meatballs*: $19.6m (16th/1979); *Little Darlings*: $16.7 (19th/1980) (Anon., 1980b, p. 21; Anon., 1981a, p. 29).

28 *Friday the 13th*: $16.5m (20th/1980) (Anon., 1981a, p. 29).

29 *Airplane!*: $38m (4th/1980); *Urban Cowboy*: $22.7m (14th/1980) (Anon., 1981a, p. 29).

30 The strategy was occasionally used by the majors in previous decades with Warner Bros., for example, opening *Them!* (1954) on 2000 screens within the space of one month (Maltby, 2003, p. 182; Cook, 2000, pp. 16–17).

31 Gomery credits the head of Universal, Lew Wasserman, with adopting this strategy for the release of *Jaws* (1998, p. 51).

32 'Box office mojo' [accessed 2 March 2008].
33 'Box office mojo' [accessed 2 March 2008].

Chapter 4

1   This chapter does not examine the contemporaneous Canadian-made teen
    slasher *Terror Train* (1980) because the timing of the film's release (September
    1980) rendered minimal its impact on the production and content of subsequent
    teen slashers.
2   'Museum of Broadcast Communications' [accessed 23 June 2008]
3   'Telefilm Canada'. [accessed 23 June 2008]
4   *The Neptune Factor*: $2.75m (51st/1973); *The Apprenticeship of Duddy Kravitz*: $1.7m
    (67th/1974). *Black Christmas*: <$1m (Anon., 1974a, p. 19; Anon., 1975c, p. 24).
5   *The French Connection*: $6.1m (13th/1971), $27.5m (22nd/All-Time, 1975); *The
    Sting*: $68.4m (1st/1974, 4th/All-time, 1975) (Anon., 1972, p. 9; Anon., 1975c,
    p. 24; Anon., 1975b, p. 26).
6   *Breaking Point*: <$1m (Anon., 1977a, pp. 14, 44).
7   The use of American settings was a key shift that distinguished the biggest hits
    of 1967–1976 from those of the early-to-mid-1960s, as Krämer points out (2005,
    pp. 28–32).
8   'Telefilm Canada' [accessed 23 June 2008].
9   *American Graffiti*: $10.3m (10th/1973), $47.3m (13th/All-time 1978); *The
    Longest Yard*: $10.1m (16th/1974), $22.6m (54th/All-time, 1978); *Rocky*: $54m
    (2nd/1977, 9th/All-time, 1978); *Smokey and the Bandit*: $39.7m (3rd/1977, 20th/
    All-time, 1979) (Anon., 1974a, p. 19; Anon., 1975c, p. 24; Anon., 1978b, p. 21;
    Anon., 1978a, p. 25).
10 *The Poseidon Adventure*: $40m (1st/1973), $42m (19th/All-time, 1978); *Earthquake*:
    $7.9m (24th/1974), $36m (24th/All-time, 1978); *The Towering Inferno*: $55m
    (2nd/1975, 11th/All-time, 1978); *The Deep*: $31m (6th/1977, 30th/All-time,
    1978); *The Spy Who Loved Me*: $22m (11th/1977, 61st/All-time, 1978) (Anon.,
    1974a, p. 19; Anon., 1975c, p. 24; Anon., 1976a, p. 18; Anon., 1978b, p. 21; Anon.,
    1978a, p. 25).
11 *Running*: $2.8m (91st/1979) (Anon., 1980b, pp. 21, 70).
12 This is shown in the 1978–1979 CFDC annual report (see Magder, 1993, p. 198).
13 *Black Christmas*: $2m (3rd/All-time); *The Apprenticeship of Duddy Kravitz*: $2.3m
    (2nd/All-time); *Meatballs*: $4.2m (1st/All-time) (Anon., 1979p, p. 47).
14 *Animal House*: $52.3m (3rd/1978, 15th/All-time, 1979) (Anon., 1979b, p. 17;
    Anon., 1979a, p. 30).
15 *The Bad News Bears*: $22.2m (4th/1976), $24.3m (59th/All-time, 1979) (Anon.,
    1977a, p. 14; Anon., 1979a, p. 30).
16 The PG-13 rating was adopted in 1984 (see Vaughn, 2006, p. 50).
17 In the mid 1980s, non-white heroes started to appear in teen slashers like *Friday
    the 13th: A New Beginning* (1985) and *A Nightmare on Elm Street 3: Dream Warriors* (1987).

[18] 'Norstar Filmed Entertainment Inc'. [accessed 2 March 2008]

[19] 'The Terror Trap'. [accessed 2 March 2008]

[20] *Dirty Harry*: $16m (5th/1972), $17.8m (103rd/All-time, 1979); *Magnum Force*: $18.3m (4th/1973), $20.1m (83rd/All-time, 1979); *The Enforcer*: $24m (8th/1977, 61st/All-time, 1979) (Anon., 1973a, p. 7; Anon., 1974a, p. 24; Anon., 1978b, p. 21; Anon., 1979a, p. 30).

[21] *Up in Smoke*: $21.2m (11th/1978, 75th/All-time, 1979) (Anon., 1979b, p. 17; Anon., 1979a, p. 29).

[22] *Deliverance*: $18m (2nd/1973), $23.4m (69th/All-time, 1979); *Race with the Devil*: $6m (37th/1975) (Anon., 1974a, p. 19; Anon., 1976a, p. 18; Anon., 1979a, p. 20).

[23] *Grease*: $83m (1st/1978, 4th/All-time, 1979) (Anon., 1979b, p. 17; Anon., 1979a, p. 30).

[24] *Ice Castles*: $9.5m (38th/1979) (Anon., 1980b, p. 21).

[25] *Rosemary's Baby*: $12.3m (7th/1968); *The Exorcist*: $66.3m (2nd/1974) (Anon., 1969, p. 15; Anon., 1975c, p. 24).

[26] *Funny Lady*: $19m (7th/1975); *A Star is Born*: $37.1m (4th/1977); *The Goodbye Girl*: $41.6m (6th/1978); *Eyes of Laura Mars*: $8.3m (34th/1978); *Magic*: $13m (24th/1979); *Dracula*: $10.5m (33rd/1979) (Anon., 1976a, p. 18; Anon., 1978b, p. 21; Anon., 1979b, p. 17; Anon., 1980b, p. 21).

[27] *Carrie*: $2.5m (67th/1976), $15m (143nd/All-time, 1979) (Anon., 1977a, p. 14; Anon., 1979a, p. 34).

[28] *Skatetown, U.S.A*: $2.35m (97th/1979) (Anon., 1980b, p. 21).

[29] *Roller Boogie*: <$1m (>124th/1979) (Anon., 1980b, p. 21).

[30] *The Graduate*: $39m (1st/1968), $49m (20th/All-time, 1980) (Anon., 1969, p. 15; Anon., 1980a, p. 24).

[31] *Phantasm*: $6m (58th/1979) (Anon., 1980b, p. 21).

[32] Soon after, the company renewed production operations (Cook, 2000, p. 325).

[33] *Death Ship*: $1.75m (104th/1980) (Anon., 1981a, pp. 50).

[34] *The Fog*: $11m (29th/1980) (Anon., 1981a, p. 29).

[35] Kernan's contention that late 1970s trailers reflected 'New' Hollywood's 'mission to avoid alienating any potential audience segment' is ideally understood as operating within the parameters of a film's general target audience (2004, p. 167).

[36] *Friday the 13th*: $16.5m (20th/1980) (Anon., 1981a, p. 29).

Chapter 5

[1] *Animal House*: $52.3m (3rd/1978, 15th/All-time, 1979); *Grease*: $83m (1st/1978, 4th/All-time, 1979); *Saturday Night Fever*: $71.4m (10th/All-time, 1979) (Anon., 1979b, p. 17; Anon., 1979a, p. 30).

[2] Donahue notes that *Squeeze Play* generated $4.3m in rentals when distributed independently in 1982 and 1983 (1987, pp. 269, 241).

[3] *H.O.T.S*: $1.4m (115th/1979); *King Frat*: <$1m (>124th/1979); *Squeeze Play*: <$1m (>124th/1979) (Anon., 1980b, p. 70).

4   *The Wanderers*: $2m (103rd/1979); *Boulevard Nights*: $1.9m (108th/1979) *Over the Edge:* <$1m (>124th/1979); *Sunnyside:* <$1m (>124th/1979); *Walk Proud:* <$1m (>124th/1979) (Anon., 1980b, p. 70).
5   *The Warriors*: $12.3m (26th/1979) (Anon., 1980b, p. 21).
6   *Skatetown, U.S.A*: $2.35m (97th/1979); *Roller Boogie*<$1m (>124th/1979) (Anon., 1980b, p. 70).
7   *Exorcist II: The Heretic*: $13.9m (22nd/1977); *The Brood*: <$1m (>124th/1979); *The Orphan*: <$1m (>124th/1979); *The Changeling*: $5.3m (62nd/1980) (Anon., 1978b, p. 21; Anon., 1980b, pp. 21, 70; Anon., 1981a, p. 29).
8   *Dracula*: $10.5m (33rd/1979). In 1979 and 1980, no independently produced vampire films generated over $1m in domestic rentals (Anon., 1980b, pp. 21, 70; Anon., 1981a, pp. 29, 50).
9   *Alien*: $40m (4th/1979); *The Shining*: $30.2m (10th/1980) (Anon., 1980b, p. 21; Anon., 1981a, p. 29).
10 The makers of some films re-contextualized elements of *Dressed to Kill*, including those behind the giallo *Night School*, the conspiracy thriller *Blow Out*, and the obsessed-stalker film *The Fan* (all 1981).
11 *Friday the 13th*: $16.5m (20th/1980) (Anon., 1981a, p. 29).
12 *Prom Night*: $6m (53rd/1980) (Anon., 1981a, p. 29).
13 *Little Darlings*: $16.7m (19th/1980); *Friday the 13th*: $16.5m (20th/1980) (Anon., 1981a, p. 29).
14 John Dunning stated: 'Frank [Mancuso Sr.] said "we're not taking [*My Bloody Valentine*] unless you get an MPAA rating"'. The film's director George Mihalka added that 'Paramount and Frank Mancuso [Sr.] were willing to do a pickup and a national distribution (. . .) as long as we could get [*My Bloody Valentine*] out for Valentine's Day [1981]' (John Dunning interviewed in 'Going to pieces', 2006; George Mihalka interviewed at 'The Terror Trap'. [accessed 23 June 2008]).
15 Both teen slashers flaunted Canadian locations because, unlike the late 1970s, masking Canadian origin hindered CFDC subsidy applications. In 1980, the University of Toronto's Institute for Policy Analysis argued that the strategy had had 'a perverse effect on Canadian film culture' (Magder, 1993, p. 190).
16 The situation was exacerbated by films that shared features with teen slashers, in particular shadowy killers featured in *Deadly Blessing*, *Halloween II* (both 1981), and *Night School*.
17 The commercial failure of *Skatetown, U.S.A* and *Roller Boogie* rendered minimal the influence of *Prom Night*'s disco music/dancing on the group of eleven.
18 *Dressed to Kill*: $15m (23rd/1980) (Anon., 1981a, p. 29).
19 The website 'the final girl' is described as 'exploring the slasher flicks of the '70s and '80s' ('The Final Girl' [accessed 30 August 2008]).
20 *Little Darlings*: $16.7m (19th/1980) (Anon., 1981a, p. 29).
21 *Foxes*: <$1m (>130th/1980); *Times Square*: $1.4m (119th/1980) (Anon., 1981a, p. 50).
22 *Caddyshack*: $20m (17th/1980) (Anon., 1981a, p. 29).
23 *The Howling*: $8.2m (47th/1981) (Anon., 1982a, p. 15).

24 By 1983, three Carpetbagger Cash-ins had generated just over $1m in US theatrical rentals. *Madman*: $1.35m; *Hell Night*; $1.31m; *Graduation Day*: $1.15m (cited in Donahue, 1987, Appendix Table A-1).

25 Average print/publicity costs were almost $5m in 1981 (Prince, 2000, p. 21).

26 *Friday the 13th Part 3: 3D*: $16.5m (21st/1982); *Friday the 13th: The Final Chapter*: $16m (26th/1984) (Anon., 1983, p. 13; Anon., 1985, p. 16).

27 Cook points to market saturation albeit from 1978 to 1983 (1992, p. 237).

28 *Raiders of the Lost Ark*: $90.4m (1st/1981); *Superman II*: $64m (2nd/1981); *Arthur*: $37m (7th/1981); *The Cannonball Run*: $35.3m (8th/1981); *The Four Seasons*: $26.8m (9th/1981); *For Your Eyes Only*: $25.4m (10th/1981) (Anon., 1982a, p. 15).

29 *Stripes*: $39.5m (5th/1981); *Cheech and Chong's Nice Dreams*: $17.6 (13th/1981) (Anon., 1982a, p. 15).

30 *Endless Love*: $15.1m (21st/1981); *An American Werewolf in London*: $11.6m (29th/1981) (Anon., 1982a, p. 15).

31 *Private Lessons*: $5.7m (69th/1981) (Anon., 1982a, p. 15).

32 *Friday the 13th Part II* initially received an X-rating which would have invalidated its conditional pickup deal with Paramount (Vaughn, 2006, p. 102)

Bibliography

Adil. (1974), 'Black Christmas', *Variety*, 16 October, 16.

Adilman, S. (1979), 'Reaction to Par's "Meatballs": a Canadian Film's U.S. "break" heartburns Canadian distribs', *Variety*, 25 April, 3, 40.

Allen, T. (1978), 'The sleeper that's here to stay', *Village Voice*, 6 November, 67, 70.

Allen, T. (1980a), '"Friday the 13th"'. *Village Voice*, 19 May.

Allen, T. (1980b), *Village Voice*, 27 August, 40.

Allis, S. (1979a), 'Spooky profits for a "cult film in reverse"', *Washington Post*, 18 March, H1, H6.

Allis, S. (1979b), 'A master of B-movies', *Washington Post*, 5 August, G1.

Alloway, L. (1971), *Violent America: the movies 1946–1964*. New York: Museum of Modern Art.

Alpert, H. (1968) 'SR goes to the movies', *Saturday Review*, 16 March, 53.

Altman, R. (1999), *Film/Genre*. London: BFI.

Alvarez, M. (1981) 'A very unmerry "Birthday" for you', *Milwaukee Journal*, 22 May, 26.

American Cinema Releasing. (1979), *Silent Scream* box office announcement, *Variety*, 30 November, 14–15.

American Cinema Releasing. (1980), *Silent Scream* box office announcement, *Variety*, 30 January, 18–19.

Anderson, G. (1980), 'The triangle tattler: the show must go on despite bad break', *Pittsburgh Post-Gazette*, 14 October, 21.

Anon. (1968a), 'Big rental films of 1967', *Variety*, 3 January, 23.

Anon. (1968b), 'Pix must broaden market: 18 percent of public; 76 percent of audience', *Variety*, 20 March, 1, 78.

Anon. (1969), 'Big rental films of 1968', *Variety*, 8 January, 15.

Anon. (1970), 'Big rental films of 1969', *Variety*, 7 January, 18.

Anon. (1971), 'Big rental films of 1970', *Variety*, 6 January, 11.

Anon. (1972), 'Big rental films of 1971', *Variety*, 3 January, 9, 67.

Anon. (1973a), 'Big rental films of 1972', *Variety*, 3 January, 7, 36.

Anon. (1973b), 'Budge Crawley views, plans; adv. pic vet's screen angels', *Variety*, 21 November, 26.

Anon. (1973c), 'Made-in-Canada blockbuster needed to buck up filmmakers', *Variety*, 21 November, 19.

Anon. (1973d), 'Tax break swings in the wind, Canada films "bleakly cheerful"; CFDC chief Mike Spencer talks', *Variety*, 21 November, 19, 32.

Anon. (1973e), 'Roeg: minimal cuts of nudity won't R tag on "Don't Look Now"', *Variety*, 5 December, 6.

Anon. (1973f), 'Astral Bellevue Pathe party in Hollywood on Canadian coprod', *Variety*, 12 December, 26.

Anon. (1973g), 'Made "Serpico", will shun mayhem, De Laurentiis: too much gore', *Variety*, 26 December, 5.

Anon. (1974a), 'Big rental films of 1973', *Variety*, 9 January, 19, 80.

Anon. (1974b), 'Updated all-time film champs', *Variety*, 9 January, 23, 54, 56, 58, 60.

Anon. (1974c), 'Critic Meacham hails "Exorcist" but scores MPAA for R rating', *Variety*,
23 January, 5.

Anon. (1974d), '"Exorcist" scoreboard: Satan, 3 — God, 0: so thinks one Catholic critic', *Variety*,
23 January, 5.

Anon. (1974e), 'Golden Globe possessed by "Exorcist"; cops four awards', *Variety*, 30 January, 7.

Anon. (1974f), 'Informally X in Boston, "Exorcist" also under criminal complaints', *Variety*,
30 January, 23.

Anon. (1974g), '"No one wants that X anymore"; hence "Fritz" sequel R, political', *Variety*,
30 January, 3.

Anon. (1974h), '"Exorcist" paces January pack; "Serpico", "Papillon" also strong', *Variety*,
6 February, 3.

Anon. (1974i), 'WB to Friedkin: "we'll buy your 10%": "Exorcist" booms Donald Rugoff',
Variety, 6 February, 5.

Anon. (1974j), 'International soundtrack', *Variety*, 28 February, 26.

Anon. (1974k), 'Nat'l board of Canada, making features that make money is no thrill to
showmen', *Variety*, 13 March, 4.

Anon. (1974l), 'International soundtrack', *Variety*, 15 May, 46.

Anon. (1974m), 'Vision IV audit after one year; cite tomorrows', *Variety*, 27 November, 32.

Anon. (1975a), 'Advance investment rates 100% writeoff', *Variety*, 1 January, 7.

Anon. (1975b), 'Updated all-time film champs', *Variety*, 8 January, 26.

Anon. (1975c), 'Big rental films of 1974', *Variety*, 8 January, 24, 75.

Anon. (1975d), 'Variety chart summary for 1974 (U.S. grosses only)', *Variety*, 7 May, 133–135.

Anon. (1975e), 'Yank re-think on Canadian pix', *Variety*, 27 August, 26.

Anon. (1975f), 'Black Christmas is Canada's no. 2 film', *Boxoffice*, 15 September, 8.

Anon. (1975g), '"Condor" soaring $134,000, LA; "Master" 105G; "Hooker" 100G; "Xmas"
$70,500; "Farewell" 60G', *Variety*, 6 October, 9.

Anon. (1975h). '"Master" $40,000 tops Chicago; "Xmas" $21,000; Ali Fight 23G', *Variety*,
6 October, 10.

Anon. (1975i), '50 top-grossing films', *Variety*, 29 October, 9.

Anon. (1975j), '50 top-grossing films', *Variety*, 5 November, 9.

Anon. (1975k), '50 top-grossing films', *Variety*, 12 November, 15.

Anon. (1975l), '50 top-grossing films', *Variety*, 10 December, 9.

Anon. (1975m), '50 top-grossing films', *Variety*, 24 December, 9.

Anon. (1976a), 'Big rental films of 1975', *Variety*, 7 January, 18, 52.

Anon. (1976b), 'Toronto's Ambassador gains rep', *Variety*, 21 January, 44.

Anon. (1976c), '"Snuff" unreels in Vegas subject to many limits', *Variety*, 26 February, 36.

Anon. (1976d), 'Maryland bans "Snuff"; distrib won't cut the gory final sequence', *Variety*,
3 March, 26.

Anon. (1976e), 'Plitt cancels "Snuff" on editorial; the Sun-Times: "films create perverted taste,
then cater to it"', *Variety*, 10 March, 5.

Anon. (1976f), '"Snuff" biz goes when pickets go', *Variety*, 24 March, 36.

Anon. (1977a), 'Big rental films of 1976', *Variety*, 5 January, 14, 44.

Anon. (1977b), 'Crown Int'l pitches for pix via indies' marketing flexibility', *Variety*,
21 February, 49.

Anon. (1977c), 'Yablans says no to "Captain Lust;" wrong for image', *Variety*, 6 July, 4.

Anon. (1977d), '20 pix at $30,000,000; is New World a "major"?', *Variety*, 30 November, 4, 28.

Anon. (1978a), 'All-time film rental champs', *Variety*, 4 January, 25, 82, 84, 86, 88, 90.

Anon. (1978b), 'Big rental films of 1977', *Variety*, 4 January, 21, 50.

Anon. (1978c), 'Akkad: low-budget diversity; awaits recoupment on $17-m "Mohammad" ($5-m.
in so far)', *Variety*, 11 January, 33.

Anon. (1978d), 'Irwin Yablans, Moustapha Akkad unite as Compass Intl. Films', *Variety*,
1 February, 28.

Anon. (1978e), 'Richard Dames haunted by "Snuff": women win re-activation against exhib for showing "murder on screen"', *Variety*, 1 March, 7.

Anon. (1978f), 'Filmways and American Intl. merging; $25–30 mil deal', *Variety*, 11 October, 3, 63.

Anon. (1979a), 'All-time film rental champs', *Variety*, 3 January, 30, 54, 56–58, 60, 62.

Anon. (1979b), 'Big rental films of 1978', *Variety*, 3 January, 17, 80.

Anon. (1979c), 'U's pickup of Canadian-made "Running" cues nationalist beef by home distribs; money talks', *Variety*, 14 February, 21, 70.

Anon. (1979d), 'While majors fly high, indie distribs go bust', *Variety*, 14 February, 50, 40.

Anon. (1979e), 'Par tries to take heat off "Warriors": toning down ad campaign', *Variety*, 21 February, 3, 26.

Anon. (1979f), '"Halloween" hit induces Avemb to get on with "Phantasm"', *Variety*, 14 March, 6.

Anon. (1979g), 'Irwin Yablans hailing "Halloween" expectancy calls Boston crucial', *Variety*, 14 March, 6.

Anon. (1979h), 'Serious gang clashes over "Boulevard" and "Warriors"; Chicanos see distortion', *Variety*, 28 March, 24.

Anon. (1979i), 'Non-sexy horror needs non-X ratings; so says Romero', *Variety*, 18 April, 37.

Anon. (1979j), 'Can. development films', *Variety*, May 9, 460.

Anon. (1979k) 'Pickups, TV, cable for 10 "Canadian development" pics yield $39, 100,000 (so far)', *Variety*, 9 May, 448, 460.

Anon. (1979l), 'Roller Boogie Advertisement', *Variety*, 27 June, 27.

Anon. (1979m), 'Brian De Palma true to "menace"', *Variety*, 29 August, 3.

Anon. (1979n), 'New generation of theatrical feature talent in Canada', *Variety*, 29 August, 55.

Anon., (1979o), 'U.S. filmgoing outstrips rise in population', *Variety*, 24 October, 1, 120.

Anon. (1979p), 'Canada-only b.o figures', *Variety*, 21 November, 47.

Anon. (1979q), '"Meatballs": Canadian coup could gross $50,000,000', *Variety*, 21 November, 46.

Anon. (1979r), 'Can. film development future', *Variety*, 26 November, 64.

Anon. (1979s), 'Check-list of 63 films', *Variety*, 26 November, 36.

Anon. (1979t), 'Local rink ties "Roller Boogie" ballyhoo peg', *Variety*, 19 December, 23.

Anon. (1980a), 'All-time film rental champs', *Variety*, 9 January, 24, 44, 46, 48, 50, 52, 54, 74.

Anon. (1980b), 'Big rental films of 1979', *Variety*, 9 January, 21, 70.

Anon. (1980c), 'Movies opening this week', *The Desert News*, 21 March, 2C.

Anon. (1980d), '"Mayors more pickup-prone"', *Variety*, 7 May, 1, 606.

Anon. (1980e), '"Prom" Rights to Avemb', *Variety*, 21 May, 27.

Anon. (1980f), 'US distrib deals for Canadian films are on an upswing', *Variety*, 28 May, 7, 36.

Anon. (1980g), 'Did "Cruising" respect rulings?', *Variety*, 25 June, 3, 37.

Anon. (1980h), 'MGM enters horror picture', *Spokesman Review*, 1 July, 15.

Anon. (1980i), 'After "Friday 13th" windfall, Cunningham explores new area', *Variety*, 9 July, 25.

Anon. (1980j), 'Plitt yanks "I Spit On Your Grave"', *Variety*, 23 July, 33.

Anon. (1980k), 'Decide "Dressed to Kill" ad copy too sophisticated, hence revision', *Variety*, 6 August, 6.

Anon. (1980l), 'People', *Ottawa Citizen*, 12 September, 35.

Anon. (1980m), 'Blood on the tracks: costumes and killings aboard the "Terror Train"', *Washington Post*, 3 October, C1.

Anon. (1980n), 'On the screen', *Deseret News*, 3 October, 12.

Anon. (1980o), '10 year diary of fast-fade "indie pix"', *Variety*, 8 October, 10.

Anon. (1980p), 'Sick films for sick people', *Chicago Tribune*, 7 November, B2.

Anon. (1980q), 'Chi tribune blasts gory X-films in R-rated clothing', *Variety*, 12 November, 6, 30.

Anon. (1980r), 'Canadians seek "any lessons" in "Meatballs" and "Prom Night"', *Variety*, 26 November, 36.

Anon. (1981a), 'Big rental films of 1980', *Variety*, 14 January, 29, 50.

Anon. (1981b), '"Prom Night" nixes pay TV for net airing', *Variety*, 11 February, 1, 36.

Anon. (1981c), 'Sean Cunningham: enough already of horror successes', *Variety*, 1 April, 6, 41.

Anon. (1981d), *PR Newswire*, 4 May. www.lexisnexis.com/ [accessed 2 February 2010].

Anon. (1981e), 'Madman', *Fangoria*, 13, June, 59.

Anon. (1982a), 'Big rental films of 1981', *Variety*, 13 January, 15, 42.

Anon. (1982b), 'Horror pics a crowded path to boxoffice, but lucrative', *Variety*, 3 March, 20.

Anon. (1983), 'Big Rental Films of 1982', *Variety*, 12 January, 13, 46, 52.

Anon. (1985), 'Big Rental Films of 1984', *Variety*, 16 January, 16, 78, 90.

Ansen, D. (1978), 'Trick or treat', *Newsweek*, 4 December, 116.

Ansen, D. and Kasindorf, M. (1979), 'Hollywood's scary summer', *Newsweek*, 18 June, 54.

Ansen, D. and Kasindorf, M. (1980), 'Hollywood's doldrums', *Newsweek*, 14 July, 74.

Armstrong, B. (2003), *Slasher Films: An International Filmography, 1960–2001*. Jefferson: McFarland.

Arnold, G. (1976a), '"Carrie": brilliant hair raising horror', *Washington Post*, 3 November, D1, D7.

Arnold, G. (1976b), 'De Palma's spectacular sleeper', *Washington Post*, 21 November, 141.

Arnold, G. (1978), '"Halloween": a trickle of treats', *Washington Post*, 24 November, B5.

Arnold, G. (1979a), '"The Warriors" — surly kids pack a box-office wallop', 18 March, H1, H6.

Arnold, G. (1979b), 'Hollywood breaks out laughing: 100 new comedies head for the box office', *Washington Post*, 22 April, K1.

Arnold, G. (1979c), '"Skatetown, U.S.A"s' roller-disco lovers', *Washington Post*, 23 November, E1, E7.

Arnold, G. (1980a), 'Caddy capers', *Washington Post*, 26 July, C3.

Arnold, G. (1980b), 'Murder by the blade', *Washington Post*, 1 October, B9.

Arnold, G. (1981a), '"Friday the 13th, Part 2": unlucky number', *Washington Post*, 13 May, B6.

Arnold, G. (1981b), 'Unhappy returns', *Washington Post*, 15 May, F4.

Arnold, G. (1981c), 'Puncture imperfect; "Blow Out": the sound of murder; Travolta & murder a la De Palma in "Blow Out"', *Washington Post*, 24 July, D1.

Arnold. G. (1981d), '"Bodies" kills clichés', *Washington Post*, 11 August, C10.

Arnold, G. Harrington, R., Hume, P., Lardner, J., Kriegsman, A. M., McLellan, J., Richard, P., and Shales, T. (1980), 'Critics Roundtable', *Washington Post*, 28 December, F1.

Austin, T. (2002), '"*Gone with the Wind* plus fangs": genre, taste and distinction in the assembly, marketing and reception of Bram Stoker's *Dracula*', in S. Neale (ed.), *Genre and Contemporary Hollywood*. London: Routledge, pp. 294–306.

Avco Embassy Pictures (1980), *Prom Night* advertisement, *Variety*, 30 July, 24.

Bailey, B. (1980), 'Terror Train works despite unoriginality', *Montreal Gazette*, 14 October, 70.

Bailey, B. (1981), 'Urban cowboys, horror flicks lead the way', *Montreal Gazette*, 3 January, 34.

Balio, T. (1993), *Grand Design: Hollywood as a Modern Business Enterprise, 1930–1939 (History of the American Cinema, Volume 5)*. London: Simon & Schuster Macmillan.

Balio, T. (1998), '"A major presence in all of the world's important markets": the globalization of Hollywood in the 1990s', in S. Neale and M. Smith (eds.), *Contemporary Hollywood Cinema*. London: Routledge, pp. 57–73.

Beamon, W. (1981), 'Don't get burned paying for "Burning"', *Evening Independent*, 12 May, 17.

Berenstein, R. J. (1996), *Attack of the Leading Ladies: Gender, Sexuality, and Spectatorship in Classic Horror Cinema*. New York: Columbia University Press.

Berg. (1980), 'Prom Night', *Variety*, 23 July, 20.

Best, A. L. (2000), *Prom Night: Youth, Schools and Popular Culture*. New York: Routledge.

Blank, E. (1981), '"Happy birthday" saves its worst for the end', *Pittsburg Press*, 16 May, 6.

Bodroghkozy, A. (2002), 'Reel revolutionaries: an examination of Hollywood's cycle of 1960s youth rebellion films', *Cinema Journal*, 41, 3, 38–58.

Bordwell, D. (1985), *Narration in the Fiction Film*. Madison: University of Wisconsin Press.

Boulenger, G. (2001), *John Carpenter The Prince of Darkness: An Exclusive Interview with the Director of Halloween and The Thing*. Los Angeles: Silman-James Press.

Boyles, D. (1980), 'Hollywood 'B's make the box office buzz', *New York Times*, 3 August, D17.

Boyles, D. (1981), 'To market, to market to peddle a shocker", *Los Angeles Times*, 4 June, H1.

Bracke, P. M. (2005), *Crystal Lake Memories: The Complete History of Friday the 13th*. Los Angeles: Sparkplug.

Buckley, T. (1981), 'A potboiler at the end of the rainbow', *New York Times*, 23 January, 8.

Burfoot, A. and Lord, S. (2006), *Killing Women: The Visual Culture of Gender and Violence*. Waterloo: Wilfrid Laurier Press.

Burns, J. H. (1981a), 'My Bloody Valentine', *Fangoria*, 11, February, 54–56, 64–65.

Burns, J. H. (1981b), 'Friday the 13th Part II', *Fangoria*, 12, April, 12–15, 64–65.

Byron, S. (1982), 'Rules of the game', *Village Voice*, 16 March, 50.

Canby, V. (1979), 'Chilling truths about scaring', *New York Times*, 21 January, D13.

Canby, V. (1980a), '"Caddyshack," "Animal House" spinoff', *New York Times*, 25 July, C8.

Canby, V. (1980b), '"Prom Night," chiller from Canada masks gore', *New York Times*, 16 August, 11.

Canby, V. (1981a), 'Happy Birthday to Me', *New York Times*, 15 May, C13.

Canby, V. (1981b), 'When movies take pride in being second rate', *New York Times*, 7 June, 19.

Carl. (1980). 'He Knows You're Alone', *Variety*, 27 August, 29.

Carl. (1981a), 'My Bloody Valentine', *Variety*, 18 February, 20.

Carl. (1981b), 'The Funhouse', *Variety*, 18 March, 133.

Carlomagno, E. and Martin, B. (1982), 'Young and independent: coming attractions from a new breed of filmmakers!', *Fangoria*, 17, February, 22–22, 46–47.

Carroll, N. (1990), *The Philosophy of Horror or Paradoxes of the Heart*. New York: Routledge.

Carroll, N. (1996), 'Towards a theory of film suspense', in N. Carroll (ed.), *Theorizing the Moving Image*. New York: Cambridge University Press. pp. 94–117.

Carroll, N. (1999), 'Horror and Humor', *The Journal of Aesthetics and Art Criticism*, 52, (2), 145–160.

Caulfield, D. and Garner, J. (1981), '"Fringe" teens versus mainstream movies', *Los Angeles Times*, 24 May, L22.

Cedrone, L. (1976), 'Maryland bans "Snuff" based on its "psychotic violence"', *Variety*, 7 April, 4.

Chase, C. (1981a), 'Lights, camera in Hollywood on the Hudson', *New York Times*, 27 March, C8.

Chase, C. (1981b), 'Frenchwoman next door talks of love', *New York Times*, 30 October, C8.

Cherry, B. (1999), 'Refusing to refuse to look: female viewers of the horror film', in M. Stokes and R. Maltby (eds), *Identifying Hollywood's Audiences: Cultural Identity and the Movies*. London: BFI, pp. 187–204.

Clandfield, D. (1987), *Canadian Film*. Oxford: Oxford University Press.

Clover, C. J. (1987), 'Her body, himself: gender in the slasher film', *Representations*, 20, 187–228.

Clover, C. J. (1992), *Men, Women and Chainsaws: Gender in the Modern Horror Film*. London: BFI.

Cohn, L. (1981), 'Gore perpetual fave of young film fans', *Variety*, 26 August, 6–7, 41–42.

Collins, J., Radner, H and Preacher Collins, A. (1993), *Film Theory Goes to the Movies*. New York: Routledge.

Columbia Pictures. (1974), *The Way We Were* box office announcement, *Variety*, 23 January, 11.

Compass International Films. (1979), *Roller Boogie* production announcement, *Variety*, 27 June, 27.

Connelly, K. (2007), 'From final girl to final woman: defeating the male monster in *Halloween* and *Halloween H20*', *Journal of Popular Film and Television*, 35, (1), 12–20.

Conrich, I. and Woods, D. (2002), *The Cinema of John Carpenter: The Technique of Terror*. London: Wallflower.

Cook, D. A. (1994), 'Auteur cinema and the "film generation" in 1970s cinema', in J. Lewis (ed.), *The New American Cinema*. Durham: Duke University Press, pp. 11–37.

Cook, D. A. (2000), *Lost Illusions: American Cinema in the Shadow of Watergate and Vietnam, 1970–1979 (History of the American Cinema, Volume 9)*. Berkeley: University of California Press.

Cook, D. (2007), '1974 — movies and political trauma', in L. D. Friedman (ed.), *American Cinema of the 1970s: Themes and Variations*. Oxford: Berg, pp. 116–134.

Corry, J. (1980), 'Spottiswoode's "Terror Train"', *New York Times*, 3 October, C10.

Corry, J. (1981), '"Hell Night": initiation rite', *New York Times*, 6 September, 51.

Cowan, G. and O'Brien, M. (1990), 'Gender and survival vs. death in slasher films: a content analysis', *Sex Roles*, 23, (3–4), 187–196.

Crane, J. L. (1994), *Terror and Everyday Life: Singular Moments in the History of the Horror Film*. London: Sage.

Creed, B. (1993), *The Monstrous Feminine: Film, Feminism, Psychoanalysis*. New York: Routledge.

Crown International Pictures. (1976), *The Pom Pom Girls* box office announcement, *Variety*, 18 August, 18–19.

Cunningham, S. (1979), '*Friday the 13th*: Production Announcement', *Variety*, 4 July, 23.

David Novak Associates Inc. (1980), 'Astral Bellevue Pathé communique de press/news release: 75 theatre Canadian Release slated by Astral: Twentieth Century Fox spends $5 million to launch "Terror Train" in 1000 theatres across the U.S.A ', 18 September. Press release held at British Film Institute, London, United Kingdom.

Dibsie, P. (1980), 'Do horror films promote violence towards women? — yes! — no!', *Reading Eagle*, 14 December, 66, 83.

Dickstein, M. (1984), 'The aesthetics of fright', in B. K. Grant (ed.), *Planks of Reason*. London: Scarecrow Press, pp. 68–86.

Dika, V. (1987), 'The stalker film, 1978–81', in G. A. Waller (ed.), *American Horrors: Essays on the Modern Horror Film*. Urbana: University of Illinois Press, pp. 86–101.

Dika, V. (1990), *Games of Terror: Halloween, Friday the 13th and the Films of the Stalker Cycle*. London: Associated University Press.

Doherty, T. (1988), 'Hollywood agit-prop: the anti-communist cycle, 1948–1952', *Journal of Film and Video*, 40, 4, 15–27.

Doherty, T. (2002), *Teenagers and Teenpics: The Juvenilization of American Movies in the 1950s* (revised edn). Philadelphia: Temple University Press.

Donahue, S. M. (1987), *American Film Distribution: The Changing Marketplace*. Ann Arbor: UMI Research Press.

Dresser, N. (1980), '"Prom Night" showing at 5 theatres, drive-ins', *Toledo Blade*, 28 July 1980, 2.

Ebert, R. (1981), 'Why the movies aren't safe anymore', *American Film*, 6, (5), 54–56.

Erb, C (1998). *Tracking King Kong: A Hollywood Icon in World Culture*. Detroit: Wayne State University Press.

Evans, S. (1981), Untitled Letter, *Fangoria*, 11, February, 6–7.

Farley, E. (1977), 'Impresarios of axploitation movies', *Los Angeles Times*, 13 November, O1.

Farley, E. (1981), 'Linda Blair: erasing the demon image', *Los Angeles Times*, 22 February, L22.

Farley, E. and Knoedelseder, W. K. Jr. (1982), 'A tangled web clogs "Chain Saw"', *Los Angeles Times*, 12 September, U3.

Frederick, R. B. (1980), '"Dressed to Kill" hits market; De Palma stays with suspense', *Variety*, 16 July, 41.

Friedman, L. D. (2007). *American Cinema of the 1970s: Themes and Variations*. Oxford: Berg.

Gage, N. (1975), 'Organised crime reaps huge profits from dealing in pornographic films', *New York Times*, 12 October, 1.

Garner, J. (1981), 'Teens blah on killer thrillers', *Los Angeles Times*, 22 August, L29.

Gasher, M (2002), *Hollywood North: The Feature Film Industry in British Columbia*. Vancouver: UBC Press.

Gateward, F. and Pomerance, M. (2002), *Sugar, Spice and Everything Nice: Cinemas of Girlhood*. Detroit: Wayne University Press.

Gateward, F. (2007), '1973 — movies and the legacies of war and corruption', in L. Friedman (ed.), *American Cinema of the 1970s: Themes and Variations*. Oxford: Berg, pp. 95–115.

Geraghty L. and Jancovich, M. (2009), *The Shifting Definitions of Genre: Essays on Labeling Film, Television Shows and Media*. Jefferson: McFarland.

Gilby, R. (2003), *It Don't Worry Me: Nashville, Jaws, Star Wars and Beyond*. London: Faber and Faber.

Gill, P. (2002), 'The monstrous years: teens, slasher films and the family', *Journal of Film and Video*, 54, (5), 16–30.

Gillette, D. C. (1976), 'Think indie producers unwise in stressing lurid films', *Variety*, 7 April, 5, 40.

Gittings, C. E. (2002), *Canadian National Cinema*. London: Routledge.

Goldstein, P. (1981), 'Mutants, monsters, apes', *Los Angeles Times*, 25 October, L7.

Gomery, D. (1998), 'Hollywood corporate business practice and periodizing contemporary film history', in S. Neale and M. Smith (eds), *Contemporary Hollywood Cinema*. London: Routledge, pp. 47–57.

Grant, B. K. (1984), *Planks of Reason: Essays on the Horror Film*. London: Scarecrow Press.

Grant, B. K. (1986), *Film Genre Reader*. Austin: University of Texas Press.

Grant, B. K. (1996), 'Rich and strange: the yuppie horror film', *Journal of Film and Video*, 48, 1/2, 4–16.

Grant, L. (1979), 'Chicanos picket "Boulevard Nights"', *Los Angeles Times*, 23 March, G19.

Greenberger, R. (1981), 'P. J. Soles', *Fangoria*, 13, June, 17–19, 65.

Grigsby, W. (1979), 'Montreal after "Meatballs": attys become producers; a reprise of recent films', *Variety*, 21 November, 50, 72.

Groen, R. (1981), 'Friday the 13th sequel: once more with the gore', *Globe and Mail*, May 4, 1981. www.lexisnexis.com/ [accessed 2 February 2010].

Gross, L. (1978), 'A woman's place is in . . . exploitation films', *Los Angeles Times*, 12 February, 34.

Gross, L. (1980a), '"Scream" trite but scary', *Los Angeles Times*, 24 January, F8

Gross, L. (1980b), '"Friday the 13th": encamped in gore', *Los Angeles Times*, 15 May, 17.

Gross, L. (1981a), 'Bloody valentine is heartless fare', *Los Angeles Times*, 16 February, E2.

Gross, L. (1981b), '"Final Exam": some answers missing', *Los Angeles Times*, 11 June, H7.

Gross, L. (1981c), 'Comical parts in "Student Bodies"', *Los Angeles Times*, 11 August, G4.

Gross, L. (1982), '"Slumber Party": gore is still gore', *Los Angeles Times*, 15 September, G3.

Grove, D. (2005), *Making Friday the 13th: The Legend of Camp Blood*. Godalming: Fab Press.

Guerrero, E. (1993), *Framing Blackness: The African American Image in Film*. Philadelphia: Temple University Press.

Hall, S. (1998), 'Tall revenue features: the genealogy of the modern blockbuster', in S. Neale (ed.), *Genre and Contemporary Hollywood*. London: BFI, pp. 11–26.

Hall, S. (2002), 'Carpenter's widescreen style', in I. Conrich and D. Woods (eds), *The Cinema of John Carpenter: The Technique of Terror*. London: Wallflower Press, pp. 66–77.

Harmetz, A. (1979a), 'Hollywood is taking aim at the funny bone', *New York Times*, 5 August, D5.

Harmetz, A. (1979b), 'Cheap and profitable movies are multiplying', *New York Times*, 24 October, C21.

Harmetz, A. (1980a), 'After 2 good summers, film business lags', *New York Times*, 26 June, C14.

Harmetz, A. (1980b), 'The selling of a film, a not-so-subtle art', *New York Times*, 23 July, C15.

Harmetz, A. (1980c), 'For films, a chilly summer warmed up', *New York Times*, 5 September, C4.

Harmetz, A. (1980d), 'Quick end of low-budget horror-film cycle seen', *New York Times*, 2 October, C15.

Harmetz, A. (1980e), 'The movie no theatres thought worth seeing", *New York Times*, 4 November, C5.

Harmetz, A. (1981), 'Robert Rehme, king of the low-budget shocker', *New York Times*, 30 November, C13.

Harper, J. (2004), *Legacy of Blood: A Comprehensive Guide to Slasher Movies*. Manchester: Headpress.

Harries, D. (2000), *Film Parody*. London: BFI.

Harrington, R. (1980), 'Bloody illusions: the cutting edge of gore', *Washington Post*, 2 November, M1.

Harvey, S. (1980), 'Can't stop the remakes', *Film Comment*, 16, (5), 49.

Hay, J. and Bailey, S. (1998) 'Cinema and the premises of youth: "teen films" and their sites in the 1980s and 1990s', in S. Neale (ed.), *Genre and Contemporary Hollywood*. London: BFI, pp. 218–235.

Heffernan, K. (2002), 'The hypnosis horror films of the 1950s: genre texts and industry contexts', *Journal of Film and Video*, 54, 2/3, 56–70.

Heffernan, K. (2004), *Ghouls, Gimmicks and Gold: Horror Films and the American Movie Business, 1953–1968*. Durham: Duke University Press.

Hege. (1978), 'Halloween', *Variety*, 25 October, 20.

Heller Anderson, S. (1982), 'The 'R' rating — a lure or a barrier', *New York Times*, 2 May, 19.

Hicks, C. (1980), 'So far — a good year for bad movies', *Desert News*, 29–30 July, C7.

Hicks, D. (1981), 'A bloody waste', *Fangoria*, 13, June, 7.

Hillier, J. (1994), *The New Hollywood*. New York: Continuum.

Hillier, J. and Lipstadt, A. (1981), *Roger Corman's New World*. London: BFI.

Hillier, J. and Lipstadt, A. (1986), 'The economics of independence: Roger Corman and New World Pictures 1970–1980', *Movie*, 31/32, 43–53.

Hills, M. (2007), 'Para-paracinema: the *Friday the 13th* film series as Other to trash and legitimate film cultures', in G. Sconce (ed.), *Sleaze Artists: Cinema at the Margins of Taste, Style, and Politics*. Durham: Duke University Press, pp. 219–239.

Holmund, C. and Wyatt, J. (2005), *Contemporary American Independent Film*. London: Routledge.

Horton, A. (1977), 'Turning on and turning out at the drive-in: an American phenomenon survives and thrives', *Journal of Popular Film*, 4, (3–4), 233–244.

Hugo, C (1980). 'American cinema in the 70s: the economic background', *Movie*, 27/28, 43–49.

Jancovich, M. (2000), '"A real shocker": authenticity, genre and the struggle for distinction', *Continuum: Journal of Media and Cultural Studies*, 14, (1), 23–35.

Jancovich, M. (2002), *Horror, the Film Reader*. London: Routledge.

Jancovich, M. (2009), '"Thrills and chills": horror, the woman's film, and the origins of film noir', *New Review of Film and Television Studies*, 7, (2), 157–171.

Jancovich, M., Reboll, A. L., Stringer, J. and Wills, A. (2003). *Defining Cult Movies: The Cultural Politics of Oppositional Taste*. Manchester: Manchester University Press.

Jenkins, P. (1994), *Using Murder: The Social Construction of Serial Homicide* New York: Aldine De Gruyter.

Johnson, E. and Schaefer, E. (1993), 'Soft core/hard gore: *Snuff* as a crisis of meaning', *Journal of Film and Video*, 45, (2/3), 40–59.

Jones, E. (1981), 'Quality decreases as profits continue', *Free Lance-Star*, 23 September, 17.

Kapsis, R. E. (1992), *Hitchcock: The Making of a Reputation*. Chicago: University of Chicago Press.

Kart, L. (1981), '"Hand", "Birthday": horror movies with a shocking lack of intelligence', *Chicago Tribune*, 19 May, A8.

Kawin, B. F. (1987), '*The Funhouse* and *The Howling*', in G. A. Waller (ed.), *Horrors: Essays on the Modern Horror Film*. Urbana: University of Illinois Press, pp. 102–113.

Kernan, L. (2004), *Coming Attractions: Reading American Movie Trailers*. Austin: University of Texas Press.

Kilday, G. (1976), 'Girl crazy', *Los Angeles Times*, 27 September, E8.

Kilday G. (1978), 'The gang's all here', *Los Angeles Times*, 10 September, L23.

King, G. (2002), *Film/Comedy*. London: Wallflower.

Klad. (1981), 'The Prowler', *Variety*, 25 November, 22.

Klain, S. (1979), 'Bill Benson sees "Boulevard" swamped in "gang war" wave', *Variety*, 28 March, 24.

Kleinhans, C. (2002), 'Girls on the edge of the Regan era', in M. Gateward and M. Pomerance (eds), *Sugar, Spice and Everything Nice: Cinemas of Girlhood*. Detroit: Wayne University Press, pp. 72–90.

Klinger, B. (1989), 'Digressions at the cinema: reception and mass culture', *Cinema Journal*, 28, (4), 3–19.

Knoedelseder, W. K. Jr. (1980a), 'The new dealmakers: killing them at the box office', *Los Angeles Times*, 9 November, N3–4.

Knoedelseder, W. K. Jr. (1980b), 'Jamie Lee Curtis: a scream queen attracts attention', *Los Angeles Times*, 16 November, Q4.

Kolker, R. (1980), *A Cinema of Loneliness: Penn, Kubrick, Coppola, Scorsese, Altman*. Oxford: Oxford University Press.

Koven, M. J. (2006). *La Dolce Morte: Vernacular Cinema and the Italian Giallo*. Lanham: Scarecrow Press.

Koven, M. J. (2008), *Film, Folklore, and Urban Legends*. Lanham: Scarecrow Press.

Krämer, P. (1999), 'A powerful cinema-going force? Hollywood and female audiences since the 1960s', in M. Stokes and R. Maltby (eds), *Identifying Hollywood's Audiences: Cultural Identity and the Movies*. London: BFI, pp. 93–108.

Krämer, P. (2002), '"The best Disney film that Disney never made": children's films and family audience in American cinema since the 1960s', in S. Neale (ed.), *Genre and Contemporary Hollywood*. London: BFI, pp. 185–200.

Krämer, P. (2005). *The New Hollywood: From Bonnie and Clyde to Star Wars*. London: Wallflower Press.

Labonté, R. (1980a), 'New films hit screens on Friday', *Ottawa Citizen*, 26 August, 38.

Labonté, R. (1980b), 'Terror Train tracks horror trend', *Ottawa Citizen*, 9 October, 202.

Labonté, R. (1980c), 'Year of the god', *Ottawa Citizen*, 27 December, 27.

Leach, J. (1986), 'The body snatchers: Genre and Canadian Cinema', in B. K. Grant (ed.), *Film Genre Reader*. Austin: University of Texas Press, pp. 357–369.

Leach, J. (2006), *Film in Canada*. Cambridge: Cambridge University Press.

Lev, P. (2000), *American Films of the 70s: Conflicting Visions*. Austin: University of Texas Press.

Levine, E, and Parks, L. (2007), *Undead TV: Essays on Buffy the Vampire Slayer*. Durham: Duke University Press.

Levine, E. (2007b), 'Buffy and the new girl order: defining feminism and femininity', in E. Levine and L. Parks (eds), *Undead TV Essays on Buffy the Vampire Slayer*. Durham: Duke University Press, pp. 168–190.

Lewis, J. (1992), *The Road to Romance and Ruin: Teen Films and Youth Culture*. New York: Routledge.

Lewis, J. (1994), *The New American Cinema*. Durham: Duke University Press.

Lewis, J. (2002), *Hollywood vs. Hard Core: How the Struggle over Censorship Saved Hollywood*. New York: New York University Press.

Lewis, P. (1989), *Comic Effects: Interdisciplinary Approaches to Humor in Literature*. Albany: State University of New York Press.

Lor. (1981a), 'Friday the 13th Part 2', *Variety*, 26 May, 21.

Lor. (1981b), 'Hell Night', *Variety*, 2 September, 14.

Lowry, E. (2005), 'Dimension Pictures: portrait of a 1970s independent', in C. Holmund and J. Wyatt (eds), *Contemporary American Independent Film*. London: Routledge, pp. 41–53.

Lyons, C. (1997), *The New Censors: Movies and the Cultural Wars*. Philadelphia: Temple University Press.

McCarty, J. (1984), *Splatter Movies: Breaking the Last Taboo of the Screen*. New York: St. Martin's Press.

McCarty, J. (1989), *The Official Splatter Movie Guide*. New York: St. Martin's Press.

McLellan, J. (1980a), '"Friday the 13th": it's all in the offing', *Washington Post*, 13 May, B3.

McLellan, J. (1980b), 'Boogie, with a touch of blood', *Washington Post*, 16 August, B2.

McRobbie, A. and Nava, M. (1984a). *Gender and Generation*. Basingstoke: Macmillan.

McRobbie, A. (1984b), 'Dance and social fantasy', in A. McRobbie and M. Nava (eds), *Gender and Generation*. Basingstoke: Macmillan, pp. 130–161.

Magder, T. (1993), *Canada's Hollywood: The Canadian State and Feature Films*. Toronto: University of Toronto Press.

Maltby, R. (1983), *Harmless Entertainment: Hollywood and the Ideology of Consensus*. Metuchen, NJ: Scarecrow.

Maltby, R. (2003), *Hollywood Cinema Second Edition*. Oxford: Blackwell.

Marshall, B. (2001), *Quebec National Cinema*. Montreal: McGill-Queen's University Press.

Martin, J. (1981), 'A bloody "birthday" picture', *Washington Post*, 15 May, W19.

Mask, M. (2007), '1971 — movies and the exploitation of excess', in L. B. Friedman (ed.), *American Cinema of the 1970s: Themes and Variations*. Oxford: Berg, pp. 48–70.

Maslin, J. (1980a), '"Friday the 13th": horror at middle-class summer camp', *New York Times*, 10 May, 14.

Maslin, J. (1980b), 'Nicholson and Shelley Duvall in Kubrick's "The Shining"', *New York Times*, 23 May, C8.

Maslin, J. (1981), 'Tired blood claims the horror film as a fresh victim', *New York Times*, 1 November, 15.

Maslin, J. (1982), '"Burning" from horror genre', *New York Times*, 5 November, C7.

Mathijs, E. (2003), 'The making of a cult reputation: topicality and controversy in the critical reception of *Shivers*', in M. Jancovich, A. I. Reboll, J. Stringer and A. Wills (eds), *Defining Cult Movies: The Cultural Politics of Oppositional Taste*. Manchester: Manchester University Press, pp. 109–127.

Middleton, J. (2007), 'Buffy as femme fatal: the cult heroine and the male spectator', in E. Levine and L. Parks (eds), *Undead TV Essays on Buffy the Vampire Slayer*. Durham: Duke University Press, pp. 145–167.

Miller, V. (1980a), 'Confessions of a horror writer', *Washington Post*, 22 June, K1.

Miller, V. (1980b), 'The guy next door writes a scream gem', *Los Angeles Times*, 29 June, Y6.

Modleski, T. (1986a), *Studies in Entertainment: Critical Approaches to Mass Culture*. Bloomington: Indiana University Press.

Modleski, T. (1986b), 'The terror of pleasure: the contemporary horror film and postmodern theory', in T Modleski (ed.), *Studies in Entertainment: Critical Approaches to Mass Culture*. Bloomington: Indiana University Press, pp. 233–242.

Molitor, F. and Sapolsky, B. S. (1993), 'Sex, violence and victimization in slasher films', *Journal of Broadcasting and Electronic Media*, 37, 233–242.

Monaco, P. (2001), *The Sixties, 1960–1968 (History of the American Cinema, Volume 8)*. New York: Charles Schribner's Sons.

Moorhead, J. (1980a), 'Summer camps hit again in "Friday the 13th"', *St. Petersburg Independent*, 12 May, 22.

Moorhead, J. (1980b), 'Silent Scream: title is best part', *St. Petersburg Independent*, 26 May, 3B.

Moorhead, J. (1980c), '"Gorp" is gluttonous garbage', *St. Petersburg Independent*, 3 June, 3.

Moorhead, J. (1981), '1980 Oscar nominees sadly hobbled nags', *Evening Independent*, 18 February, 21.

Morris, G. (1993), 'Beyond the beach: AIP's beach party movies', *Journal of Popular Film and Television*, 23, (1), 2–11.

Morrisroe, P. (1980), 'Hard-core horror hits the mark!', *Montreal Gazette*, 6 September, 101.

Motion Picture Association of America. (1977), 'The code of self-regulation (revised cdn, 1977): declaration of the principles of the code of self-regulation of the motion picture association' (reprinted in Lewis, 2002, 307–314).

Muir, J. K. (2000), *The Films of John Carpenter*. Jefferson: McFarlane.

Murphy, A. D. (1975a), 'Audience demographics, film future: loss of youth adjustment due', *Variety*, 20 August, 3, 74.

Murphy, A. D. (1975b), 'Demographics favoring films future: "aging of 60s teens a factor"', *Variety*, 8 October, 3, 34.

Murphy, A. D. (1976a), 'Pinch picture playoff: majors can't supply full year's product', *Variety*, 17 March, 1, 34.

Murphy, A. D. (1976b), '300 indie films pace production: invest $100 — mil outside majors', *Variety*, 9 June, 1, 32.

Naremore, J. (1998), *More than the Night: Film Noir in its Contexts*. Berkeley: University of California Press.

Neale, S. (1981), '*Halloween*, suspense, aggression and the look', *Framework*, 14, 25–29.

Neale, S. (1990), 'Questions of Genre', *Screen*, 31, (1), 45–66.

Neale, S. (1993), 'Melo talk: on the meaning of use of the term "melodrama" in the American trade press', *The Velvet Light Trap*, 32, 66–89.

Neale, S. and Smith, M. (1998), *Contemporary Hollywood Cinema*. London: Routledge.

Neale, S. (2000), *Genre and Hollywood*. London: Routledge.

Neale, S. (2002), *Genre and Contemporary Hollywood*. London: BFI.

Nolan, J. M., and Ryan, G. W. (2000), 'Fear and loathing at the cineplex: gender differences and perceptions of slasher films', *Sex Roles*, 42, (1–2), 39–56.

Nowell, R. (2011), '"The ambitions of most independent filmmakers": indie production, the majors, and *Friday the 13th* (1980)', *Journal of Film and Video* (63), 2.

Paramount Pictures. (1981), *Friday the 13th Part II*: box office announcement, *Variety*, 6 May, 30–31.

Paseman, L. (1980), '"Scream" provides a good basic scare', *Eugene Register Guard*, 24 January, 2C.

Paul, W. (1994) *Laughing Screaming: Modern Hollywood Horror & Comedy*. New York: Columbia University Press.

Pendakur, M. (1991), *Canadian Dreams and American Control: The Political Economy of the Canadian Film Industry*. Detroit: Wayne State University Press.

People. (2000), *2001 People Entertainment Almanac*. New York: Cader Books.

Pevere, G. (1995), 'Middle of nowhere: Ontario movies after 1980', *Post Script*, 15, (1), 9–22.

Pinedo, I. C. (1997), *Recreational Terror: Women and the Pleasures of Horror Film Viewing*. Albany: State University of New York Press.

Pollock, D. (1978a), 'Hollywood hemorrhaging [sic] Dracula films; in one he visits Gotham and gets mugged; 8 new scripts', *Variety*, 14 June, 6.

Pollock, D. (1978b), 'How to survive majors' summer clout: on Al Belkin indie game plan', *Variety*, 5 July, 5, 26.

Pollock, D. (1979), '"Cruising" in "war zone"; finished on sked, bow set', *Variety*, 12 September, 6.

Pollock, D. (1980), 'Second most successful film: scary news: it's "Friday the 13th"', *Los Angeles Times*, 27 June, G11.

Pollock, D. (1981a), 'The man with the Midas touch', *Los Angeles Times*, 7 April, G1.

Pollock, D. (1981b), 'Body count means counting bucks', *Los Angeles Times*, 6 May, H1.

Powers, S., Rothman, D. J. and Rothman, S. (1996), *Hollywood's America: Social and Political Themes in Motion Pictures*. Boulder: Westview.

Prince, S. (2000) *A New Pot of Gold: Hollywood under the Electronic Rainbow, 1980–1989 (History of the American Cinema, Volume 10)*. Berkeley: University of California Press.

Read, J. (2000) *The New Avengers: Feminism, Femininity and the Rape-Revenge Cycle*. Manchester: Manchester University Press.

Reiser, K. (2001), 'Masculinity and monstrosity: characterization and identification in the slasher film', *Men and Masculinities*, 3, (4), 370–392.

Rich, F. (1977), 'Discomania', *Time*, 19 December. www.time.com/time/magazine/article/0,9171,945860,00.html [accessed 28 August 2010]

Robbins, J. (1982), 'Survey says public likes sci-fi but really loves comedy', *Variety*, 22 September, 22.

Rockoff, A. (2002), *Going to Pieces: The Rise and Fall of the Slasher Film, 1978–86*. Jefferson: McFarland.

Romao, T. (2003), 'Engines of transformation: an analytical history of the 1970s car chase cycle', *New Review of Film and Television Studies*, 1, (1), 31–54.

Rubin, M. (1999), *Thrillers*. Cambridge: Cambridge University Press.

Russell, J. (2009), '"A most historic period of change": the Western, the epic and *Dances with Wolves*', in L. Geraghty and M. Jancovich (eds), *The Shifting Definitions of Genre: Essays on Labeling Film, Television Shows and Media*. Jefferson: McFarland, pp. 142–158.

Sandler, K. S. (2002), 'Movie ratings as genre: the incontestable R', in S. Neale (ed.), *Genre and Contemporary Hollywood*. London: BFI, pp. 203–208.

Sandler, K. S. (2007), *The Naked Truth: Why Hollywood Doesn't Make X-rated Movies*. New Brunswick: Rutgers University Press.

Schaefer, E. (1992), 'Of hygiene and Hollywood: origins of the exploitation film', *The Velvet Light Trap*, 30, 34–47.

Schaefer, E. (1994), 'Resisting refinement: the exploitation film and self-censorship', *Film History*, 6, (3), 293–313.

Schaefer, E. (1999), *Bold! Daring! Shocking! True!: A History of Exploitation Films, 1919–1959*. Durham: Duke University Press.

Schaefer, E. (2004), 'Gauging a revolution: 16mm film and the rise of the pornographic feature', in L. Williams (ed.), *Porn Studies*. Durham: Duke University Press, 2004, pp. 370–400.

Schaefer, E. (2007), 'Pandering to the "goon trade": framing the exploitation audience', in G. Sconce (ed.), *Sleaze Artists: Cinema at the Margins of Taste, Style, and Politics*. Durham: Duke University Press, pp. 19–46.

Schatz, T. (1983), *Old Hollywood/New Hollywood: Ritual, Art, Industry*. Ann Arbor: UMI Research Press.

Schatz, T. (1993), 'The New Hollywood', in J. Collins, H. Radner and A. Preacher Collins (eds), *Film Theory Goes to the Movies*. New York: Routledge, pp. 8–36.

Schickel, R. (1976), 'Cinema: a movable feast', *Time*, 8 November. www.time.com/time/magazine/article/0,9171,918515,00.html [accessed 28 August 2010].

Schneider, S. J. and Shaw, D. (2003a), *Dark Thoughts: Reflections on Cinematic Terror*. Lanham: Scarecrow Press.

Schneider, S. J. (2003b), 'Murder as art/the art of murder: aestheticizing violence in modern cinematic horror', S. J. Schneider and D. Shaw (eds), *Dark Thoughts: Reflections on Cinematic Terror*. Lanham: Scarecrow Press, pp. 170–194.

Schneider, S. J. (2003c), *Fear without Frontiers: Horror Cinema Across the Globe*. Goldalming: Fab Press.

Schneider, S. J. (2006), 'The madwomen in our movies: female psycho killers in American horror cinema', in A. Burfoot and S. Lord (eds), *Killing Women: The Visual Culture of Gender and Violence*. Waterloo: Wilfrid Laurier Press, pp. 237–250.

Schnurmacher, T. (1980), 'Local group gets Saturday chance', *Montreal Gazette*, 26 June, 69.

Schoell, W. (1985), *Stay out of the Shower: The Shocker Film Phenomenon*. London: Robinson Publishing.

Schreger, C. (1977), 'Majors drain off theatre cash, indie distributors now forced to upfront demand: Tenser', *Variety*, 23 March, 28.

Schreger, C. (1979a), 'Movie profits good regardless of film', *Victoria Advocate*, 3 January 1980, 16.

Schreger, C. (1979b), 'Hail, hail, the gang's not here', *Los Angeles Times*, 9 April, E12.

Schreger, C. (1979c), 'A wheel trend', *Los Angeles Times*, 4 July, D6.

Schulman, B. J. (2000), *The Seventies: The Great Shift in American Culture, Society, and Politics*. Cambridge: Da Capo Press.

Sconce, J. (2007), *Sleaze Artists: Cinema at the Margins of Taste, Style, and Politics*. Durham: Duke University Press.

Scott, J. (1979a), 'Horror movie sophisticated far beyond its low budget: Halloween mines forgotten fears', *Globe and Mail*, 19 January. www.lexisnexis.com [accessed 2 February 2010].

Scott, J. (1979b), 'Last embrace a wilted bouquet', *Globe and Mail*, 5 May. www.lexisnexis.com/ [accessed 2 February 2010].

Scott, J. (1979c), 'Unpredictable stranger a classic nerve-jangler', *Globe and Mail*, 22 October. www.lexisnexis.com/ [accessed 2 February 2010].

Scott, J. (1980), 'Prom Night: seven clichés of success', *Globe and Mail*, 17 September. www.lexisnexis.com/ [accessed 2 February 2010].

Scott, J. (1980b), 'Terror Train simply terrible', *Globe and Mail*, 15 October. www.lexisnexis.com/ [accessed 2 February 2010].

Scott, J. (1981a), 'Cage II and Charlie Chan hold more true horror than valentine', *Globe and Mail*, 16 February. www.lexisnexis.com/ [accessed 2 February 2010].

Scott, J. (1981b), 'Canada sparkles without tinsel', *Globe and Mail*, 26 May. www.lexisnexis.com/ [accessed 2 February 2010].

Scott, K. (1980), 'Horror film duo offer maximum violence', *St. Petersburg Times*, 24 September, D3.

Scott, V. (1979), 'Disco dancing on wheels in "Skatetown"', *Sarasota Herald-Tribune*, 4 August, 24.

Scott, V. (1981), 'Merchant of menace', *Hollywood Reporter*, 16 May.

Seymour Borde and Associates. (1979), *Summer Camp* box office announcement, *Variety*, 27 June, 31.

Shales, T. (1981), 'Stiff "Saturday"', *Washington Post*, 23 November, C2.

Shary, T. (2002a), *Generation Multiplex: The Image of Youth in Contemporary American Cinema*. Austin: University of Texas Press.

Shary, T. (2002b), 'The nerdly girl and her beautiful sister', in F. Gateward and M. Pomerance (eds), *Sugar, Spice and Everything Nice: Cinemas of Girlhood*. Detroit: Wayne University Press. pp. 235–250.

Shary, T. (2005), *Teen Movies: American Youth on Screen*. London: Wallflower.

Sheffield, S. (1981), '"Happy Birthday to Me" has its jolts', *Boca Raton News*, 19 May, 7.

Shirley, D. (1978), 'The gang is back: seven films about rowdy youth rumble toward the screen', *Washington Post*, 15 October, L1, L12.

Siskel, G. (1974), 'Black Christmas', *Chicago Tribune*, 6 October, B6.

Siskel, G. (1976), '"Carrie" has style but violence carries the day', *Chicago Tribune*, 9 November, A7.

Siskel, G. (1978a), 'First "Star Wars" imitation orbits around the trashy', *Chicago Tribune*, 7 November, A5.

Siskel, G. (1978b), '"Halloween": some tricks lots of treats', *Chicago Tribune*, 22 November, B7.

Siskel, G. (1979), 'Movies '78', *Chicago Tribune*, 7 January, D3.

Siskel, G. (1980a), '"Friday the 13th:" more bad luck', *Chicago Tribune*, 12 May, A9.

Siskel, G. (1980b), '"Silent Scream"', *Chicago Tribune*, 3 June, A5.

Siskel, G. (1980c), 'Prom Night', *Chicago Tribune*, 21 July, A6.

Siskel, G. (1980d), 'Brutal attacks on women: films take a turn for the worse', *Chicago Tribune*, 21 September, D6.

Siskel, G. (1981a), 'A week-by-week preview of 45 summer films', *Chicago Tribune*, 24 May, E18–E20.

Siskel, G (1981b), 'Siskel's flicks picks', *Chicago Tribune*, 5 June, B10.

Siskel, G. (1981c), 'Final Exam', *Chicago Tribune*, 9 June, A6.

Snelson, T. (2009), '"From grade B thrillers to deluxe chillers": prestige horror, female audiences, and allegories of spectatorship in *The Spiral Staircase* (1946)', *New Review of Film and Television Studies*, 7, (2), 173–188.

Sobchack, V. (1987), 'Bring it all back home: family economy and generic exchange', in G. A. Waller (ed.). *American Horrors: Essays on the Modern Horror Film*. Urbana: University of Illinois Press, pp. 175–194.

Sowa, T. (1981), 'New breed of horror unleashed', *Spokesman-Review*, 18 April, D14.

Spiros Associates. (1980), 'Proud to have been part of Paramount's success', *Variety*, 3 September, 14–15.

Stabiner, K. (1979), 'A look at filmmaking on the cheap', *New York Times*, 11 February, D15.

Stalling, L. (1975), '"Black Christmas" is taut thriller', *Daytona Beach Sunday News Journal*, 14 December, C6, C9.

Stanfield, P. (2001), *Hollywood, Westerns and the 1930s: The Lost Trail*. Exeter: Exeter University Press.

Steinberg, L. E. (1979), '"Murder at Disco Down" production announcement', *Variety*, 9 May, 253.

Step. (1980), 'Friday the 13th', *Variety*, 14 May, 14.

Sterritt, D. (1980), 'His low-budget films have a punch', *Christian Science Monitor*, 13 March, 18.

Stokes, M. (1999), 'Female audiences of the 1920s and early 1930s', in M. Stokes and R. Maltby (eds), *Identifying Hollywood's Audiences: Cultural Identity and the Movies*. London: BFI, pp. 42–60.

Stokes, M. and Maltby, R. (1999), *Identifying Hollywood's Audiences: Cultural Identity and the Movies*. London: BFI.

Summers, K. C. (1979), '"Meatballs" is made for kids', *Washington Post*, 13 July, W24.

Szulkin, D. A. (2000), *Wes Craven's Last House on the Left: The Making of a Cult Classic*. Guilford: FAB Press.

Tasker, Y. (1993), *Spectacular Bodies: Gender, Genre and the Action Cinema*. London: Routledge.

Taylor, T. (1978), 'Same old animals, same old house', *Washington Post*, 11 August, D17.

Thomas, B. (1977), 'The director is savoring his "School" days', *Chicago Tribune*, 29 May, A6.

Thomas, B. (1980), *Associated Press*, 27 February AM cycle. www.lexisnexis.com/ [accessed 2 February 2010].

Thomas, K. (1975), 'Gothic tale of a "Black Christmas"', *Los Angeles Times*, 6 August, F12.

Thomas, K. (1976), 'Teen-age hijinks in "Pom Pom Girls"', *New York Times*, 10 September, F16.

Thomas, K. (1978), 'Slaughter, fear in grisly "Halloween"', *Los Angeles Times*, 27 October, F22.

Thomas, K. (1980a), 'The gory horror of "Prom Night"', *Los Angeles Times*, 18 August, G14.

Thomas, K. (1980b), 'Stylish, scary fun on "Terror Train"', *Los Angeles Times*, 3 October, H19.

Thomas, K. (1981), '"Hell Night" terror takes the pledge', *Los Angeles Times*, 4 September, G13.

Totaro, D. (2003), 'The Italian zombie film: from derivation to reinvention', in S. J. Schneider (ed.), *Fear without Frontiers: Horror Cinema Across the Globe*. Godalming: Fab Press, pp. 161–173.

Tudor, A. (1989), *Monsters and Mad Scientists: A Cultural History of the Horror Movie*. Oxford: Basil Blackwell.

Turan, K. (1980), 'Fleeing from the curse of cult movies', *Washington Post*, 27 January, G1.

Tusher, W. (1977), 'Dangers of non-major filming; drift from 'sex' and 'violence'; bad guesses never hit market', *Variety*, 22 June, 5, 46.

Twentieth Century Fox Film Corporation. (1980), *Terror Train*: marketing announcement, *Variety*, 13 August, 28–29.

Twitchell, James B. (1985). *Dreadful Pleasures: An Anatomy of Horror*. New York: Oxford University Press.

Tzioumakis, Y. (2006), *American Independent Cinema: An Introduction*. Edinburgh: Edinburgh University Press.

Unger, A. (1980), '"Sneak Previews" — a sneak hit on public stations', *Christian Science Monitor*, 19 December, 19.

Universal Pictures. (1974), *American Graffiti*: box office announcement, *Variety*, 16 January, 13.

Vatnsdal, C. (2004), 'Happy Birthday to Me bash 'n' Slash', *Fangoria*, 238, November, 72–77.

Vaughn, S. (2006), *Freedom and Entertainment: Rating Movies in the Age of New Media*. Cambridge: Cambridge University Press.

Verrill, A. (1976), 'Preposterous sex dimensions, and Russ Meyer's hang-ups', *Variety*, 10 November, 27.

von Maurer, B. (1980), '"Prom Night" passes horror test, but fails as a first-rate thriller', *Miami News*, 22 September, 4B.

Waller, G. A. (1987), *American Horrors: Essays on the Modern Horror Film*. Urbana: University of Illinois Press.

Walentis, A. (1980), '"Silent Scream": Denny Harris creates above-average chiller', *Reading Eagle*, 2 March, 72.

Warner Bros. Pictures. (1974a), *The Exorcist* box office announcement, *Variety*, 9 January, 14–15.

Warner Bros. Pictures. (1974b), *Magnum Force* box office announcement, *Variety*, 16 January, 12–13.

Warner Bros. Pictures. (1975a), Release Slate, *Variety*, 14 May, 34–37.

Warner Bros. Pictures. (1975b), *Black Christmas* box office announcement, *Variety*, 20 August, 17–18.

Warner, L. (1980), 'Horrors! it's getting to be no joke', *Los Angeles Times*, 24 August, R5–R6.

Wasko, J. (1995), *Hollywood in the Information Age: Beyond the Silver Screen*. Austin: University of Texas Press.

Wasser, F. (1995), 'Four walling exhibition: regional resistance to the Hollywood film industry', *Cinema Journal*, 43, (2), 51–65.

Watkins, R. (1980), 'Demented revenge hits world screens', *Variety*, 15 October, 33.

Wee, V. (2005), 'The *Scream* trilogy, 'hyper-postmodernism' and the late-nineties teen slasher film', *Journal of Film and Video*, 57, (3), 44–61.

Wee, V. (2006), 'Resurrecting and updating the teen slasher: The case of *Scream*', *Journal of Popular Film and Television*, 35, (2), 50–61.

Weiler, A. H. (1975), 'Murky whodunit "Black Christmas" at local theatres', *New York Times*, 20 October, 45.

Wells, P, (2000), *The Horror Genre: From Beelzebub to Blair Witch*. London: Wallflower Press.

Westrop, H. (1980), 'Bouncy "Fame" heads list of new films', *Ottawa Citizen*, 9 October, 203.

Whitehead, M. (2000), *The Pocket Essential Slasher Films*. Harpenden: Pocket Essentials.

Williams, A. (1984), 'Is a radical genre criticism possible?', *Quarterly Review of Film Studies*, 9, (2), 121–125.

Williams, C. (1980), 'Horror fad finally fading', *Toledo Blade*, 16 November, E1.

Williams, L. (1999), *Hardcore: Power, Pleasure and the 'Frenzy of the Vizible'* (expanded paperback edn). Berkeley: University of California Press.

Williams, L. (2004). *Porn Studies*. Durham: Duke University Press.

Williamson, R. (1981), 'Holiday tales of terror', *Los Angeles Times*, 19 April, L31.

Wood, R. and Lippel, R. (1979), *American Nightmares: Essays on the Horror Film*. Toronto: Festival of Festivals.

Wood, R. (1983), 'Beauty bests the beast', *American Film*, 8, (10), 63–65.

Wood, R. (1984), 'An introduction to the American horror film', in B. K. Grant (ed.), *Planks of Reason: Essays on the Horror Film*. London: Scarecrow Press, pp. 164–200.

Wood, R. (1986), *Hollywood from Vietnam to Reagan*. New York: Columbia University Press.

Wood, R. (1987), 'Returning the look: *Eyes of a Stranger*', in G. A. Waller (ed.), *American Horrors: Essays on the Modern Horror Film*. Urbana: University of Illinois Press, pp. 79–85.

Wyatt, J. (1994a), 'From roadshowing to saturation release: majors, independents and marketing/distribution innovations', in J. Lewis (ed.), *The New American Cinema*. Durham: Duke University Press. pp. 64–86.

Wyatt, J. (1994b), *High Concept: Movies and Marketing in Hollywood*. Austin: University of Texas Press.

Wyatt, J. (1998), 'The formation of the "major independent": Miramax, New Line and the new Hollywood', in S. Neale and M. Smith (eds), *Contemporary Hollywood Cinema*. London: Routledge, pp. 74–90.

Wyatt, J. (2005), 'Revisiting the 1970s' independent distribution and marketing strategies', in C. Holmund and J. Wyatt (eds), *Contemporary American Independent Film*. London: Routledge. pp. 229–245.

Ynac, J. (1996), 'More than a woman: music, masculinity and male spectacle in *Saturday Night Fever*', *The Velvet Light Trap*, 38, 39–53.

Audiovisual resources

'Bob Clark unabridged', (2002), DVD Extras, *Black Christmas*. Critical Mass Releasing Inc.

'Filmmakers commentary', (2001), DVD Extras, *Madman*. Anchor Bay Entertainment.

'Filmmakers commentary', (2003), DVD Bonus Materials, *Halloween: 25th Anniversary Edition*. Anchor Bay Entertainment.

'Going to pieces: The rise and fall of the slasher film', (2006), THINKfilm.

'*Halloween*: a cut above the rest', (2003), DVD Bonus Materials, *Halloween: 25th Anniversary Edition*. Anchor Bay Entertainment.

'Return to Crystal Lake: making *Friday the 13th*', (2003), DVD Extras, *Friday the 13th*. Warner Bros UK.

'Sneak previews', (1980), Broadcast 23 October.

'Three all-new featurettes', (2009), DVD Special Features, *Silent Scream*. Scorpion Releasing.

Online Resources

'Box office mojo'. URL: www.boxofficemojo.com

'The final girl blogspot'. URL: www.finalgirl.blogspot.com

'Hysteria lives! 10 Years of slasher trash with panache!'. URL: www.hysteria-lives.co.uk

'Museum of Broadcast Communications'. URL: www.museum.tv

'Nexis news search'. URL: www.lexisnexis.com

'Norstar Filmed Entertainment Inc'. URL: www.norstarfilms.com

'TeleFilm Canada'. URL: www.telefilm.gc.ca

'*Time* magazine archives'. URL: www.time.com

'Terror trap: a museum of horror and thriller films from 1925 to 1987'. URL: www.terrortrap.com

Index